That Men Would Praise
the Lord

That Men Would Praise the Lord

The Triumph of Protestantism in Nîmes, 1530–1570

ALLAN A. TULCHIN

UNIVERSITY PRESS

2010

OXFORD
UNIVERSITY PRESS

Oxford University Press, Inc., publishes works that further
Oxford University's objective of excellence
in research, scholarship, and education.

Oxford   New York
Auckland   Cape Town   Dar es Salaam   Hong Kong   Karachi
Kuala Lumpur   Madrid   Melbourne   Mexico City   Nairobi
New Delhi   Shanghai   Taipei   Toronto

With offices in
Argentina   Austria   Brazil   Chile   Czech Republic   France   Greece
Guatemala   Hungary   Italy   Japan   Poland   Portugal   Singapore
South Korea   Switzerland   Thailand   Turkey   Ukraine   Vietnam

Copyright © 2010 by Oxford University Press, Inc.

Published by Oxford University Press, Inc.
198 Madison Avenue, New York, New York 10016

www.oup.com

Oxford is a registered trademark of Oxford University Press

All rights reserved. No part of this publication may be reproduced,
stored in a retrieval system, or transmitted, in any form or by any means,
electronic, mechanical, photocopying, recording, or otherwise,
without the prior permission of Oxford University Press.

Library of Congress Cataloging-in-Publication Data
Tulchin, Allan A., 1968–
That men would praise the Lord : the triumph of Protestantism in Nîmes, 1530–1570 /
Allan A. Tulchin.
   p. cm.
Includes bibliographical references and index.
ISBN 978-0-19-973652-2
1. Reformation—France—Nîmes. 2. Nîmes (France)—Church history.
I. Title.
BR372.N56T85   2010
274.4′83706—dc22   2009038183

9 8 7 6 5 4 3 2 1
Printed in the United States of America
on acid-free paper

*To my wife, Judy, and to our children,
Hillel and Lena,
with much love*

O give thanks unto the Lord, for he is good:
    for his mercy endureth for ever.
Let the redeemed of the Lord say so,
    whom he hath redeemed from the hand of the enemy;
And gathered them out of the lands,
    from the east, and from the west,
    from the north, and from the south.
They wandered in the wilderness
    in a solitary way;
    they found no city to dwell in.
Hungry and thirsty,
    their soul fainted in them.
Then they cried unto the Lord in their trouble,
    and he delivered them out of their distresses.
And he led them forth by the right way,
    that they might go to a city of habitation.
Oh that men would praise the Lord for his goodness,
    and for his wonderful works to the children of men!
For he satisfieth the longing soul,
    and filleth the hungry soul with goodness.

                                  —Psalm 107:1–9

Acknowledgments

Many thanks to the University of Toronto Press and to Duke University Press for publishing versions of Chapter 5 and Chapter 7. As I wrote this book, many people and institutions kindly assisted me, for which I feel enormously grateful. I received a fellowship and travel funding from the Department of History at the University of Chicago, which helped support me while I was in France, and more recently the Camargo Foundation lodged me for a semester while I completed the project. Shippensburg University gave me a semester's leave so that I could accept the fellowship. Six months as an Ahmanson-Getty Fellow at UCLA were crucial to drafting Chapter 7. I also benefited from five weeks at Calvin College in Grand Rapids, Michigan, attending a seminar on Calvinism sponsored by the National Endowment for the Humanities. Karin Maag and Raymond A. Mentzer Jr. directed the seminar, which provided an excellent opportunity for me to learn from them and the other attendees. Ray has helped me from the beginning of my research. I also received much good advice and practical assistance from Gabriel Audisio and Colin Lucas. M. Alain Venturini, director of the Archives Départementales du Gard in 1993–1995, when I lived in Nîmes to research this book, kindly let me see originals of documents that are normally only accessible via microfilm. Similarly, Michel Jas, then pastor of the Grand Temple in Nîmes, permitted me to photocopy materials which ordinarily do not circulate. My friend Tim Pollack-Lagushenko suggested the comparative section in the conclusion and read it with a fine critical eye. Intellectually, my debts are far too many to enumerate, but I must acknowledge Constantin Fasolt and John Padgett, members of my dissertation committee, and Bill Sewell, my dissertation director. I have been very lucky in my teachers.

Finally, I thank my parents, who not only made it all possible, but who always had faith in me. My father gets a special thanks for reading drafts of every chapter of my dissertation, frequently twice. Mom, Dad, Abe: I owe you so much.

Contents

Introduction, xiii

1. Nîmes: A Sixteenth-Century City, 3
2. The Creation of a Protestant Community: Nîmes, 1530–1547, 27
3. Growth and Crisis: Nîmes's Protestants, 1547–1559, 49
4. The Religious Crisis Begins, 1559–1560, 71
5. The *Cahier de Doléances*, 1561, 97
6. The Consolidation of the Protestant Movement, 1561–1562, 121
7. Rising and Falling: The Protestant Movement in Nîmes, 1562–1570, 155

Conclusion: The Reformation in Nîmes in Comparative Perspective, 181

Appendix A: The Evolution of the Protestant Movement in Nîmes, 1560–1562, 201

Appendix B: Constructing the Notarial Database, 203

Notes, 221

Bibliography, 269

Index, 289

Introduction

In just a few years in the latter part of the 1550s and early 1560s, under the inspiration of John Calvin, perhaps two million French people turned from the Catholic religion of their ancestors and embraced Protestantism, founding hundreds of Reformed churches in many parts of the country. When they renounced their allegiance to the pope, they caused the most momentous change in the religious life of the country since the conversion of Constantine over a thousand years earlier. Converts to Protestantism put their lives at risk, since the punishment for the crime of heresy was being burned at the stake by the royal courts. Worse, the massive conversions of the late 1550s and early 1560s were directly responsible for the outbreak of a forty-year civil war.

In perhaps no other region of France was the Protestant movement more successful than in Bas-Languedoc, centered on Nîmes. In Nîmes, more than three-quarters of the town's population eventually embraced what France's Catholics called the "supposedly reformed religion." Nîmes became the heart of Protestant France, comparable to Manchester for the industrial revolution or the Vendée for the counter-revolution of 1793. Not only was religious change in Nîmes profound and abrupt, it was violent. By the end of the 1560s, Protestant zealots had reduced every church in town, save one, to rubble. To support their side in the civil wars, Nîmes's Protestant leaders sold off the relics from the town's churches to pay for cannons. Nor were deaths confined to the battlefield. In Nîmes in 1567 and

1569, Protestants murdered more than two hundred of their Catholic opponents, according to contemporary estimates. Some townspeople may have been religiously indifferent, but the overall impression is of deep commitment, even fanaticism.

My primary goal in this volume is to explain these startling, extraordinary, and bloody events. By studying Nîmes, I intend to give readers a sense of how and why the Reformation occurred. My approach to answering this question is to study how Protestant ideas spread through a community, and why some people and groups were highly attracted to Protestantism while others were not. The Reformation is generally considered to be one of the most important episodes in European and even world history. Many readers will therefore not need to be persuaded that my project is worthwhile. Even if the Reformation were not important, however, the events are so dramatic that they still might command attention, especially if I have managed to write with sufficient verve. In either of these cases, an introduction to this book might be unnecessary. However, I also wish to give readers some backstory on how I came to write it, and to make some broader theoretical points that inform the book. Other explanations, especially those primarily of scholarly interest, have been tucked into the notes. The conclusion, which proposes some general parameters for evaluating the success or failure of the Reformation in France, is also somewhat more academic in tone. In the main text, however, I have emphasized narrative and readability and reduced explanation to a minimum.

I came to France and to history early, before I was a teenager. France is my father's fault: until he retired, he was an art professor, and as a result I spent a week in the Louvre at age eight. On that trip, I also fell in love with the Place des Vosges, and seeing its late sixteenth-century architecture may have had some role in the genesis of this book. As a child, my passion was maps; I used to pore over the atlas for hours and doodled imaginary topographies at every opportunity. History became my favorite subject once I read Colin McEvedy's series of historical atlases, published by Penguin; the combination of maps plus narrative hooked me for good, and my favorite was the early modern volume. But college was where I really decided to specialize in the period. That was due to David Underdown's superb teaching. I was also fascinated by the existential questions that Europeans had posed in the sixteenth and seventeenth centuries, which were oddly analogous to the questions I was asking myself. I grew up in New York City in an apartment complex whose residents were largely elderly Jewish garment union members, most of whom spoke English only with a heavy accent. The head gardener had numbers tattooed on his arm. My own background is Jewish but secular. As I found my way in the wider world, I wondered how to balance tradition with change, and how to cope with those whose views are radically different from my own. I concluded, as I drew closer to the Jewish religious tradition, that I gravitated toward the Huguenots at least in part because it was a way to study a religious minority coping with suffering without quite the pain it would have caused me to study modern Poland. In the pages that follow, I have tried to temper my instinctive pro-Protestant bias, especially since many of them were also murderers.

Although I now consider myself a fairly religious person, I have tried to keep my religious views out of this book. I also have tried to avoid imposing religiosity on my subject matter. I chose the epigraph for this book to give readers a sense of the longing for God that was at the heart of the Protestant experience for many sixteenth-century French people. However, although most sixteenth-century people were religious, their level of religious faith and knowledge varied. Heterodoxy is very well attested, of both exceptional individuals like the miller Menocchio, famously studied by Carlo Ginzburg, and even whole communities. To take one prominently cited example, in the thirteenth century, in the area around Lyon, St. Guinefort was well loved. Guinefort, however, was a dog, the faithful companion of St. Roch. Guinefort was particularly remembered because he saved St. Roch's life by bringing him food every day when he was sick with the plague.[1] We should neither ignore such folk beliefs nor despise them from the heights of our modern sophistication. Actually, moderns can hold beliefs quite as strange as any. Perhaps the most surprising personal experience I have had of this was when in the synagogue social hall I met a woman who asked me about myself. When I explained that I was writing a book about the Huguenots, she was delighted and told me that I should interview her, because she had been a Huguenot in a past life. Similarly, people in the sixteenth century held a wide variety of theological views, some of which were far from orthodox, or even Christian. Faith and knowledge were not necessarily correlated: people could be devout and not knowledgeable or the reverse. Skepticism also existed, and some people attended church irregularly if at all. I hope this is not surprising. Rather than assume that people in the sixteenth century must have converted for purely theological reasons, I have preferred to listen to what they had to say about it, and compare it with other evidence. My technique has been to try to pinpoint when they converted and then examine what they were talking about at the time. I have also considered what other motivations they may have had. In some cases, conversion was a courageous act, as the many martyrs of the period demonstrate. In others, it was highly convenient. Material circumstances must be considered when evaluating whether people's stated motives were genuine.[2]

Now that I have alerted readers to potential bias on my part, I also wish to point out briefly two distinctive aspects of the theoretical underpinnings of this book. One is less visible to the casual reader but still important, namely, the use of sociological and anthropological models of religious conversion. The second, also important and far more obvious, is my interest in quantitative approaches to historical analysis.

Sociologists and anthropologists have devoted a great deal of attention to religious conversion. I have found much of this literature useful in conceptualizing the Reformation in Nîmes, although to my knowledge it has never been cited by Reformation historians.[3] Where I have found helpful analogies in the social-scientific literature, I have added appropriate endnotes and sometimes a brief discussion in the text. I wish to make it clear here, however, that I do not aspire, unlike some sociologists, to write rules of general validity for all societies, across time and space.[4] Like many anthropologists, I am agnostic to skeptical about the usefulness of such rules. As Robert Hefner, an anthropologist, notes, the complex interactions involved in religious conversion are too messy to be reduced to "sociological fact."[5]

Probably the most influential concept in the psychological literature on conversion is cognitive dissonance, namely, the principle that people do not like to believe two incompatible things at the same time. The term was coined by Leon Festinger, an American psychologist, and his colleagues in *When Prophecy Fails* (1956). In that book, Festinger analyzed a religious movement which had to accommodate its views to the failure of the planet to be destroyed according to the leader's timetable. The term has since entered into the language and driven a great deal of psychological research. Despite its popularity, as far as I know it has never been considered in the context of the Reformation in Europe. This is particularly surprising since the term was coined in the context of a study of a religious group.[6] But the term is relevant, beginning with the very notion of a "reformation." Since in the sixteenth century most people thought that it was a terrible criticism to call an idea "new," cognitive dissonance theory would suggest that religious innovators had to believe that their ideas were not really new, but rather that they were a return to ancient principles.

One consequence of cognitive dissonance is that the conversion process is difficult, because converts are in limbo and have elements of two systems of thought in their heads at the same time. People therefore have to pay a significant psychic cost for conversion, although this is presumably lessened when everyone around them is doing likewise. Those people with a low tolerance for cognitive dissonance may well hesitate before converting and then rush through the process as quickly as possible once they decide to do it. One way they ease these strains is to become eager proselytizers, since the willingness of others to follow their beliefs validates their own choices. Despite these rebirth pangs, when people are sufficiently upset by other problems, the cognitive dissonance of not converting may exceed the dissonance of conversion. If they are sufficiently disgusted with their current theology, or its representatives, it may be easier to exit the current religious institution rather than attempt to change it for the better. Still, both choices are available, and different people will choose different responses based on the nature of the problem and their own temperaments.[7]

Cognitive dissonance does not affect everyone equally. Some people can pass from one world view to another with great regularity and no apparent discomfort. I knew a born-Jewish woman (now deceased, alas) who went through vegetarian, communist, and Christian Science phases. But most people find such drastic changes stressful. Certainly, her husband did. Rather than one conversion model, it is more likely that there is a repertoire of possible responses to particular situations or conflicts. Cognitive dissonance plays a part, but so do peer pressure and other more culturally specific issues. Some recent studies stress the distinction between "sudden" and "gradual" conversions, for example.[8] Similarly, mass conversion is not simply individual conversion multiplied: Nîmes was not a city of thousands of Calvins or Luthers, so the mass conversion there was a qualitatively different phenomenon.[9] Religious conversion in the modern world cannot be compared to sixteenth-century Nîmes for hypothesis testing or rule building under these circumstances. Nonetheless, I still find anthropological accounts helpful because they suggest models of conversion that might not otherwise occur to me. Ethnographers also have easy access to much more detailed information about the societies they study than I do.

The other distinctive methodological aspect of this book is its use of quantitative techniques, using relational databases and a limited amount of social network analysis. These techniques may remind some scholars of the mid-twentieth-century *Annales* school of French economic and social historians. Since then, many historians have criticized the *Annales* school. As a result of the "linguistic turn" in historical studies cultural history became much more fashionable. For me, the biggest problem with *Annales*-style history is its tendency to emphasize structure over agency, immobility over change. This is antithetical to history as a story of human development, and dull to read. Oddly, many cultural historians seem to have forgotten that the *Annales* school also produced cultural history. The founders of the *Annales* were Marc Bloch and Lucien Febvre. But Bloch wrote *The Royal Touch* and Febvre wrote *The Problem of Unbelief in the Sixteenth Century,* books that are cultural history by any reasonable standard. Michel Vovelle, the Annales School historian whose *Piété baroque et déchristianisation en Provence au XVIIIe siècle* (1973) is probably the single greatest influence on this book, used quantitative and qualitative techniques to examine important historical change. This book attempts to marry *Annales*-style quantitative techniques and cultural history. Generally, there is good reason to favor a middle ground rather than either an extreme sociological or an extreme linguistic determinism. Events are constituted on a spectrum, both socially and linguistically. Some phenomena are probably impervious to linguistic or cultural analysis, on the one hand, or quantitative analysis, on the other, but both techniques have their uses. Indeed, when both methods lead to similar results, the conclusion is particularly convincing.[10] Finally, it is the interconnectedness in people's lives between ideas and structures that makes history interesting.

Despite C. P. Snow, there is no necessary opposition between the sciences and the humanities, tables and texts. Indeed, I would echo and extend the remark of Otto L. Bettmann, founder of the well-known Bettmann Archive of visual materials, who once wrote that "[i]t is a fact that words and pictures go well together."[11] Numbers and words can be mutually enlightening, too. One of the classic techniques of professional history is the confrontation of documents: that is, since most categories of documents have built-in, systemic biases, scholars can use different kinds of documents to help overcome the inherent blind spots of each. It is precisely because words, numbers, and pictures are such different ways of knowing that using them together can be so productive. To avoid scaring off any numbers-phobic readers, however, I have generally used graphs rather than tables. For those who want the numbers, I have put some crucial ones in Appendix A. Methodologically, I hope to show how juxtaposing numbers and texts enriches both.

History cannot be reduced to numbers, but numbers and computers do have a role to play in historical analysis. This is more true today than ever: the computer revolution is probably the most important social and economic change of the past generation, and it seems positively churlish for historians not to take advantage of computing power. It is now possible to do things with a desktop computer in seconds that would have taken weeks in the days of mainframes and punch cards. Under the onerous constraints of that era, crude hypotheses and banal results were sometimes inevitable. Much more sophistication is possible today. It is time to remedy historians' neglect of quantitative research, although that does not mean that the techniques of cultural history should be abandoned. I do not propose a simple return to the *Annales* school paradigm. Rather, cultural history needs to be brought back into dialogue with social history to produce a rounded picture of the past. This study therefore does not eschew narrative and literary sources. It attempts to tell a story, and that story is told largely through the surviving literary sources, buttressed by quantitative data where they are available. Happily, I have found that juxtaposing quantitative and literary evidence has generally been fruitful rather than frustrating. I hope that readers will agree.

Plan of the Book

Chapter 1 gives an overview of Nîmes's governmental, religious, and other institutions and its economy. It gives the percentages of the employed population working in the city's various trades, and specifies which were the richest and most prestigious. In Nîmes, lawyers and officials, almost always trained in the law, were the most influential people: for example, the first consul, equivalent to the mayor of Nîmes, was by statute invariably a lawyer.

Chapter 2 discusses the history of the town from 1530 to 1547. Protestant ideas probably entered Nîmes via its university and college of arts, led by Claude Baduel, an early Protestant and native of the town. At first, Nîmes's Protestants were disproportionately wealthy artisans and cloth workers. This group was probably inspired by Calvin's theology, notably his interpretation of the Lord's Supper. These early Protestants were sufficiently literate that they were open to the Protestant message, yet were not so prominent in Nîmes society that they felt their interests were aligned with those of the crown. They were also probably under little surveillance, compared to Nîmes's wealthy and influential lawyers and officials. Since the French monarchy was closely aligned with the Catholic Church, it was impolitic for high officials to embrace Protestantism. It was also the policy of the Parlement of Toulouse, which was the most important institution trying to repress heresy, to try to eliminate Protestantism by executing its most prominent adherents. By 1547, the Protestant movement in Nîmes had a sense of itself, since we possess a letter from "the church of Nîmes" to Calvin discussing the Lord's Supper, and in the early 1550s Nîmes's two Protestant notaries, Jacques and Jean Ursi, stopped using Catholic formulas in wills and marriage contracts.

Although the formation of a self-consciously Protestant community in Nîmes was an important step, in the 1550s the movement was still small and its members still feared for their lives. Nîmes's first Protestants found it difficult to gain adherents outside their relatively narrow circle before the early 1560s. Chapter 3 details how this situation changed when a political and economic crisis proved to be a heaven-sent opportunity. In 1557, a flood nearly wiped out the town and destroyed the harvest. Since biblical times, floods have been viewed as God's judgments on sinful nations, and in this case the catastrophe added weight to the Protestant argument that Nîmes needed moral renewal.

This was only the first of four harvest failures in a row, at a time when the town's relationship with the monarchy was also under severe strain. The crown, in an effort to avoid defeat in its wars with the Hapsburgs, imposed high new taxes, forced loans, and forced the town to pay heavy fees to preserve its judicial privileges.

As described in Chapter 4, despite these measures, France was defeated, and King Henri II was killed in a freak accident at the peace conference. His not-quite fifteen-year-old son then came to the throne, but he only lived a year and was succeeded by his ten-year-old brother. The Protestant movement capitalized on an angry population and a newly weakened monarchy by arguing that Calvinism's political and social teachings pointed the way out of France's crisis.

Chapter 5 shows how Nîmes's Protestant movement's local leaders demonstrated the potential of their program by writing a list of grievances, or *cahier de doléances,* to be sent to the French Estates General. In the cahier, they stated that religious reform was a necessary first step toward political and social renewal, "so that we can properly reform and build all other matters on this foundation." They then connected religious reform to contractualist principles of limited government: the crown's fiscal problems, they argued, should be solved by taking lands and money from the Catholic Church. Furthermore, the Estates General should meet regularly, with the right to declare war, ratify peace, and consent to all taxes. The cahier was a crucial catalyst for the success of the Protestant movement in Nîmes and part of a nationwide Protestant campaign. This is a conclusion that has not been recognized previously. I will show that, in the immediate aftermath of the cahier's adoption, lawyers and then officeholders decided to convert to the new religion. Over three hundred people signed the cahier, including many of the elite and people who were new to the Protestant movement. It was also an important event in the history of the Nîmes Protestant church: the church's governing board, the consistory, held its first official meeting and elected its first officers only eight days after the passage of the cahier.

Chapter 6 describes how it became impossible for Nîmes's government to repress the movement once significant numbers of the elite had converted. Even committed Catholics were reluctant to prosecute their friends, neighbors, and relatives. The Calvinist leadership then began conducting mass meetings, which whipped up a climate of near-revolutionary enthusiasm. Protestant mobs seized churches and smashed idolatrous images. The movement's social concerns can be clearly seen in wills: beginning in the second half of 1561, there was an outpouring of legacies to the poor, clearly suggesting that Nîmes's Protestants were concerned about the needy. Eventually, over three-quarters of the town converted. Protestant ideas now altered Nîmes society from top to bottom, in domains ranging from political allegiances to family life, as the newly energized population acted to recreate their society according to their religion's ideals.

Ironically, this drive for moral reformation ended in a bloodbath, as described in Chapter 7. The French crown, determined to repress heresy, engineered several coups to keep the newly Protestant elite out of power. Eventually, the Protestant leadership grew frustrated with this state of affairs, and in two bloody uprisings in 1567 and 1569 orchestrated a massacre of many members of the Catholic minority, particularly its leadership and clergy. Extensive source material survives for the 1567 massacre, called the Michelade. Both massacres show that Protestants in power were just as murderous as Catholics, despite the celebrated arguments of Natalie Z. Davis in *Society and Culture in Early Modern France* (1975). Nîmes's Protestants even destroyed most of the city's Catholic churches, explaining, "The nests must be destroyed, so that the birds will not return." As a result, Nîmes became a Protestant-dominated town.

In the conclusion, I compare Nîmes with other cities in France and Western Europe to create a typology of towns to explain why the Protestant movement was more successful in some than in others. I conclude that variation among towns was not random, but rather, regularities can be seen when the movement is considered across time and space. I argue that Nîmes's Protestants benefited from the Roman law culture of southern France and from the remoteness of royal authority. Cities like Aix and Toulouse, which had parlements, tended to stay Catholic because the judges, who were the richest and most powerful residents, identified their interests with those of the Most Christian King, as the kings of France were called. Similarly, Paris, whose economy depended on the proximity of the court, and Champagne, dominated by the Catholic Guise family, were resistant to heresy. Southern French towns, because of their tradition of independence, their political structure, and their Roman law inheritance, were especially receptive to Protestant ideas.

Some Notes on Conventions in This Book

Money. France in the sixteenth century used the Roman system of money (which was also used in Britain until 1971); there were 20 sous in the livre tournois (tours livres were the standard), and 12 deniers in the sou. However, although the smaller coins were minted, no livres were, and instead other coins, most commonly florins and écus, circulated. Because bullion content fluctuated and local conditions varied, calculating equivalencies is notoriously difficult. Judging from equivalencies given in wills in Nîmes, in this period a florin equaled 15 sous, and an écu d'or soleil (or écu sol) equaled 45–50 sous. In order to avoid confusion, all figures in this book have generally been converted to livres at a rate of 46 sous to the écu, which appears to have been the most common rate of exchange for Nîmes in this period.[12] In cases where there is any ambiguity, this has been noted. I have used the conventional signs £ for livres, s. for sous, and d. for deniers.

Names. In the text and the index, I have modernized the spelling of names for consistency, but I have retained the original spellings in the notes. In most documents from the ancien régime, women's last names were (a) the same as their fathers,' not their husbands'; and (b) given a feminine ending: if a woman's father's last name was Chevalier, her last name was Chevalière. I have retained these forms.

Dates. In Nîmes in the mid-sixteenth century, the first day of the year was March 25. In order to avoid confusion, I have altered dates in the text to conform to the contemporary Western custom that the year begins on January 1, while in the notes documents are given with a slash between the original year and the modern equivalent of the date, for example: 2 February 1555/56.

Translations. All translations, unless otherwise noted, are my own. I almost always provide the original French, however, usually in the endnotes. Since the original is available, I have occasionally permitted myself a certain freedom to compress when translating, to spare the reader. Sixteenth-century language is frequently legalistic and repetitive, so someone will not say "they have broken the law," but instead "they have broken the laws, statutes, decrees and ordinances of the king." This may have sounded rhetorically impressive when delivered at a town council meeting, but can be quite tiresome on the printed page.

That Men Would Praise the Lord

I

Nîmes

A Sixteenth-Century City

The Reformation began nearly five centuries ago. The French Revolution seems very distant to most people today, but for someone living in 1789, the Reformation was even further in the past than the Revolution is for us. One must therefore always remember that the daily life and habits of thought of people in sixteenth-century France were very unlike our own. It is part of the historian's task to serve as a guide to the past, pointing out the vanished structures, sights, and feelings of long ago. This chapter will introduce the city of Nîmes in southern France, its streets and institutions, its people, and its economy in the middle of the sixteenth century. It will focus on four topics: (1) the province of Languedoc and its institutions; (2) the physical and human geography of Nîmes and the region; (3) the institutions of the town: the government, the church, education, arts and culture; and (4) Nîmes's economy.

The Province

Nîmes was one of the leading cities of Languedoc, and before describing the city in detail, it is worth describing this important southern French province and some of its more prominent institutions. The province was one of the largest in France, occupying about 17,500 square miles (45,000 square kilometers), about 10 percent of the kingdom. It was the home of less than 10 percent of France's total population of about

19 million. Languedoc, like much of the Mediterranean, was probably somewhat more urbanized than Northern Europe on average, but less urbanized than northern Italy or the Low Countries. For tax and other purposes, the province was divided into twenty-two civil dioceses, which corresponded only approximately to bishoprics.[1] Geographically, it was a land of great contrasts, from the mountains of the Pyrenees to the plateaus of the Massif Central, from the river valleys of the upper Garonne to the sandy Mediterranean and marshy Camargue at the mouth of the Rhone.

Languedoc had originally been ruled by counts with a substantial degree of autonomy, but had become part of the royal demesne of the kings of France in the thirteenth century, in the aftermath of the crusade against the Albigensian heresy. The governor of the province in the mid-sixteenth century was Anne, baron de Montmorency; he was succeeded by his second son, Henri de Montmorency-Damville, in 1563. The Montmorencys were one of France's most important noble houses. The governor usually lived at court, rather than in the province. In his absence, Honorat de Savoie, comte de Villars, was the lieutenant general of the king. Montmorency also appointed a deputy, Guillaume, vicomte de Joyeuse, called the *lieutenant du gouverneur* or *lieutenant du roi*.[2]

The elite of Languedoc understood French, but the ordinary language of the region was Oc, or Occitan, one of a number of provençal dialects spoken in the southern half of the country (called the Midi in French). Major cities in Languedoc included Béziers, Carcassonne, Montpellier, Narbonne, Nîmes, and the largest and capital city of the province, Toulouse. Montpellier and Toulouse had famous universities, the former especially celebrated for its faculty of medicine, the latter for its faculty of law.[3]

In addition to its university, Toulouse also housed the high court, the *parlement*, for the province of Languedoc. France was divided into a number of districts, each with its own parlement, of which Paris was the largest and most prestigious. The Parlement of Paris had to register all laws and royal edicts in order for them to become valid, although the king could force the parlement to register a law by appearing personally before the parlement at a *lit de justice*.[4] The Parlement of Toulouse, although not as powerful, was the final court of appeal for all legal cases in a wide region, including Nîmes and all of Languedoc, the county of Foix, and some other territories along the Spanish border. Since the parlement was the highest court in the province, it generally dealt with the most serious cases, as well as with appeals. In particular, it was responsible for cases of heresy and related crimes, such as blasphemy. It was unusual for the parlement, a civil court, to have jurisdiction over heresy, a religious crime: elsewhere in Europe, heresy was usually tried in ecclesiastical courts, most famously those of the Inquisition. Despite their lay status, the judges of the parlement were mostly good Catholics who were eager to repress Protestantism. The parlement did not always sit in Toulouse: like all of the major parlements, it occasionally sent a delegation on circuit to hold *grands jours* elsewhere in the province, bringing justice closer to the people and strengthening royal authority. The Parlement of Toulouse occasionally sent judges to hold *grands jours* in Béziers, Le Puy, and Nîmes.[5]

The other major institution of government in Languedoc was the Estates General of the province, its legislature. Each of the three Estates into which the realm was customarily divided—the clergy, the nobility, and the commons—was represented in it. Specifically, the Estates consisted of twenty-two bishops, twenty-two nobles, and forty-four representatives of the towns. The towns tended to send their leading officials. Unlike the national Estates General, in which each Estate constituted one house of the legislature, the Estates of Languedoc met as one body. Since the representatives of the towns had much better attendance records than the noblemen, in theory they could have dominated the proceedings, but in practice the privileged orders, especially the bishops, expected and received great deference. Unlike most representative institutions in early modern Europe, which tended to meet irregularly, the Estates of Languedoc met every year. Unlike most modern legislatures, the Estates had no fixed capitol building, meeting instead in a different city each session. In 1547, they met in Carcassonne; in 1548, in Montpellier; in 1549, in Beaucaire; in 1550, in Montpellier again; in 1551, in Pézenas; in 1552, in Nîmes. In this respect, they were similar to early modern royal courts, which were itinerant until they became too large and cumbersome to move their staffs. The Estates gained more from moving about than from staying in one place. Among other things, moving calmed regional jealousies. The Estates were a portable chat room: people went to the sessions to take counsel as well as to pass legislation. From the crown's point of view, the most important purpose of the Estates was that they voted taxes, including the *taille,* a land tax; *crues* (supplements asked for in time of war); payments in lieu of military service; payments for fortifications; and so forth. Although the Estates met annually, there was little question that they would ratify the king's tax requests. Indeed, the Estates were sufficiently obedient that the crown would sometimes include the revenues from the province in its calculations before the Estates had even voted them.[6]

Geography and Population

Nîmes was a substantial place in the sixteenth century, with a population of perhaps 10,000, although this, like many sixteenth-century population figures, is only an educated guess. For the purpose of comparison, Nîmes was probably about the same size as Bristol, Newcastle, Leiden, Leipzig, Siena, Geneva, or Nîmes's neighbors Arles and Montpellier. In France today, Nîmes ranks just outside the twenty largest cities; this was probably also true in the mid-sixteenth century. The king of France and the bishop of Nîmes were co-lords of the city, but over the course of the Middle Ages, Nîmes had largely succeeded in eliminating the bishop's authority. For all practical purposes, Nîmes was a free city: it was beholden to no *seigneur* (lord), and no great noble family controlled the town's political destiny. The most important nobleman in the region was Antoine, comte de Crussol, but his extensive lands were centered on Uzès (about 25 miles north of Nîmes), and he rarely intervened in Nîmes's affairs. The leaders of the town could therefore pursue an independent course, based on their perception of the city's interests, within the limits set by the larger political structures of the province and the kingdom.[7]

Nîmes is located a bit more than 25 miles (40 kilometers) north of the Mediterranean and somewhat more than 25 miles southwest of Avignon. It is about 30 miles (50 kilometers) northeast of Montpellier and about 70 miles (120 kilometers) west of Marseille. Nîmes's walls enclosed a shield-shaped area, that is, a triangle with a flat top and rounded sides, with the top oriented to the north. Administratively, the town was divided into six *quartiers* within the walls and several suburbs outside them. Within the walls, the city was divided in half along a line that ran north-south down the middle. On the west side, proceeding from north to south, were the Bocarié haute, Bocarié basse, Garrigues, and Méjan quarters. On the east side of town were the Prat and Corcomaires quarters.

Nîmes did not enjoy a particularly salubrious reputation. In the middle of the fifteenth century, an observer commented:

> The city is humid, and further, very poorly founded and constructed. Its marshy soil is mortal for men of three temperaments: those who are sanguine, melancholy, and phlegmatic. It is true that this same soil is appropriate for the choleric, who, by nature, are more burning than fire; but these are but a rare exception. The town was and is very badly built. The houses are, for the most part, rudely constructed with boards, and therefore very subject to fire. It is, moreover, subject to horribly impetuous winds and afflicted with so many maladies that, for one hundred inhabitants, you will not find one—we have verified it—over sixty.[8]

Despite this grim description, Nîmes enjoyed many visitors in the sixteenth century. Royal personages made ceremonial visits, merchants peddled their wares, students stopped by on their way to the University of Montpellier, and troops passed through on their way to the wars. Many travelers stopped to see the sights along their way, since Nîmes was already famous in the sixteenth century for its Roman amphitheater, *les arènes de Nîmes,* and its numerous other monuments from classical antiquity.

Most travelers probably arrived in Nîmes on the via Domitiana, the Roman road that paralleled the Mediterranean coastline. The road connected Italy to Spain: it led from Arles and Beaucaire, on the Rhone, to Béziers and Narbonne, passing through Nîmes. Nîmes was located so far inland because south of it was the Camargue, a vast expanse of low-lying marsh and mud formed by the delta of the Rhone River. The Roman road deliberately skirted this wild region, crossing the river farther upstream, to the north. As travelers walked or rode the Roman way, they passed through miles of *garrigues,* rather poor, chalky soil that lies between the coastal sand dunes and the low mountains of the Cévennes farther inland. Originally, only trees and Mediterranean semi-arid scrub, including thistles, grew on it, and therefore the *garrigues* near Nîmes had been used almost exclusively for common pasture. In the second quarter of the sixteenth century, however, the authorities began to become alarmed. The population was growing, and peasants were gradually taking over the land to grow grapes, olives, and grain. In 1520–1521, the Parlement of Toulouse addressed the issue of deforestation, and in 1539 and 1546 the Estates of Languedoc commented that "the country is being entirely cleared of wood."[9]

Although the major road paralleled the coast, the major movement of people was perpendicular to it, from the poor and overpopulated mountains and upland areas of the Cévennes and the rolling hills that parallel them down toward the city of Nîmes. Indeed, of the 2,083 people recorded as getting married in Nîmes's notarial registers between 1550 and 1562, just over one-quarter (535) of them recorded that they were not born in Nîmes. In reality, the percentage of immigrants was almost certainly higher, possibly one-third. Since young adults tended to immigrate, Nîmes may have had a slightly youthful feel, like a college town today. The densest concentration of immigrants was from a region bounded by Nîmes, Uzès, Alès, and Anduze, although there was a smattering of residents from all over France and occasionally beyond. To give just a few admittedly exceptional examples, Pierre Canu, a carpenter, came from Troyes; Barthélemy Prouhomme, a farmworker, was from Lantosque (about 20 miles north of Monaco) in the then-independent duchy of Savoy; and Marie d'Allié was originally from Paris. Her husband, Jean Giebert, was a farmworker from Grenoble. Most people came from closer to Nîmes, however. At the top of the valleys of the Cévennes, where they meet the flat plateaus known as the *causses,* northwest of Nîmes, immigration fell off rapidly. The town of Florac, at the base of the Causse

Méjean, about 65 miles (110 kilometers) northwest of Nîmes (now in the *département* of Lozère), may be considered the farthest point from which people regularly immigrated to Nîmes.[10]

The Cévennes are a range of mountains reaching a height of 5,000 feet (1,525 meters). They frame the northwest side of the Rhone delta. They are largely composed of granite and limestone; because the limestone is soft, underground rivers and springs abound, and rivers drive deep, narrow gorges through them. The tops of the *causses* are flat, windswept, and barren, only suitable for pasture. Peasants planted olives in the lower elevations and chestnuts in terraces lining the steep sides of the valleys. There were also mulberry trees, to feed the silkworms for the budding silk industry, although their numbers would increase dramatically only in the seventeenth century.[11] Nucleated villages abounded in the plains, but with the higher elevations sheep and goats took over, and the isolated farm, known as a *mas,* became the typical form of human habitation. Many of Nîmes's artisans worked to transform the products of the Cévennes' animal husbandry into useful products: weavers wove wool into cloth, tanners transformed hides into leather.

Travelers journeying west along the via Domitiana from Beaucaire entered Nîmes via the Gate of Augustus, passing one of the city's suburbs, the faubourg de la Couronne, on the left as they approached the city. Near the Crown Gate that gave the suburb its name was an Augustinian monastery. Two other roads, which led in the direction of Avignon and Uzès, converged at the gate's entrance, and the Carmelite monastery was located there as well. The gate and the walls on this side of town dated from Roman times. A royal fort, the château, was situated just inside the gate. It held a small detachment of troops. Travelers headed northeast along the via Domitiana from Béziers, Narbonne, or Montpellier first crossed a bridge over the Cadereau, a small stream that flowed just west of town. They arrived in Nîmes via St. Anthony's Gate, passing two more suburbs, the faubourg St. Antoine and the faubourg de la Madeleine, on the left. Travelers arriving from the southwest also passed the monasteries of the Franciscan Observantines, or Cordeliers, and the Poor Clares, since they were in the western suburbs. The walls on the west side of town were medieval, and the Roman amphitheater loomed over them from inside. It was just to the right of the gate, in the southwest corner of town. During the Middle Ages, the amphitheater had been subdivided into houses, and many people, mostly poor, lived in it. Inside the amphitheater there were even two small churches, St. Martin des Arènes and its dependency, St. Pierre des Arènes.[12]

Anyone wishing to get a good view of Nîmes in the sixteenth century, however, would have done best to see it from the north, since on that side the town was overlooked by hills. Mont Cavalier rose 200 feet above the city, and near its summit stood the Tour Magne, the 106-foot-high remains of a Roman watchtower. From the top, Nîmes stood revealed behind its walls (medieval on this side as well). Northeast of the tower there were more hills, with windmills on top of them. Looking south toward the city, in the foreground, before the walls, there was another suburb, known as the faubourg des Precheurs because of the Dominican monastery there. The northwest gate to the city was called the Porte des Jacobins, in their honor. (Jacobins was another name for Dominicans, after the rue St. Jacques in Paris, where their first monastery was located.) At the base of the hill was the spring that was the reason for the town's location, the ruins of the Roman building known as the Temple of Diana, and the convent of the Benedictines of St. Sauveur de la Fontaine. Nearby was the Franciscan monastery. The spring fed a small stream, the Gau, that flowed into town, powering several mills and filling the moat that protected the city's walls on the east and west. The water then flowed southeast toward the Mediterranean. Beyond the walls, the most visible sights were the towers of the town's cathedral and the clock tower, but one could also see the roofs of many of its buildings, including another important Roman monument, the temple known as the Maison Carrée (the Square House), and perhaps the nearby church of St. Étienne de Capdueil. In all, there were fifteen churches and chapels, including the cathedral, within the town's walls.[13]

Institutions

Travelers were probably most interested in seeing the town's many Roman monuments. These are still visible today, but unfortunately only a few sixteenth-century buildings still stand. Of the town's churches, only a portion of the cathedral's facade and the small chapel of St. Eugénie survive. Some private houses also remain.[14] In any case, the empty buildings hardly convey the lives of those who once resided and worked within them. Most of the important institutions in Nîmes performed their functions within specific physical spaces: the town council met at the Hôtel de Ville; the professors, called regents, of the University and College of Arts lectured in the college's building; and so forth; and the locations of these buildings are known even if they no longer exist. Almost all of them were within the city walls and thus quite close to each other. The hospital was the one exception to this rule, since it was located for hygienic reasons in the faubourg St. Antoine. In the sixteenth century, it would have been possible to take a short walking tour and see each of the town's major institutions in its habitat; and with a little historical imagination, it is still possible to do so.

Nîmes's most prestigious institution, the *présidial*, was located in the Méjan quarter, at the south end of town. Let us imagine that our stroll through sixteenth-century Nîmes began there, at the *palais de justice*. It was located across the street from the amphitheater. Our imaginary tour will then continue clockwise around town, stopping at each institution, approximately in order of precedence.[15]

Nîmes had long been the seat of a *sénéchaussée*, a royal court, but on October 25, 1552, it was remodeled into a new category of courts, a présidial. King Henri II had created the first présidiaux by royal ordinance in January of that year. There was considerable opposition to their establishment. France's most important courts, the parlements, resented having their own jurisdiction thus circumscribed. Judges earned a salary, but much of their income came from charging the public for their services; in the courts, the payments were called *épices* (spices). Reducing the jurisdiction of the parlements had direct effects on the judges' finances. The Parlement of Paris led a protest, and the others, including the Parlement of Toulouse, joined with equal vigor. The localities, by contrast, generally liked the présidiaux, since authority was being transferred to them from the distant parlements. The king's motive for their creation was quite straightforward: he made money by selling offices to ambitious subjects. The practice of selling offices, or venality, had existed for a long time, but the crown first adopted it wholesale in the sixteenth century. François I greatly extended the system, and Henri II enlarged it even further. Many people attacked venality vociferously: Jean Bodin commented in his *Method for the Easy Comprehension of History*, "they appoint thieves and criminals for public office, and for the collection of revenue, so that they sap the people's resources and blood."[16] But new taxes were at least equally unpopular. The real difficulty with the system was that selling offices was more like borrowing money than actually raising it. People bought offices for the same reason they buy government bonds today: the government got the principal, and the buyers got the interest. Since the judges of the parlement had paid for their offices, on the assumption that they would receive a certain income, they were particularly unhappy that the crown was altering the terms of the deal. Henri was unmoved. By creating présidiaux, Henri was creating hundreds of new offices at a stroke, and he needed the money. He was therefore prepared to antagonize the parlements, and they eventually surrendered.

Initially, présidiaux were given civil jurisdiction in cases where the sum at issue was less than either £250 (without appeal) or £500 (with the right of appeal), as well as limited appellate and some criminal jurisdiction. These rules were modified over the course of the century: in 1557, for example, the limits on the size of suits were extended to £1,000 and £1,200. The exact composition of the court, including the number of councillors, varied over the years. In Nîmes, and other cities where *sénéchaussée* courts already existed before présidiaux were created, the two institutions were merged, so that officials from the *sénéchaussée* became part of the présidial. In 1560, the Nîmes présidial was composed of the president, Guillaume Calvière; twenty-two other judges and *conseillers;* two *procureurs du roi* (royal prosecutors); and the *avocat du roi* (the king's lawyer), who assisted them. Just as in the Parlement of Toulouse, there tended to be close personal and familial relations among the members of the présidial: for example, Jean-Poldo d'Albenas, an important local humanist and author, was a *conseiller,* and his first cousin Jean d'Albenas was the principal lieutenant. The members of the présidial were the most prestigious officials regularly resident in the town, and they took prominent positions, in their special robes and hats, in all official ceremonies and other municipal occasions.[17]

The court's existence was also important for the local economy. As will be discussed below, many of the fortunes of the town's leading families derived from the law. Thomas Platter, when he visited in the 1590s, thought that there were 2,000 lawyers in Nîmes, an obvious exaggeration; including other members of the legal fraternity—notaries, clerks, and so forth—he was probably exaggerating by a factor of five.[18] Nonetheless, they were of vital importance. Many people also took advantage of the opportunity to buy from Nîmes's merchants when judicial business forced them to visit.

Continuing north from the présidial palace, our tour passes by the amphitheater—where you should watch not only underfoot, to avoid the muck on the streets, but also overhead, since stones occasionally fall off the amphitheater and hit passersby—before reaching the rue Fresque. The rue Fresque was also known as the rue de la Juiverie, since the Jewish quarter was located there until the Jews were expelled in the fourteenth century. Walking several blocks north along the rue Fresque and then making a right turn, you arrive rapidly at the second most important local institution, the city hall. It was called the *maison de la ville* or the *maison consulaire* in honor of Nîmes's leading political figures, the consuls. Here, the municipal council regularly met, after the town crier, accompanied by trumpet calls, had dutifully announced the meeting. City hall was located in the Bocarié haute quarter. The crier and the rest of the town's civil servants wore special long robes with long sleeves and with the arms of the city displayed on their shoulders, in order to emphasize the dignity of their offices and those of their masters, the city fathers.[19] Nîmes was governed by consuls, a style of government that was typical for southern and southwestern France. On November 14, 1476, an accord put an end to bickering over the distribution of offices and appears to have widened the number of families who participated, but Nîmes's government was by no means democratic, even by the standards of the era. The system established by the accord of 1476 was as follows: the city government consisted of four consuls and twelve *conseillers* (councilmen) comprising the *conseil ordinaire* (ordinary council). They were divided into four groups or classes: (1) lawyers; (2) bourgeois, merchants, and doctors of medicine; (3) notaries and artisans; and (4) *laboureurs* (wealthy farmers). For second consul, they were required to nominate either (a) four bourgeois, (b) four merchants, or (c) four medical doctors; and for third consul, they were required to nominate two notaries and two artisans. In 1552, for example, the four consuls were Tanequin Raymond, seigneur de Brignon, a lawyer; Vincent Mazel, a merchant who lived in the Corcomaires quarter; Guichard du Brana, a surgeon who also lived in the Corcomaires quarter; and Étienne Guiraudon, a *laboureur* who lived outside the walls in the faubourg des Precheurs.[20]

In contrast to many French cities, where at least male guild members could vote, in Nîmes municipal officers were chosen by the existing consuls and *conseillers*. In this sense, the town council was more like a board of trustees than a modern democratic assembly. Each year, the current and immediate past consuls and *conseillers* voted for four candidates from each group. The consul in each category was then selected by lot from among the top four vote getters. This was a dramatically staged and popular event. On the appointed day, usually in November, the town's officials ordered the doors of the Hôtel de Ville opened, and a large body of citizens came to see who would be selected. A boy of around seven years old made the choice. He was given a bag containing four wax balls, one of which was colored silver. He reached into the bag and handed one ball to each of the four candidates for each consulship; whoever got the silver ball was the winner and thus the consul for the following year. The consuls then selected twelve new *conseillers*, three in each category, for the next year. (Originally, the new officials took office in March, but in 1553 it was decided to switch to January 1.)[21]

Usually, Guillaume Calvière, the president of the présidial, or another judicial official acted as chair of the meetings, while the first consul, or in his absence the most senior consul present, spoke first, announcing the subject of the meeting and initiating the discussion. There were at least three different kinds of sessions, namely, the ordinary, extraordinary, and general and extraordinary (*conseil ordinaire, conseil extraordinaire,* and *conseil général et extraordinaire*), depending on the importance of the issue. Important meetings were usually open and well attended when the public was concerned about the issues to be considered. In quiet times, the council met about once a month, but could have sessions every few days when there was enough important business to justify it.[22] Council members usually deferred to the first consul. Under the governance of its first consul, Nîmes was nearly a dictatorship of lawyers, and their only institutional rivals were the judges, to whom they deferred and before whom they argued, on the présidial court. The consuls served a mediating function between the people and the state.[23]

To get to the next stop on our tour, the royal château, we cross the town heading east via the rue des Cardinaux to the Place du Château. The castle itself, the seat of royal authority in Nîmes, was on the east side of the square. In times of peace, it functioned as the jail for debtors or for people awaiting trial, who were watched over by the jailer, in this period Jean Fabre. Weapons were stored there, and when small bodies of royal troops came to town, they were quartered there as well.[24] From the château, it is only a short distance via the Place de la Belle Croix to the Place de la Cathédrale, the center of town and of Christian worship in Nîmes. The large square in front of the cathedral was also an important marketplace, so if you became hungry while on your walking tour, you could find something to eat. Of the various churches in Nîmes, the cathedral, dedicated to Notre Dame and St. Castor, was the largest and by any measure the most important. It was certainly the most prestigious and also, perhaps, the most loved: at any rate, more people asked to be buried there than in any other church in town. (Other popular churches included the Dominican, the Augustinian, St. Madaleine, the Observantin, St. Étienne de Capdueil, and the Carmelite.)[25]

The bishop of Nîmes from 1496 to 1514 was Guillaume Briçonnet, who was succeeded by his nephew Michel, who remained bishop until 1554. He was then succeeded by his nephew Claude. Only in 1561, at the height of the crisis of the Reformation, did the dynasty of Briçonnets end in Nîmes, when Claude Briçonnet exchanged places with Bernard d'Elbène, bishop of Lodève. All three Briçonnet bishops were relatives of the famous Guillaume Briçonnet, bishop of Meaux, who was interested in humanist ideas and whose circle included several clerics who later became Protestants. However, the Briçonnets of Nîmes were far less active pastors than the bishop of Meaux and were only infrequently resident. The bishop of Nîmes's deputy, or *vicaire*, was more important in the life of the town, since he was normally on the spot making decisions. In the late 1540s and early 1550s, after the retirement of the long-serving Robert Delacroix, the *vicaire* was Michel Suau, who was then replaced by Jean du Caylar.[26] From time to time, there was friction between the bishop and the canons of the cathedral. One instance was when the canons attempted to elect their own bishop instead of Guillaume Briçonnet in 1496. But these sorts of disputes were commonplace in sixteenth-century France.

There was undoubtedly some anti-clericalism in Nîmes, but there is no reason to believe that it was greater than elsewhere. The canons had been cloistered until

1539, when they obtained a bull of secularization from the pope, releasing them from their monastic vows. The bull also reduced the number of canons from 81 to 20. There have been suggestions that the act of secularization demonstrates a lack of zeal on the part of Nîmes's clergy. There is little evidence, however, that the clergy in Nîmes were any more or less dedicated than those in other places. Certainly, they were quite prepared to attack heresy, as will be seen later. Effectiveness is, however, determined by a combination of zeal and resources. It is reasonable to wonder whether Protestantism had an advantage in Nîmes because the Church had fewer personnel available to combat heresy than in other regions. Unfortunately, it is not easy to determine whether this was the case. Over 100 priests can be identified in Nîmes in the period, and probably there were substantially more. Still, there appear to have been 400–500 members of the clergy in Troyes—admittedly a city of more than twice Nîmes's size. (If these figures are correct, there were between 16 and 20 priests per 1,000 people in Troyes; Rouen had a similar percentage, while Madrid had even more.) By contrast, Troyes had ten churches and three abbeys, so by that measure Nîmes, with fifteen churches, was well provided for.[27] The church in Nîmes as an institution, although not the most dynamic in Christendom, was reasonably able and well equipped—but well-endowed and -staffed institutions can still fail to attract an enthusiastic following.

Measuring popular piety is difficult: even when records survive, individual piety is subjective, and abstracting piety to a large group of people only compounds the problem. Furthermore, as Protestants repeatedly pointed out, external actions do not necessarily correspond to inward beliefs. However, it is only the external acts, not the feelings that inspired them, that can be measured; and although sixteenth-century Protestants might have disagreed, surely external acts have some significance. In many small gestures and in a few actions that have entered the historical record, the people of sixteenth-century Nîmes displayed the telltale signs of their Catholic upbringing and education, which the Protestant church would eventually try to eliminate. So, if we cannot determine how pious the people of Nîmes were compared to other French towns, we can at least hope to understand to what degree they followed certain Catholic customs. Unfortunately, even here, measurement is difficult and comparison tricky. There are no reliable sixteenth-century figures for church attendance, for example.

Wills provide some evidence of popular piety, since they contain bequests for masses after death and gifts to the poor. As they lay in their beds, believing themselves close to death, people in Nîmes frequently chose to give money to the Church for the repose of their souls after death. They sometimes also offered to give alms, usually food or clothing, to poor people, who in exchange would march in the funeral procession and pray for their benefactors. In the later sixteenth century in Dijon, about one-third of artisans asked for at least one mass to be said for their souls; in Reims and Avignon, the percentage appears to have been distinctly higher. In Nîmes, the percentage varies widely from year to year, and from notary to notary; as will be discussed further below, one family of notaries in Nîmes, the Ursis, were almost certainly early Protestants. In the period 1554–1560, from which many non-Ursi wills survive, between one-third and nearly three-quarters of testators chose to leave money for masses, depending on the year, and between an eighth and a third of them chose to leave money for the poor. Insofar as piety can be measured, then, Nîmes was a reasonably pious community.[28]

A brief walk from the cathedral back to the Place de la Belle Croix and then down the Grand' Rue on the east side of town leads to the University and College of Arts. It was founded by royal patent in 1539, the same year the cathedral chapter was secularized. When it was founded, the council gave the college the building of the old St. Mark's hospital, which had a suitably academic form since it was structured around a central courtyard. The council later bought several adjoining houses for the college's use. The college got off to a somewhat rocky start. Over the next decade, there were considerable administrative changes, lawsuits, and accusations of heresy (discussed below). By the early 1550s, things had quieted down considerably under the rectorship of Guillaume Tuffan, a native of Nîmes and the head of the College of Narbonne at the University of Paris before taking up his Nîmes appointment. Assisting him were a handful of other professors, who taught philosophy and mathematics in addition to the classical languages. Latin was the language of instruction, except in the early grades. The college was not a true university, since it did not have any of the requisite graduate faculties of law, medicine, or theology: it was only an undergraduate institution, akin to a modern American liberal arts college. Although it is difficult to know how many students were at the college at any one time, over the course of the 1550s and early 1560s, nearly fifty can be identified. Most of them came from Nîmes or the vicinity, although several came from Provence and a few from Dauphiné, Piedmont, Normandy, and the Limousin.[29]

Below the level of the college, Nîmes had a number of schools. The town itself and the Carmelite monastery ran the most important ones; several others, including one run by the cathedral, were reserved for future priests. Tutors were common, especially in elite families. Sons usually stayed in school until age fifteen, when they were apprenticed to a trade. For boys in the artisan class or higher, education was relatively common: in Montpellier in the 1570s, almost all of the merchants could sign their names, and more than three-fifths of the artisans could do so. Wool carders were also highly literate, but masons were not. Agricultural workers were only rarely literate. Education for girls, of course, was much rarer than for boys, and university education was entirely closed to them. It appears that university education was relatively widespread in Europe in the sixteenth century and that 2–3 percent of young men attended—a figure not matched until the twentieth century. But the figures are not as reliable as one would like.[30]

If you walked south from the college buildings down the Grand' Rue, then west across town along the rue du Marché aux blé into the Place du Marché (Market Square), you could then leave town by the Porte St. Antoine and proceed into the suburbs, specifically the faubourg St. Antoine, where the hospital was located. (You could also stop in the square to buy food, if you had not already bought something in front of the cathedral.) Nîmes had several hospitals, which also served the poor, in the Middle Ages. The town council had succeeded in consolidating most of them into one municipal Hôtel-Dieu in 1483, and it continued this policy, adding the Charité de St. Césaire in 1546. (In addition, there was also a hospital for lepers, separated from those suffering from other illnesses.) In these efforts at consolidation, Nîmes was precocious but hardly alone: Aix-en-Provence, for example, succeeded in consolidating all of its hospitals by 1531. The Hôtel-Dieu was in the suburbs, but just outside the city walls. It consisted of two floors, the lower for men and the upper for women. The hospital also housed abandoned children, called "the bastards of the hospital." The city paid for the rector and for a surgeon to treat the patients. A priest was available as well, and there was also an endowment for an *avocat des pauvres,* a legal aid lawyer for patients and for poor people generally. In March 1550, the consuls came on an inspection tour; at that time, the building held five men, six women, and seven orphaned children. Still, there were other poor people and children hanging about the marketplaces and in front of the churches, begging for charity from passersby.[31]

Unlike in many other cities and towns in Europe, there were no guildhalls in Nîmes in the early 1550s. In the Middle Ages and into the early sixteenth century, Nîmes had a large number of confraternities, guilds organized by profession, usually under a patron saint. The leather workers of Nîmes created a confraternity under the patronage of St. Crépin and maintained a chapel to the saint in the cathedral. The wool carders' patron was St. Blaise, and their chapel was in the Carmelite church. Confraternities commonly met regularly to discuss the business of their trades and also to have banquets, usually on the feast days of their patron saints. In 1540, the Nîmes city council, obeying the royal Edict of Villers-Cotterêts, which had been announced the year before, ordered the suppression of all guild confraternities and ordered that their assets be transferred to the new college. It seems that most towns did not enforce the edict, and even in Nîmes it is not entirely clear how thoroughly the edict was enforced, since the town council continued to negotiate with the various food trades in the 1540s and 1550s. However, the confraternities were firmly linked to Catholicism, with their chapels in the churches and patron saints, and none of them seems to have survived the Reformation. It is possible that the town council inadvertently aided the Reformation by its actions: in suppressing the confraternities, the council destroyed an important link between ordinary people and the Church.[32]

Travelers wandering around Nîmes might wish to purchase a book, and indeed Nîmes possessed some literary life. In particular, some townspeople appear to have been interested in Renaissance humanism. Two of Nîmes's booksellers, Jean Lucquet and François Bernard, were also publishers in a modest way: Bernard published a volume on legal procedures for the use of lawyers filing motions with the Nîmes présidial, and Lucquet published an oration in praise of the college and the présidial written by Ferrand de Bez. Lucquet also put up one of the first Renaissance-style facades in Nîmes for his house. Bernard died in 1556, and his son of the same name succeeded him in business. In the early 1530s, one enterprising Nîmes bookseller, Léonard Danyot, a close friend of Bernard, had even tried his hand at printing editions of the breviaries of the Abbey of Saint-Gilles and the diocese of Uzès. In all, there were probably around ten booksellers in Nîmes in the 1550s.[33] There were also a number of local authors, most notably the humanists at the college and Jean-Poldo d'Albenas, the author of the first description of Nîmes's Roman antiquities, the *Discours historial de l'antique et illustre cité de Nismes,* first published in 1559. Several Nîmes residents, including d'Albenas, also published translations of Spanish, Italian, and Latin works.[34] Thomas Platter, the traveler mentioned earlier, probably bought a copy of the *Discours historial* on his visit to Nîmes in 1596 and used it as a guidebook, since he commented that it described the city's monuments in "a very interesting way." There was also a circle of local antiquaries interested in Roman coins and medallions, as part of the developing field of numismatics. When another traveler, the important engraver and early collector of Roman coins Hubert Goltzius of Bruges, came to Nîmes in 1560 on a search across Europe for coins for a book on the subject, he conferred with a number of the city's residents, including the vicomte de Joyeuse, who was visiting the town; Bernard Vallat, a well-to-do leather worker; and, unsurprisingly, Jean-Poldo d'Albenas.[35]

Economy

Most cities during the Renaissance provided a number of standard services for the surrounding villages and countryside. They served as local marketplaces where produce could be sold and various commonly needed goods could be acquired. Most towns had local clothing manufacturers, metalworkers, smiths and farriers (horseshoe makers and those who shoed horses), merchants, and so forth. Every community had to provide certain basic services for its inhabitants, so there were always butchers, bakers, innkeepers, masons, carpenters, and furniture makers. There were also those who provided specialized and professional services, including doctors, surgeons, apothecaries, jewelers, and, especially in Mediterranean Europe, notaries, who wrote up contracts and put them into legal form. Larger towns and cities were usually administrative centers. The courts, financial administrators, and the provincial governor often resided in them. Large towns also had distinctive local products that could be sold in the international marketplace—perhaps an esteemed local fabric, or leather, or a unique manufacturing process.

In sixteenth-century Nîmes, men needed to work. Undoubtedly, most women worked, and worked hard, either in the household or outside for pay, but men were identified as the primary breadwinners. Most men did not produce all the food and other products they and their families needed to live on. Rather, they worked for pay, and used the money they made to buy the things they needed. Their livelihood therefore depended on the strength of the local economy. The economy of Nîmes depended on four main sectors: agriculture, clothing and leather, trade, and government, and it was upon these sectors that the population depended. If the industries that brought money into the city failed, many people were thrown out of work, and the ripple effects rapidly spread to other businesses throughout the city. In the sixteenth century, when the line between making a living and destitution, disease, and malnutrition or starvation was much finer than today, anything that could adversely affect the economy was viewed with something like panic. Figure 1.1 shows the percentages of men working in the various sectors of the economy, derived from an analysis of the people who appear in the wills and marriage contracts surviving in the registers of the town's notaries between 1560 and 1562.[36]

In contrast to some cities in Northern Europe, agriculture in Nîmes was vital not only because it provided the food people needed to eat, but because it directly employed a large percentage of Nîmes's adult male population. Something like one-third of all men got up in the morning and walked out to the fields to work. It must have made for a great deal of bustle at the town's various gates as they all passed through. This percentage is broadly comparable to other towns in the Midi. Emmanuel Le Roy Ladurie, for example, found over 20 percent of

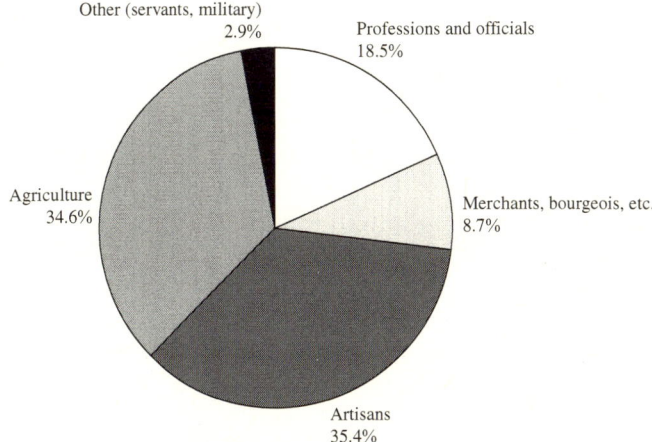

FIGURE 1.1. Occupational distribution of adult men in Nîmes, 1550–1562.
Source: ADG, Series IIE.

the population of Montpellier to be *travailleurs;* the comparable figure for Nîmes is just under 25 percent.[37] Tax records indicate that grain, wine, olives, and grazing were the most common land uses in the area, although there does not appear to have been much specialization. No one is described as a wine grower (*vigneron*), for example, and there were only a few shepherds, probably because most of them spent their time in the mountains with their flocks. The most common terms used to describe agricultural workers were *laboureur* and *travailleur,* corresponding roughly to the old English terms yeoman and husbandman. The first designated someone who owned most of his own land and supervised others, while the second meant an underling, someone who worked the land for other people. It was common for people to spend some of their time on their own land and some of it working for others, so these designations were somewhat fluid. There were also gardeners, *jardiniers,* who grew fruits and vegetables which were then sold in the markets. They could own their own land or tend the gardens of wealthy people. One of the four consuls who governed the city was always a *laboureur,* but as mentioned earlier he always occupied the fourth and least important position. *Laboureurs,* although the top of the hierarchy of agricultural trades, were not particularly wealthy nor of high status in the town.

Most towns in the sixteenth century employed a substantial part of the population in clothing manufacture, and Nîmes was no exception. Nîmes was geographically favored for both wool and leather production, since large upland areas nearby were suited to raising cattle and sheep. Everyone needed clothes, and making them consumed an enormous amount of energy. The raw material (linen, wool, silk) had to be processed (wool had to be combed, for example), dyed, spun into thread, woven, then cut into pieces and sewn to make shirts, breeches, dresses, smocks, aprons, and other items. Each of these processes was normally a separate trade. Cloth, once woven, was a major element of international trade, as were some other components of clothing (ribbon and lace, for example). Cloth was relatively lightweight and therefore easy to transport: as a result, there was every reason to concentrate the intricate dance of production in a small area and distribute the finished product in a large one. Even if, as was the case in some cities, guild restrictions encouraged the dispersion of some parts of the process to the countryside, cloth making was always strictly dependent on a center, unlike wood or stone work, which had to be done locally in every commune and hamlet. Within the cloth-making trades, there was a definite hierarchy of wealth: drapers and hosiers near the top, then shearers, tailors, and dyers, with weavers and wool carders near the bottom. In the leather trades, there were fewer distinctions and less wealth generally, but furriers were, unsurprisingly, rather better off than the rest. There was great variety within these occupations, however, and status also depended on whether one was a master, in charge of the shop, a journeyman, or an apprentice. In Nîmes, about one-fifth of the male population worked in clothing and leather, with somewhat more than half of that in clothing.

At the upper ends of the trades, some of the masters were occupied in trading goods produced elsewhere as well as selling their own production. As a result, there were fine gradations among a wealthy artisan, a merchant, and a bourgeois, that is, a man who had retired from active trading and lived entirely off his investments. Usually, the more money a man made, the further removed from production he became, and therefore the bourgeois were generally the wealthiest of the group. Nîmes in the sixteenth century had a significant percentage of such men—if we include a few other high-status professions, including brokers, retailers, and jewelers, merchants and bourgeois added up to slightly more than 8 percent of the adult male population—and they were important in local government, although not generally at its highest levels. The top positions in local government were dominated by men of the law, who accounted for a similar percentage of the population but who were, on average, much richer.

It was normal in southern France and Mediterranean Europe, broadly speaking, for lawyers to be at the top of the urban hierarchy, and Nîmes was no exception. Lawyers were the richest group of legal professionals; notaries and clerks were more like merchants in social status. In Nîmes, where the most prestigious local institution was the présidial court, the preeminence of lawyers is not surprising. They moved relatively easily through the same world as the officials, with whom they shared the same educational background and with whom they interacted daily in the courts, although the officials were substantially more affluent. The economic effects of the court were not only direct, but indirect. Although Nîmes was not as dependent on government as Washington, D.C., and Springfield, Illinois, are today, it was much less a commercial capital than Lyon or Florence. It was, above all, an administrative center.[38]

Since marriage contracts survive for women who married men in most of the various trades, dowry figures can be used to give an overall ranking of professions in Nîmes. By this measure, officials ranked at the top of the social scale. Along with them ranked some families who were starting to move into the ranks of the nobility by purchasing noble land, châteaux, and seigneurial rights. Tanequin Raymond, the first consul in 1552, was a good example of this: he held the title of seigneur de Brignon. This did not mean that he was a true member of the nobility, as contemporaries understood the term. People referred to true aristocrats by their titles of baron, comte, marquis, etc., without mentioning their family names. Still, these seigneurs-by-purchase, officials, and their families ranked at the top of local society, and their wives came with dowries averaging over £1,200. Directly after seigneurs and officials in the hierarchy of wealth and status came lawyers: the women they married had dowries, on average, of over £900. This was significantly above those of even wealthy merchants and bourgeois, who received dowries of, on average, £200 and nearly £500, respectively. Farmers

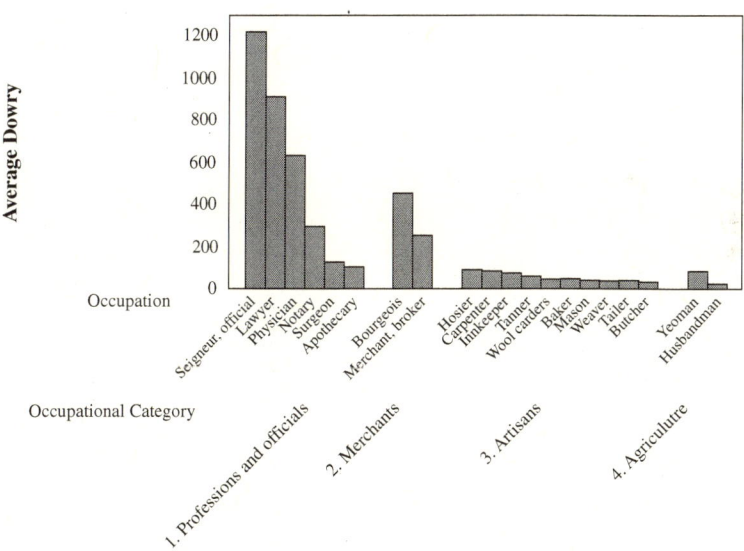

FIGURE 1.2. Average dowries given to men in selected occupations, Nîmes, 1550–1562. Source: ADG, Series IIE.

and agricultural workers ranked at the bottom of the scale (yeomen married women who had an average dowry of £86, husbandmen just over £30).

As a rough measure, it would be reasonable to describe dowries of more than £200 as wealthy, £100–£200 as upper middling, £50–£100 as middling, and below £50 as poor. Thus, professionals, officials, and bourgeois would rank as rich, while merchants, notaries, other men of the law—clerks and *praticiens*—and apothecaries would be in the upper-middling group. On the border between the upper middle and the middle would be members of a few high-status cloth trades, including drapers, mercers, embroiderers, and velvet makers. The middle would consist heavily of cloth tradesmen, with leather workers, including saddlers and tanners, in the upper half and hatters and wool carders at the lower end. Also prominent in the upper half of the middling group were *laboureurs;* booksellers, although few in number, belonged there as well, as did some members of the carpentry trades, locksmiths, and potters. In the lower reaches of the middle group were the food tradesmen: bakers, butchers, innkeepers. The poor consisted of building tradesmen, such as masons, carters, and, most of all, poor agricultural laborers.

Dowries can be used to give an approximate social rank even to people who were not getting married, based on which marriage contracts they witnessed. Weddings were fairly stratified, and the witnesses to marriage contracts with large dowries tended to be wealthier than those who witnessed the contracts of more modest people. In the end, it proved possible in my research to use the dowry information to create a wealth index and to assign a "social status" number and rank almost every person who appeared in the surviving wills and marriage contracts. (The details are described in Appendix B.) The technique produced slightly different results than using dowries directly. A person with a social status of more than 200 qualifies as wealthy; 100–200 as upper middling; and 50–100 as middling. People with a social status number of less than 50 were probably quite poor.[39]

People tended to marry within their own station, broadly construed. For 274 marriages where the occupation of the groom and the bride's father are both known, and both parties came from Nîmes, it was generally at least twice as likely for people to marry within their broad occupational grouping as outside it. Agricultural workers tended to marry the daughters of other agricultural workers, men of law the daughters of other men of law, and so forth. It is noteworthy that officials, professionals, and bourgeois moved largely within a separate realm: officials never married into the lower-ranking artisanal and agricultural trades, and even professionals and merchants did so only rarely. Artisans tended to marry among themselves, and the same was true of agricultural workers, although there was some degree of mixing. Cloth workers were the most likely to marry out. However, it should be pointed out that these figures were calculated by occupation, not by wealth, and the different cloth trades included a particularly wide economic spectrum: some members were fairly well-off, while others were quite poor. Some cloth workers were therefore good marriage prospects even for the well-to-do, while others would have had to look to other poorer people to find suitable partners.

Marriage choice was not only horizontally stratified. Marriages also reinforced the vertical ties that bound the social order, since in marriages, wealthy people

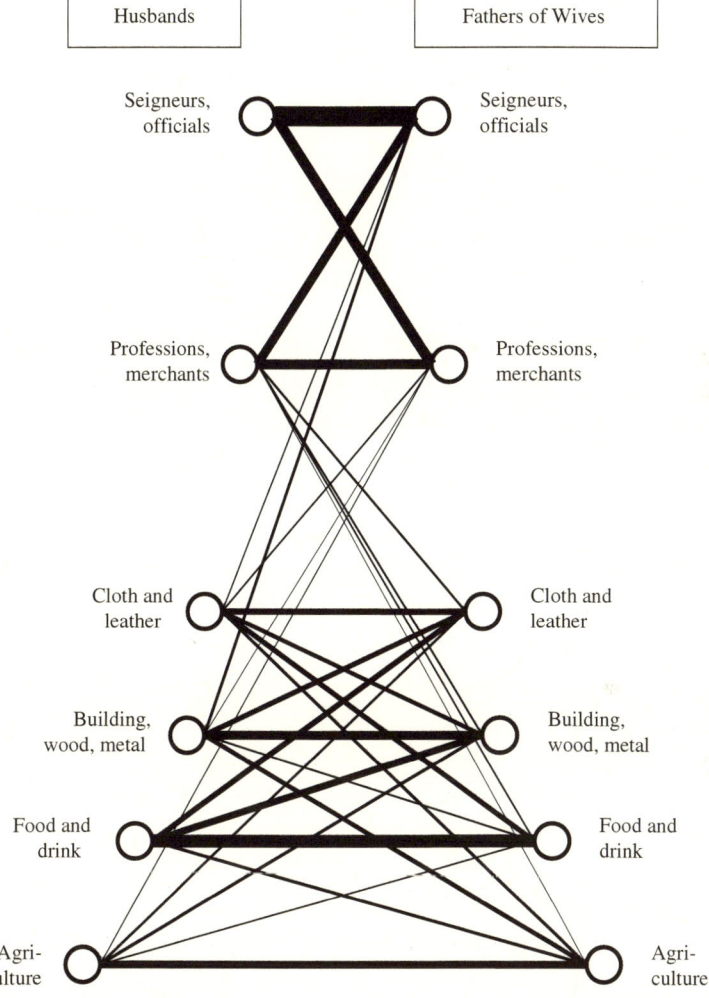

FIGURE 1.3. Marriage stratification in Nîmes. The pyramid places wealthier groups, as measured by dowries, proportionately closer to the top. Thicker lines represent proportionately more marriages. Based on a sample of 274 marriages in which the occupations of both parties are known, and both come from Nîmes. Source: ADG, Series IIE.

could provide a great deal of aid to humbler relatives and employees. Wealthy men and women frequently provided dowries for their servants: Antoinette Cordilh married a respectable yeoman, a *laboureur,* no doubt in part thanks to a substantial dowry of £50 plus the use of some land. Of that, she received £20 from her master and mistress, Jean Barrière and Jeanne Deran. Barrière was a doctor of laws and seigneur de Vestric; other members of his family were members of the présidial court. He may also have provided the priest, since one of the witnesses was Father Benoît Barrière, another relative.

Even when masters did not provide the dowry directly, their maidservants frequently owed their dowries to their ability to save significant sums out of their earnings. Jeanne Caruc, for example, managed to acquire a dowry of £48 from her earnings working for Mathieu Campanhan, the lieutenant of the criminal court.[40] Furthermore, the signing of the marriage contract was an occasion for celebration, marked by a ceremonial meal, and masters could provide a suitable space for the reception. The meal was probably held after mass, perhaps linked to the announcement of the banns, since 43 percent of marriage contracts were signed on Sunday. The contract of marriage between Alphonse Portal, a gardener, and Marguerite Fabre, for example, was signed in the "large garden of Gilles Bonaud [his employer] under the large parquet," presumably referring to a reception room that had steps down to the garden. These halls were also a common place to conclude the contract—presumably Portal and Fabre used the garden because of his profession, or perhaps because the weather was good enough that day so that the reception could be held outside. Of course, some people, usually fairly poor ones, did not have wealthy patrons. They frequently used an inn instead, or sometimes the garden of the Order of St. John of Jerusalem. Masters and other prominent people generally appear first in the list of witnesses, too, indicating their superior position and the role they played in helping the couple.[41]

The data on marriage suggest that the top of the social pyramid was fairly unified, rather than Lawrence Stone's description of England as consisting of multiple elites, each at the top of a separate hierarchy, such as commerce, the law, or the aristocracy. (He called this the "San Gimignano model," after the Tuscan hill town that is dotted with late medieval towers.)[42] Social network analysis confirms this. For the 249 most important families in Nîmes (a total of 674 people), I used the information from the database of marriage contracts and wills to create a tree of relationships linking families and dividing them into factional groups. The crucial issue is that, in Nîmes, as has generally been reported for Western Europe, most families asked people who were close to them to sign as witnesses to their wills and marriage contracts. In addition to personal friendships, these ties also reflected family alliances, since families repeatedly asked each other to be witnesses to each other's contracts. Thus, it was possible for me to compile lists of which families were closest to each other. The result might be visualized as a web, with dots representing the families and lines connecting them. The computer algorithms that created the factions work on the principle of dividing the population into groups while "cutting" as few ties as possible. (The process of selecting the individuals, dividing them into families, and creating the factions is discussed in more detail in Appendix B, which also includes a table giving the statistics on which this paragraph is based.) If you look in a broad way at Nîmes's elite families in the sixteenth century, they divided up into 6 main factions and 17 small, distantly related out-groups. The bigger factions were located at the center of the elite, so the biggest faction had 56 families and was the wealthiest, on average. It also had the highest betweenness. *Betweenness* is an important measure used by sociologists to quantify which people, families, or institutions are most well connected to others. A family that knows every other family in one faction, but has no connection to other factions, will not have particularly high betweenness compared to a family that acts as a go-between among several different factions. In Renaissance Florence, for example, the Medicis had extremely high betweenness because they were the only family that linked older aristocratic families to newly wealthy ones. This was a crucial asset in the Medicis' rise to power. More generally, people who are seen as particularly trustworthy have high betweenness. Such people are respected by everyone. They are also exposed to a much wider set of points of view than people who have ties with only one part of the community. They are thus natural politicians and power brokers who can help to form coalitions of interests. People with high betweenness are likely to rate appeals to the public interest highly. This gave Nîmes's elite considerable added strength, since the leading families were well connected to many parts of the society, making it easier for them to receive information and exercise influence.[43]

In many ways, sixteenth-century Nîmes was like other southern French towns of the period. Shared elements included the consular system of government, the large percentage of agricultural workers among the population, and the importance of men of law in governance. Some of these features almost certainly influenced the course of the Reformation in the town: (1) Nîmes had a unified social hierarchy, with clear direction from the top, namely, its lawyers and officials. This contrasted sharply with the social structure commonly found in northern French towns, which were dominated socially and politically by guilds. There, converting one occupational grouping did not necessarily help when it came to converting the others. In Nîmes, the conversion of lawyers and officials greatly facilitated the conversion of the rest of the town, because they were so influential. (2) Calvinism may also have had a particular appeal to the men of the law who governed Nîmes, both because Calvin's theology had a legalistic turn (discussed further below) and because lawyers had to have a sophisticated literacy that gave them the ability to appreciate the intricacies of theological debate. (3) Beyond Nîmes, the configuration of the local economy also facilitated the growth of Protestantism. Townspeople had extensive connections with the city's rural hinterland, since the town's leather and cloth trades depended on supplies from the Cévennes. This helps to explain why Protestantism spread so successfully to the countryside, as will be discussed in more detail in the conclusion of this book. (4) Nîmes's sense of connection to classical Rome probably helped to spread humanist, and then Protestant, ideas. Calvinist rectitude may have had a particularly strong appeal to consuls who saw themselves as the heirs of Cato and Cicero. Latin could be a double-edged sword, however, since Catholic propaganda also relied on ties to Rome, the Rome of St. Peter's as well as of the Colosseum. In general, Roman traditions were stronger in southern France than elsewhere, and they may have been especially strong in Nîmes. (5) Finally, it is probable that people in Nîmes had a certain predisposition to Protestantism because they were inclined to be suspicious of central authority. Paris was far away for most residents of the Midi.[44]

But none of these factors are even necessary, let alone sufficient, conditions to explain the startling success of the Reformation in Nîmes. The Protestant movement, when it came to Nîmes, encountered an old society with fixed institutions through and with which it would have to work. The town's social organization gave the movement some opportunities and foreclosed others, but nothing in Nîmes's political, economic, or social structure preordained the success of the Protestant movement. Nîmes's Protestants successfully evangelized the bulk of their fellow-citizens. This was a profound and lasting change, altering the city's religious, political, social, and economic behavior for the next four centuries. But the movement succeeded, as the following chapters will show, because its leaders proved masterful at seizing the moment and exploiting a particular historical crisis.

2

The Creation of a Protestant Community

Nîmes, 1530–1547

The people of Nîmes in the early 1530s were good Catholics, loyal to their king and the pope. Fifteen years later, although this was still largely true, their attitudes and circumstances had changed significantly. Intellectually, Nîmes was affected by what historians have traditionally labeled Renaissance humanism. Ideas like those of Erasmus seem to have been particularly attractive. There was a new moralism to public life, renewed interest in the Roman past, and a new commitment to education. Materially, the major change was a significant decline in living standards, a trend which only accelerated in the following decade. It was in these conditions that the first converts to Protestantism appeared, and over the next decade, the movement's ideology matured and it found its leaders. By the late 1540s, the town harbored a small but significant Protestant minority.

A New Moralism

One sign of the new moralism in public life was a new attitude toward public prostitution. In the later Middle Ages, Nîmes, like most towns in Languedoc, had a licensed public brothel, which paid an annual rent to the town. In the later fifteenth century, the owner of Nîmes's brothel was Gabriel de Laye, a lawyer and prominent citizen: he was first consul and was sent as a representative to the king when he visited Montpellier in 1490. In this period, it was customary for the madam to publicly offer a cake for charity on Ascension Day; on at least one occasion, in 1480, the consul thanked her with a kiss.[1] The existence of the licensed public brothel was to some extent a sign that ordinary people didn't like prostitutes in their vicinity, since it kept them confined to one location rather than permitting them to wander about. At the same time, it was apparently no disgrace to be the owner.

In the sixteenth century, however, people began to change their minds about the morality of legalized prostitution. In Germany, where municipal brothels were also common, they were frequently abolished as part of the Reformation. In Languedoc, people's attitudes started to change earlier. In the late fifteenth century, authorities in Toulouse began to close its brothel in times of plague, and in 1528 the town decided to use the money that the brothel owner paid, which they felt was tainted, to support the work of the plague hospital. Ordinary people's attitudes also began to change: in 1532, people began to report to municipal investigators that certain women were "nothing but" prostitutes. At around the same time, the authorities began to clamp down on prostitutes from the official brothel, punishing them for even minor offenses. In Nîmes, municipal authorities first temporarily closed the brothel, citing health concerns, in 1522. They closed it definitively in 1532 and turned it into a hospital. This new suspicion of institutionalized prostitution gradually spread throughout the region. In the 1550s, the public brothels of Alès, Castelnaudary, and Montpellier were all closed, and finally, the Edict of Orléans in 1561 forbade all brothels in France. In Castelnaudary, the house was referred to as the *maison de débauche,* thus indicating that moral concerns, not merely issues of health, were behind the decision.[2]

In another sign that a changing moral landscape was making people nervous, shortly after the closure of the brothel, Nîmes faced its first heresy scare. The Nîmes city council hired a priest each year to preach a series of sermons for Lent. In 1532, they chose an Augustinian monk who was resident in the town. However, on March 30, the day before Easter Sunday, an official of the Parlement of Toulouse ordered the preacher's arrest. The city council was sufficiently concerned that it met to discuss the issue on Easter Sunday.[3]

Nîmes's elite was small and its consuls, led inevitably by lawyers, tended to set a legalistic tone. They also tended to think alike, because they inherited from their predecessors a set of prerogatives, perquisites, and problems. Because they had legal training and a high sense of their own dignity, they felt they knew what was right, and wanted the freedom to act accordingly. Nîmes stubbornly pursued some legal cases—against the crown, for example—for generations, and each first consul thus inherited the same ever-increasing files and the same institutional animosities. The first consuls were lawyers, and consequently they were usually sharply observant and precise, if lengthy and ponderous, in speech. Likewise, they excelled at constructing arguments from facts, but only to defend views they already held. They were protective of their privileges, disdainful of advice, and suspicious of outsiders. They were deferential to the king only in the abstract. At the same time, they were paternalistic and felt obligated to help Nîmes's poorer citizens, so long as others showed proper deference to them.[4] When "their" monk was arrested on the day before Easter, their reaction was not fear that their reputations might be tarnished by his misdeeds. They were not concerned that they had ignorantly allowed heresy to be preached for weeks before the most holy day of the Christian calendar. Rather, they were outraged that the parlement would dare to question their judgment, although the parlement was in charge of prosecuting heresy cases.

In the council's emergency deliberations, everyone argued that the monk's views were admirable, not heretical, and they tended to suspect the clergy's motives and performance. Pierre de Malmont suggested that someone was "jealous" (*quelques uns hont conseu envie contre luy*) of the monk because he got to preach in the cathedral, and insisted that he preached "good doctrine." Instead, he felt the town was "scandalized" because the monk had not preached at vespers. Since the monk might need money to defend himself, the town should give him £40. Pierre Robert, a judicial official, suggested that they should make sure that the monk was innocent by consulting with clerics, but also stated that he had "preached well." The council had little doubt that they had not made a mistake.

Jacques d'Albenas agreed with Robert and also fulminated against the clergy. He suggested, "And one should go summon and require Monsieur the bishop of Nîmes to preach the Word of God or have some other good and worthy priest preach in Nîmes, and require him to give hospitality to the poor, and reside in his . . . episcopal residence."[5] Others agreed. (This feeling that the Church was not doing enough about poverty also recurred in later years.) Although there is no evidence of Protestantism in Nîmes's elite at the time, clearly they were not entirely satisfied with the Catholic Church. When their choice was criticized, they went on the attack. They were not deferential.

King François I Visits

In the 1530s, Nîmes's leaders became more interested in humanism, which helped to pave the way for Protestant ideas. In particular, they became more interested in Nîmes's Roman past. One way to get a sense of what the people of Nîmes felt about their society is to examine the town's feelings about the king, as they were displayed when he visited the town as part of his progress to Marseille in the spring of 1533. He traveled to celebrate the marriage of his second son, the fourteen-year-old Henri, duke of Orléans, to Catherine de' Medici, of the famous Florentine family. As usual with royal marriages, the king's motive was political: he wished to ally his family, the Valois, with the papacy. Clement VII, the pope, was Catherine's uncle. (Of necessity, this meant cooler French relations with England, since King Henry VIII and the pope were quarreling over Henry's desire to divorce Catherine of Aragon.) The king's progress south was slow: he left Lyon at the end of June, and deliberately detoured via Riom, Clermont-Ferrand, and Toulouse, rather than heading straight down the Rhone.[6] The marriage took place on October 28.

King François I had long admired Italian art and architecture and was responsible for fostering Renaissance styles in France. He also shared the Renaissance's admiration for the classical world and established four lecturers in Greek and Hebrew in Paris. This endowment was later the nucleus of the Collège de France. For his visit to Nîmes, the town's leaders therefore chose to take François on a guided tour of the town's Roman monuments.

François approached Nîmes from the south, along the old Roman road from Montpellier. The city council followed his progress and made plans to receive him. They did not want outsiders to learn what they had planned, so they resolved that each councillor must swear to keep the town's plans for his visit a secret. The streets were lined with tapestries and strewn with sand to beautify and clean them. The council was clear that the most important message they wanted to convey in the festivities was that Nîmes was a great city because of its Roman heritage. Their approval of Rome, and their self-congratulation as Rome's descendants, knew no bounds. First of all, they were lawyers, and French law, especially in southern France, was derived from Roman law. They proudly called their leaders consuls. Second, they were well aware that their town possessed the finest collection of Roman monuments in France. Jean-Poldo d'Albenas's *Discours historial de l'antique et illustre cité de Nismes* (1559) included, in addition to many illustrations of Nîmes's Roman monuments, several poems in praise of the city boasting of its ancient heritage.[7] They were proud that Nîmes was one of the oldest towns in the country.

The council ordered the erection in a square at the southern end of town of a classical column, topped with a salamander, the king's personal symbol. When the king arrived, the town received him with a civic procession where the officials, in new robes and in order of importance, trooped out to meet the king before the Jacobin Gate on the north side of the city. To provide a suitable gift for their sovereign, the townspeople hired a craftsman to make a model of the town's famous Roman amphitheater in solid silver, weighing thirty marks (more than sixteen pounds); it didn't arrive on time and had to be given to King François later. Members of the king's retinue also received suitable presents. The enormous expense of the reception—over £8,000, more than a year's taxes paid to the crown—was paid by all of the towns in the civil diocese (the region around Nîmes, considered as a unit for tax purposes). Despite the elaborate preparations, the king's visit exceeded expectations: François climbed to the very top of the Tour Magne, then went on his knees and used his own handkerchief to wipe away the dust so that he could more easily read the Roman inscriptions, thus showing an interest that contemporaries noted with shock and delight. He had truly honored their town: he had gone down on bended knee before its Roman monuments! François I further recognized Nîmes's Roman heritage when he granted Nîmes a new coat of arms after his visit: the design was based on a Roman medallion that had recently been discovered near the town, bearing the ancient name of the city, Nemausus. The town council, when it ordered the erection of a column in François honor, intended to convey a similar message about the city's Roman virtues: the column conveyed antiquity, gravity, and the town's fealty to the crown. François's visit to Nîmes's Roman monuments during his tour demonstrated his respect for Rome and for everything the residents held dear: their town, their heritage, their liberties, and their law. It was a gesture that resonated profoundly with Nîmes's governing elite. One of François purposes in his travels through provincial France was to cultivate a sense of personal connection between himself and his subjects, and in Nîmes he amply succeeded.[8]

François I's religious policies were complicated by competing considerations. He was firmly Catholic. However, as part of his enthusiasm for the new learning, he was also open to certain reforms, along Erasmian lines. Politically, he was allied with the German Protestant princes against Emperor Charles V. From François's point of view, Charles was using the religious issue as an excuse for political aggrandizement. Thus, there was an incentive for him to engineer a reconciliation among the churches, along Erasmian lines. The Protestants would return to the fold, and the Catholic Church would reform itself. On François's return to Paris, conservative Catholic theologians at the Sorbonne annoyed him by attacking his sister Marguerite de Navarre's book, *Mirror of the Sinful Soul* (*Miroir de l'âme pécheresse*). This made him even more interested in a compromise distinct from fanaticism on either extreme. He sent an emissary to inquire about the possibilities. Philip Melanchthon, Luther's closest associate, sent a conciliatory reply, but just at this moment Protestant radicals chose to testify to their faith in a most dramatic way.

On the night of October 17–18, 1534, Protestants put up posters all over Paris, a number of other cities, and even in the royal château at Amboise, where François's was staying. Modern scholarship has shown that Antoine Marcourt, the pastor of Neuchâtel in Switzerland, wrote the text. The posters denounced the "horrifying, great and intolerable abuses of the papal Mass." The text argued that transubstantiation was absurd: despite Catholic doctrine, Christ was not resacrificed in the Eucharist. The rite was merely symbolic, a remembrance. This argument directly attacked the core of the everyday religious experience of ordinary Catholics. Its theology clearly marked it as the work not of Lutherans, but of the more radical Zwinglians. How did radical heretics manage to desecrate so many of the public squares in Paris without being seen? Even worse, how did they get past the guards in the royal château? These acts suggested that, if they wanted, they could even harm the king as he slept. The "affair of the placards" horrified Parisians, and the government embarked on a wave of repression. Parisians undertook a penitential procession, and by the end of November, six convicted heretics had been burned alive.[9]

In the early years after 1517, French people had little knowledge of Luther, and theological differences were relatively blurry. Only 20 editions of works by Luther were published in French before his death in 1546, compared to 2,946 in High German. Over the next generation, theological distinctions gradually became clearer. After the affair of the placards, the most important text to proclaim Reformed ideas was John Calvin's *Institutes of the Christian Religion*, which first appeared in 1536 in Basel. Calvin had been forced to leave Paris in the wake of the affair, and he moved from Basel to Geneva shortly after the *Institutes* appeared. Except for 1538–1541, he lived in exile there for the rest of his life. The *Institutes*, with its crisp definitions and limpid style, was powerful propaganda for the Protestant cause. Its first edition sold out in record time. Calvin revised and expanded it several times, until the final editions of 1559 (Latin) and 1560 (French). It was a sixteenth-century bestseller.[10]

Textbooks sometimes erroneously summarize Calvin's theology by saying that he believed in predestination. However, Calvin's explanation of the Lord's Supper, or Eucharist, was what people found intellectually exciting in the sixteenth century. Although Parisians were first exposed to the existence of Zwinglianism in the affair of the placards, Martin Luther and Huldrych Zwingli had argued with each other in print over the issue in the late 1520s, and a face-to-face meeting in 1529 had failed to resolve the dispute. Discussions and negotiations continued after Zwingli's death in 1531. Calvin's view, although ultimately more acceptable to Zwinglians—the two streams of thought eventually merged to form the Reformed churches—was on its face a compromise between Lutheran and Zwinglian views. Luther argued for a view called consubstantiation: he asserted that because the Eucharist communicated a sense of Christ's presence to the believer, Christ was present *in* the sacrament, in the same way that iron contains heat, and was not merely *behind* it. This was close to the straightforward meaning of "This *is* my body" and to Catholic views. Zwingli insisted that the sentence was figurative. Based on other biblical passages, he argued that the correct meaning was "This signifies my body." The Eucharist was just a sign, a pledge akin to a wedding ring. He also pointed out that the next sentence in Matthew was "Do this in remembrance of me," and if Christ were present, he would not need to be remembered. Finally, if Jesus was seated at the right hand of the Father, how could he be located in the bread? The communion bread was only special because of its context: it was associated with the remembrance of God's promise.

Calvin was anxious to reconcile these two conflicting positions, especially since for him the correct administration of the sacraments was one of the principal distinguishing marks of the true Church.[11] Calvin agreed with Zwingli that the sacrament was a mere sign. No actual miracle occurred. At the same time, he pointed out that there was a real link between a sign and the thing it signified. They were distinct but inseparable. Calvin could not accept that Christ had a "local presence" in the Eucharist, because the two were distinct. The bread is not Christ. But the sign could not enter the mind without calling up the image of Christ's promise. The sign therefore communicates Christ's presence, and to deny that relationship stripped the sign of its meaning. Furthermore, the sacrament is a special event in its own right and is not merely subordinate to preaching. Unlike other signs, sacramental signs do not merely bring the meaning of the thing for which they stand into our minds: rather, they communicate or enact the truth or reality of the thing. As a metaphor to aid in understanding Calvin's conception, one might propose a pair of wheels connected by an axle. One wheel is the bread or wine, the other God's grace. The whole forms an inseparable unit, since one wheel cannot turn without the other, but each wheel is nonetheless distinguishable.

Although the differences between Luther's, Zwingli's, and Calvin's conceptions of the Eucharist, on the one hand, and the Catholic Church's, on the other, were subtle, some of the consequences were not. The rite was fundamental. The mass brought the entire community together, and the Eucharist was the focus of the mass. For most Catholics, the elevation of the host, when the priest raised the bread and the chalice prior to blessing it to perform the sacrament, was the holiest event of their week. Corpus Christi celebrations, where the host, the consecrated bread, was carried through the streets in a decorated box called a monstrance, and important personages were ranked by their closeness to it, imbued the social hierarchy with divine sanction. Only if there was a local presence of Christ in the bread, could one gain an aura of sanctity by walking close to it. For Calvin, however, the act of giving the host to the laity was sacred, the host itself was not. People could not receive grace by seeing the host displayed in a box. The dispute over the Eucharist was therefore over the most important social symbol in early modern Europe.[12]

A New Commitment to Education

Beginning in the 1520s, in yet another sign of the spread of humanist ideas in Nîmes, the city council began to expand and improve the town's school. The school had existed for many years and was largely run by the town, although the *précenteur* of the cathedral insisted that the town only had the right to suggest potential teachers to him, since he had the final say. The council sometimes examined the candidates' learning before appointing them; they usually had master's degrees. In 1524, because more students were studying Latin, the council agreed to add a second teacher to the school. The councillors knew about the latest trends in humanist education: beginning in 1528, prospective teachers had to pass an oral exam on two sections of Pliny's *Natural History* (on the geography of Aquitaine and Persia) at a council meeting before the city would agree to give them contracts. Commentaries on Pliny were an important innovation of Renaissance humanists, and at around the same time, at the University of Wittenberg, Philip Melanchthon added Pliny to the curriculum as part of the reforms that followed the Reformation there.[13]

In 1530, the council decided to increase the salaries of the teachers and to eliminate tuition fees. The result appears to have been a significant increase in the size of the school and, along with it, an increased workload for the teachers. The same year, Imbert Pécolet became the head of the school. Pécolet was born in Béziers and did his studies at the University of Montpellier, where he matriculated in 1527. Nîmes's school blossomed under his charge, and in 1534, he proposed a major expansion. He asked the city council to permit him to set up three classes—for beginning, intermediate, and advanced students—and to require the students to board at the school, so that he could teach Latin by the immersion method: the students would be required to speak in Latin, even at the dining table. Some members of the city council were in favor of the proposal, but this ambitious plan was rejected, although he was retained as principal. Shortly thereafter, Pécolet tried to lock some of the younger students out of the common areas on the ground floor of the building, since the council had refused to fund his plan. After the council ordered him to desist, he relented, but in 1535, when a capable candidate, Benoît Cosme, presented himself, the council appointed Cosme to be the head of the school and demoted Pécolet to his assistant, in charge of the youngest children. Pécolet therefore decided to leave. The council, which respected him despite their disagreement, agreed to rehire him should he return.[14]

In 1536, Henri II d'Albret and Marguerite, the king and queen of Navarre, visited Nîmes. The citizens of Nîmes took the opportunity to petition Queen Marguerite, who was celebrated for her learning, to intercede with her brother King François on their behalf to create a university.[15] In the spring of 1537, Pécolet returned, and the council, meeting on April 15, 1537, offered to reappoint him to his former post. Pécolet agreed to teach three classes to the older students—in Virgil, Cicero, and dialectics—for which he would have them read Aristotle in Greek and in Latin; to teach grammar to the younger children; and (perhaps a sign of Protestant tendencies) to read the gospel on Sundays. The council did not accept his offer entirely, reducing his fees to £100 (instead of the £150 he demanded) and adding that he should make Latin the language of instruction in the classroom. Furthermore, Judge Jean Robert of the criminal court noted that only the bishop or his deputy could authorize the reading of the gospel. By contrast, the council decided that Pécolet should lead the students, two by two, to all civic processions, chanting litanies. His term was to be, exceptionally, for two years, beginning on Michaelmas, September 29, 1537.[16] It was at this point that the Church intervened.

When the town consuls presented Pécolet to the precentor of the cathedral on October 7, 1537, for the formality of approval, they were met with rebuff. The precentor announced that Pécolet should submit to a public disputation; in the midst of the proceedings, he further decided that Pécolet should be forbidden to teach, under penalty of excommunication. At this point, the bishop's deputy came in to announce that Pécolet was "of doubtful faith." When the city council tried again on October 15 to present Pécolet for approval in his position, the precentor insisted on having a notary record his refusal. The following Sunday, October 21, when Pécolet attempted to go to mass, he was barred from entry. In the face of such firm action, the city council began legal proceedings and also attempted to name another man, Gaspar Caihas, whom they described as "appropriate and adequate," as interim head of the school until the Pécolet matter was resolved.[17] The Church, however, remained obdurate. The bishop's deputy immediately objected to Caihas because, unlike a tonsured cleric, he wore a beard. Furthermore, not enough information about him was known, except that he was an associate of Master Batalerius, who was a fugitive, and of Pécolet. The cantor of the cathedral could provide persons for the school who were "appropriate, adequate, and not suspect."[18] He added that several heretics had been condemned, but the consuls "want to obstruct this." If they wanted to protest further, he would see them in court. The consuls continued to defend their prerogatives against the Church, but it became impossible to insist that

Pécolet was a good Catholic, since he fled to Geneva. He then became a professor of Hebrew at Lausanne, where he resided from September 1538 until his death. (Note that Pierre Viret, one of Calvin's chief lieutenants, was the town preacher of Lausanne. In later years, Viret had a special relationship with the Nîmes Protestant community. Perhaps Pécolet forged the link between them.) Caihas did manage to assume the mastership of the school, although his tenure was not successful: the students apparently preferred the lectures given by Father Alexandre Antoine, and Caihas stayed in office for only a year.[19]

The Church had reason to be satisfied with the outcome of the Pécolet affair, since it had apparently succeeded in ridding Nîmes of its first heretic. But perhaps Pécolet had managed to infect others in Nîmes with heretical ideas before he left, since it was just at this time that other heretics began to emerge. At the same time as the Pécolet affair, the Parlement of Toulouse ordered Bernard Bach, a farmer, and Arnaud Alizot, a merchant, arrested for heresy. Both of them fled the jurisdiction before later returning to Nîmes. Alizot eventually became an overseer of the Reformed Church when it was officially inaugurated in 1561. Alizot was also connected to several other important early Protestants in Nîmes, including Antoine Moleri, an apothecary, and Jean Ursi, a notary: the early core of the movement had begun to form.[20] The consuls continued to ignore the presence of heretics in their midst. If they noticed them, it would permit outsiders to meddle in their local affairs and would require them to turn in their neighbors. Indeed, although there were exceptions, most towns in sixteenth-century France seemed to have wished to avoid dealing with religious controversy, or to avoid referring to it too directly if they did have to deal with it. Even at a much later stage, for example, the Nîmes city council pretended that any heretics in town were "certain individuals from the region and nearby places [who] came to this town."[21]

The University and College of Arts

Meanwhile, the town, through various representatives, continued to press François I to authorize the University and College of Arts in Nîmes. The king did so in letters patent of May 1539. At least part of the reason that François agreed to authorize the college was that the town had hit on the happy idea of appointing Claude Baduel to be the rector of the new college. Baduel was a native of Nîmes, a professor at the formidably Catholic University of Paris, and a protégé of Queen Marguerite de Navarre. He agreed to take a lower salary than he had been earning in Paris, and the bishop of Nîmes, at the queen's request, agreed to assign the new college a benefice worth £300 a year.[22]

If the Nîmes city council wanted to avoid further religious controversy, however, the choice of the scholar Claude Baduel to be the first rector of the new college was an error. Despite his bona fides, he too was a Protestant. Before teaching at Paris, he had studied at Wittenberg with the learned but undeniably Lutheran humanist Philip Melanchthon. Furthermore, he was a friend of Jean Sturm, the Strasbourg Reformer, with whom he had studied at the University of Louvain, before leaving for Germany. He did also have some Catholic connections: after leaving Wittenberg, he journeyed to Bruges and met the Catholic humanist Juan Luis Vives, before going to Strasbourg to study with the well-known Reformer Martin Bucer. While there, he also became friendly with John Calvin. However, Baduel was fundamentally a scholar of the classics, not a theologian, and was prepared to temporize on religious issues.[23] He described his own attitude during this period in a book on education:

> All of our ills spring from the same source: mistaking the law of God and of Christ. . . . It took warnings, exhortations from Divine Law to bring back youth to modesty, virtue, duty, so that this Holy Law became the light and the rule of their studies. It was possible to do this in a measured way, with discretion, without dangerous disputes, without discussing matters under debate today. I have never wished to introduce these quarrels into the schools: the still-tender spirits of these children and young people should not be distracted from their work. But in the Psalms, in the Proverbs of Solomon, in the writings of the apostles, the most appropriate precepts can be found to form children in honesty and in the fear of God.[24]

In short, Baduel believed it was possible to hold to a broad, nonsectarian Christianity, and he was interested more in good morals than in theological niceties.

The new university attracted many students, and everyone was pleased with its success. Whatever his associations, Baduel was certainly a prestigious appointment to the new college, and its other faculty were well regarded. In a selfless move, which Baduel would later regret, in 1541 he ceded primacy in the institution to another learned scholar, Guillaume Bigot. Inviting Bigot to Nîmes was Baduel's idea: Bigot had taught Baduel Greek at Louvain, and ever since, Baduel had greatly admired his teacher. Bigot, by all accounts, seems to have been brilliant but extremely difficult to deal with, and by the end of 1542 they were quarreling bitterly. Bigot did not hesitate to use Baduel's religious views against him as they battled to control the university.

Since Baduel was a native of Nîmes, it was easier for him to win the city council's sympathy when their quarrel broke out. His marriage to Isabelle

Rozelle, contracted on April 17, 1543, also helped him. The bride's father, Rostang Rozel, was the governor of Aigues-Mortes, and his sons Pierre and Charles became prominent men of the law in Nîmes. Clearly, Baduel's education had moved him considerably up the social scale: his father was a merchant. The witnesses to the contract were also members of the Nîmes elite: Jean de Sauzet, doctor of law and a judicial official; Pierre de Pavée, esquire and seigneur de Servas; and Jean Barrière, licentiate in law. The marriage probably also helped the nascent Protestant movement: Pierre and Charles Rozel eventually became important Protestant leaders, and Sauzet was an important early Protestant. However, the other witnesses were not closely identified with the early Protestant movement, and the marriage contract includes the traditional Catholic formula that the marriage "will be performed in the sight of Holy Mother Church."[25]

On the national scene, however, the authorities wished to define what was good doctrine and what was not. In Paris, the crown acted to enforce orthodoxy in the 1540s with considerable vigor. First, in 1543, the Sorbonne passed a set of articles defining Catholic belief. This was not an abstract codification, but specifically responsive to Protestantism: it affirmed transubstantiation, the cult of the saints, free will, and other contentious doctrines. For example, it asserted, "The communion of the Eucharist, in the two species of bread and wine, is not necessary for laypeople."[26] The articles were then incorporated into a royal edict and registered with all of France's parlements. Royal troops also massacred the heretical Waldensian peasants of the upper valley of the Durance. (The Waldensians, founded in the 1100s, eventually merged with the Reformed.)

In 1544, although consistently supported by the city council, Baduel, either out of fear or because he was tired of the struggle, took a position under Cardinal Sadoleto at Carpentras. After a year and a half, however, he decided to return. The troubles continued, with Bigot now suing the city council, and Baduel departed a second time—this time to Montpellier—before returning to Nîmes in 1547. In the summer of that same year, Bigot in turn was forced to flee, accused of a vicious attack on a man who had been carrying on an affair with Bigot's wife. Nîmes's leaders were delighted: surely Bigot, now in disgrace, would lose his case, and their man, Baduel, would finally win. But Bigot leaped into the fray with two unanswerable arguments: a pardon from the king for the assault on his wife's lover, and evidence of Baduel's heresy. In the end, neither Bigot nor Baduel was the victor: although Baduel was removed as rector, he was allowed to stay on as a professor, retaining his old salary. Bigot eventually gave up his post, accusing the Nîmes authorities of heresy, too, and left for Montauban. Baduel, feeling the effect of a rising tide of persecution and identifying more and more with the Reform—he wrote a letter in June 1550 to

Melanchthon that "we have no other consolation than that which comes from the Word of God or the church of Geneva, our close neighbor"—left France. His name appears in the list of arrivals in Geneva on August 24, 1551. The Nîmes city council eventually appointed Guillaume Tuffan to head the university. He was also a prestigious appointment, since his previous position had been principal of the College of Narbonne at the University of Paris. He seems to have preserved a careful neutrality in religious matters.[27]

It seems likely that Baduel's peril inhibited the growth of the Nîmes Protestant movement to some extent, both because Baduel appears to have been a leader in it and because his troubles must have served as a warning to his friends. Furthermore, on April 13, 1543, the Parlement of Toulouse condemned nine residents of the *sénéchaussée* of Beaucaire and Nîmes—mostly residents of the nearby town of Beaucaire—for heresy. Nonetheless, Protestant agitation continued. In October 1545, someone vandalized a painting of the Virgin Mary, which had been placed on the altar of one of the chapels in the cathedral. The city council, showing a zeal it had not demonstrated in the preceding conflicts, ordered a general penitential procession, which the entire population was ordered to attend. Few people from Nîmes itself were arrested in the 1540s, however, and little is known of them, except for one, Jean Morlet, a leather worker. He was a friend of Baduel, and Baduel praises him highly in his letters. According to Baduel, Morlet was arrested due to the treachery of a woman. Baduel extols him by saying:

> This man is one of those who, fearing God and living in a holy fashion, are nonetheless subject in this life to calumny and injustices. Such is the common condition of all those who live piously. This is the cross, carried first by Christ and imposed afterwards on those men who have been transformed in His image and called to resemble Him. "Happy is he who is thoughtful of the poor and needy; in bad times may the Lord keep him from harm."[28]

The implication is that Morlet was particularly known for his charity. This was especially important in Nîmes during the mid-1540s.

Declining Standards of Living

The people of Nîmes faced growing economic problems in the sixteenth century. Throughout Languedoc, the population was growing substantially by the standards of the day, on average about 11.5 percent per decade between 1500 and 1570. In an age overwhelmingly dominated by agriculture, and with little technological change, population increases meant that people needed to bring more land into cultivation to feed themselves. Peasants, looking for land, naturally turned to vacant areas, notably the *garrigues* (see Chapter 1). Unfortunately, the Mediterranean basin around Nîmes was ill suited to more intensive agriculture. The *garrigues* were scrub and yielded little relative to the amount of labor invested. People also moved up into the Cévennes mountains looking for more land, but by the early 1550s, the mountain areas near Alès, Anduze, and Le Vigan were as populated as the plain of Nîmes. Another alternative was to cut back on luxury crops in favor of grain, and some peasants did follow this course: the percentage of land devoted to wine production fell as vines were plowed under to make way for wheat. But this was only marginally helpful: what was really needed was rich soil that could stand up to more intensive production. Unfortunately, the only region that had unexploited riches was the Camargue, the marshes at the mouth of the Rhone. There was some expansion of agriculture there, but the only way that farmers could bring the marshes under the plow was to drain them. The technology existed to do so, although it was expensive; the problem was that the people who tried it got malaria and a variety of deadly water-borne diseases. Since there was little good new land to cultivate, farmers found it increasingly difficult to buy land for themselves or their children. Unlike other regions of France, notably Poitou, which saw larger landholding, in sixteenth-century Languedoc land was increasingly subdivided, and fewer and fewer people were able to make a living from their plots as the average size of the plots fell. There was also some tendency for the wealthy to buy up fertile land located near administrative centers like Nîmes and Montpellier. Although no one benefited from the bad economic times, the land crisis widened the gap between rich and poor.

As the population rose, more and more people competed for fewer and fewer jobs. Once a peasant's holding became too small to sustain his household, he naturally turned to outside work to increase his income, as did the rest of the family. This increased the labor supply, and thus there was a certain amount of increased migration, particularly of the landless destitute, to the cities. The result was that prices rose faster than wages. Many agricultural workers were paid in kind, based on a percentage of the crops they harvested. According to figures from the canons of La Bastide-Redonde, near Narbonne, in the fifteenth century, it was common for reapers to be paid one-tenth of their sheaves. By the 1540s, the reapers received one sheaf in twelve. Eventually, reapers' wages dropped to one sheaf in eighteen. On the same farm, the steward's wages barely increased between 1480 and 1557, although over that time span the price of wheat doubled. Money wages did increase in general, but not nearly as fast as prices. From the late fifteenth to the late sixteenth centuries, the average wages for stonemasons, carpenters, and agricultural workers (*travailleurs*) tripled, but grain prices sextupled. In an environment where bread was the main food source, and food the most important component of the cost of living, the effect was disastrous. Plus, it is likely that the other necessities of life increased in parallel. In short, the average person's standard of living was cut in half.

The effects of the population increase were relentless, but not continuous: the price increases were jagged, and each increase provoked a new crisis. In some years, the weather cooperated, the harvest was good, and people might have thought that good times were returning. Each bad year, however, brought a new crisis of subsistence, and each time a greater proportion of the population was in jeopardy, since each succeeding peak of prices was higher than before, and they never quite fell to where they had been. People could hardly fail to suffer under such conditions. Gradually, families ate a less varied diet, and in particular the consumption of meat per person fell by half between the late fifteenth and the late sixteenth centuries. Bread became the major food for an ever-greater percentage of the population, and the quality of the bread also declined. Today, only a small minority in industrialized countries suffers from protein deficiency, and people are encouraged to reduce their meat consumption to avoid heart disease. In the sixteenth century, when protein consumption was much lower, hygiene and health care were primitive, and most people had backbreaking jobs in agriculture involving hard physical labor, the effects of a further reduction of protein consumption on health were severe. Overdependence on bread for calories also led to vitamin and other deficiencies. The results were lowered resistance to disease and an increase in the death rate. The wealthy benefited to some extent from these economic changes since they were employers of labor, and rising populations kept down labor costs. They certainly never lacked food to eat. Nonetheless, the lowered standard of living meant that there was less money to go around: there were fewer people who could afford to buy the goods the artisans produced, fewer customers for the lawyers and doctors, and so forth. The rich suffered less, but it is hard to make money in a falling market. For the poor, whose existence was already precarious, the falling standard of living was disastrous. As people get poorer, they devote a larger percentage of their incomes to food. The poor therefore suffered particularly from higher grain prices. Even the not-so-poor felt the pinch when the standard of living fell as dramatically as it did in the sixteenth century. They might scrimp and save, and double up in their beds, but they could at least hide their suffering behind closed doors. In contrast, the swelling numbers of the destitute were immediately visible: they swarmed in the streets, especially where other people were likely to be, in the squares and in front of the churches, begging for bread.[29]

Throughout the period, in an effort to ease these economic problems, the Nîmes town council set food prices, specifically for meat, bread, and fish. The town council was prone to declare, for example, that bread should be sold "without ever varying the price." Since bread prices are still regulated in France in the twenty-first century, this should hardly be surprising, but it is worth noting if only because the council's repeated interventions suggest that the town's elites took their responsibility for the general welfare seriously. The bakers, in turn, were prone to insist that their survival depended on a price increase.[30] Sometimes, the council intervened to assist tradesmen, or to preserve public order. For example, when the women who sold fish complained that people were shoplifting from their stalls, Jean Lansard, a notary who served as a consul on a number of occasions, suggested that they needed to come up with a more suitable place for the fish market, and that the fishmongers had to be constrained to sell only in the one place, so that policing could be effective. Eventually, in an effort to ameliorate the sanitary problems that the fish market caused, the council decided to move it to the Place de la Belle Croix, in the northeast corner of town. At the same meeting, the council decided, after much debate, that the farmer's market for vegetables needed to be moved to the Place de la Cathédrale and supervised, because the stall holders did not have enough space, and arguments were breaking out over the placement of stalls. The next year, there was again talk of "frauds and monopolies" in the fish trade, and again the council intervened.[31]

Attempting to hold the line on prices led to conflicts with the town's food trades. The town council had a particularly difficult relationship with the butchers, apparently caused at least in part by the perception that the butchers were outsiders. The butchers were frequently absent from the city because they were also responsible for raising the animals, and at certain times of the year would bring them down to town from the pasture lands in the Cévennes, graze them for a while in the scrub around Nîmes, the *garrigues,* and then slaughter them. They had an annual contract with the town, which included the prices they could charge for each kind of meat. As meat consumption fell per person, the butchers were having a hard time making a profit, and they resented the town council's efforts, which made it even harder. Frequently, they refused to slaughter at the prices offered and demanded pasturing rights in the *garrigues* that the town council was loath to provide. In March 1548, the council, frustrated with "the malice and obstruction of the butchers, who are accustomed to annoy the town every year by raising the price of meat," tried a new tack, and resolved to establish municipal butchers. Apparently, this did not work, because the following year the consuls were again in negotiation with the butchers, who were again insisting on raising the price per pound of mutton and pork to ten deniers and of beef to seven deniers.[32] When the town attempted to hold its ground, no one would respond to advertisements for the butchers' contract, even when the council made announcements in the nearby towns of Sommières, Lunel, Aigues-Mortes, Saint-Gilles, and Beaucaire.[33] This led to a long discussion. Denis de Brueys, the criminal court judge, was of the opinion that the town should accede to the higher prices that the butchers had earlier demanded (10d. and 7d.). Guillaume Calvière, the president of the présidial, preferred to attempt to borrow £1,000 and appoint municipal butchers. The council divided between the two suggestions. Pierre Rozel, later an important Protestant figure, proposed a compromise, suggesting that the council should accept the butchers' offer for the present, but borrow £600 for the following year, and use the money to hire others, so long as they could promise to supply meat at a better price. Eventually, they decided to permit the consuls to make the best deal with the butchers that they could. But the problem would not go away, and the next year the butchers were again the subject of complaints. In 1556, Antoine Maltraict, a notary, asked for a bulletin board with meat prices posted, so that shoppers could compare. Other groups also had difficulties with the butchers from time to time: on September 22, 1558, Nicolas Bodet, a merchant and candlemaker, complained that the butchers sold all the fat to foreigners. The council concluded that the butchers should be ordered to supply Bodet and other candlemakers with tallow.[34]

The Problem of Poverty

For the Nîmes city council, the major problem in the mid-1540s was poverty, not heresy. The harvest of 1546 was particularly bad, resulting in the second-highest grain prices of the period. The most significant social consequence of the harsh economic times seems to have been a sharp increase in poverty, and the city council discussed extensively how to deal with the suffering that resulted. These discussions are interesting for two reasons. First, they show the magnitude of the problem in the way that statistics on grain prices cannot. Second, perhaps more important, by reading these debates it is possible to get a sense of the city councillors' attitudes toward poverty. As will be seen later, many early Protestants in Nîmes seem to have had great concern for the poor.[35]

One reasonable place to begin to look at how the town dealt with the issue of poverty is to examine the meeting of April 3, 1547, when the council held an extended discussion on the subject. As was traditional, the first consul, Pierre Rozel, set out the problem, explaining on behalf of his colleagues that the poor, looking for "alms for the honor of God," were congregating at people's doors and in front of the churches, which he believed was dangerous because there were "many contagious diseases."[36] Something had to be done from both a moral and a practical standpoint. Pierre Robert voiced his suspicions that some of the poor, although they were working, sent their children out to beg, and some even brought in children from outside the town to work the streets as beggars. The criminal court judge, Jean Robert, was exasperated, saying that "on the conduct of the poor there have been many deliberations of the consuls, in the present consular building, which demand only to be put into execution."[37] (Presumably, he knew that the discussions had been in the same building because he had been present to hear them, over and over again.)

Others suggested that the issues needed further study. Jean Joussaud, a lawyer,[38] commented that Nîmes needed to send two men, one to Avignon and one to Montpellier, to report back how those cities were dealing with the problem. Vidal Vernière, a rich merchant and an important Nîmes political figure,[39] added on a practical note that there were also many poor girls in the city, and someone should organize a system to place them in domestic service. Jean Lansard, the notary mentioned earlier, was concerned about financing poor relief. He pointed out that, following a royal ordinance, the confraternities had been suppressed, and the money in their endowments had been transferred to the poor hospital, but there was money remaining that should also be dedicated to the same purpose. At the same meeting, there was also discussion of how much to pay the preacher whom the town hired every year for Lent. Apparently, the councillors were particularly pleased with him, because several members suggested giving him a bonus. But Pierre Guilhon, a farmer, seemed more interested in bread than preaching, saying that the "rich and leisured" (*riches et bienaisés*) should pay any bonus, and not the poor.

The meeting ended inconclusively, and the council returned to the same issue at the next meeting, on April 17, 1547.[40] This time, the consuls moved immediately to consider action. They directed their frustrations at those "who do not want to feed the poor" and proposed that the wealthy should be put on a list to share the expense of supporting the needy. But a balance needed to be struck: the poor, for their part, should be prevented from begging at townspeople's doors and officers should be appointed to prevent it. Furthermore, perhaps a guard should be put at the town gates, presumably to prevent more poor people from coming in. Robert des Georges, an important Nîmes political figure and later one of the most important members of the Catholic minority, agreed that those who were refusing to support the poor should be forced to help; indeed, two men should be appointed to oversee the problem, but there was no need for guards at the gates. Honoré Richier, one of the lieutenants of the chief judge (*juge-mage*), agreed and added that the money that could be used to pay guards should instead be used to pay for the overseers of the poor. Pierre de Malmont, a leading Nîmes politician, was particularly angry at people who were not contributing their fair share, saying that they should be sued.[41] Eventually, it was decided to hire two men to watch over the poor, who would tell outsiders to continue on their way "while giving them [some] alms" (*en leur faisant donner l'aumosne*) and who would keep the local poor away from people's doors.

Unfortunately, the system did not run smoothly, and by August 14, 1547, the council was discussing the matter yet again. Some of the wealthy who had poor people assigned to them were refusing to pay, and their charges were therefore again demanding alms in the streets and in the town's Roman arena. The consuls were of the opinion that four persons should be appointed to go over the poor rolls, ordering the recalcitrant to pay, but at the same going street by street to make sure that the people on the list were "truly needy" (*vrays pouvres*). Louis Savion, a doctor of laws,[42] wanted to make clear that townspeople were not required to take the poor into their homes, unless they wanted to, but they had to pay them the money that they needed for food. He was happy to provide help—but at a distance. Jacques Bonaud, at this point an old man and one of Nîmes's most distinguished lawyers and legal scholars, felt that the apportionment was inequitable, saying that the lists needed to be revised, to take some away from those who had too many poor people assigned to them and add to those who had too few.[43] Guichard du Brana, a surgeon and former third consul, disagreed with the system: they needed a poorhouse, and everyone should give as much charity as they could afford, "without ordering anybody" (*sans contraindre personne*). Geoffre Pascal, a wealthy merchant who eventually served as consul three times, sounded an anti-clerical note: he felt that it was the job of the clergy to deal with the problem, and only the rich (*aisés*) should pay, without burdening "the poor people" (*les pouvres gens*), presumably in this instance meaning the less well-off. Despite these cantankerous notes of disagreement, most of the speakers agreed with the consuls that the poor rolls needed to be revised again, and their recommendation was followed.

These debates suggest the general parameters of thinking in Nîmes about the poor, and the concerns expressed in 1547 would recur throughout the period. People in Nîmes were xenophobic and believed that shiftless outsiders were flocking to Nîmes to take advantage of the town's generosity. No one was prepared to provide more than token assistance to outsiders. There was some suspicion even of Nîmes's own poor and a general concern that only the "truly needy" should benefit.[44] Still, overall, there was more concern over whether the burden of the poor was being equitably distributed than suspicion of the poor themselves. There was a particular solicitude for poor children and a general recognition that they needed to be trained so that eventually they could obtain employment by, for example, putting them in service or teaching them how to work with silk. Occasionally, there was some implied criticism of the clergy, apparently provoked by the thought "isn't this their job?"[45] But the predominant assumption was that the town had an obligation to provide for its own. Although the members of the city council were generally of high rank, they were also public-spirited and genuinely concerned about the plight of the poor. If they were also concerned about how much it might cost to pay for it all, it was because they had no plans to avoid their obligations.

Nîmes had a poor hospital, and discussions of its needs demonstrated similar attitudes. Council members worried that the "bastards," as the abandoned children were usually called, in the hospital were properly fed, housed, and clothed.[46] The town went to the trouble of putting up a wall around the hospital because there were too many people visiting the poor people who were lying sick there, "and therefore the plague is of longer duration." Although much of the money for poor relief came from charitable legacies, the council was prepared to consider taking money out of the town's general revenues when there was a shortfall. At the same time, if a woman was known to have abandoned a child, and thus put it to the charge of the public purse (as supposedly the chambermaid of the prior of Cassagnolles did), she was likely to be put on trial.[47] Similarly, the councillors were not happy to see someone abandoned by their family: they called the son of Thomas Reboul, a former servant of the town administration, to explain to them why he wasn't taking care of his father, who was so sick he was unable to speak and who had been abandoned in the public hospital. He promised "to do that which a son is obligated to do for his father." Nor were the councillors themselves exempt from helping to pay for poor relief: the council resolved that anyone who missed a meeting should pay a £5 fine "to the poor of the hospitals." Eventually, the town decided that the consuls were too busy to look after the hospital themselves, and the council decided to appoint and pay for a director to administer it. Guichard du Brana was chosen to be the first administrator, despite his comments in 1547, which suggested that he was not in favor of the compulsory system that the town continued to use to pay for poor relief.[48] His qualifications as a surgeon may have led to his selection.

A Protestant Community Begins to Form

Over the course of the 1540s, the Protestant movement in Nîmes slowly grew. Protestants also began to think of themselves as a separate group, rather than as a group of Christians with a particular spirituality in common. Baduel was probably the leader: at least in his letters, he doesn't refer to anyone else as the leader. It is, however, interesting that in its first surviving letter to Calvin, dated July 14, 1547, the church of Nîmes wrote collectively, and anonymously, although Baduel himself addressed letters directly to Calvin on other occasions. (The letter was also addressed to Calvin's colleague Pierre Viret.) Jacques Ursi, the notary, can be identified as the writer of the letter by his handwriting. He was likely only the amanuensis, not the author. In their letter, Nîmes's Protestants spoke of communicating with the people of the church of "Utica," which probably refers to the town of Uzès, and therefore the community in Nîmes may have drawn, at least to that extent, some support and comfort from the atmosphere in the region. The bulk of the letter, which is a reply to a now-lost letter from Calvin to them, concerns the question of the Lord's Supper:

> When we came upon the section dealing with the Lord's supper and the Eucharist we were particularly happy. For even before we had already been convinced that none [of your teachings] are innovations, but now we are completely certain. We would like you to recognize, Christian man, that your letter gave such strength to those who are troubled by the vain traditions of some people, that we owe a considerable debt to you on this account. For the widespread rumor that the rite of the sacrament amounts to an innovation was calmed and cured.[49]

Thus, as a result of their study of Calvin's writings, they now felt comfortable administering the sacrament in the Genevan fashion.

It is not surprising that at this stage of the Nîmes Protestant church's development, Eucharistic disputes would erupt. It was vital to the church's future growth and success that Calvin was able to explain to Protestants' satisfaction that his new definition of the sacrament was in accord with the view of the early Church fathers, rather than an invention of his own. It is not entirely clear whether the Protestant community in Nîmes had actually celebrated the Lord's Supper, however, since there is no evidence that they had the services of a minister to administer the sacrament. It is possible that Pierre d'Airebaudouze, an archdeacon of the cathedral who fled to Geneva in 1553, was already affiliated with the group and served as its minister (see below).[50] Nonetheless, even discussion of the Eucharist marked a significant step for the early Protestants, since Eucharistic doctrine was such a crucial line separating Protestants from Catholics. Resolving these theological disputes was a significant moment in the creation of a Protestant identity.[51]

Although the Nîmes Protestant movement had resolved its theological question, it immediately faced a new difficulty: a dramatically altered political climate. For on March 30, 1547, only three months before the church of Nîmes wrote to Calvin and Viret, King François I had died, at the age of fifty-two. The cause was probably a urinary tract infection, possibly aggravated by syphilis.[52] So ended the life of the man to whom Calvin had dedicated the first edition of the *Institutes*. Henri II, his son and successor, would prove far more evil than his father, from a Protestant point of view.

3

Growth and Crisis

Nîmes's Protestants, 1547–1559

In the 1530s, there were Protestants in Nîmes, but there was no Protestant community. By the end of the 1540s, there was a Protestant community in Nîmes, but it was a small minority. Both Christian imperatives and the instinct for self-preservation suggested that this was an unfortunate state of affairs. The Protestant community's major goal in the 1550s was to increase its numbers. The community appears to have had moderate success throughout the decade, but it was the later 1550s and especially the early 1560s that brought its triumph.

Increasing Persecution

The early 1550s appear to have been an important turning point for Protestantism in Nîmes. At the beginning of the decade, there is one small indication that there may have been change in the air, when the Dominicans explained to the town council on March 12, 1550, that they needed to sell a piece of land because "the people is not at present as moved to fervent devotion . . . as it once was," and therefore alms had fallen off.[1] In 1551, the parlement ordered a crackdown on heresy and in late December convicted twenty-four people from Nîmes, the highest number reached before 1560. The parlement's records seldom note the occupations of the accused heretics, but information from Nîmes's surviving wills and marriage contracts can help to fill in the missing pieces. In 1551, the accused who can be identified were two priests, two important men—Claude Baduel and Jean d'Albenas, whose son probably became a member of the présidial court—two merchants, a saddler, an apothecary (Antoine Moleri), three wool carders, a farmer, and four women, including Isabelle Rozelle, Baduel's wife, and two wealthy widows, probably from the same family: Isabeau de Montcalm, and the widow of the seigneur de Servas, whose name was probably Françoise de Montcalm. The parlement also indicted "Étienne Ursi"—the court probably meant to indict either Jean or Jacques Ursi, both notaries, since the name Ursi is very unusual. It is hard to generalize about a few individuals, especially since the accused who cannot be identified were probably less well-to-do than those who can. Still, it appears that these early Protestants came from the middling class, with some wealthy people and a few from agricultural occupations and the food, building, or metal trades. In 1550, Claude Baduel, in a letter to Melanchthon, explained that the church was composed for the most part of humble people:

> Jean Chambard [a pseudonym for Calvin], whom I met in Strasbourg at Bucer's residence, and whose piety, knowledge, and spiritual energy you know, consoles us in our distress by his grave and frequent letters. And when I say us, I speak also of good and pious person[s], men and women, for the most part of modest condition; for the poor have always shown more fidelity to the Gospel. This communion of saints, this fraternal sympathy in the midst of such great dispersal of the Church, fortifies us and permits us to remain standing by the grace of the Lord and by the consolation of the spirit. That is what I feel bound to tell you, in as few words as possible, of our studies and of the state of our Church.[2]

It seems unlikely that Baduel would have omitted mentioning influential converts, if there had been any. Nor does it seem likely that the Nîmes Protestant community was particularly large. Rather, by stressing that "the poor have always shown more fidelity to the Gospel," he was putting the best face on the situation he could.

Looking at the overall pattern of heresy prosecutions, it appears that before the early 1550s, the Protestant movement in Nîmes was small: the first suspect appears in the records in 1537, and after that there is little evidence of heresy in Nîmes until the 1550s. This contradicts Bigot's wide-ranging allegations during his dispute with Baduel and the town's authorities in the preceding decade. Certainly, the Parlement of Toulouse prosecuted heretics during the 1540s, but few of them came from Nîmes, and it is highly unlikely that the parlement could have overlooked them. The movement appears to have had less success in Nîmes than elsewhere in the 1540s, but it did much better in the 1550s, based on the evidence from the Parlement of Toulouse. In the 1540s, fewer than 4 percent of the people prosecuted by the parlement came from Nîmes, while 10 percent of the people prosecuted in the 1550s did.[3] Generally, it seems reasonable to assume that the parlement was responsible when prosecutions increased across the board, as they did in 1551, while when the figures for Nîmes diverged from the norm, it was probably due to changing local conditions. As a result of the crackdown, one man from Nîmes, Étienne Angelin, was executed. Overall, there may have been as many as four more executions ordered, all of them later in the 1550s, but only Angelin's is certain.[4] On the assumption that cases that reached the parlement were more serious, only persons tried in Toulouse are counted here as Protestants, although there were also some minor cases handled by the présidial of Nîmes. Consider the case of Jean Vallat, for example: he was arrested in 1553 for harvesting his crops on St. John's Day. He expostulated that the harvest was urgent, and others had done likewise. Vallat, in short, may have been a bad Catholic rather than a good Protestant. Vallat may not have been particularly law-abiding: either he or his brother of the same name subsequently knifed his brother in a quarrel over their father's inheritance. Still, he was later persecuted, as a Catholic, in the Michelade. (His brother Roland was a Protestant, however.) In any event, there were few such cases.[5]

In a small community like Nîmes, it was hard to keep a heresy investigation secret. Suspected Protestants frequently heard that they were known to

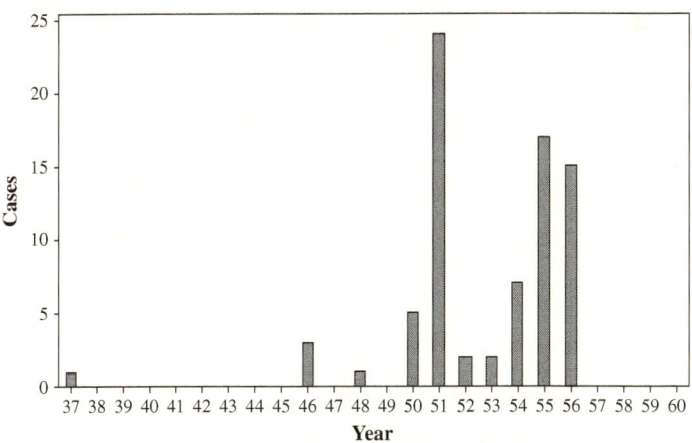

FIGURE 3.1. Heresy cases from Nîmes before the Parlement of Toulouse. Source: ADHG, Series B.

the authorities before they were arrested. Since the punishment for heresy was harsh, many of them chose to flee the country, especially if they had skills that they could use to survive abroad. Fleeing French Protestants naturally chose to follow Calvin to Geneva, and eventually a large refugee community formed there. The Genevan government kept good, although not exhaustive, records of all the arrivals, and these survive for the years 1549–1560 and again for a period in the 1570s.[6] These records provide further evidence that the Protestant community was probably very small before the early 1550s, since no one from Nîmes arrived in Geneva in 1549 or 1550. (It is worth remembering, however, that we know that there were refugees before 1549, since Imbert Pécolet, for example, fled in 1537.) Afterward, growth in the community was steady (see figure 3.2). Other inferences are also possible, including increased persecution for one, although the figures for prosecutions are not parallel enough to justify that as a conclusion. For example, of the twenty-four people prosecuted in 1551, only two, Claude Baduel and his wife, Isabelle Rozelle, arrived in Geneva that year, although two others, Antoine Moleri, an apothecary, and Pierre d'Aspères, a merchant, arrived later in the decade (in 1554 and 1557, respectively). In any case, the figures are consistent with the notion that, before the early 1550s, the Nîmes Protestant community was small.[7]

The parlement, by ordering so many prosecutions in their city, forced the Nîmes town councillors to recognize that there was a problem with heresy in their midst. The consuls, however, continued to believe that the parlement was overreacting, and there was no real cause for concern. If anything, they were more worried about the town's reputation than about the dangers of heresy.

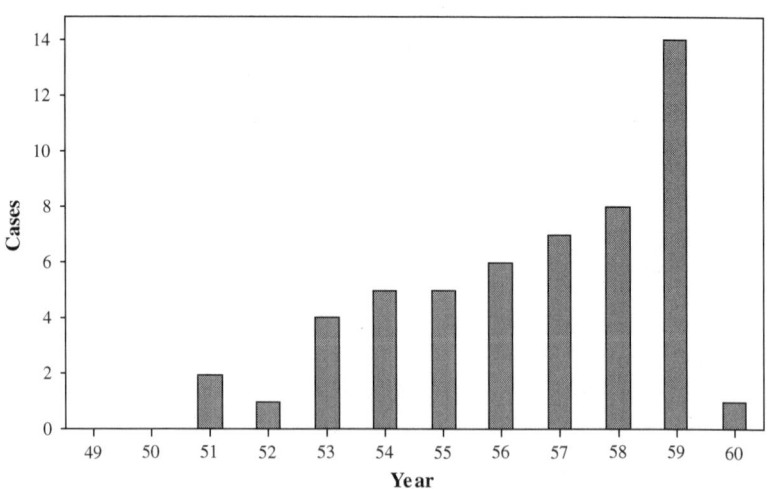

FIGURE 3.2. Refugees to Geneva. Source: Geisendorf.

They knew full well that the city's prosperity depended on royal favor, and a reputation for disobedience could be immensely harmful. On November 22, 1551, Denis de Brueys, the first consul, decided that the council needed to debate the issue. He admitted that the town was accused of being contaminated with "the Lutheran sect," but he insisted that there were no heretics in town, or if there were, the heretics consisted only "of a few individuals, not inhabitants or residents." Rather than the need to take action against the heretics, he insisted, the real worry was that the king would hear and be displeased, which would be "greatly prejudicial and damaging," and so he proposed sending representatives to tell him that the rumors "were not true" and finding out who was spreading the rumors. The council continued to discuss the issue when it met several weeks later, on December 13, but was even more circumspect: speaker after speaker rose to express his concern about the "defamation" without ever mentioning the word "Lutheran": Jean de Sauzet was even opposed to dealing with the matter at all. Eventually, they sidestepped the issue nicely and resolved to send representatives to tell of the "obedience which the inhabitants of this town have always shown toward His Majesty, his orders and his officers."[8]

There was more cause for concern than the council was prepared to admit. Just as the authorities in Toulouse started to pay attention to the Protestant movement in Nîmes, the Company of Pastors in Geneva also began to take an interest in it. Although the company had known of the movement in Nîmes for years, it had never before felt that it was worthwhile to devote scarce resources to Nîmes and to risk lives in missionary work. Now, the movement in Nîmes had reached a sufficient size that Geneva sent the first preachers to the area. They arrived in Nîmes in March 1552 and preached outside the town, on a hill high above it to the north, behind the Roman watchtower, the Tour Magne. The seneschal soon discovered what was happening and sent the bishop's agent to arrest them. The parlement also sent two officials to investigate. The preachers apparently also included one local priest, Pierre d'Airebaudouze, an archdeacon of the cathedral. The d'Airebaudouze family was extremely prominent in Nîmes and in Anduze, where it originated. The head of the family was Baron d'Anduze, and other relatives became members of the présidial court, but that did not shield Pierre d'Airebaudouze from prosecution. He was able to flee to Geneva, and once there, he married Françoise de Montcalm. He did not completely avoid punishment, however: the présidial ordered the confiscation of all of his goods. All of the preachers from Geneva also escaped, but preaching stopped. The parlement ordered all of the suspected preachers tried in absentia and had them burned in effigy in April. The authorities probably thought they had dealt the movement a fatal blow, since preaching, although it continued from time to time elsewhere in the diocese, seems to have ceased in Nîmes itself.[9]

A Growing Movement

Although the preachers had little time to spread the word, many people had come to listen, and the experience seems to have galvanized the nascent Protestant community. Two notaries in Nîmes, Jean and Jacques Ursi, appear to have adopted Protestantism early: Jacques Ursi probably wrote the 1547 letter to Calvin; Jean Ursi was a friend of the early Protestant Arnaud Alizot, and his will also has strong Protestant tendencies.[10] In the early 1550s, something decisive seems to have happened in the community, undoubtedly aided by the preaching in 1552. As a result, the Ursis and their clients decided to stop using Catholic formulas in the wills and marriage contracts they drew up and signed. They were still reluctant to commit themselves, however, since they also refrained from using Protestant formulas. In this way, they could express their deepest convictions while preserving deniability in case the authorities inquired. The changes they made were gradual, showing increasing theological sophistication. Protestants particularly disliked certain phrases that embodied the Catholic ideas that most sharply diverged from their own. They stopped using those first; only later did they stop using more subtly Catholic clauses. Figure 3.3 shows that the first sign of incipient Protestantism was that people making their wills with the Ursis stopped asking Mary and the saints to pray for their souls. Since only God could save your soul (the *sola gratia* principle), there was no point in praying to intermediaries, and Protestants were especially disturbed by what they felt was the extreme, excessive devotion to Mary in Catholicism. The community seems to have agreed on that change in 1551, even before the first preachers arrived from Geneva. By 1553, the year after the preachers had come to town, brides and grooms stopped pledging that "the wedding will be performed [*s'accomplira*] in the sight of Holy Mother Church." The implications of that phrase were somewhat more subtle. All Protestants certainly believed they were part of the church of all Christians. More precisely, they believed that they were the authentic heirs of the first Christians. It is possible that it was the Roman implications of the phrase that disturbed them, but more likely they were concerned that the phrase implied that marriage was a sacrament, a notion that Protestant theology rejected. It is also noteworthy that both of these changes involved removing feminine imagery from the notarial acts.

Protestant objections to the sign of the cross, which testators customarily made as a preamble before introducing their bequests, were more subtle. Catholic wills usually began by stating, "First, [he or she] made the sign of the cross, saying, 'in the name of the Father, and the Son, and the Holy Spirit, Amen.'"

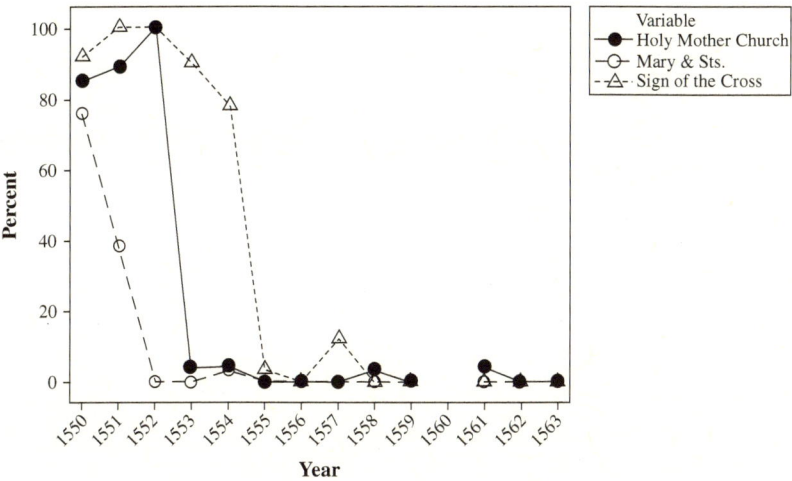

FIGURE 3.3. Use of Catholic phrases in Ursi contracts. Source: ADG, Series IIE.

The sign of the cross was an ancient Christian symbol, going back to the early Church. It is interesting to note that early on, a fairly high proportion of people making their wills with the Ursis (compared to other notaries) made the sign in Latin, rather than in French, saying, "In nomine patris, et filii, et spiritus sancti." This suggests that the Ursis' clientele was relatively theologically sophisticated. However, use of the sign declined over time. Protestants in Nîmes came to suspect the sign of the cross because of its meaning in medieval Catholic theology, which had defined it as a "sacramental." *Sacramentals* were sacred acts that conferred blessing, although since they were not instituted by Christ, they did not convey grace in the same automatic way that the true sacraments did (other sacramentals included using holy water, burning incense, and giving alms). The sign of the cross was therefore implicated in the whole sacramental system, which Protestants rejected. They came to this realization slowly, however, partly because making the sign was strongly rooted in daily life and practice. Some Protestants felt that it was appropriate to say the words, but not to make the gesture. (A handful of people chose to retain the gesture but omit the words.) Words conveyed meaning directly, and proclaiming the Word was a good Christian thing to do. This compromise position became the norm in 1553 and 1554, only to disappear thereafter. The act was too enmeshed in its Catholic context: the break had to be complete. If Protestants in Nîmes had not yet affirmatively decided on how the rituals of the life cycle should be performed, they were increasingly clear about what they rejected.

Although there were clear signs of growing Protestantism in Nîmes in the early to mid-1550s, the municipal authorities continued to ignore the issue. When the parlement sent representatives to the town council on April 4, 1554, to demand a list of names of heretics, the town council agreed to do so, but the members said that they did not know of any.[11] Later that same year, however, Protestant sources—but not the surviving records of the Parlement of Toulouse—state that Pierre de Lavau, originally from a village near Toulouse, was arrested while preaching in Nîmes. Condemned to death, he was taken to the Place de la Couronne, where he was executed. Dominique Deyron, a Dominican priest, escorted him as he went. Deyron was supposed to continually mutter in his ear, urging him to repent so that he would not go to hell. But Deyron, a secret Protestant, actually urged him to be steadfast and to believe in eternal life. Deyron was overheard and eventually fled to Geneva. (Deyron's arrival in Geneva can be independently confirmed.) Deyron's loss was a particular blow to Nîmes's Protestant community: he had been an active preacher and a learned priest, having received a doctorate in theology from the University of Paris.[12]

In the second half of the 1550s, although there were no reports of preaching in Nîmes itself, there were preachers in the area. In 1556, there were reports of preachers in Anduze, St. Jean du Gard, Sauve, and Le Vigan. The following year, Denis de Brueys, the *lieutenant criminel* of the présidial, was sent to investigate, along with representatives of the parlement, and several people were arrested. In Anduze, a monk, Claude Rozier, of the Order of the Cordeliers, was arrested, and he was executed in Nîmes on August 22: his tongue was cut out, and he was then burned alive. The town of Anduze had hired Rozier as its Lenten preacher; afterward, fearing arrest, he had fled to Geneva and had married there, but he had unwisely chosen to return. A notary in Anduze commented that Rozier died "a true martyr, continuing to sustain the [true] religion" (*moureust en vray martir, sostenant toujours la religion*). Many people were probably moved by such bravery in death.[13] A significant number of Nîmes residents also appeared before the parlement in 1555 and 1556; only the year 1551 had more prosecutions.

The Protestant movement was fortunate enough to gain at least three of Nîmes's booksellers as recruits. They were particularly useful for the cause. Both Jean Lucquet and François Bernard the younger became leaders of the Protestant movement in Nîmes when the movement elected its first officers in 1561. Another bookseller, Antoine Gouzet, left Nîmes in 1557 for Geneva.[14] Even in the late 1550s, however, contemporaries found it difficult to determine the boundary between orthodoxy and heresy. In late March 1558, a canon of the cathedral, Jean Alesti, who was later murdered for his Catholicism, seized four books from Bernard, including Pierre Estiard's *Alphabet; ou, Instruction chretienne pour les petits enfans*

(Lyons, 1556). The présidial called Alesti in to explain in what way the book was heretical. Alesti replied that "he found nowhere mention of confession as a necessary thing, as being one of the sacraments of the church." But the officers of the présidial replied that the book was printed in Lyon, by a named printer, and that it had also been printed in Paris and Toulouse, so how could it be forbidden? In fact, the book was heretical, but in the confused situation that prevailed, the court had reason to be cautious. Nonetheless, it did question Bernard to determine whether he had any books printed in Geneva or elsewhere with anonymous authors or printers and if he had any Bibles. Apparently, he denied having any. The court therefore released him, but ordered him not to sell any prohibited or suspicious books. The cathedral canons were also not as careful as they could have been, despite Alesti's attempt to incriminate the bookseller. Shortly after this incident, it seems the cathedral chapter hired a Dominican named Mutonis to preach on the rogation days. Mutonis became a Protestant preacher in Nîmes only three years later.[15]

Outside the proto-Protestant milieu, there were also significant changes in notarial formulas, revealing a certain softening of Catholic orthodoxy, although the essentials were unchanged until the crisis years of 1559–1562. Throughout the 1550s, between half and three-quarters of all testators continued to ask for the saints to pray for them. However, the number of people asking for the prayers of the Virgin Mary dropped: after 1552, there was no year in which even half the testators mentioned her. Still, until 1561, more than 80 percent of testators still made the sign of the cross, and 90 percent of people wanted to be married

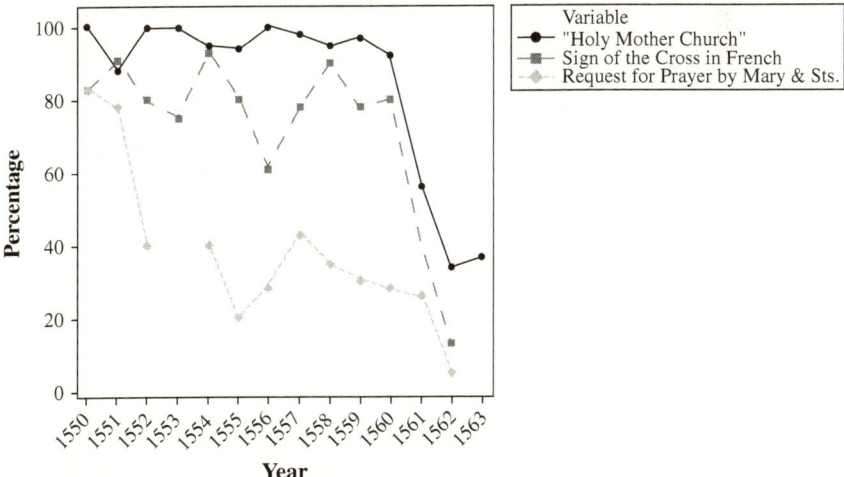

FIGURE 3.4. Catholic phrases in non-Ursi notarial acts. Source: ADG, Series IIE.

in the "Holy Mother Church." In short, after the initial advances of the early 1550s, further conversions seem to have proceeded relatively slowly. There were some significant defections even among the elite, but the bulk of the population at all levels remained Catholic.

Considered in isolation, the evidence of the register of immigrants in Geneva, the heresy figures from Toulouse, and the notarial figures from Nîmes might not suffice to measure the growth of Protestantism in Nîmes. But each gains strength from the others. There seems to be a consensus of the three that the Protestant community in Nîmes was small until the early 1550s, then grew significantly over the course of the decade until the real breakthrough, the tremendous growth of the late 1550s and early 1560s. This pattern of growth is highly suggestive, given France's history and that of Nîmes. One obvious explanation looks toward the perceived breakdown of royal authority once a child, François II, ascended the throne in July 1559 and the further disruption caused by his death in December 1560. Philip Benedict has written perceptively of the "necessary social 'space'" that Protestantism needed to develop.[16] This is perhaps too passive a formulation to fit the picture in Nîmes; as will be shown below, it would be more accurate to say that the Protestant movement skillfully exploited the spaces available to it. But the economic and political strains of the later 1550s favored the growth of dissident movements, if they could find a way to mobilize discontent among the general population and local elites.

The Social Profile of the Early Protestant Movement

Who were the early Protestants? The Ursis' clientele give some general indications. Their clients tended to be much poorer than those of most other notaries: if the ten notaries whose surviving registers contain ten marriage contracts or more are ranked by the average value of the dowries their registers contain, Jean Ursi ranks seventh and Jacques Ursi ninth. Ursi clients included far fewer officials and professionals than average; about the average number of artisans, merchants, and bourgeois; and somewhat higher than the average number of weavers and other non-leather cloth workers, as well as a particularly high number of agricultural workers. It is also possible that the Ursis' clientele were younger than average: although the Ursis wrote 53 percent of the surviving marriage contracts, they accounted for just under 40 percent of the wills. But the best information on the composition of the early Protestant movement comes from three sources: the list of people who immigrated to Geneva, the register of those who were prosecuted by the Parlement of Toulouse, and a list of heretics prepared by the Nîmes présidial court on May 18, 1560 (see Chapter 4). Since all three give fragmentary information, they have to be compared with information in Nîmes's wills and marriage contracts. After eliminating people who appear on more than one list, forty-eight early Protestants can be identified: forty-seven men with known occupations and one woman.

In some ways, these data suggest that early Protestants represented a cross section of Nîmes society: they included farmers, professionals, and artisans (for a complete breakdown, see Appendix A). Nonetheless, the surviving records indicate that early Protestants were less likely to come from agriculture and much more likely to be high-status artisans (merchants and bourgeois) or to work in the cloth trades than the population as a whole. As discussed in Chapter 1, I performed social network analysis for the top 249 families in Nîmes. Seventeen of these families had at least one early heretic among their members. The 17 families had somewhat higher betweenness than average (1.28 compared to an overall of .9 for all families) and were scattered among the various factions without any noticeable clumping.[17] Without putting too much emphasis on these figures, they do suggest that the early Protestants were well poised for future growth, since they were well connected and not tied to a particular faction. The occupational figures should also be treated with some reservations, since figures derived from the combination of the three lists only give a sample: clearly, there were more than 47 Protestants in Nîmes in 1560. If the sample suggests what percentage of Protestants were artisans, it does not show what percentage

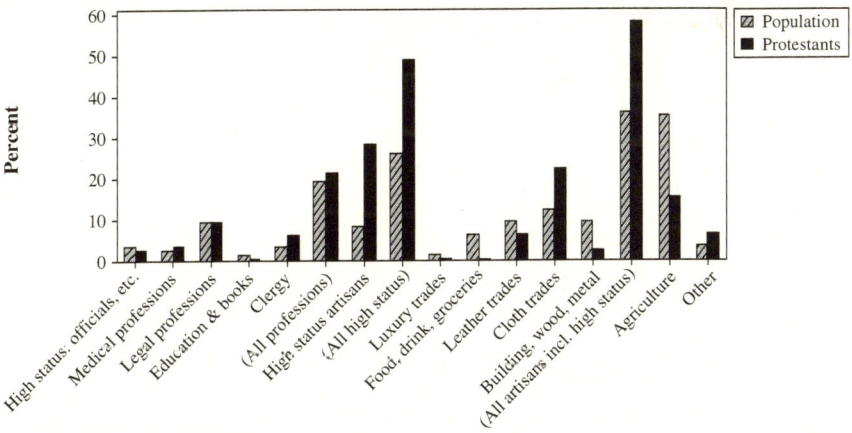

FIGURE 3.5. Early Protestants compared to population. Sources: ADG, Series IIE, ADHG, Series B, Geisendorf, Puech.

of artisans were Protestants or, more broadly, what percentage of the town as a whole had converted. A complete explanation for this profile is probably impossible: for one thing, we are dealing with the very first adherents of the movement here, and such hard-core Protestants are likely to have been the most ideologically and religiously motivated adherents. When they wrote to Calvin, they indicated that his Eucharistic theology was their overriding concern. Even without that information, it is clear that they joined at a time when doing so meant at least to some degree separating themselves from most of their neighbors. There is also no indication that conversions were clustered in the years 1540 or 1545, when grain prices were especially high. Unfortunately, more precise information is difficult to obtain because the small movement left few signs of its existence and virtually no internal records. The picture derived from the statistics is nonetheless consistent with Claude Baduel's description, discussed earlier, and to that extent both gain in credibility.

The statements we can make with confidence are largely negative. Among those below a certain level of education and literacy, including the ability to speak French, it was probably difficult for the movement to penetrate, especially given the constraints under which it was operating in its earliest years. By contrast, the authorities in Toulouse were known to be targeting the top of the social pyramid, which may have inhibited recruitment at the highest social levels. Just as wealthy families that gave their daughters large dowries had to use greater calculation when marrying off their children (see Chapter 1), they had to think about their religious affiliations carefully: they had more to lose. So upper-middling sorts, below the level of the elite, might have been particularly able to receive the message and less intimidated about embracing it. Certainly, the group was not especially prestigious on average: not one early Protestant ever became a town consul, for example. Some early Protestants were members of prominent local families, however, including the d'Albenas, the de Malmont, de Sauzet, and the Chabot families. Thus, although the early Protestants were not prominent, they were well connected. Given the small sample, it is difficult to draw significance from yet-smaller subgroups, but it is nonetheless tempting to point out the presence of three members of the Catholic clergy, who presumably brought some theological sophistication to the nascent movement.

Although we have no diaries or sermons that reveal the motivations of the earliest Protestants in Nîmes, there is nonetheless some evidence of their way of thinking. Many of the earliest Protestants were linked to local intellectuals, that is, Baduel and Pécolet. This suggests that they were interested in theological ideas. The church of Nîmes's first letter to Calvin, with its narrative of theological discussions, suggests this as well. Early Protestants also tended to use the Ursis as their notaries. Ursi wills in the early 1550s, before Catholic formulas dropped out, were especially pious: in 1552, 83 percent of them included provisions for masses after death. (In 1550, it was 76 percent, in 1551, 75 percent.) Ursi testators were more likely to leave money for masses than were those who patronized other, Catholic notaries. In 1558, the year with the highest percentage, 73 percent of non-Ursi wills included provisions for masses.[18] This suggests that the earliest Protestants were at least as pious as the average person, if not more so: they came from a highly devout milieu. Finally, because the group was small in the early days, it took a strong character to join, one with a certain indifference to risk. Although the available evidence is hardly conclusive, it suggests a group that was intellectual, pious, and committed.

Economic and Political Strains, 1557–1560

At the end of the 1550s, even nature seemed to conspire to add to Nîmes's economic difficulties. Sometime between one and two o'clock in the afternoon of September 9, 1557, a tremendous thunderstorm burst over the city. Several houses were struck by lightning, but that was hardly the most important damage. The rain, mixed with hail, continued until eight that evening, causing floodwater to cascade down the sides of the hills to the north and west of town, and turning the road to Sauve into a river that wrought enormous damage to the town and the fields around it. A mill at the Madeleine Gate, to the west of the town, was destroyed, taking with it the gate and the bridge over the town moat. The town's walls were left in tatters, with gaping holes where the water had poured through. There must have been little worth salvaging on the ground floors of the houses: the water covered the courtyard of the University and College of Arts to a height of six feet, even though the courtyard was elevated above the level of the street. (The students recorded the height with a mark on the wall, which was still visible in the eighteenth century.) The damage to the city, however, was perhaps not the most important consequence of the disaster. In the countryside, the hail did tremendous damage to the crops, while the cascading waters eroded the topsoil and deposited stones and portions of destroyed houses in its place. It incidentally proved a boon to local antiquaries, as it scoured the soil to reveal Roman remains, including coins and inscriptions, previously buried in the earth, but they were probably the only beneficiaries. A contemporary commented that "it seemed like a new Flood." If there was any doubt as to the portentousness of the event, it was immediately noticed that Nostradamus had, in his usual cryptic fashion, predicted it.[19] For the people of

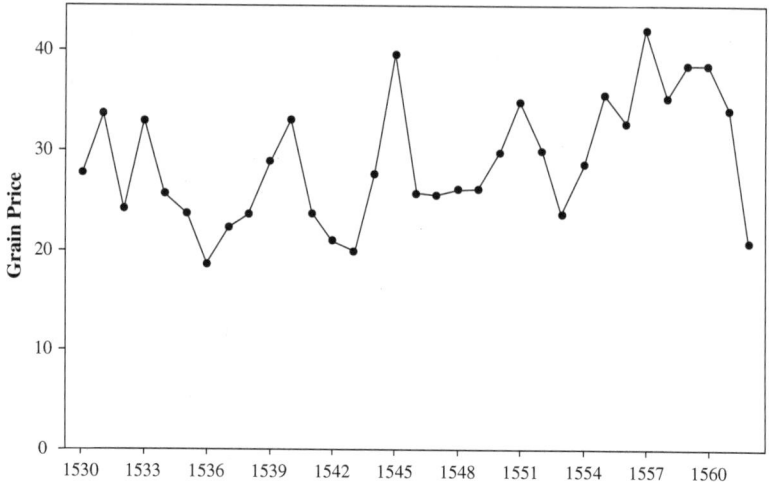

FIGURE 3.6. Grain prices, 1530–1562. Source: Le Roy Ladurie, *Paysans*.

Nîmes, accustomed to seeing the hand of God in the events of the world, this disaster must have seemed a warning to mend their ways before it was too late, just as the Flood had been a punishment for humanity's sinfulness.[20]

Indeed, the flood was a portent of sorts, because it came near the beginning of an extended period of poor harvests, hard times, and high prices. One basic phenomenon, rising grain prices, distinguishes the later 1550s from the previous decades. Grain prices in the region in the 1530s averaged 26.12s. per *setier* (a setier is about 1.4 bushels); in the following decade, they remained roughly the same, 26.83s. For 1557–1561, the average was 37.73s.; 1557, the flood year, had the single highest average price of the period, over 42s. Of the six years in the period when grain prices topped 35s., only two of them (1545 and 1555) were outside the period 1557–1560.[21] The extended period of high prices with no letup put tremendous strain on the town's ability to cope.

The Town Council Attempts to Respond

If the effects of the high prices are difficult to appreciate in the abstract, the town council's discussions of the issues suggest that they were of the utmost importance to contemporaries. Concerns about the grain supply recurred from time to time but were concentrated in the late 1550s. There was some discussion about grain prices in 1553, for example, but it was in the later half of the decade that the issue began to preoccupy the council. On January 20, 1557, the first consul, Guillaume Martin, opened the meeting by noting that "because of the high cost of grain and other products, because of the barrenness [of the land] and the scarcity, there are a great number of poor people." The town council resolved to buy 400 *salmées* (slightly less than 2,300 bushels) of grain, in order to prevent scarcity. By March, the situation had not improved, and the council resolved to buy another 200. To prevent unrest, the council also ordered the town gates guarded day and night. In June, however, they resolved to buy 400 *salmées* more, this time by requisitioning money from the richest 100–120 families in town.[22] Then, in September, came the flood.

By the following winter, the council was close to panic. The storm had destroyed the harvest:

> [B]ecause of the fear of the harvest failure, the consuls must first secretly find out what amount of grain is available in town from those who deal in it, buying and selling; and afterwards consult with the bakers and others selling bread to find out how much they will use between now and the next harvest, and whether they have sufficient provisions, or how much they lack, and how much the poor inhabitants, artisans and others will need.

Even middling sorts—artisans—were in jeopardy. Furthermore, as the consuls noted at the same meeting, royal demands were in direct conflict with their efforts to ease the pain. The crown was demanding 12,000 charges (approximately 62,000 bushels) of grain for the war against the Hapsburgs, which was driving up the price and raising the specter of greater shortages later in the season.[23] Nor did the pressure let up in 1559: in July, the council noted, still frightened, that there was danger of "great public outcry and riot" because of the poor harvest, and there were "a great many poor people who are stripping the harvest," stealing the almost-ready grain before the farmers could reap it themselves. (This reduced the total yield and added to the scarcity.) The town council ordered an inventory of all the grain in town and prohibited all sales without a permit. Although it did not immediately prohibit the export of grain, it did authorize the consuls to do so should it become necessary. In October, the council considered "if it would be good to seize the grain of outsiders who are in town."[24] In November, the council was relieved to learn that a merchant from Beaucaire was offering to sell up to 1,000 charges of grain, at 10 florins per charge, and it immediately appointed commissioners to inspect the grain and negotiate the price. In December, Jacques Le Vellais, a wealthy merchant, offered to sell the town 600 charges of grain; the town gratefully accepted. But the following week, it was noted that Le Vellais's contribution was not enough, and something must be done so that "the town be provided for and not fall into scandal." The council granted authority to the consuls to borrow money to purchase more grain, at their discretion. These efforts were unavailing, however, as the hard times continued into the winter. In February 1560, the council was talking again of the possibility of "great sedition and outcry," if grain were not purchased. The Dominican monks were also in difficulties, and the council agreed to reduce their tax (*taille*) payments.[25]

One of the ways in which the council tried to improve the local economy, and presumably to alleviate unemployment, was to encourage new trades—usually through tax abatements. Again, these measures were concentrated in the late 1550s. In 1556, the council agreed to furnish a house and workshop to Hugon Parat, a pin maker, and to exempt him from taxes for five years. He promised to take on an apprentice each year, without charge. In November 1557, the consuls recommended that the town exempt its only cooper from taxes, arguing that, because of the town's poverty, they should be encouraging new industries. The council agreed. At the same meeting, it agreed to provide Antoine Bonfar, a velvet maker, £25 to make repairs to his workshop. (Some years before, the council had agreed to subsidize him by building him a workshop, since no one else in town practiced his trade, but the one they had provided him was not lit well enough.) The town also agreed in 1557 to hire a woman from Avignon to teach the girls in the foundling hospital how to make thread from silkworm cocoons. This is the first mention of silk production in Nîmes, which eventually became a crucial industry for the local economy.[26]

From 1547 until the later 1550s, when the town council discussed the poor, they were usually talking about the poor of the hospital, suggesting that the problem was relatively contained. Starting in 1557, however, due to bad harvests and the flood, poverty became once more a problem of the streets. In January, the council noted that "there were a great number and quantity of poor people," and it "would be good to know the number and afterwards lodge them in private houses or at least give them something so that they can support themselves until good times return." The council divided up the town into neighborhoods (*quartiers*) and appointed twelve notables to compile a survey of the poor within each district, calling on the clergy and all other "notable personages" (*notables personnages*) to assist them.[27] In March, the council was still concerned about the number of the destitute, as well as the high price of grain.[28]

The following February (1558), the council noted that "there are many abandoned children," and by March the grain that had been bought for the poor in the hospital was nearly exhausted, presumably because more people were receiving aid than had been expected. By the fall of 1559, the poor hospital was also running out of money from its endowments, and the council deliberated using town money instead and suing the clergy if no assistance from them was forthcoming. In December of the same year, the council noted that "there are an enormous number of poor people, about eight hundred or so, and that every day more outside poor are arriving." Because of the dearth, it was necessary to verify again how many were "truly poor" (*vrayment pouvres*) and to find out their parishes of origin. The council nominated a large and extremely influential group, including all of the outgoing and new consuls, other distinguished citizens, and several priests, to do this. The council also decided to send six wives of notable citizens to help attend to the poor lying sick in the hospital.[29] The gesture was no doubt intended at least in part to be symbolic, to encourage a sense of solidarity between the town's poor and its elite. But it was also intended in earnest. The council tried, given its limited means, to do its best by its citizens. Despite the council's efforts, however, it is hard not to connect at least some of the roiling passions of the immediately following period with a sense of frustration and a desire for renewal.

Politics and Taxes

While the citizens of Nîmes had reason to be happy with the efforts of their local leaders to respond to the emergency, they had far less reason to be happy with Henri II, their king in distant Paris. They felt that his job was succoring them, his people. They did not understand why he was more concerned with waging war against the Hapsburgs, although the king's position was quite understandable. France was nearly surrounded by Hapsburg possessions. If Nîmes, after experiencing so many difficulties, wanted financial support in the late 1550s, Henri, facing ever-increasing financial troubles, expected Nîmes and other loyal cities to give assistance rather than to receive it. The crown did need help: the endless wars eventually led to bankruptcy and the unfavorable Treaty of Cateau-Cambrésis in 1559. France gained little in the negotiations, and Henri was widely criticized for the results. He had achieved almost nothing after making war against the Hapsburgs more or less continuously for seven years. France had been fighting intermittently for most of the century.[30] While the treaty damaged the crown's prestige, at least in Nîmes, the crown's actions while Henri was still alive had at least as much to do with the ensuing upheaval as the timing of his death.

Nîmes, as one of the major cities in the province of Languedoc, paid significant taxes to the crown. Like many towns, it was exempt from the land tax, but did have to pay extraordinary taxes, and in this period, every year was an extraordinary year. It also paid other sums from time to time, as required. Some of these were legally and morally questionable, as will be described

FIGURE 3.7. Taxes paid to the crown, 1547–1562. Source: ADG, Series C.

below. These increased significantly in the later 1550s. While tax payments generally averaged about £3,000 per year before 1550, they never dropped below 4,000 thereafter, and averaged over £6,500 between 1551 and 1562. Again, the later 1550s were the highest years of all. Townspeople must surely have resented the high taxes—over £12,000—they paid in 1558, a year of tremendous economic difficulty in the aftermath of the flood. Although receipts rose throughout the country in this period, the effect was even more brutal in Nîmes than elsewhere. Total net French revenue, already high, averaged £5.9 million in 1551–1556, and increased 14 percent to about £6.7 million in 1557–1558. In Nîmes, the average tax bill in the period 1551–1556 was £5,714 per year, but in 1557–1558 it ballooned 56 percent, to £8,916. As a result, Nîmes and the surrounding villages started to fall into arrears, and the civil diocese had to send out repeated appeals for payment. In the fifteenth century, it appears that Normandy was heavily taxed, while the crown treated Languedoc somewhat more gently, but precise figures for such regional disparities in the sixteenth century are unknown. In any case, people in Nîmes were not likely to be altruistic enough to accept large tax increases on the grounds that they had previously been undertaxed. They only saw that their taxes were increasing brutally and disproportionately.[31]

Taxation was not the only source of friction with the crown. Sixteenth-century France was an extremely litigious society, but one case more than all others consumed the attention of the Nîmes town council. It concerned the ownership of the *garrigues*, the scrub land around the town. Both the town and the crown claimed ownership of it, and no one knew who had jurisdiction over it. This was particularly important since, although the *garrigues* had been used since time immemorial as commons, and in particular for gathering wood, with the growing population, it was being encroached upon for agriculture. In 1549, the council noted that "outsiders and foreigners who come from the mountains" were taking the wood and selling it, so that "soon there will be no wood for this town's use." Furthermore, once these individuals cleared off the wood, they were cultivating and selling the land without ever registering the property for tax purposes. The land was also used for grazing, and of course the encroachments were bad for the cattlemen, who complained that they were "constrained to abandon their cattle and let them die of hunger."[32] As the seemingly endless case edged toward a conclusion, various powerful court officials wanted a piece of the action. Robert LeBlanc, the ordinary judge (*juge ordinaire*) of Nîmes, wrote from Paris to the town council in 1557 that it would be well to bribe the *procureur général du roy*, one of the king's judicial officers, with a payment of 1,500 *écus d'or sols* (£3,450). The town, stipulating that it was a one-time payment, agreed.[33]

Finally—after more than fifty years of pursuing the case—in 1558 the crown offered a settlement, probably provoked by the financial exigencies of the Hapsburg wars. (The bribe paid in 1557 may also have helped.) It offered to give the town the *garrigues* as a fief of the crown, with generous rights, for a token annual lease and a one-time payment of 2,000 écus, or £4,800. The town accepted the offer, and arranged to pay for it by taxing the residents of the *garrigues* half the cost, with the rest to be borne in common.[34] The two substantial payments, totaling over £8,000, represented a large sum of money, even compared to the town's annual tax payments (see above). The timing—since 1557 and 1558 were years of great economic stress for Nîmes—could not have been worse. Although the town's irritation may have been heavily tinged with relief, given how long the case had lasted, it is likely that the affair left a bitter aftertaste.

Not only was the crown seemingly out to get every drop it could, by whatever means, it even seemed at certain points that it wished to destroy what remained of the local economy. The law and the courts were important to Nîmes, as the high percentage of lawyers in the population, already discussed in a previous chapter, would indicate. Because the volume of judicial business depended heavily on the extent of the courts' jurisdiction, the Nîmes town council was always zealous in attempting to prevent any other city in the area from obtaining its own courts. However, the crown always had a certain interest in creating new courts, because the new offices could then be sold, which would produce a significant amount of revenue. In 1544, for example, the

Nîmes town council sent the first consul to Toulouse, on hearing a rumor that Le Puy, once again, was trying to become the seat of a new seneschalsy and likely to succeed. Similarly, in 1551, when there was a proposal to subdivide the seneschalsy into multiple parts, the council immediately dispatched a delegation to the royal court to discover what was afoot. Of course, in 1552, when présidiaux were established throughout the kingdom, Le Puy wanted one established there, and equally naturally, Nîmes opposed the idea. Two years later, in 1554, both sides were at it again. This time, having obtained two royal decrees prohibiting Le Puy from obtaining a présidial, the Nîmes council proposed putting copies in the archives as evidence, should the matter ever come up again.[35]

The Nîmes town fathers might then have expected to have seen the end of the matter. But in 1558, right when Nîmes could least afford it, Le Puy renewed its quest for a présidial of its own. For suitable financial remuneration, the crown was prepared to consider the idea in its own time of fiscal strain. According to the Nîmes town council deliberations, Le Puy in fact "lent" (these sorts of loans were rarely paid back) the crown £30,000 in exchange for the award of the présidial. Everyone, not just the lawyers and judges, was concerned: the whole region agreed to petition the king to reconsider, since "by this act the inhabitants would be deprived of the commerce and trade which they have with the inhabitants of the mountains [of the] pays du Velay, the Vivarais and Gévaudan."[36] Initially, the Nîmes town council offered to take over the loan, but that proved insufficient: eventually, the town was forced to pay £10,000 to reverse the royal decree. The town council, no doubt exasperated, insisted that it was only prepared to pay if the resulting decree were "perpetual and irrevocable."[37] In the end, faced with the costs of covering the £30,000 loan and the £10,000 gift, the council attempted to escape from the loan:

> Reimbursement would be Impossible, either in whole or in part, because the inhabitants, if it pleases Him [the king], cannot pay, given their poverty and Impotence, because of the great expense that they have borne hitherto to support the king in his great and urgent affairs of war, and because they have undergone, about two years ago, a deluge, and Unbelievable ruin of the greater portion of their town, their possessions and goods.[38]

Considering that the town had enormous difficulty paying its taxes in 1558, and was laboring under the payment to the crown resulting from the settlement of the *garrigues* legislation, this complaint seems entirely believable. Despite all of Nîmes's efforts, and the £10,000 bribe, the king put through the legislation creating a new présidial for Le Puy. It appears that Nîmes was able to avoid paying the £30,00 loan. This was small consolation: despite all their efforts, the Nîmes city fathers had lost, and one of the town's most important sources of revenue suffered a major blow.[39]

If high taxes, bribery, and large payments in hard times did not do enough damage to the relationship between the people of Nîmes and their prince, the crown, increasingly desperate for cash, courted additional resentment by resorting to further, illegal expedients in the search for revenue. It first demanded significant forced loans that wealthy citizens were ordered to pay. On November 22, 1551, for example, Chief Judge Gaillard de Montcalm had announced that "the king has been forced into war again by our Holy Father the Pope and by the Emperor, and therefore it is necessary for the king to amass a large sum of money for the support of the great costs of the war." The king announced that he needed to borrow 2.4 million écus (about £5.5 million) from his subjects. The Nîmes council agreed eventually to do its part, once it found out how others were organizing to meet the obligation. The following year, the council was forced to permit troops to lodge in town, but noted that it was agreeing only for one time, without setting a precedent, and vowed to protest if the town were not reimbursed.[40]

Because of all the town's other burdens, however, when the crown made further demands, the council became recalcitrant. On May 6, 1558, the council received a new demand for a forced loan of 1,000 écus (about £2,300) from each of ten inhabitants and 500 écus (about £1,150) from thirty more, for a total of 25,000 écus, or £57,500. Royal commissioners would collect it. This time, the consuls simply refused, saying they "did not know of any inhabitants rich enough to borrow or lend to the king even a much lesser sum." But the following month, they were concerned because "there were those who were finding it impossible or difficult to pay their taxes," and therefore they resolved to turn to the wealthy (*les plus aysèz*) to lend the town money so that the taxes could be paid.[41] This does not indicate that the council was lying in its response to the forced loan, since the total of the loans the king demanded added up to many times the town's annual taxes. On an individual level, only five surviving marriage contracts in Nîmes in the period 1550–1562 specify dowries of £2,300 or greater.[42] Nonetheless, it was unusually daring for the town council to refuse flatly to respect a royal request, and this suggests a hardening attitude. The town had, with great difficulty, paid its taxes, including the considerable increases. It had paid to try to prevent the establishment of a new présidial at Le Puy, and it had agreed to the settlement of the legal case over the *garrigues*. That was more than enough.

The political and economic strains in the later 1550s in Nîmes were not the only proximate causes of the Reformation. But it would be hard to claim that the town's problems were irrelevant to the growth of Protestantism there, because the same years of economic and political stress were crucial to the growth of the Protestant movement. Henri II's government, by its insensitivity to Nîmes's problems, had engendered a wave of discontent. Its failure in war had only increased its unpopularity. His domestic policies were also unpopular with French Protestants. In June 1559, while at Écouen, Henri II announced that, now that the war was over, he was going to devote his energies to eliminating heresy from the kingdom. He embarked on a savage campaign of persecution. He also devoted his attention to the peace treaty and the attendant celebrations. The peace was cemented by two marriages: Philip II of Spain married Henri's daughter Elizabeth, and Emmanuel Philibert, the duke of Savoy, married Henri's sister Marguerite. Henri organized a grand tournament as part of the festivities. He loved pageantry, and himself participated, fighting under the colors of his mistress Diane de Poitiers. While jousting with the captain of his Scotch Guards, Gabriel de Montgomery, Montgomery's lance struck the visor of Henri's helmet. A fragment broke off and entered Henri's left eye. The wound became infected. The best physicians of the day could do nothing for him, and after ten days of agony, he died. His subjects, on the whole, had disliked him: his foreign policy had been an expensive failure. Now, his death permitted all of the anger to come out, especially since his eldest son, now King François II, was just fifteen years old. Protestants saw the hand of God in his fate, and their deliverance.[43]

4

The Religious Crisis Begins, 1559–1560

When Henri II died, he left France weakened abroad and burdened with debt. After his death, the Protestant movement grew. The situation was difficult in many localities, and beginning in early 1560, Nîmes's officials had to turn from issues of grain prices and taxes to concentrate on halting the newly aggressive Protestant movement. The présidial court moved fairly energetically to quash heresy, although it was hampered in several respects. Government was not very efficient in the sixteenth century, and it was particularly difficult to threaten people with jail and execution in a small town like Nîmes, where the victims of religious persecution were likely to be one's neighbors, friends, and relatives. Furthermore, the présidial needed an armed force to act, and the town council, the court's traditional partner in government, was reluctant to provide it. The town council's members were more closely linked to the Protestant movement than were the présidial's members, and several of the consuls for 1560 in particular were Protestants or closely related to them. Despite these difficulties, the présidial, under strong pressure from royal officials, did succeed in keeping Protestant agitation to a minimum in the first half of the year. Then, the crown switched first to a more permissive policy, which undid all the présidial's efforts of the spring, and then back to harsh repression. The crown's erratic behavior alienated the populace and the town's leadership alike. By November 1560, Nîmes's authorities were in disarray and the town council was nearly in open revolt. Royal officials then staged a coup by manipulating Nîmes's voting procedures to put Catholics into office as consuls for the coming year, but their actions gravely weakened the town's institutions. Henri's policies and the rise of the Protestant movement had increased political tensions. His death and the young François's accession to the throne weakened the crown. As a result, the opponents of the crown's political and religious policies were emboldened, and in Nîmes the first permanent minister arrived to preach the word. As in 1776, 1789, or 1989, people believed they had crossed over a threshold into a new era. The very uncertainty of the political future encouraged people to contemplate their society and its essential underpinnings.[1]

Conflict at the Center

Throughout France, Protestantism had made substantial gains in the late 1550s. Beginning in 1555, the Geneva Company of Pastors formalized its activities and began a systematic missionary effort, largely directed toward France. By 1557, Protestant assemblies were attracting hundreds of people in Paris, as well as the attention of the authorities. Despite harsh and increasing persecution, in May 1559 the movement held its First National Synod, in Paris. (There is no evidence that Nîmes sent any representatives to this gathering.) This meeting marked a new maturity in the French Protestant movement. The delegates to the synod approved a Confession of Faith and an ecclesiastical discipline, which gave French Protestantism a structure and governance. Calvin's ideas were instrumental in both, and both documents largely followed Genevan models. Henceforth, Protestantism would be an organized, disciplined body, a convincing alternative to its rival, the Catholic Church. After Henri's death, as the kingdom headed toward civil war, the crown became more concerned with what to do about the Protestants than with any other issue in domestic or foreign politics.[2]

Henri II's declaration of war against heresy at Écouen had frightened French Protestants greatly, and they hailed his death as a liberation and a divine judgment on him for his policies. After Henri's death, the court rapidly became bitterly divided, and royal policy became incoherent as factions gained and then rapidly lost ascendancy. King François II was only fifteen years old, which meant that technically he was of age (French kings became adults at age fourteen), but in practical terms he was extremely susceptible to influence. In any case, on previous occasions, guardians had sometimes governed in a king's name until he reached the age of twenty, which led to further wrangling. One important player in the subsequent squabbles at court was Henri's widow,

Catherine de' Medici. She tended to pursue a moderate policy toward the Protestants, and over time came to be mistrusted by extremists on both sides of the religious divide. Her position was powerful but ambiguous. The leading figure in the kingdom should in principle have been Antoine de Bourbon, king of Navarre. He was entitled to a role in government because he was the first prince of the blood. Also, his queen was Jeanne d'Albret, daughter of Marguerite de Navarre. Jeanne would convert to Protestantism in 1560, becoming the most important Protestant noblewoman in the kingdom. (Her son would become King Henri IV.) But Antoine de Bourbon was in Guyenne, in the southwest of France, at the time of Henri's death, and he was neither energetic nor politically astute. Instead, François, duc de Guise, and his brother Charles, the cardinal of Lorraine, seized the reins of power. They soon became highly unpopular, both because they were outsiders (the Guise family came from Lorraine, then in the Holy Roman Empire) and because they monopolized patronage. They were remarkably greedy. Protestants in particular disliked them because they were zealous defenders of Catholic orthodoxy and persecutors of heretics. The Protestants initially focused their hopes on Navarre, and there were many letters exchanged between France and Geneva discussing how to get rid of the Guises and install the first prince of the blood in power, but Navarre proved to be a weak reed. Instead of working to improve his position at court, he preferred to travel south, escorting the king's sister Elizabeth de Valois on her way to marry King Philip II of Spain. As a result, Protestants began to hope that Navarre's younger brother Louis I, prince de Condé, would lead the fight against the Guises.

The anti-Guise nobles at court became increasingly frustrated as the Guises consolidated their hold on power. The Guises' opponents felt that the house of Lorraine's behavior was illegal, and yet the only way to stop it was to get the king to dismiss the Guises from their offices, or to call a session of the Estates General, which had the right to install a new royal council. But by this point, the Guises so monopolized the young king's time that he was largely isolated from the rest of the court. From the opposition's point of view, the Guises had made the king virtually a prisoner, and therefore the only way to get to the king to put forward their own plans for the kingdom was to make him their prisoner instead. Calvinist noblemen, doubly angry with the Guises since they were being both persecuted for their religion and deprived of pensions and offices, were the most anxious to rectify the situation. On February 1, 1560, a group of these extremist nobles met in Nantes to plan how to kidnap the king and imprison the Guises. It is possible that some of them thought that, if they had the opportunity to speak at length to the king, he might even convert to Protestantism. Jean du Barry, seigneur de La Renaudie, was the chief organizer of the scheme. Calvin disapproved of him and his plans, but La Renaudie nonetheless attracted supporters by telling them that he had Geneva's support. The Guises soon discovered the plot, and La Renaudie was killed on March 18. The plot, known as "the conspiracy of Amboise," was over. The Guises immediately used the incident to paint the Protestants as seditious traitors who were prepared to attack the person of the king, although in the main the Protestant churches, following Calvin's lead, had resisted participating. Arnaud de Maillane, a minor French nobleman, spent a considerable amount of time in Provence and Languedoc, and he had asked the Protestant community in Nîmes to assist. The church refused, both because the majority disapproved of the enterprise and because the members felt that they could not afford to spend the money. A minority of hotheads, however, were in favor of the project.[3]

In the immediate aftermath of the Amboise incident, the Guises put through a new edict that reiterated earlier prohibitions against illicit heretical assemblies and added that officials who failed to prosecute violators would themselves be subject to removal from office. Nonetheless, after the immediate excitement of discovering the conspiracy had waned, the airing of such widespread discontent weakened the Guises' power, and Catherine de' Medici saw an opportunity to exercise her influence on behalf of moderation. She threw her influence behind a new decree, the Edict of Amboise. It offered amnesty for all heretics except conspirators and Protestant pastors, on condition that they renounce their false ideas and return to the Catholic Church. Over the following months, political maneuvering continued at court, where both Catherine and Gaspard de Coligny, admiral of France, who was becoming the most prominent Protestant spokesman, were trying to lessen the Guises' grip on power. When François Olivier, the chancellor of France, died, Catherine and Coligny succeeded in nominating a moderate, Michel de L'Hospital, to replace him. One of the new chancellor's first acts was to lobby for the Edict of Romorantin, issued on May 18, 1560, which removed cases of heresy from the civil courts and put them in the hands of the Church. Ecclesiastical courts did not have the authority to execute people, so this was a significant relaxation of policy. Furthermore, the edict reestablished a distinction between heresy and sedition: it only banned "illicit assemblies and public forces," and such offenses were removed from the parlements to the présidial courts for trial. Many people interpreted this ambiguous phrase to mean that only armed assemblies were prohibited, and peaceful ones were therefore licit. The Parlement of Paris, a generally conservative body, was scandalized that its right to hear appeals from the présidiaux was being limited and that its jurisdiction was being handed over to the ecclesiastical courts, but it finally registered the edict nearly two months later, on July 16. But L'Hospital had antagonized the parlement for no good reason, since the edict was never enforced.[4]

When the royal council met in August, the moderates again managed to prevail, and the council decided to call the Estates General to meet on December 10, 1560, and an Assembly of the Clergy to meet on January 20, 1561. The council hoped that the two bodies could find solutions to the kingdom's most pressing problems. The Estates could impose new taxes, and thereby ease the continuing fiscal problems caused by the debts incurred in the wars which had ended the previous year. The assembly might find a satisfactory formula that would permit the reunification of the churches. Protestants were overjoyed. In the aftermath of this apparent victory for the anti-Guise forces, some Protestants decided that it was time to destroy the Guises completely and that the kingdom was theirs for the taking. On the night of September 4, 1560, Edmée de Maligny, one of the conspirators of Amboise earlier in the year, attempted to seize Lyon. Some moderates, like Navarre, were appalled, and they successfully prevailed on Maligny to desist. Navarre's brother Condé may have been more deeply involved. The young king was furious. He ordered a sharp turn toward repression, and Catherine was powerless to intervene. François ordered Condé's arrest as soon as he could be captured. Royal forces arrested Condé on October 31, and he was apparently condemned to death. Throughout the fall, harsh anti-Protestant measures continued, but then fate again intervened. The king had a series of fainting spells, which turned out to be caused by an incurable fistula in his ear. He died on December 5. His younger brother, ten years old, succeeded to the throne as Charles IX and then presided over the meeting of the Estates General convened by his brother. Since Charles was a minor, this time there was a regency, which put Catherine back in control, as co-regent with Navarre. The repression of the fall soon eased, and the crown tacked back once again toward a more moderate policy. Condé was released. François's reign had lasted less than a year and a half, but the damage had been done. In the midst of fiscal and religious crises, royal policy had bordered on the schizophrenic. Under these circumstances, local government lacked direction, and the authorities in places like Nîmes, which faced the same strains on a smaller scale, were confused and alienated.[5]

New Opportunities for Protestantism in Nîmes

Until the late 1550s, the Protestants of Nîmes were a small minority of the population and held relatively little political power. Over the preceding decade, they had increased their numbers, gained in organization, and developed a coherent understanding of theology, but they had not been able to break out of a relatively confined section of society to gain the mass conversions necessary if they were to become Nîmes's dominant religious group. At the end of the 1550s, the difficulties that provoked near panic for Nîmes's government provided new opportunities for Protestantism to expand. The movement had finally reached the size needed to maintain a minister, who could then push the community to a new level of growth, sophistication, and influence. It would have been unreasonable to hire a minister unless the community was big enough to support him; at the same time, a minister could consolidate the gains already made and help to build the congregation.

In order for the Protestant movement to take advantage of these opportunities, it needed to defy the law and begin mass preaching to solicit large numbers of new members. Preaching was a superb vehicle for Protestants because it was consonant with Protestant ideals and because it was a well-established custom. Protestant theology insisted emphatically that faith was conveyed through understanding God's promises to humanity, and a true church had to convey that message to the people. Calvin and Viret were two of the greatest preachers of the age. But preaching was not a Protestant innovation. People in sixteenth-century France were accustomed to sermons and enjoyed them; preaching therefore attracted people who were not yet socialized into Protestant ways. Protestants usually had no access to local churches, which were in Catholic hands. But preaching outside of church was not shocking to people; sermons had always been held outside in good weather, since a good preacher frequently drew a larger audience than a church could hold. The preacher would set up in a church cemetery or public square, in a corner from which the wind would carry his voice toward the audience. A rope usually separated men from women. Although sermons attracted large crowds, they were to some degree a middle-class passion: the poor appear to have been more attracted to mystery plays. Sermons could be quite taxing on the mind and the body. They commonly lasted at least an hour, and some went on for much longer. Listeners sat if they could, but most stood. Preachers frequently complained that their audiences were distracted, that they refused to repent, or that they were more interested in flirting across the rope than in listening. Nonetheless, the right preacher could hold an audience spellbound, and there was a cumulative effect. If a preacher could gather a large crowd, each person's emotions were reflected in the faces of their neighbors, magnifying the minister's words. A great sermon, delivered on the right theme, could convert an entire community.[6]

In a largely oral culture, Protestantism's success depended on good preaching. The movement therefore needed competent, respected, and energetic ministers who could give stirring sermons. Good ministers could also provide leadership and direction to the Protestants of a particular locale. The small groups of dissenters frequently needed focus, and they required trained personnel if they were to become stable, institutionalized church communities. At the end of the 1550s, both the leaders of the Protestant movement in Nîmes and the Company of Pastors in Geneva must have concluded that the time was ripe. The leadership of the Calvinist movement in Geneva therefore agreed to send a minister to assist the Nîmes community, and on September 29, 1559, Guillaume Mauget, the first permanent pastor of the Nîmes Protestant church, arrived in town. He would guide the church through its early years. At the same time, or shortly thereafter, it is probable that a second pastor, named Arnaud Banc (apparently using the pseudonym of Pierre de la Source), arrived. Of Mauget's background, little is known, although it is most probable that he was born in Guitres, in the Bordelais. Banc appears to have been a colleague of Pierre Viret in Lausanne.[7] Their arrival marked the beginning of a new phase in the history of the Protestant movement in Nîmes.

Eventually, Mauget would give sermons in Nîmes's streets to hundreds of people. He began much more cautiously, however, continuing the small-scale meetings that had begun before his arrival. A contemporary diarist notes that he "began to preach in a few houses secretly," that is, to the Protestant community only. He had to secure his base. There are no lists of those who attended, nor are there any surviving sermons. If Protestant meetings in Nîmes were like those elsewhere, they took place behind heavily curtained windows, in small groups. The pastor had little time to proselytize, since it took most of his time just to tend to his flock. There is little information about where he preached. Another source suggests that he preached "at night, in the house of the lawyer Cabot," probably Pierre Chabot, who was later named an overseer (*surveillant*, an early term for *ancien*, elder) at the first meeting of the Protestant Consistory in 1561.[8] There is one other piece of evidence that may indicate some of Mauget's other contacts in Nîmes in this early period: the will which Jacques Maurin, a gardener, made on October 30, 1559, only a month after Mauget's arrival. The will was described as having been "done at the house in the garden of the great park of Mr. Tristan de Brueys, royal advocate in the présidial court." Among the witnesses were Jean Maurin, locksmith; several other gardeners; and Guillaume Mauget, merchant of Guitres, in the Bordelais. It is unclear if there was any family relationship between Jacques and Jean Maurin, but in any case Jean Maurin's house was where the first recorded meeting of the Protestant Consistory was held. It seems likely that Mauget was called in to comfort the sick man and therefore also was available to be a witness to the will. It is even possible that Mauget was present because he was preaching in the garden. It also seems plausible that de Brueys knew that a Protestant minister was visiting his gardener on the grounds of the estate; if he was not himself already a Protestant, he was at least unwilling to denounce his employee.[9]

Nîmes's Government Responds to Heresy

Shortly after Mauget arrived in Nîmes, the Protestant community had a stroke of luck. In the elections that autumn, several Protestant candidates won the lottery and were selected as consuls for the following year, 1560. Of the four consuls selected, the first consul, François Bonail, was probably a Protestant, and the third and fourth consuls, Jean Mombel, a notary, and Pierre Cellerier, a wealthy yeoman (*laboureur*), were almost certainly so, although halfway through the year Cellerier was replaced by Claude Granon, a Catholic. Granon was unlikely to be a powerful figure on the Catholic side since the fourth consul had little authority and his daughter had married Étienne Dumas, who was a Protestant. (At some point before 1561, Mauget also preached in the garden of Étienne Alexi, Dumas's mother, in the Jacobins neighborhood, outside the city.)[10] The second consul, Jean de Lubac, a retired apothecary, was a firm Catholic. On the Protestant side, both Mombel and Cellerier were weak Protestants lacking in zeal; Mombel was eventually criticized by the Protestant governing body, the consistory, because he "attended mass during the time of persecution."[11] The resulting slate of consuls contained no hard-liners, and they were disposed to pursue a relatively neutral policy, preserving the peace and attempting to restrain both sides.

The présidial court was the principal institution responsible for enforcing the law, and it was therefore immediately concerned when preaching moved out into the open. From its point of view, Protestant meetings were a public disturbance. The présidial could not act entirely on its own: it needed the town council's help to provide the necessary force. The council could order the city's guards to shut the town's gates, for example. By late March 1560, the consuls were hearing alarming rumors of growing Protestant activity in Nîmes and in the region. On March 29, the consuls decided that the town needed to take action to prevent the situation from getting out of hand. Bonail, de Lubac, and Cellerier therefore came to a meeting of the présidial court. They pointed out that there had been disturbances in nearby provinces, including Dauphiné and Provence, and it would be a good idea to nominate a "captain," as a military leader for the town. The captain would survey "cabarets and taverns, public places and private homes if necessary." The officials were unwilling to admit exactly what they feared. The closest they came to saying what they meant was when they suggested that the captain should chase away all vagabonds and masterless men, prevent all "illicit assemblies," and make sure that no one bore arms in the street. A number of présidial members, including Pierre Vallete, who later became an important member of the Catholic party in Nîmes, agreed heartily, and asked the consuls whom they would suggest for the job. Pierre Robert, who had held the post on previous occasions, explained that he was no longer up to the task. The consuls suggested Jean Maure and Jean Bertrand, two wealthy merchants, and the présidial agreed. This decision was apparently not followed by any action.[12]

The consuls and members of the présidial had reason to act somewhat cautiously. In early 1560, the crown proclaimed the Edict of Amboise, which promised amnesty for heresy. News of the edict reached Nîmes in March. The leaders of the Protestant movement were hardly likely to get a more favorable moment nor town officials more favorably disposed to the new religion. Furthermore, the edict suggested that the crown was softening its repressive policies, and emboldened Nîmes's Protestant community to start preaching more openly. Mauget by this time had also established himself and gotten to know his flock. As a result, he felt that it was time to begin preaching during the day, so that he could attract people who had not been informed in advance. Until the movement came at least somewhat out into the open, it would be hard to attract new people to Protestantism.[13]

Despite the Edict of Amboise, the town's authorities were not prepared to permit such blatant defiance of the law. Even the Protestant consuls, lacking in zeal, afraid of royal displeasure, and unsure of their base of support in the council, were loath to pursue a frankly Protestant policy. As soon as public preaching began, the consuls and the présidial began to consider what should be done. On April 1, the bishop's deputy, Jean du Caylar, showed up at a meeting of the présidial to complain that "there was a rumor running round the town of certain disorders and rebellions, affairs against the Church in certain nearby regions, and although it was nothing but words for the moment," he was concerned about the upcoming Palm Sunday procession. Pierre Vallete, the *procureur du roi* at the présidial, noted that he had heard there had been "assemblies and conventicles" that were being held by day and by night. He insisted that they had to take action against the guilty and "radically extirpate" heresy. The présidial had the town crier announce that assemblies, and the bearing of arms, were prohibited. Following Vallete's suggestion, it also ordered all of the town's officials, including the consuls, to attend the upcoming Easter celebrations and not to leave town during the festivities. That said, on the eleventh the présidial assured the vicomte de Joyeuse, the lieutenant of the king in Languedoc, that it was unnecessary for him to intervene, although at the same time they ordered the consuls to keep the town gates shut at all times.[14]

Two days later, the présidial met again. The April 13 meeting consisted of the members of the présidial, namely, the judges, lieutenants, and councillors, as well as the *gens du roi* (the king's men), that is, lawyers who represented the crown in legal cases. The town consuls were also apparently supposed to be present, although only three of the four showed up (Mombel was absent). A leading

Catholic, Jean Baudan, wrote a letter to the présidial denouncing Protestants. Pierre Vallete accused a merchant, Arnaud Alizot (called La Ramée), of having assemblies in his house. Another member of the présidial, Honoré Richier, added that "Aliot [and] Ferrandon" were also guilty. Alizot had indeed been named an overseer at the first meeting of the consistory, while Ferrandon was probably Jacques Savy, a fairly obscure yeoman (*laboureur*) whose nickname was Ferrandon. Everyone who spoke agreed that the court needed to move against the heretics, but there was some division about how stern a position the court should take. The first speaker was Jean d'Albenas, the principal lieutenant, who insisted that the existing ordinances should be enforced rigorously and the town crier should remind the townspeople that all assemblies were forbidden. He added that the criminal lieutenant should investigate and turn over anyone he found to the *procureur du roi* for prosecution. Men-at-arms should be hired to give the officers sufficient force to carry out their mission, and strangers should be expelled from town. Honoré Richier, a councillor and the second speaker, advocated a harder line. He agreed with all of d'Albenas's suggestions, but added that Ferrandon should be arrested forthwith, without waiting for the criminal lieutenant to investigate. Jean de Fons, Tanequin Besserier, and Jean-Poldo d'Albenas, all councillors, agreed with Richier. Pierre Saurin, another councillor, then rose to agree with Jean d'Albenas, presumably meaning that he was opposed to arresting Ferrandon. Although Saurin did not specify why he was opposed to immediate arrests, it was not because he was inclined to Protestantism: he eventually became a prominent leader of the Catholic minority in Nîmes. It is more likely that he was uncomfortable arresting people on mere hearsay, which violated normal judicial procedures. Denis de Brueys put forward an intermediate position. He agreed with d'Albenas that the *juge-mage* should investigate before arresting anyone, but suggested that the officers and town consuls, as well as the *procureur du roi*, Pierre Vallete, should be fined £10,000 if they failed to prevent the assemblies. That way, those responsible would be compelled to act. The majority was not prepared to punish failure so harshly. Jean de Montcalm, the *juge-mage*, agreed with Richier, the hard-liner, and, since that was the majority's will, it became the decision of the court. The firmer side won out, but the présidial had shown it was reluctant to punish any of its own if its policies did not succeed in quelling the troubles. Most members of the présidial continued to be diligent and committed to repressing heresy. It is difficult to determine if any members of the court were Protestants, but if they were, they realized there was nothing they could do to stop the court from prosecuting heresy. A few of those who were Protestants may have made a silent protest against the présidial's increasingly harsh policies: they absented themselves from the court's meetings. They were not yet strong enough to alter the présidial's policy.[15]

On April 15, the présidial decided it needed to meet with all of the major local institutions to discuss the widening crisis. It voted to demand the presence of the consuls and the town's leading citizens, on pain of fines and imprisonment, at a meeting to remind them to use force to repress dissent. In addition, the religious authorities were requested to assist in identifying the culprits, which was a bit more surprising, given the long history in Nîmes of suspicion between lay and clerical authorities. Asking for the clergy's assistance was also a way of sharing the responsibility for an onerous task. Fearing that these measures were insufficient, however, the présidial members also changed their minds and decided they needed help from the crown. This was a radical step, since it was unusual for a local body to encourage, or even to tolerate, such interference. Local communities had good reason to resist asking royal officials for military assistance, since royal aid could lead to troops quartered in the city, which any city in sixteenth-century France tried to avoid at all costs. The next day, the court wrote to the vicomte de Joyeuse, asking him to come to aid them. Apparently, there were further disturbances during that day, for they wrote him a second time at the end of it. On the sixteenth, they met again and decided to write to the members of the présidial who were absent from the city, demanding their presence immediately, and on the seventeenth, concerned about assistance the heretics might be receiving from the outside, they also resolved to write to nearby authorities to ask them to enforce the laws. The flurry of writing suggests increasing panic. It was much less painful for the présidial to write letters than to arrest friends and neighbors.[16]

Throughout all these discussions, the town council remained silent (it had last met on February 25).[17] On April 18, Jean d'Albenas, the principal lieutenant, made some shocking allegations against the consuls: he had heard the day before that they had "removed arms from the city hall and given them to the inhabitants." Although the judges of the présidial may have had good reason to doubt the intentions of several of the consuls, in this instance it appears they were mistaken. The consuls, summoned to declare on oath whether they had done so, insisted that they had not, except for four suits of armor that had been used as part of the Easter procession and that had already been returned. They were ordered on pain of a £10,000 fine to ensure that no arms leave the town's possession, except for police purposes. The présidial also noted that Jean de Lubac, the second consul, had a bad leg and was therefore unable to be in charge of the keys to the city, and it urged the consuls to appoint someone to be in charge of guarding the city at their next meeting. The présidial repeated that all strangers needed to be expelled immediately. Finally, it wrote to the royal prosecutor (*procureur general du roi*) of the Parlement of Toulouse, informing him that there had been disturbances (caused by "seditious people from

Provence and Dauphiné, our neighbors"), and they had written to Joyeuse because they were afraid that they would not be able to handle them. The présidial members still were under the impression that outsiders were disturbing their city or, at least, wanted to preserve that illusion when speaking to royal officials. Nonetheless, the court promised to try to do its best. The same day, however, Jean de Montcalm, the *juge-mage*, wrote another letter to the prosecutor, explaining that the judges would jeopardize their lives if they tried to move on their own. The royal authorities were not disposed to accept any excuses, however, and ordered the présidial to stop the assemblies itself and arrest those responsible.[18]

The présidial met again on the morning of the nineteenth, and began by discussing a letter from Joyeuse, who was demanding to know the state of affairs. Pierre Robert, the *lieutenant viguier*, complained that he had spent the night on guard, as he had been ordered to do, but that it was not his job and he wished to be excused from doing it. Jean d'Albenas spoke next, saying that Denis de Brueys was "absent from this company, [since he is] busy today," but they needed to tell Joyeuse the precautions they had taken, and therefore de Brueys needed to write a statement by the following morning, explaining what he had done. He added that Robert needed to do likewise. Although d'Albenas's language apparently excuses de Brueys, it is likely that he intended a threatening tone to his speech: he meant to imply that the présidial needed to report some of its less-energetic members to higher authority. D'Albenas went on to say that the consuls needed to consider whom they should nominate to be the captain in charge of the guard. Other speakers reiterated the point that they must communicate with Joyeuse as soon and as fully as possible, mixed with some recriminations as each speaker insisted that he had done his duty and that, as Pierre Vallete, the *procureur du roi*, protested, "it was not and would not become his duty to take charge of the entire problem." At the end of the meeting, three of the town consuls showed up to say that, following the instructions the présidial had given them the day before, they would meet later in the day to discuss the appointment of a captain for the city.[19]

The consuls kept their promise. Later that day, the town council acted, albeit cautiously. Without mentioning the issue of the assemblies, it began the process of selecting a military leader for the town. The tone of the meeting was quite different from that of the meetings of the présidial. At the beginning of the debate, the *viguier*, Pierre Robert, announced that he no longer wished to be captain of the town, due to his advanced age. The town council concluded by stating that "in the state of tranquility that the town is [in] at present there is no great need to provide for a captain." Just to be on the safe side, however, since there had been troubles nearby, they appointed Robert's son of the same name, who was also his lieutenant, to the post. The council, following long-established precedent, was prepared to take some precautions against heresy, but it was still reluctant to admit that there were any actual heretics in town. Nîmes's council still held the belief, common to municipal leaders elsewhere in France, that the illusion of unity had to be maintained at all costs.[20]

Five days later, on April 24, Joyeuse, the king's lieutenant in the province, arrived in Nîmes. He immediately summoned the présidial into session under him to give its account of the continuing disturbances. Jean de Montcalm, the *juge-mage,* and Denis de Brueys, the criminal lieutenant, explained that "there had been some assemblies by night with forbidden weapons, with a large number of strangers or unknowns," but they had been unable to discover who was responsible, except for Alizot and Ferrandon. They did know that people were going to hear a preacher, to pray, and to sing the psalms. Their policy of expelling strangers from the city had succeeded in getting many to leave, and there had been no more assemblies where people had been armed. However, they had been unwilling to arrest Alizot and Ferrandon, because they were afraid of a rebellion if they tried. Joyeuse urged them to uncover the names and addresses of those responsible, "without favoring or exempting anyone, no matter what his station," but also without using falsified depositions. The list of culprits had to remain absolutely secret, presumably in order to avoid tipping off the heretics and allowing them to escape.[21]

Joyeuse also told the town council that he had come to Nîmes because he had been informed that there had been "some carrying of arms and assemblies," which he was intent on stopping. On April 25, the council met to consider how to respond. The consuls were hardly eager to admit that there was anything the matter, insisting on their loyalty and admitting only that "if there have been any assemblies they were not in public." Further disclaiming responsibility, they suggested that perhaps outsiders were meeting in the town, but if there was any problem, the captain of the town could handle it. This time, they named François de Montcalm, seigneur de Saint Véran, as captain, rather than Pierre Robert, the *lieutenant viguier.* But Montcalm immediately declined the post. In the interim, several people volunteered to help guard the gates.[22] At the next meeting, on May 18, still needing a captain to take overall charge of restoring order, the council finally chose Pierre Suau, called Captain Bolhargues, an archer of the royal guard who was a native of Nîmes.[23]

After two days in Nîmes, Joyeuse decided what he thought of the situation in the town, and he did not like what he saw. He was sufficiently concerned that he wrote to the king. He was extremely dissatisfied with the behavior of both the présidial officials and the town council. He agreed with the town officials when he suggested that, on Easter Monday, "many strangers, from nearby villages and elsewhere," had come to town and marched about by night, accompanied by townspeople, all carrying weapons.[24] Joyeuse recounted to the king that when he heard rumor of the assembly, he immediately went to Nîmes to restore order. He had heard from "good testimony" (*bons témoignages*) that three ministers from Geneva had been in town since Holy Week (April 7–14), celebrating the Lord's Supper and baptizing. Three ministers seems an exaggeration; in any case, it cannot be substantiated. Joyeuse went on to severely criticize Nîmes's officials. He concluded, after meeting with the officers of the présidial, that they were sharply divided: some were loyal, while others were "seditious," and he feared that the latter were the majority. He also decided that the town council's loyalists were "insufficient."[25] Joyeuse ordered all strangers out of the city and, as he described it, began "laying down the law to the magistrates of the city, as well as to the consul[s], as to what they have to do for your service." But, he added, he could not keep order with the troops that he had, especially given that the surrounding countryside was equally suspect.[26] Just like the présidial, he was reluctant to accept complete responsibility for ending the assemblies. Joyeuse may have become suspicious of Nîmes's officials because they responded resentfully to his high-handed attitude, rather than because they were Protestants. Local officials invariably assumed that the town was theirs to govern, a private domain. Nor were they likely to want to take strong action to suppress a movement that had a significant number of supporters, perhaps including some of their own friends and relations. After all, despite all his bluster about "laying down the law," Joyeuse himself hesitated to take action without significant reinforcements. Towns in sixteenth-century France were usually governed by carefully managed consent, and only rarely by force.

After a brief pause, probably due to Joyeuse's visit, Protestant organizing continued. On May 13, there were further accusations at a présidial meeting that there were assemblies at the houses of François Felix, a lawyer or merchant, and the heirs of Ferrandon, who appears to have died in the interval. At that meeting, Robert de Brueys alleged that they were singing the psalms in French, which he suggested should be made illegal. No one else was prepared to adopt this opinion, however, which would probably have led to mass arrests of hundreds of people.[27] Taking a firm but less extreme position, Jean d'Albenas urged that the culprits be identified and that they should write to the Parlement of Toulouse, and to Joyeuse to inform him, and ask for new edicts forbidding the assemblies. Anyone taking in a stranger, including all servants and tutors from outside of town, should be fined and imprisoned. All assemblies of more than four households should be banned. The consuls "and principals" of the town must be commanded "on pain of their lives" not to permit any assemblies. Finally, Pierre Robert, the *lieutenant viguier*, should be ordered "to give to the court each day, his doings and procedures, guarding the town, [and also] for the past two months; and if the day passes and he does not make his report he should be restrained in the château [i.e., imprisoned] until he has obeyed."[28] The présidial had finally realized that Robert, who had complained to the council only three weeks earlier about how hard it was to stay on guard all night, was in all probability a secret Protestant. Honoré Richier agreed with d'Albenas, but added that the town needed troops to enforce the new measures. Joyeuse should be asked "to provide in such a way that the authorities have force to execute the decrees and punishments that will be handed down." There was general agreement on d'Albenas's ideas, and the severe new decrees were issued, but there was disagreement on whether to approve Richier's addition, and the measure went to a vote. Since most towns in sixteenth-century France hated to have royal troops billeted among them, this controversy is not surprising. However, the vote did not particularly divide along religious lines: Jean d'Albenas, a prominent future member of the Catholic minority, voted against asking Joyeuse to provide troops, while Jean de Fons, who eventually converted to Protestantism, voted for Richier's more hard-line proposal. With many absentees, the measure passed by five votes to four.[29]

One week later, on May 20, the présidial met again, this time to move against the Protestants once and for all. Pierre Suau, whom the town council had newly chosen to be the town's captain, appeared before the présidial to explain that he needed to close the town's gates, except for two which would each be guarded by six men. Now that it finally had military authority, the présidial could take firmer action. The présidial agreed with Suau, and then ordered arrest warrants for thirteen Protestant leaders. Some of these warrants touched close to home, including the *lieutenant viguier,* Pierre Robert; the son of the présidial councillor Jean de Sauzet, also named Jean; Maurice Favier, a *greffier* (court official); the fourth consul's son-in-law Étienne Dumas (probably a farmer); and councillor Jean-Poldo d'Albenas's brother Vidal, also a *greffier.* Most of the others were also of high social standing, including Antoine Copier and François Felix, both lawyers; Estienne Ranchon, a notary; Gabriel Prades, a merchant; the tutor to Robert's children; a locksmith; and, once again, Arnaud Alizot and Jacques Savy, called Ferrandon (respectively, a merchant and a *laboureur*—apparently they did not know Savy had just died).[30] The présidial also wrote to Joyeuse and the parlement again, informing them that they had taken control of the Dominican monastery, because assemblies had taken place there, and had arrested a *greffier* and a *praticien* (clerk).[31] Unfortunately for the présidial, in a tightly knit community like Nîmes, it was difficult to keep the arrest warrants secret, although the présidial tried to move swiftly. Later the same day, and then the next morning, the présidial officers attempted to execute the arrest warrants. They also searched the houses, looking for weapons and forbidden books. Not a single one of those named was present, although several had left weapons behind, and a copy of a satire mocking the Church, *Description de la Palharde,* was found in the house of Jean de Sauzet the younger.[32] On the twenty-second, the court therefore wrote to the surrounding jurisdictions, asking them to seize any of the fugitives if they could be found.[33]

The following day, May 23, the town council met and heard a letter from Joyeuse, warmly congratulating the town's efforts and adding that the king could only be more pleased if it managed to arrest any of the agitators, especially any of the Protestant ministers. Unfortunately, it also received a letter the same day from the constable, Anne de Montmorency, of directly opposite import. He threatened to put a garrison into the town if the seditious assemblies did not cease. He was not interested in activity, only in results. The town council resolved to continue to have Suau guard the town, but agreed, on a motion by Jean d'Albenas, the principal lieutenant of the présidial, to "have spies around the town."[34] On May 25, Denis de Brueys recommended to the présidial that "given the last letter from Monseigneur de Joyeuse," it should compile a list of every known heretic and call them in for questioning. The présidial proceeded to do so, listing seventy-one suspected heretics in all (the composition of this group was analyzed in Chapter 3).

In June, records for the présidial court cease for six months, so it is difficult to assess the development of its policies. For the first half of 1560, however, the Nîmes présidial, although hampered somewhat by the town council, moved energetically to quell the Protestant movement, which for the first time was sufficiently large to risk calling attention to itself. When Protestants organized assemblies by day, the présidial first issued decrees against them, then moved against the leaders, and then attempted to compile a list of all of the Protestants so that they could be arrested. The présidial did not have much success in making the arrests, but it would be unreasonable to suspect that its failure was deliberate: the Parlement of Toulouse, a bastion of orthodoxy, achieved no more. Furthermore, although the présidial failed to arrest the Protestant leaders, the attempt was successful in hampering the Protestant movement. Once the influential Protestants on the présidial's list had fled, the Protestant movement called a halt to preaching, at least publicly.

Liberalization

On June 7, the town received news of the Edict of Romorantin, which greatly liberalized the laws governing heresy. Under these circumstances, the présidial apparently decided to relax the pressure on the Protestant movement, and the movement was quick to take advantage of the changed climate.[35] The authorities in Nîmes were happy to be permitted to take a more lenient tone. By this point, Nîmes's authorities were distinctly feeling the pinch of their position as intermediaries between the citizenry and the crown. The town council in particular did not relish taking action to repress heresy, which would be opposed by a significant and vocal fraction of the people, but it was also aware that a failure to act could have unpleasant consequences. If the crown took action, it would likely mean that the whole town, not just the heretics, would suffer. In early June 1560, the Nîmes town council heard a rumor that its worst fears would be realized: troops might be coming to occupy their town. The town council was less willing to accept troops than was the présidial for two reasons. First, the council was undoubtedly more subject to Protestant influence. Second, if the troops came, the council, not the présidial, would be responsible for paying for them. To find out if the rumor were true, the council wrote to the duc de Guise, who led the most powerful Catholic noble family in France and who was at this point the dominant political figure at court. In their letter to Guise, the members insisted that they were obedient subjects of His Majesty, but they did not want troops quartered in their town. The duc de Guise only increased their fears when he replied disingenuously, saying that "concerning the fear that you have that troops will be sent to you, we have never heard of it, insofar as such things do not occur except in places where there has been an apparent connivance of the people and institutions of the city."[36] He wanted to know what side was the town council on. The town council was undoubtedly feeling the pressure from both sides, since the Protestant movement was not disposed to relent either. In June, just when Guise was writing to the council, Protestants began preaching again. The movement had apparently felt that it was too dangerous to do so after the attempted arrests, but decided after Romorantin that it could begin again, although less publicly than before. Some radicals wanted to go even further, but their view did not prevail.[37]

On September 2, the town council met again, this time to respond to Catholic complaints, presumably provoked by the renewed preaching. Almost everyone present at the council meeting wanted to make some suggestion, since no one wanted to be accused of ignoring the situation nor of being in collusion with the heretics. At the same time, no one really wanted to be in charge of repressing heresy, since it was clear that it would be a difficult task, and if it did not work, the crown would blame whoever had taken the initiative for the failure. Then, royal troops would occupy the town. Jean du Caylar, the bishop of Nîmes's deputy, came to the meeting and read a letter, noting that "notoriously in this town, day and night, there are assemblies with sermons and preaching full of blasphemy against God and his holy sacraments, and administering them." He closed his letter by offering all reasonable help from the diocese to repress the assemblies. His letter put the diocese on record as offering its help, but if the council accepted the offer, it would be admitting that it was its job to repress the assemblies, and it would be responsible for any failure. The consuls had no desire to take on the task. In order to have convenient targets should they need to duck their responsibility, they had taken the precaution of asking two representatives of the présidial court, the *juge-mage* and the criminal lieutenant, to attend the meeting. After du Caylar spoke, the consuls immediately replied, insisting that they thought it was "the judicial officials," that is, the présidial, who were in charge of repressing heresy, although it was the consuls' job to provide the force necessary, which they had done. The *juge-mage* and the criminal lieutenant then replied. They realized that they had been handed the responsibility, and they were also not anxious to undertake it. They resisted the implication that it was their responsibility to end the disturbances. They agreed that something needed to be done, but they had written letters to the duc de Guise, the constable, and other high officials, and a response could be expected shortly. While waiting, they could also write to Joyeuse. In short, they preferred to wait and let higher officials solve the problem. The special lieutenant of the présidial, Jacques de Rochemaure, added, "everyone must take it as his duty to speak to the other inhabitants of the town, and to use all gentleness to prevent any agitation among themselves, and to restrain themselves in obedience to the king and his justice."[38] Repressing heresy was everyone's responsibility. Honoré Richier, another member of the présidial, agreed that they should write to Joyeuse, and in addition, the consuls had to provide for guards at the gates. When it came to using force, which would be particularly unpopular, he wanted the town council to take the lead. The members of the town council, including several future members of the Catholic party who were present, ignored this suggestion, since it implied that eliminating heresy was the council's responsibility. Most simply suggested that the council send representatives to confer with Joyeuse, although the two Pierre Rozels, father and son, added that they should await the decisions of the forthcoming Estates General, the father commenting, "all of this must be conducted with prudence."[39] The Rozels were proposing a strategy of masterful inactivity. It is possible that there was something behind this reference, since the Protestant party subsequently placed its hopes in the 1561 meeting of the Estates (see Chapter 5). But Rozel senior also recommended writing to Joyeuse.

Clearly, the situation worried the town's officials: the meeting had dissolved into mutual finger-pointing, and no one had a coherent policy to propose. There was one Protestant member of the council, Roland Vallat, a leather worker, who thought he saw an opportunity in this confusion. Since the authorities were clearly worried that they could not crush the Protestant movement, why couldn't they consider joining it? He therefore gave a long and interesting speech, the first out-and-out Protestant speech at a council meeting. The records describe his perspective:

> [I]nsofar as the town of Nîmes troubles itself with what it need not, according to him, [then] the remedy is very simple to find, since [the council] could listen, without any scandal, since according to him the head of the assembly, who is called the minister, will present himself to Messieurs at their good pleasure, whether in a secret place or in public, and [submit to] the decision of those who hear him, for it will do nothing to quarrel about guessing whether the things which he preaches are true or not.[40]

His proposal somewhat resembled the debates held in some German cities. City councils that permitted such debates were essentially proclaiming Protestantism: the Protestants were never permitted to lose. Nîmes's city council was not yet Protestant, however, and in any case had less freedom of maneuver. Vallat's suggestions were outside the other members' frame of reference, and no one took them up. It is nonetheless worth considering this speech further, because it contains an element that seems crucial to the Huguenot sense of self: the conviction that one is speaking a truth so transparently clear that no one who hears it can fail to be persuaded by it. Vallat's pedantic tone as he defined the term "minister" and the certainty that the council would be able to tell from "the things which he preaches" whether they "are true or not," implied a distinctly different sense of politics and of men's role within society than the intensely circumspect, legalistic language of most councillors.[41] Early meetings of the Protestant Consistory show the same frank simplicity of speech. One of the most characteristic institutions of the Reformed movement was the *grabaud*, self-criticism sessions where the members of the consistory forthrightly told each other what specific faults (anger, poor attendance, wife-beating) they needed to correct.[42] Early Protestants like the first deacons were impatient. They wanted to force the pace of change. The bluntness of their speech represented, in part, a reaction against the secrecy that, for a time, they were compelled to maintain. But the ideology of the movement was also important here: they were equally suspicious of rituals and symbols, because they lacked the immediacy of direct speech. Hard-line Protestants like Vallat disapproved of the council's behavior. It was wrong to pass the buck so elaborately, to behave with such circumspection. People like Vallat were direct. They did not keep silent. Vallat may have hoped that the councillors, after they had proposed such weak and vacillating policies, might have found a bold course something of a relief.

The council, however, had no interest in taking up such a radical suggestion; instead, it preferred to continue the broad outlines of its previous policy. The consensus of the council was clearly to write to Joyeuse, letting him know what was going on:

> For the last several days, there have been some assemblies in private houses, by day, without [anyone bearing] arms, with a certain minister who preaches to a great troop of people of every condition, townspeople and strangers, praying and chanting the psalms of David, without any insult, sedition, and trouble.[43]

This letter, written on September 3, does seem to mark a certain shift in the council's attitudes. Vallat had some cause to rejoice. Instead of attacking heresy, the council's language tended to exonerate the Protestant movement. It admitted to more knowledge of the assemblies than it had before, and it mentioned the minister gingerly but respectfully. Unlike the bishop's letter, the council's letter did not suggest that the assemblies were blasphemous; instead, it noted that people were chanting the psalms—surely a holy thing to do? It also clearly stated that the meetings were peaceful, and no one was carrying weapons. It is hard to say, however, whether this was due to a shift in the council's views, a change in public opinion in the city, or the council's perception of the line taken by the crown after Romorantin. The council made a mistake if it was relying on Romorantin, however, since the crown returned to more repressive policies in the fall of 1560. Since royal policy was constantly shifting, Nîmes's authorities found it difficult to obey the crown's wishes, and the council was repeatedly caught wrong-footed.

Joyeuse, whether following the new royal line or his own views, returned a harsh response to the letter from the council. He was determined to repress Protestantism in Nîmes, although the movement in Nîmes, unlike that in Lyon, had shown no particular tendencies toward violence. In his reply, he stated firmly that "it was not for the people to invent and use a new religion, without the authority and permission of the king, and it was prohibited by his edicts to have assemblies, with arms or without." That, of course, was the nub of the issue and a far more contested point than Joyeuse's language would indicate. Furthermore, Joyeuse added, the town had promised to prevent further disturbances, and it was on this basis that he had written favorably to the king and the constable on its behalf. He would have to write them again, telling them "the contrary, to his great regret." Nîmes would have to pay the penalty of his displeasure. The town's behavior was both illegal and a personal affront. More to the point, 400 men-at-arms were on their way, under the command of the constable, and Nîmes would soon be put under military occupation.[44]

The council did not heed the warning. Instead of attempting to clean its own house vigorously, so as to avoid outside intervention, it responded to Joyeuse's strong language by recommending measures so insubstantial as to be merely unconvincing gestures. Pierre Rozel the elder urged again that only two of the town gates should be left open, and the keys be put in the hands of the second and fourth consuls. That measure, at least, was more than a gesture, since de Lubac and Granon, the officials in question, were Catholics. Strangers should not be permitted inside the walls, but be required to lodge in inns in the suburbs, and innkeepers should confiscate any weapons they carried, to be returned only on their departure. (Certain prohibited kinds should be confiscated entirely.) Innkeepers should report any visitors to the authorities within one day of their arrival. Rozel again emphasized that the town had to mount guards by night. Finally, suggesting that it was difficult to assemble the general and extraordinary council, he recommended appointing deputies: Pierre de Brueys, Jacques Ferrand, Pierre d'Assas, Pierre Baudan, Pierre de Fabrica, Jean Bertrand, Pierre Boys, and Laurens Tutelle. Charles Rozel agreed. Although Pierre and Charles Rozel were future Protestant leaders, not all of those on Pierre's list were Protestants.[45]

Robert des Georges then rose to suggest that all suspect persons should leave the council chamber before the group proceeded.[46] This was the first open suggestion that there were heretics inside the council chamber, although Rozel's proposals had implied as much. Calvière, the president of the présidial, who was chairing the meeting, immediately demanded that des Georges name those whom he suspected, which des Georges refused to do, saying that "he did not know" but "he had heard it said" that some of those present had been at the assemblies. It was their fault that royal troops were descending on the town, and they should desist, or at least, the cost for the troops' upkeep should be borne only by the guilty. This also broached a sensitive issue. The authorities had generally tried to pretend that outsiders were largely responsible for the troubles, at least in part in order to preserve the fiction of local unity. Des Georges's suggestion was sharply divisive. He further recommended that they should send representatives to the king and give him a list of the guilty, so that they be forced to pay, and suggested four representatives: Jean Malmazet, an elderly lawyer; Jean Lansard; Pierre Boys, bourgeois; and Laurens Tutelle. Antoine Roverie agreed.[47]

The final proposal put on the table was Jean Lansard's. He suggested that the religious and judicial authorities warn the guilty, and if the assemblies did not cease, then they should "have recourse to the vigorous approach." In the end, the majority agreed with Rozel's proposal, except that they nominated him to replace de Brueys. They swore, hands held high, to prevent "any assembly and force of arms."[48] Finally, they wrote to Joyeuse to say that they did not understand how he could say that there had been anyone bearing arms, although it was true that there had been assemblies. They said that it was impossible to stop them without bloodshed, since "they are a greater number of people than ever before." They also admitted, rather incautiously, that some of the gentlemen attending had worn the swords appropriate to their rank. Again, instead of responding to the new, firmer royal line, the council responded by becoming more defiant. For the first time, the council added a sentence that seemed to support the new movement: it said that "there are no longer as many larcenies, murders, rapes or other insolences, which used to be committed more often than at present," suggesting that the assemblies were improving the town's moral tone. It would endeavor to find provisions for the troops, although the harvest had not been good for the past several years. In short, its answer left much to be desired from the crown's point of view: it excused, even defended, the assemblies and submitted to Joyeuse's authority only grudgingly. Joyeuse replied, thanking them for the provisions, but he added that he could not understand how "in what touches the service of his majesty and the obedience that you owe him, you speak of limitation."[49] Joyeuse was still trying to communicate that the era of toleration inaugurated by the Edict of Romorantin had ended. He would need to use more than words to be heard.

The Crown Takes Action

The town council accomplished little for most of September and October, instead writing letters and sending various delegations to plead the town's cause before leading royal officials, including Honorat de Savoie, comte de Villars, the lieutenant general of the king, who was in the province to preside over the Estates, which were meeting in Beaucaire, just to the east of Nîmes. The town's representatives were not successful. Villars informed them that the town had "a bad reputation." He added that there were only two sides, the king's or against him, and if they resisted, "although it was a commonplace that Nîmes would perish by water, he suspected that they would perish by blood and fire."[50] At the same time, rumors were flying that there were plans afoot for the heretics to join together for an attack on Lyon. Villars, following the new royal line and concerned about the temper of the province, had not arrived alone at the meeting of the Estates of Languedoc: he was accompanied by troops. The Estates, however, held on October 11, took a staunch pro-Catholic attitude, and Villars was pleased with their decisions. He took the opportunity, while he was there, to burn a cache of Protestant books. He was still upset by Nîmes's reluctance to crack down on heresy, and he wrote a letter to Montmorency, the governor of Languedoc and constable of France, complaining about the town's behavior. He also dispatched the Marshal de Saint-André, of the Mondragon family, with three companies (*enseignes*) of infantrymen to secure Montpellier. Saint-André arrived on October 15; the Protestant minister immediately fled, and the bishop emerged from hiding.[51] Villars appointed Saint-André and Louis l'Estrange, vicomte de Cheylane, both with the title of governor, over the towns of Aigues-Mortes, Montpellier, and Nîmes, as part of a general campaign to pacify the province.[52]

On October 22, bowing to the pressure, the Nîmes town council finally tacked back toward repression. The council resolved:

> To prohibit to all, inhabitants of the town or otherwise, to have illicit assemblies and conventicles for preaching, or otherwise to come together, offer for such their houses or lands, or any favor in any fashion, on pain of having their houses (used for the assemblies) razed, and to be banished, as violators of the peace and public tranquility, and punished according to the penalties of the royal edicts. And any persons who know and discover any such assemblies, whether clandestine or public, [are] required to reveal them, on pain of being adjudged as guilty and subject to the same penalties.[53]

Furthermore, it named four captains with 100 men each to police the town: Robert Brun, seigneur de Castanet; François Barrière, esquire (*écuyer*); Bernard Arnaud, seigneur de La Cassagne; and Jean Abraham, bourgeois. They were to serve under two commanders, François de Montcalm, seigneur de Saint Véran, and Joseph Dolon, seigneur de Ners and treasurer, with Jean Michel, a former soldier, as sergeant major.[54]

These decisions, although impressive sounding, concealed continuing resistance. In particular, the officer corps had distinct Protestant tendencies. Jean Abraham was probably still a Catholic, since in December 1560, he was permitted to vote in the elections for consul, but he later turned Protestant. By contrast, both Brun and Bernard Arnaud stood as guarantors for the Protestant community in late November. Montcalm and Barrière eventually converted as well, but it is unclear when. Dolon's and Michel's religions are unknown.[55] The council nonetheless ordered them to present themselves for Saint-André's approval and to swear allegiance. Indeed, it ordered every head of household in town to swear, for themselves and on behalf of their families and their tenants, on pain of banishment. Innkeepers were again ordered to confiscate the arms of all strangers, and lanterns were ordered set up at all intersections, under the direction of Pierre Baudan, a bourgeois, and Arnaud Bonneterre, a merchant. The council also organized a committee to provide the necessary supplies for the royal troops. The committee, which might be stuck with the bills for the troops if it proved unable to collect the payments due from the town, included a number of prominent Catholics, among them Robert des Georges, as well as some future Protestants.[56]

At a brief meeting the following day, October 23, the consuls arranged lodgings for l'Estrange, who was expected shortly. Once he arrived, L'Estrange presided over the next meeting of the council, on the twenty-ninth. He began by announcing that "he did not intend to specify anyone in particular, but that by all means he intended to hold every resident within God's commandments, the ordinance of his Church, of the Holy Father the Pope, as has been customary heretofore, under the obedience of our sovereign Most Christian prince the king." The consuls spoke next, saying that the town had suffered "great and fantastic expenses for soldiers," and the council would have to decide how to find the money to pay for them and whether to send an emissary to the king to ask that the town be relieved of the garrison. They reminded the council that Villars had ordered everyone to turn in their arms. Then they read a letter from François de Pavée, seigneur de Servas, attacking Bauzille Roverie and Jean-Poldo d'Albenas for defaming Nîmes by alleging at court that the town was full of "wicked Lutherans" and that "the town and its people must be put to fire and sword."[57]

Roverie, who had already returned from Paris and was present, responded by saying that he had merely handed over a letter from some of the canons of the cathedral detailing "everything that was going on in this town, including the [Protestant] weddings and burials by day, publicly." The words were meant to sting. He said he had met Saint-André in Lyon, and he did say to him that "if he sent one officer with fifty men, they could drive off everyone, because justice slept, and the consuls connived [at heresy]; but [to allege that he had suggested that] the town be razed, or be taken, to raze it, that was false." He offered to pay someone to go to the court to confirm his statements, and a canon, Jean de Peberan, also spoke on his behalf. But the council decided that it was unnecessary, and it should merely send someone to the court to assure the king of the town's obedience. The damage to the town's reputation had already been done. The council also agreed to make a list of everyone in town to apportion the charges owed for the garrison.[58]

By this point, the town council had passed from mere foot-dragging to something more like active opposition. L'Estrange had no doubts: something needed to be done to bring this important institution into line. However, his next move was probably not dictated by any particular act of the council, but rather by the calendar. Elections were normally held in December, and a new council with new town consuls would take office on January 1. Should the current membership elect its successors, as the town's charter provided, the new council could easily prove at least as obstreperous as the old. To forestall this possibility, a group including Bernard Barrière, the *procureur du roi* on the présidial, and Father Jean du Caylar, the deputy of the bishop of Nîmes, hatched a plan for special, early elections in late November, at which only Catholics could vote. The governor was only too happy to oblige, and the election was held on November 23, 1560. The assembly chose four persons for each office, and, according to the usual procedure, the winning candidates were selected by lot. Interestingly, Pierre Rozel the elder was elected as one of the four candidates for first consul despite the heresy in his family. But he did not win the lottery. The four new consuls were Jean Malmazet; Pierre de Fabrica, a *greffier;* Pons Blanc, a merchant; and Guillaume Ferrussac, a *laboureur*.[59]

In the continuing battle for public opinion, however, this electoral plan was unlikely to gain friends for the Catholic cause. Nîmes's traditional liberties and privileges were held sacred by just about every citizen, and even the proponents of the early elections were clearly somewhat embarrassed by the proposal. Barrière, the *procureur du roi,* was careful to spell out in a letter to the comte de Villars that the special arrangements would not set a precedent. It is also at least possible that some of the Catholics who refused to show up to vote did so because they were uncomfortable with the procedure. Pierre de Brueys, a lawyer who took part in the election and was therefore presumably Catholic, asked that his objections to the procedure be noted for the record, along with those of some of the consuls, who had named him as their representative. It seems likely that the consuls deliberately chose a Catholic to present their objections precisely to emphasize that supporting the town charter was not a matter of religious partisanship.[60]

In the short run, the early elections were undoubtedly effective: they produced a more reliable (from the crown's perspective) municipal leadership. Ultimately, however, the crown's lack of a coherent policy was disastrous. The monarchy could not achieve its goals by alternating between quasi-official toleration and repressive measures of questionable legality. A firmer, more consistent, but legal policy might have been more effective. The crown's policies allowed Protestants to claim that the monarchy was acting true to form: tyrannically. The decision to force the election of Catholic consuls destroyed the council's legitimacy and led to the collapse of Nîmes's government.

5

The *Cahier de Doléances*, 1561

In the immediate aftermath of the coup d'état in Nîmes, Governor l'Estrange had good reason to be pleased, since he had achieved two important aims. First, he had gotten the town council to alter course suddenly after months of recalcitrance and to put more stringent measures against heretical assemblies on the books. Second, he had put new leadership in place to carry out the new measures. But l'Estrange was urgently needed elsewhere, since the whole region was apparently turning Protestant, and few troops were available to suppress the heresy. So on November 25, two days after the elections, he cut a deal to obtain payment for his troops, by contracting with wealthy members of the Protestant community: if they paid £6,000, the garrison would be withdrawn. Seven Protestants agreed to stand bond for the sum. Interestingly, given that the representatives had to have means and prestige, only two were seigneurs and one a lawyer; the others were a merchant, an apothecary, a clerk, and a farmer. Nîmes's officials gave the contract official recognition in some sense, since it was signed at the home of Jean de Montcalm, the *juge-mage* of the présidial, and Jean Mombel, the third consul, wrote up the contract as the notary.[1]

Nîmes's officials, in support of the Catholic cause, had agreed to make the Protestant community pay for the royal troops. Given the Protestant movement's growing size and influence, this took some daring. Unfortunately for the consuls, the crown soon decided to make the town pay more large sums to repress heresy in the region. On November 28, the consuls summoned the town council into session to hear a letter they had received from Jean-Poldo d'Albenas. He informed the council that he had been delegated by the comte de Villars to provide supplies for the troops in the vicinity of St. Jean du Gard in the Cévennes, which had arrived to suppress Protestant assemblies and generally to quell dissent. He ordered the authorities in Nîmes to help provide for the troops' maintenance by shipping grain, hay, wine, and meat to the town of Anduze. Villars had his reasons: wild rumors were circulating. Judging from a letter he wrote to the duc de Guise, Villars thought that thousands of Nîmes residents had gone up to the mountains to organize themselves into military units and were planning to return and seize power. There is no evidence that anyone in Nîmes was aware of the rumor, nor any possibility that it was true. The council, in its ignorance, immediately decided to protest, since it saw no reason why the town should have to pay to support troops elsewhere, and the town would be required to pay not just the price of the supplies, but the considerable cost of transporting them.

Even the second consul elect, Pierre de Fabrica, and Pierre de Brueys, who were both Catholics, agreed to go to Villars to protest. Their religion did not trump their loyalty to their community. They agreed, however, that in the meantime they would attempt to find the supplies. They noted that, although the commission specified that only the Protestants should have to pay, the town had already had to borrow money to supply its own garrison, since the Protestants were too poor to provide enough money.[2] Here was the crown's difficulty in a nutshell. Repressing heresy cost an enormous amount of money, and it was impossible to get the sums required out of the Protestants of the region. But if the crown demanded large sums from the rest of the population, it only alienated them and drove moderates and the undecided into the Protestant camp.

The same day, the consuls urged the governor not to impose the payment on Nîmes's Protestants. They brought with them four Protestant representatives, who argued that it was unfair for their members to pay, and the richer members of the community had fled. Furthermore, it was more reasonable to make Anduze and its neighboring villages pay, since they had "made similar assemblies and persisted longer than anyone." Protestant solidarity apparently stopped at Nîmes's gates. The governor denied most of their requests, and the Protestant representatives immediately announced their intention to protest the entire decision to Villars. The town's representatives split the difference, agreeing with neither the Protestant party nor the governor. Instead, it would be more reasonable to make Anduze pay, but if any Nîmes residents had to pay, it should only be the Protestants, not the whole town.[3] If the consuls had to take sides, they would stand with Rome and the king. At the last town council meeting of the month, on November 24, the consuls organized a guard of 200 "non-suspect" persons.

Governor l'Estrange, on behalf of the crown, had handpicked Nîmes's consuls for their religious and political loyalty. But even if the royal and Catholic cause had been their only priority, they could not simply force the town to obey them. Cost precluded the use of military force, which would in any case further antagonize the population. Nationwide, the crisis compelled the royal council to consider other alternatives, and in August 1560 it decided to call for the election of representatives to a meeting of the Estates General. The meeting in December 1560 created a new political climate.[4] It also enabled Nîmes's Protestants to organize more effectively than ever before.

The Calling of the Estates General

When the royal council decided to summon the Estates General and a separate Assembly of the Clergy, it hoped to solve the twin obstacles facing the kingdom: an empty treasury and religious dissension. This was a desperate measure. The Estates had last met in 1484 and had refused to authorize sufficient taxation by the crown. After that failure, French monarchs became unwilling to go to the trouble and expense of calling them, and the French Estates became the least-often consulted national legislature in Europe. Of the major European countries, France was the only one whose Estates did not meet between 1484 and 1560. The council's decision to call the Estates in 1560 was thus a measure both of the council's noble aspirations and of the monarchy's dire needs. However, in the dangerously unsettled circumstances that prevailed in 1560, it was probably less risky to call the Estates than to try to impose taxation by fiat. Since there was already a danger of rebellion, the council did not want to recommend harsh measures that would only further inflame public opinion.[5] It took several months to organize the elections, to allow time for messengers to send the orders throughout the country, and for the representatives, once elected, to arrive at the appointed city. In the end, there were two meetings of the Estates, one beginning on December 13, 1560, at Orléans, and the other during the following August (1561) at Pontoise, near Paris.

Although it would have been risky not to call the Estates, the long preparations for the two sessions diverted the crown's attention and hindered it from taking action at a crucial time. Furthermore, calling the assemblies started a process whose end could not be foreseen. No one could know whether the Estates would vote to provide the new taxes that the crown needed, nor whether the Assembly of the Clergy would find a formula for compromise that would ease the kingdom's religious divisions. Finally, when the crown called the meeting of the Estates, it also set off a furious bout of local political maneuvering. Each locality was required to write a list of grievances, a *cahier de doléances*, proposing suggested improvements for the Estates to consider. The local cahiers were then combined into one list when the Estates met, and the king then approved or rejected each provision. In Nîmes, there is no record of a cahier for the Orléans session, but the Protestant movement organized an impressive campaign around the adoption of the cahier for the Pontoise session. The movement capitalized on the economic and political discontents that began in the late 1550s and proposed a massive plan for political reform. As members of a persecuted minority, it was natural for Nîmes's Protestants to push for a more limited government. By drawing up the cahier, they managed to link their concerns with the broader problems facing the community. The Protestant proposals proved to be wildly popular, attracting support from hundreds of Nîmes residents, many of whom had not previously been aligned with the Protestant movement. On the national level, the crown never adopted any of the measures that Nîmes proposed in its cahier. But in Nîmes itself, the Protestant movement's campaign around the cahier created the conditions for the new religion's eventual success.

The Estates, consisting of 455 deputies, assembled at Orléans. The querulous representatives first wondered whether their writs of election were still valid. The young King François II had died only days earlier. Could representatives called by one king meet under the authority of another? Perhaps new elections were necessary. The crown was unwilling to wait, however, and after some debate, the Estates agreed to sit. Michel de L'Hospital, the chancellor, opened the session by urging national unity under royal authority. Everyone needed to obey the king, who owed his crown to God alone. Heretics, however, needed to be brought back "par la douceur, et non par la rigeur" (gently, not by rigor) to the true faith. His goal was to assert royal power, but he also made sure to flatter the Estates.[6]

The three Estates began to negotiate the election of a Speaker common to all of them, who would present their grievances, but they found it impossible to come to an agreement. The nobility wanted to elect Antoine de Bourbon, king of Navarre, but the clergy felt that he was too tainted by heresy to be acceptable. Rivalries between various noble houses made it difficult for the nobility to come up with another choice to present to the clergy. In the end, the nobility was unable even to submit one cahier for itself, unlike the other two Estates. Some of the nobility submitted quasi-Protestant cahiers, where they urged that doctrinal disputes be decided by reference to the

Bible, while others insisted that they wished to live and die under the rules and doctrines of the Roman Catholic Church. The Third Estate submitted its united cahier to the king on January 10, 1561. It was sharply anti-clerical. It proclaimed that religion, which should be the principal glue that bound the nation, had become instead the reverse, and the principal cause of this calamity was the "inexcusable negligence and insupportable faults" of the clergy. Far too many of the clergy were ignorant, greedy, and lazy. Indeed, the majority were at fault in certain ways. Moreover, the Third Estate requested that the traditional exemption of the clergy from taxation should be ended.[7]

The Estates were cantankerous, but the crown was also partly at fault. The monarchy did little to influence the contents of the cahiers: unlike the cannier Tudor kings in England, the French crown failed to use sympathetic members to plant "government" provisions into the grievances. Furthermore, only on January 13, after the Estates had finalized the cahiers, did the crown open the discussion of the financial question. In order to impress on the representatives how much it needed the new taxes, the crown made no attempt to hide the extent of the problem and offered to open its books for the representatives' inspection. The danger of this course was that the members of the Estates might take the view that the extent of the debt only proved how disgustingly profligate Henri II had been. Only the clergy cooperated, and nominated thirteen delegates to examine the books. The bishop of Évreux announced the results on January 20: the kingdom's debt amounted to £43.5 million, approximately four times annual revenues. Even the clergy insisted, however, that they did not have the authorization to grant new taxes, since their commissions only mentioned submitting grievances. This attitude harkened back to an older conception of the representatives' role, originally prevalent in England as well. According to this theory, the members of a parliament were really delegates, under the instructions of their cahiers and unable to treat any matter not contained in them. In England, members of Parliament gradually came to enjoy full power (*plena potestas*) to make whatever arrangements seemed best to them. The clergy at Orléans were claiming that they lacked this power. Negotiations between the crown and the Estates continued for another week, to little effect. The crown decided to accept the deputies' arguments, dissolve the assembly, and call for new elections in which the representatives would be specifically empowered to discuss the financial question. In the meantime, to gain goodwill, the crown acceded to most of the proposals in the national cahiers of the three Estates. There were two main exceptions. Catherine de' Medici, acting as regent for her son Charles IX, vetoed provisions that tended to reduce royal revenues.

She also rejected some provisions in the First Estate's cahier which called for harsh measures against heresy.

At the end of the month, Chancellor L'Hospital called the Estates together and presented the crown's proposals for new taxes, which would last for six years. In the king's name, he asked the Church to redeem loans based on the royal domain and various taxes, amounting to £15 million. The nobility's share would be to pay a tax on salt. In areas where salt was not taxed, other feudal levies were substituted. Finally, the Third Estate was asked to approve an increase in the *taille* and a wine tax. Now that the Estates knew what they had to think about, the chancellor dismissed the assembly and ordered new elections for a smaller, more manageable body, which would meet at Melun. The meeting was originally scheduled for May 1, 1561, although it had to be postponed several times. When the letters patent ordering the elections were issued on March 25, they specifically forbade the local and provincial Estates to discuss the structure of either government or religion. The national Estates finally met, three months later than originally planned, on August 1.[8]

In the middle of the session of the Estates, Catherine announced a new edict which further liberalized the laws against Protestants. The amnesty for heresy was extended, for the first time, to Protestant preachers. It also even included an acceptance of assemblies where people had borne arms. The Protestant movement was naturally delighted; it also seems to have begun a process of consultation in order to come up with a platform that it could propose in local communities when they met to draw up their new cahiers. Unfortunately, the details of these consultations are obscure because there are few surviving records, except a draft memorandum listing possible provisions. These were then incorporated more or less faithfully into local cahiers where the Protestant movement was influential. On March 10, the Second National Synod of the Protestant Church had met and, among other decisions, endorsed a short program for the Estates, including several key provisions from the draft. In Paris, Protestant representatives also influenced the city's cahier, which included some similar provisions. In Nîmes, the Protestant movement drew up a cahier that is particularly similar to the surviving draft memorandum. The Nîmes Protestant movement had organized the campaign in order to achieve its goals at the meeting of the Estates, but the cahier also proved to be a superlatively successful organizing tool at the local level. The Protestant cahier is therefore crucial to the history of the Reformation in Nîmes because it is the fullest exposition of Protestant ideas and because the struggle to adopt it was crucial to the success of the Protestant movement. In the cahier, Nîmes's Protestants, given an opportunity by the economic and fiscal problems of 1557–1560, finally found a set of arguments that resonated with the town's elite.[9]

The Introduction of the Nîmes Cahier

Nîmes's Catholic consuls were guaranteed to oppose any cahier the Protestant party proposed. However, the consuls' political position was quite weak, since they had been imposed by force and the crown was deeply unpopular. By now, Nîmes's elite, shaken by the political and economic stresses of the previous four years, emboldened by the weakness of the central government, and excited by the vision of political and religious reform presented in the cahier, was ready to move. When, on March 15, 1561, the council met to consider the cahier, the town's first consul was absent, due to a convenient illness. The proposals were introduced instead by Louis Bertrand, a wealthy, prominent Protestant, explicitly a member of the nascent party:

> M. Louis Bertrand declared, in his own name and on behalf of his supporters, and asked the honorable sirs the President and consuls to assemble the present Extraordinary Council, in order to remonstrate concerning the honor of God, the king's service, and the repose and tranquility of the People, and to report this to the local Estates of this province of Languedoc... and to the Estates General.[10]

This opening of Bertrand's speech gives considerable insight into his political views. By using the term "remonstrate," he showed his low opinion of the consuls. He may also have been suggesting that since, without the reforms he was proposing, the people would be unhappy, the consuls might face violence if they rejected his proposals. He also clearly thought that the cahier was of extreme importance. At a rhetorical level, he described the cahier as concerning God, the king, and the people. More concretely, and in defiance of established procedure, he proposed that the Nîmes cahier should be considered not just at a local or provincial level, but by the entire nation, representatives of which would assemble at the Estates General.

Bertrand's position was strengthened because he was accompanied by 136 named citizens, making the session one of the best attended in contemporary records. The 136 included many members of the upper crust, but many also of the more middling classes, including bakers, tanners, and students at the College of Arts.[11] The town consuls attempted to delay consideration of the cahier by pointing out, "There were no members of the ordinary council [the smaller, more elite body] present, as is well-known," and, in a well-calculated appeal to the town's tendency to jealously guard its local rights and privileges, to proceed "could be prejudicial to the [local] transactions, statutes, and ordinances."[12] The consuls were arguing that the supporters of the cahier were out of order, as well as arguing that the cahier itself was poor policy: the cahier should be rejected both on procedural and on substantive grounds.

The chair of the council meeting, normally the president of the présidial court, had the right to decide whether a motion was in order. The president, Guillaume Calvière, had been notably absent from the intensive series of présidial meetings the previous spring, where the court debated how to suppress heresy. Calvière's views in this period are therefore hard to determine, although his absence may by itself indicate disapproval of its anti-Protestant approach. In any case, in this instance he ruled in favor of the Protestant party and disallowed the consuls' objections, insisting that "in [the councillors'] absence [the debate] should continue." Again, the consuls restated their objections, adding that they needed time to consider the articles of the cahier, which they had not seen before and which the first consul should review, since he was "a man of letters." Calvière did not accept this argument, since the absentees had been duly notified, "both by the sound of the bell, and individually by the [town's] servants; and in order not to retard the affairs of the king, he commanded the consuls to give their opinions." When given the chance to express their opinions on the document that they had done their best to table, the consuls—presumably because they were afraid to condemn a document in front of more than a hundred people who supported it—refused, saying only that it should be referred to a committee. They also insisted that any list of grievances should only go to the provincial, not the national, Estates. In the end, however, they lost every point.[13]

Several conclusions can be drawn from all of this. Though Bertrand represented only one faction of the community, it was a well-mobilized and enthusiastic one. While the support of the council's presiding officer, Calvière, certainly helped, the importance of the crowd who turned out in support of the cahier can hardly be overstated.[14]

The cahier provided an outlet for all of the frustrations that Nîmes's elite had been feeling since the flood of 1557, including some age-old irritations that had new urgency, given the town's difficult circumstances. Nîmes's town council had long been concerned about the town's poor. Its concern contained a strong element of enlightened self-interest, since the members were at the top of the local society, and those on top can only lose when there is political instability. Thus when, because of the fiscal and economic strains of 1557–1560, Nîmes's governing legal elite found itself increasingly unable to relieve the hungry, they bitterly resented the crown's illegal fiscal demands, which hit their pockets hard and hindered their commendable efforts to help the town's poor. They were self-righteously appalled by the wastefulness of royal policies, which racked up debts and only led to military defeat. Nîmes's Protestant movement argued successfully in the cahier that these problems were linked, and the root cause was moral corruption. The situation could only be remedied by religious reform and rigorous controls on royal power. The cahier carefully skirted certain controversial religious questions, so that Catholics, particularly those of an Erasmian or reform-minded stripe, could sign it in good conscience. Many of the cahier's proposed constitutional reforms had been proposed long before, and some of the provisions might seem arcane to us. In the end, the crown did not agree to make the changes that were recommended. Nonetheless, the cahier electrified contemporaries. Undoubtedly, people were particularly attracted to it because it was passed at a crucial political juncture. The economic situation was still quite bad. The regent, Catherine de' Medici, had just granted the Protestant movement a greater degree of liberty than it had ever had before. Furthermore, the crown had just admitted that it was in grave financial difficulties. People who wanted political reform had reason to hope that the crown would actually agree to major concessions in exchange for the new revenues it desperately sought. In the end, however, the cahier affected Nîmes's citizens profoundly, but did little to change France's government.[15]

The cahier was composed of five parts: (1) the means to settle the king's debts, (2) the regulation of the king's expenses to prevent future deficits, (3) the reform of the Christian religion, "on which foundation all other reform is built," (4) the elimination of judicial abuses, and (5) the maintenance of law and order.[16] The most pressing issue was the debt, and most French people assumed that the Church would have to contribute much of the money necessary to reduce it. At the same time, as the Orléans session of the Estates General had shown, many Catholics were upset with the Church hierarchy. Some wished to redistribute the Church's funds away from overly wealthy bishops toward urgent needs, including preaching and charitable foundations. In the discussions leading up to Pontoise, some anti-clericalism was in the air, and many communities were in favor of making the Church pay. At Amiens, for example, the cahier urged that "the king must take for his own profit annates and the revenues of vacant benefices,"[17] while the *prévôté* of Paris said:

> It was most reasonable that those who held the best part of the wealth of this kingdom, such as the men of the Church who possess fat benefices which are not much burdened (not including the poor vicars and other poor holders of benefices who have great difficulties living off of them), should assist with one third or two parts [i.e., one-half] of the revenue of their benefices.[18]

In another sign of Catholic anger, the Third Estate of the seneschalsy of Toulouse, in its cahier for the Orléans meeting of the Estates, insisted that no mercy should be shown to heretics, but bitterly condemned the clergy and called for reducing tithes.[19] Even by this standard, the Nîmes cahier was unusually detailed and blunt. It expressed no sympathy for "poor vicars" and insisted instead that severe impositions on the clergy would "affect no one" or would "affect the fewest and will not be resented." It incorporated both the above provisions from the Amiens and Paris cahiers and more:

> In order that it will not be necessary to further burden his people . . . it would be good to use two means, one which is of no concern and affects no one, the other which affects the fewest and will not be resented. The first is to take of the revenue of the confraternities, the bells, the half, or a third, or better all, in each and every temple, and the relics. The second is to take one third of the revenue of benefices worth more than £1000, and the annates and the revenue of vacant posts . . . and similarly, to take the temporal jurisdictions of the churchmen, which they cannot hold in good conscience, even according to the decretals. And the king can derive money from them by bestowing them on his vassals, receiving military service in time of war, and customary rights which the king can commute in exchange for cash, which would amount to greater sums than might be thought.

Given the hard economic times, it is not surprising that the authors of the cahier were also concerned about growing poverty and urged that, in order to "warm the hearts of men to charity and alms," either one-quarter or one-third of Church revenues should be diverted "for food for the poor." Secular men should be put in charge of administering the poor funds.[20] This was a comprehensive attack on the Church's revenues and jurisdiction. It went beyond a reorganization for the Church's own benefit, as proposed by the Toulouse cahier, and indeed far beyond the light shearing proposed by the town of Amiens.

Protestants, both in the draft memorandum and in the Nîmes cahier, were anxious to attack the Church and particularly disposed to single out areas where they thought the crown and the public were likely to agree with them. For example, twenty years before, the royal Edict of Villers-Cotterêts had ordered the abolition of confraternities.[21] The Protestant movement therefore felt it had good reason to attack the confraternities, and since Nîmes had been one of the few towns that implemented the edict, at least in part, the provision was likely to arouse few objections there. Similarly, the authors of the cahier took care to attack the wealthiest members of the Catholic hierarchy and the ecclesiastical courts, which were widely resented in sixteenth-century Europe. The cahier attacked the Church's most unpopular features. Still, by any standard, the Nîmes cahier was radical. It is particularly noteworthy that the cahier refers to churches as "temples," the Protestant term.[22] Using "temple" in the cahier may have been a way of getting more people in Nîmes accustomed to the term and a faint suggestion that France's churches belonged to the kingdom's pious Christian subjects—the invisible Church universal, that is the Protestants—rather than to the institutional Catholic Church. In sum, it is hard to avoid concluding that the cahier meant to harness a deep, visceral anti-clericalism among its supporters and, presumably, potential supporters.

Other provisions, whether directly religious or not, may have particularly appealed to a Protestant sensibility. The cahier asks, for example, that "[n]o reproach, question, nor molestation, should be done to any person whatsoever, under color of a conspiracy," referring to the earlier conspiracy of Amboise. It also suggests that the Protestant-leaning king of Navarre should have a prominent role in the governing of the kingdom. Less directly, a Protestant suspicion of hypocrisy can perhaps be seen in the cahier's singling out of "the calumniator and the false witness" for special mention.[23] Some commentators have argued that Calvinism was particularly concerned with ensuring that proper hierarchy was observed within the family, and certainly the Nîmes cahier asks for reforms of the system of trustees (*tuteurs* or *curateurs*) for orphaned young people and of dowries.[24] Neither subject is mentioned in either the Toulouse or the national *cahiers de doléances* for the Orléans Estates General meeting, so it is possible to argue that such concerns reflect strictly local sensibilities. The cahier aimed to preserve hierarchy through sumptuary laws and by restricting gaming to men of leisure, excluding "any man of mechanical occupation, or manifestly lacking the wherewithal." In a manner consistent with both Protestant and Catholic reformers, the cahier also attacked dancing and theatricals.[25]

The cahier's generally moralizing tone may also owe something to cognitive dissonance. In the context of a conversion experience, which is inherently destabilizing, the yearning for consistency may be particularly strong. Such experiences are exhilarating, but also frightening, and converts may wish to retain as many of their comfortingly familiar ideas as possible. As their views rapidly alter, their family and friends and the converts themselves (if they are sufficiently introspective) might well wonder, what's next? Looked at from this point of view, this attempt to reinvigorate what today might be called traditional family values makes sense as an attempt to counterbalance Protestantism's innovations in theology and practice. The cahier restated some moral propositions with which it was hard to disagree and then attached them to a popular but more controversial political and religious program. By doing so, the cahier writers seem to have created what some modern social scientists would call an *emergent norm*. Such moments, such as prayer meetings where more and more people apparently start to "testify" spontaneously and announce that they have now found the Lord, can have powerful emotional consequences for participants. The effect is like a cascade of peer pressure, by the end of which even initially reluctant or skeptical members of the group can be swept along in a wash of feeling. This seems to have been the case in Nîmes. The meeting to discuss the cahier created a context in which it seemed like the entire community ratified a collective belief and agreed on a program even though, had a formal vote been taken, this might easily have proven not to be the case. Indeed, the cahier discussion included little doctrinal or other information about the group to which people were in effect pledging their adherence. Presumably, the cahier signers were learning about Protestantism from the mass meetings and preaching going on in Nîmes, but preaching at such events was also likely to focus on moral uplift and attacks on the corruption of the Church, rather than on the careful exposition of precise theological differences.[26]

While Protestant views are visible in numerous ways in the Nîmes cahier, some of the most explicitly religious clauses are surprisingly circumspect. It does say that "if we return to God, and serve Him purely, according to His Word," God will reward France with military victory, just as he did for the Israelites. But the notion of the word of God is not strictly Protestant. Again, in asking for a national council to reunite the Church, anticipating the Colloquy of Poissy later in the year, the Nîmes cahier asks for the representation of "all those who speak French," presumably so that Genevans could be included, and that issues be decided, not by tradition, but "by the word of God alone."[27] Other clauses ask for prayers to be conducted in the vernacular, the freedom to read the Bible, the end of payments to Rome, and for the people's ministers to urge them to sing hymns and the psalms. At the same time, bishops should be ordered "not to depart from the exposition of Scripture to set one against another, but only and simply to instruct the people in the pure word of God." But the key clause, demanding tolerance, is careful not to be too direct, asking that "those who believe they cannot take part in the ceremonies of the Roman Church should be given means to be instructed and taught in the Word of God, for fear lest they fall into atheism."[28] This could almost be misinterpreted as a demand for special instruction for the wayward, to bring them back into the fold, rather than as a demand for a separate church of their own. And finally, consider this clause:

> Similarly, to oppose the light of truth to the thick darkness of ignorance, which has filled the air and the earth unto this day, and to give an opening to everyone to know and understand their salvation, the catechizing of children and rustics should be restored, if the king pleases, to such effect that they will be clearly and simply instructed in the articles of our faith, of the Law of the Ten Commandments, of the way to pray to God for the explanation

of the Lord's Day's sermon, and taught purely the dignity, the end, and the use of the holy sacraments, to all who are of age and capable of understanding.[29]

Considering that there was a major dispute between Protestants and Catholics over how many sacraments there were, this is quite imprecise. It is, however, remarkably similar to two provisions in the Orléans cahier, which ask for sermons on the Decalogue and on the "institution, virtue, and effect of the sacraments."[30] The Nîmes cahier also avoids questions of ecclesiology: there is no suggestion that the hierarchy should be remodeled to eliminate the bishops or the monasteries. The cahier avoids detailed statements on the sacraments, their meaning, and church organization, the most contentious issues dividing Catholics from Protestants. By contrast, requests for Bible reading, although eventually considered irredeemably Protestant, were not out of the question for reform-minded Catholics in the early sixteenth century. Thus, the Nîmes cahier, although drawn up by Protestants, because of its careful phraseology might have been acceptable to some reformist Catholics.

Why was the language of the religious clauses in the Nîmes cahier so ambiguous? Of course, a too-open Protestantism might have provoked persecution, but heresy only half-concealed seems hardly useful protection. Protestants in Nîmes faced a terrible dilemma, since they wished to escape trial for heresy yet felt a passion to give witness to their faith, to spread the good news. In the environment of the time, furthermore, half-concealed digs may have taken on a special, symbolic significance, like the veiled criticisms of samizdat, which later seemed timid. But the Nîmes cahier went much further than others did. The delegates at Orléans did not attack the Church in order to justify conversion to a new religion. Instead, they were angry that the Church, in its bloated inefficiency, had been unable to prevent the rise of the new heresy. Toulouse was equally concerned by the "long absence, ignorance and boundless avarice of many prelates," and its cahier suggested that Church revenues should be seized and turned to more useful purposes, like funding preachers and schools.[31] This was still notably different from Nîmes's cahier, which advocated that the crown confiscate much of the Church's wealth in order to reduce the state's debts. The authors of Nîmes's cahier would also presumably not have approved of confiscating some of the Church's wealth to fund preachers: that measure was designed to help Catholicism more effectively combat heresy.

Some Protestants hoped for a reconciliation with the Catholic Church, although in practice what this meant was they hoped that the Church would capitulate to their demands. Perhaps we should understand the demands to regulate the bishops' sermons, rather than abolish their office, in the light of the Protestant party's extravagant hopes at this time. Fundamentally, the cautious language must be understood politically: Nîmes's Protestants did not wish to give the opposition any ammunition. This was a sign of their political sophistication. While it may have been unrealistic to expect that the Catholic Church would capitulate to Protestant demands for reform, it was perhaps more reasonable to hope for conversions among less firmly committed Catholics. By demanding reforms, rather than the liquidation of the Church, the Nîmes cahier laid the groundwork for a later breach should the reforms not be adopted. The cahier was a document with unmistakable Protestant leanings, designed to appeal to the Protestant community, with a certain amount of ambiguous language that could also appeal to moderate, reform-minded Catholics, and a grand call for a sweeping reform of government and society designed to appeal to Protestants, Catholics, and those in the middle.

The Nîmes cahier advocated radical pruning of Church assets, and its proposals for limiting royal power were hardly less dramatic. The Nîmes cahier did not merely advocate that the clergy pay for the king's debts. It suggested that royal expenses be reduced and measures taken to control them in the future. Gifts and pensions to members of the court needed to be reduced, tax officials needed to be more closely scrutinized, and, during the king's minority, no war should be declared nor any tax imposed without the approval of the Estates. Furthermore, the Estates should be convened on the king's majority, "to see better in what state are the king's affairs and how affairs have been conducted during his minority," and at least every ten years. In future, the monarchy should be much more tightly scrutinized, and joint decision making should replace the personal rule of the monarch. Such demands were hardly new: the Estates General had in fact suggested at its last meeting, in 1484, that it should meet every two years.[32] Similarly, it was hardly surprising that the authors of the cahier thought that royal advisers during a king's minority were liable to line their pockets from the public purse. It was always easier to attack the king's evil counselors than the king himself. Still, the provision for regular meetings of the Estates was important: it represented a serious commitment to the idea of a greater popular voice in national affairs. Although there was considerable precedent for the constitutional views expressed in the Nîmes cahier, not all contemporaries agreed. The Toulouse cahier recommended that the jurisdiction of the Estates of Languedoc be divided in two to reduce the travel expenses for the communities that paid them.[33] The cahier also used the Catholic consuls' resistance against them, arguing the populist case that cahiers should not be concocted by local elites alone, "sans y appeler le peuple" (without calling the people).

The cahier's predilection for conciliar forms is also apparent in its suggestion that the kingdom should be governed by a council of sixteen or eighteen, to include the princes of the blood and the principal ministers of state, until the king reached his majority. Royal acts should be signed "Par le roy, à la relation de son conseil," and there should be provisions against nepotism. The crown should also send out commissions in advance of provincial Estates, so that local meetings could draw up cahiers, "so that the king may dispense his grace and justice unto the least of his subjects, according to his holy desire and will."[34]

In some areas, however, it is clear that the Nîmes cahier was less radical, or more circumspect, than, for example, the Languedoc cahier. Both the Nîmes and the Languedoc cahiers called for the end of all judicial fees, or *épices,* but only in Languedoc did they go so far as to insist that "[n]o judicial office shall be sold."[35] If no lucrative fees were attached, it would be hard to imagine why people would be interested in selling an office. Perhaps the authors of the Nîmes cahier felt that mentioning the sale of offices would impugn the members of the présidial court, all of whom had bought their offices. The Nîmes cahier also recommended: "In order that they [the judges] can honestly support themselves, according to their estate and the importance of their offices, good and competent salaries should be assigned to them so that they may work without regret."[36] Some of the provisions in the Nîmes cahier may have excited interest because they reflected local concerns. For example, section 4 of the Nîmes cahier asked that all jurisdictional boundaries be fixed, with the goal of preventing its rival Le Puy from getting a présidial. It also asked that surplus jurisdictions and officials and "long and useless formalities" in legal proceedings be eliminated. Similarly, the cahier asked for royal regulation of the butchers, who (as discussed above) had consistently irritated the town council over the years.[37]

Given the detail of some of the legal reforms that the cahier proposed, it is amply clear that people well versed in the law were involved in writing it. It does not, however, exempt them from criticism. The cahier accused notaries, for example, of "great infidelity and corruption" and suggested that their number be reduced. This is particularly noteworthy since Jacques Ursi, an early Protestant, was a notary with a large clientele. It criticized lawyers as well:

> [E]specially the impudence of advocates, who advise and sustain an ill cause, is insufferable, which they cannot do without shame and a great weight on their conscience, nor the audacity and equivocation of those who consume all the time in outrages and false facts which they allege against the parties.

There is, however, some reason to be skeptical about these protests. The cahier did not advocate a social revolution, which would have reduced the power of the lawyers and legal officials who dominated Nîmes. In its last clause, it suggested that authority should be concentrated in the hands of the présidiaux and the municipal councils, that is, in the members of the traditional ruling elite.[38] It is nonetheless worthwhile to consider why such harsh language was included. The cahier was undoubtedly a compromise, and it is possible that these denunciations welled up from below, and the elite cynically permitted them knowing that the actual proposals were to their benefit. The artisans who comprised the early leadership of the movement, and who were relatively removed from access to power, may have held such resentments and written them into the cahier. But it seems more probable that the elite shared in a certain ambivalence, even guilt. If they did not, it would be somewhat difficult to explain why they converted: self-satisfied people, especially cynical ones, are not obvious candidates for conversion. Furthermore, the Nîmes elite had considerable reason to feel guilty. They had failed in their paternalistic roles as protectors of the town. Floods and bad harvests were perhaps not their fault, but when times were bad their duty was to make up for them. Yet they had been unable to moderate extreme royal fiscal impositions, and the town's empty treasury and granary were thus in some sense their responsibility. They felt at the same time responsible for the town's problems and unable to solve them. Nîmes's advocates and notaries may have actively agreed with denunciations of lawyers and notaries in general, although each one probably excepted himself.[39]

The Nîmes elite thought habitually in paternalistic terms and expressed these kinds of sentiments repeatedly in town council meetings. Their language was also shot through with a particular kind of humanistic morality. This probably owed something to the legal mind, formed as it was by Justinian's Code, as well as to the town's burgeoning pride in its Roman heritage and the presence of the humanist scholars at Nîmes University and College of Arts. The cahier's language was tinged with it when it expressed its concern that "children and rustics" should be instructed in "the Law of the Ten Commandments." A humanist principle—the distinction between the deserving and the undeserving poor—can also be seen in the provisions for charity, which, as noted above, urged that Church funds be diverted to the poor while at the same time making it clear that lazy people should be forced to take up a trade.[40] As has been noted by many scholars of the period, this kind of language is as much humanist as Calvinist; if Nîmes's elite were already imbued with humanist values, it helps to explain why they converted. Calvinism reinforced the moral viewpoint to which they already adhered, thus easing any cognitive dissonance they may have felt. The cahier was a program to restore moral order to the kingdom. In that sense, even the "secular" parts of the cahier were really religious.

The cahier's ideology was wildly popular. After the adoption of the cahier, two hundred more people, many of whom were of quite low status—wool carders, soldiers—added their signatures to the bottom of the document. The most important thing about the cahier is not the occupational breakdown of its signers, but the sheer number of those who signed. This was the closest Nîmes came to a referendum on the Reformation, as frequently happened in Germany's imperial cities.[41] Still, it is interesting to compare cahier signers with the breakdown of "early Protestants" derived from Toulouse heresy prosecutions, immigrants to Geneva, and the présidial list of May 18, 1560 (discussed in Chapter 3; for both sets of figures, see Appendix A). If that list gives a profile of the movement as of early 1560, it suggests that signers of the cahier included more members of the elite, although otherwise the two groups are broadly similar. Crucially, members of the legal professions were 15 percent of those who signed the cahier, but only 9 percent of the early Protestants, and the high-status group of seigneurs and officials was also better represented among the signers than among the early Protestants. It was essential for the Protestant movement to gain the support of the lawyers, since they were the most important group in the town council. On the face of this evidence alone, it is possible to argue that lawyers may have been prominent among cahier signers merely because the cahier was a political document that was presented in the town council, where lawyers were prominently represented. But for reasons discussed below (in Chapter 6), it is more likely that the changing percentages really do represent the changing character of the Protestant movement.

Once the lawyers joined the Protestant movement, Protestants would no longer fear that the council would enact measures to suppress their preaching and other activities. Compared to the early Protestants, among the cahier signers high-status artisans—merchants and bourgeois—were not as well represented, and the percentage of those in agriculture was lower as well. It is not clear whether the national Protestant movement succeeded in its attempts to organize support for its draft cahier, but in Nîmes the effect was remarkable. The campaign was successful in attracting a large number of people and in particular the kind of influential people who had so far been somewhat reluctant to join. With the success of the cahier campaign, the movement passed a significant milestone on its way to becoming the dominant religion in Nîmes.

Some people who signed the cahier were no doubt already Protestants, but others were perhaps only on their way to becoming so, and a few probably signed despite being Catholics. No présidial members signed, while two consuls of 1560 did: Pierre Cellerier and Jean Mombel, both of whom had probably been Protestants for some time. Among the signers were Pierre Rozel the elder and Jean Voluntat, bourgeois, two of the thirty-two "non-suspect" voters who had been allowed to vote for the new consuls the preceding November. Thirty of the two hundred equally "non-suspect" city guards nominated in December also signed.[42] This pattern suggests that the cahier was indeed successful in its goal of persuading previously uncommitted people to support the Protestant cause: people who had been considered reliable Catholics only the preceding fall chose to sign a document promulgated by the Protestant movement. It suggests that the Catholic cause was rapidly losing ground and that the Protestants had indeed scored a notable success with the cahier. There are other reasons to believe that the agitation over the cahier was part of a broader Protestant campaign designed to pull in support from the larger community. The movement took additional measures to convert others to its cause: Protestant preaching reached a new pitch of excitement just at this time, and the Protestant Consistory was organized on March 23, only eight days after the tumultuous meeting of the town council.[43] Whoever was responsible for drawing up the cahier knew what provisions would be likely to energize Protestant sympathizers and what would be likely to persuade the undecided and even some Catholics to join the Protestant cause.

The Nîmes Cahier in Provincial and National Politics

After adopting the cahier, the town council forwarded it to the provincial Estates General of Languedoc, whose session opened on March 20, 1561, in Montpellier, only five days after the approval of the Nîmes cahier. Pierre Chabot, a radical Protestant, represented Nîmes. According to one contemporary account, at first he was not permitted even to address the assembly, but the clamor of the crowd outside the hall eventually persuaded the delegates to give him a hearing. Chabot later explained that the other delegates of the provinces had insisted that he could not discuss his proposals, because "there [at the Estates meeting] only the funding of the king's debts was to be discussed." The delegates to the Estates were merely following Catherine's orders, but Chabot was less obedient.[44]

Nonetheless, the Estates did consider far-reaching proposals for reform. Claude Terlon, a lawyer and the *capitoul*[45] of Toulouse, suggested that "the most prompt expedient would be to take all the temporal goods of the Church, reserving to those who hold benefices the houses and lands adjacent to their benefices." Furthermore, he proposed that any assets that remained after the crown's debts had been paid off should be given to commissions of town officials to administer on the Church's behalf. As Emmanuel Le Roy Ladurie has pointed out, this would have made the clergy into salaried state employees, a local version of the procedures eventually adopted by the French Revolution. Terlon was not an out-and-out Protestant, as indeed his proposal to reorganize the Church's finances shows: he was more interested in reforming the Catholic Church than in demolishing it. Nonetheless, the Church could hardly have been pleased with his proposals. The Church was particularly perturbed because Terlon's views were rather the norm than the exception: the deputies at Montpellier adopted his proposals, and they named him the representative of the Third Estate of Languedoc to the Estates General of Pontoise.[46] The delegates treated Chabot's proposals much more gingerly. Rather than reject them, which would have inflamed Protestant opinion both within and without the chamber, they arranged instead to have Antoine de Crussol, vicomte d'Uzès, a great landowner and leading Protestant, take charge of Chabot's complaints and present them at the Estates General meeting. Achille Gamon, a contemporary and a Catholic, noted that there was a wide spectrum of opinion, with some eager to have Chabot punished as "a disturber of the public peace." But lines were generally blurred. As a Catholic, his description of the contemporary mood has special significance:

> An air of reform, which the preachers of the new religion made seem necessary, seduced some; the license which it encouraged corrupted the others, and in the uncertainty, or, more accurately, the ignorance about the Catholic religion and the Reformed religion that prevailed, people did not know which of the two to cleave to, and which pastors to follow.[47]

In this fluid, liminal atmosphere, then, the Nîmes cahier was useful as a propaganda document to convince the uncertain to join the Protestant cause.

Preparations for the Estates continued through the spring and early summer; the sessions had originally been scheduled to start on May 1, 1561, but were delayed. The clergy met separately from the other two orders. Its session began on July 31, 1561, at Poissy. The following day, the king and the queen mother opened the new Estates General. Instead of meeting at Melun, the session was moved to the nearby town of Pontoise; about eighty delegates attended. The session lasted just under a month, closing on August 27. The nobility and the commons were reluctant to vote new taxes. The nobility proposed with breathtaking effrontery that the clergy should pay two-thirds of the outstanding debt, the commons the remaining third, and they should pay nothing. The commons, equally ungenerous, felt that the clergy should pay the entire sum. Both recommended measures that the Nîmes cahier had also endorsed, including the right of the Estates to consent to peace treaties and declarations of war and the scheduling of regular (biennial, in this case) meetings of the Estates. The clergy, thoroughly concerned by the antagonism that the other two Estates had shown, agreed to pay more than £9 million over ten years. As a result, the crown felt better disposed toward the clergy, who had shown themselves cooperative, than toward the other Estates, which had demanded much in exchange for little. The nobility and the commons, angry at both the crown and the Church, had attacked both at once, rather than husbanding their energies. Their strategy lacked shrewdness.[48]

The Effect of the Nîmes Cahier on Local Politics

The immense popular enthusiasm for the Nîmes cahier shows that it captured the public mood brilliantly, even though its goals were impossibly ambitious. Public opinion in Nîmes favored restraints on an extravagant monarchy and reform of the Church, which was believed to be rich but not performing its duties. These were simplistic solutions, but the problems were real. The Protestant movement's strategy was somewhat shortsighted in its thinking: if its primary goal was to weaken the Church, it was a mistake to antagonize the king at the same time. From a national perspective, it was foolhardy for the Protestant movement to pursue political reform. On the local level, however, it seems likely that it would have sacrificed much of the enthusiasm for the cahier if it had abandoned its proposals for increasing the power of the Estates. It was in order to attract the fluid center of local public opinion, then, that the cahier adopted a number of popular, traditional reforms. It is also probable that the movement's own deep-seated anger at the crown prevented it from allying with the monarchy, even against the Church. The Protestants could not readily disentangle the two. Finally, at least on the local level, the structure of the Protestant church was based on an elected council, a consistory, rather than on the more hierarchical structure of the Catholic Church. It would have been grossly inconsistent for the movement to advocate a representative council structure in one sphere and not the other. The result was that the movement campaigned for a document that was perfect for gaining converts in Nîmes, but not successful in gaining support at court. It would have been more expedient to gain the crown's support if it were possible, but the odds of a royal conversion were never good. In any case, the other choice was the more principled position.

Furthermore, the cahier's overarching structure was quite traditional. Politically, the cahier represented a classic contractualist view of politics, where the king and his subjects had mutual, unequal responsibilities, but the king was supposed to rule under significant legal restraints. On the whole, the effect of the cahier, had its provisions been adopted, would have been to weaken the power of the crown, although in exchange the king would have been rewarded with a general redistribution of Church revenues, lordships, and jurisdictions. Had the crown received sufficient new revenues, it would have become relatively independent of the Estates since it would not have to ask them for supplies. But this threat was unrealistic. It was unlikely that the crown could ever acquire so much land from the Church that it would have enough money to finance itself during wartime. The cahier's proposals requiring the Estates' assent to declarations of war would also have severely limited the crown's traditional prerogative to make foreign policy.[49] Nonetheless, these proposals were only a starting point, and with further negotiations, they could have proven the basis for an attractive bargain for the crown. In its original form, however, the cahier was more a statement of principles than a completely realistic proposal. In particular, it seems likely that Protestants emphasized deliberative structures like the Estates because they were opposed to the kingdom's hierarchical structure, which resembled that of the Church. The French Protestant church's own structure, with its local and national synods, mimicked the provincial and national Estates and the system of councils that governed most towns.

Eventually, the leaders of the Protestant movement in Nîmes realized their mistake. At the next meeting of the town council, on November 13, there was a discussion of the cahier and its purposes. The November meeting was called in response to popular agitation and in spite of the consuls, and it was the hard-line Protestant Pierre Chabot who appears to have been a leader in the agitation and who was the first to speak. He first had to duel with the consuls about whether the meeting should be held, but he then turned to the question of the cahier, "in which," among other articles, "there was a request for the purpose of asking for Protestant churches, and that those who wanted to live according to the Word of God could assemble to be instructed in it."[50] At least in retrospect, then, the cahier was seen as an unambiguously Protestant document. The town council, however, did not see the cahier as simply a petition on behalf of the Protestant community. Rather, it formulated the cahier's request as an exchange, asking for religious concessions in exchange for cash, and specifically that the king work with the formula agreed to by the Estates. Similarly, the council resolved to send deputies to the Languedoc Estates to continue the negotiations. They gave the delegates these instructions:

> To accord to His Majesty all taxes that he may please to command be levied on the province of Languedoc to satisfy his debts, charges, and the affairs of the kingdom, with the allegiance that true and faithful

subjects of His Majesty must give, sparing nothing, and for the share payable by this town. And insofar as the delegates of the Third Estate of this kingdom assembled in the last Estates General, held in the town of Pontoise, in their list of grievances, for the reasons contained therein, agreed that, in order to satisfy those who wished to live in the purity of the Gospel, under the king's obedience, a temple should be assigned to them in every town.[51]

Between the spring and the fall, there had been a crucial change in emphasis. In the cahier, the Protestant movement was prepared to antagonize the crown and the Church at the same time. By the fall, the leadership had recognized that its religious goals required that an alliance be struck. They may not have been entirely in earnest, since the country was already headed for civil war. That is, they offered to sacrifice their demands in the cahier, but they may not actually have expected to have to fulfill the offer. By making it, however, they positioned themselves as loyal subjects and attempted to put the onus for the hostilities on the Catholic party. Still, it is hard to imagine that the cahier would have been more popular had it included offers to the king to pay significant tax increases. Had Nîmes's elites thought carefully about the issues, they might have realized that the cahier was not a practical political program. By then, they were perhaps too frustrated and angry to care, and the Protestant movement's tactics—the revival-meeting tone—helped to generate an intense, emotional atmosphere. The result was that large numbers of people signed the document without fully considering how it might affect Nîmes's religious life. Their precise religious views probably varied considerably. But while political discontent may have motivated some people to join the movement, their new religious identity became sufficiently important that they were prepared to forgo the very political reforms that had motivated them initially. Their anxiety then led them to encourage others to join. They had accepted a community, not just a program, and only with time did they fully come to understand the precise dogmas and rites of their new faith and recognize that their previous religion had been idolatry.[52] In the interval, the cahier had succeeded in one crucial way: the Protestant party, despite its outlaw status, had persuaded the majority of the town's elite to sign a document it had written.

In the preceding decade, primarily to pay for the king's wars, the people of Nîmes had seen taxes rise year after year, during a period of flood, harvest failures, grain shortages, rising prices, and falling standards of living. The crown had also extorted money repeatedly by threatening to divide the Nîmes présidial's jurisdictions, which would have hurt the local economy. So it is reasonable to imagine that some of the provisions of the cahier, for example, curbing royal power, fixing the boundaries of judicial districts, and regulating meat prices, won the support of local people because they were upset by recent events. The cahier of 1561 is an indication of how and why the economic and political strains of 1557–1560 helped the growth of the Protestant movement. The Protestants succeeded in linking Nîmes's economic and political problems to a religious ideology that promised reform in church and state, whose political philosophy, doctrine, and ecclesiology were a coherent response to the problems of the day. Protestantism was not a mindless reaction to misery: it was aimed at people who were not themselves hungry. In 1561, Nîmes's elites were angry and emotional, and they had reason to be: the town had been in grave difficulties for four years, and now the nation was in jeopardy of civil war. Had they been fully rational, they would have realized that the proposals in the cahier were not practical politics, since the king could hardly be expected to agree to them. Instead, the cahier evoked a more visceral response because it expressed Nîmes's elites' views of how the kingdom ought to operate. However impractical, this vision was powerfully seductive.[53]

Despite the enormous excitement the cahier generated, it alone did not ensure Protestant success, for several reasons. First of all, the case for the link between Nîmes's problems and Calvinism was not self-evident: it had to be made, and skillfully. This link could not have been forged if the Protestant leadership had not also used mass prayer meetings and sermons, more personal approaches, and powerfully symbolic acts, such as iconoclasm. The Protestant leadership's success in converting the elite demonstrated their ability to organize people and helped to remove the obstacles—the persecution—that had hindered the new church from broadcasting its ideas in public and in private. Second, the events of March 1561 did not ensure success by themselves. It took another year of intense activity for Protestantism to become the majority religion in Nîmes, and several years more for the Protestant party to achieve control over the town. The cahier marked a crucial breakthrough, but it was only the beginning.

6

The Consolidation of the Protestant Movement, 1561–1562

At the March 15, 1561, meeting of the Nîmes town council, where the Protestant-sponsored *cahier de doléances* was passed, Nîmes's Protestants won a major victory. The group had put itself at the head of a popular movement in favor of political and religious reform. The cahier had generated enormous enthusiasm and prominent new converts. The adoption of the cahier also had one important political effect: Nîmes's Catholic consuls, presumably fearing further incidents, neglected to call another meeting until the following August (the longest gap between meetings in the records). As a result, the consuls' ability to mobilize the town's institutions to combat heresy was gravely limited. However, the Protestant movement still faced major impediments: it still had neither churches of its own in town nor an institutional structure, and Nîmes's government was still in the hands of Catholic consuls. Furthermore, many of those who had signed the petition for the cahier were not yet completely committed to the new church, were not necessarily knowledgeable about its doctrines or ceremonies, and did not have clear identities as Protestants. The leaders of the movement had to create active Protestant institutions, in part so they could inculcate new rituals and patterns of behavior into the recruits who continued to flock to the mass meetings and preaching. The Nîmes Protestant leaders' goal was to institutionalize Protestantism in Nîmes so that even those people who did not have strong religious views would come to see their daily lives shaped by Protestant institutions. In this, they were successful, and within a year or two, only hard-core, committed Catholics remained.

The Composition of the Protestant Movement in Early 1561

On March 23, 1561, eight days after the Protestant movement forced the city council to adopt the cahier for the Estates General, the movement held its first official meeting. The proximity between the two events indicates how formative the cahier campaign was for the Nîmes Protestant movement. The Protestants called the meeting to organize the consistory, the governing body of the new church. Pastor Mauget presided as the assembly chose its officers: four deacons (*diacres*), and overseers (*surveillants*), tithingmen (*dixeniers*), and criers (*advertisseurs*) for each of ten districts that they defined in the town and suburbs. (The divisions did not correspond to the six quarters into which the town was divided.) Each overseer was given one crier and two tithingmen to assist him. The consistory also resolved at the end of that month that there would be an assembly—presumably, a meeting for prayer and preaching—each day, and it would be held in each district in sequence; the deacons would ensure that each district assembled for prayers every Sunday.[1] These measures suggest that the consistory was anxious to secure itself by using networks of neighborhood relations, so that the Protestant church would be solidly anchored in the community.

Much of the consistory's time in the first weeks of its existence, through the early part of May, was devoted to choosing officers. Many men were nominated to more than one office, so that, for example, Arnaud Alizot was elected to be an overseer as well as the treasurer of the poor fund. Of the approximately seventy officers, fifty-three, or about 75 percent, can be identified from notarial records. (Some of the remaining references are fragmentary, so it is difficult to estimate the exact number of people under consideration.) Occupational data about them are given in Appendix A.

While there were similarities between the occupational distributions of early Protestants and of the Protestant leadership in 1561, there were also some significant differences, notably, an increase in representation from the legal professions. The percentage of farmers, already low, dropped further, as did the percentage of merchants, bourgeois, and men from the textile trades. But the rise in the percentage of lawyers, notaries, and clerks suggests that Protestants had been successful in recruiting from this important group over the preceding year. As was noted above in the discussion of the signers of the cahier, this is particularly significant given lawyers' important place in Nîmes's social hierarchy. In particular, it helps to explain why the town council was so reluctant to move against heresy in 1560, especially in the latter half of the year: Protestantism was making too many inroads. It is also hard not to see a link between the political agitation—the cahier in particular—and the dramatic increase in lawyers among the Protestant movement, although whether the influence of the lawyers led to the political program of the cahier, or vice versa, or both, is hard to say. In any event, the Protestant movement and the legal elite came to share the same goals. The figures also suggest why the rigged elections of late 1560, which were bound to antagonize the political classes, were so spectacularly ill timed: they alienated a key group at a point when many of its members were making up their minds about which side they would join.[2]

The occupational percentages for the Protestant leadership (obtained from consistory records) correspond to those of the signers of the cahier, as recorded in the Nîmes town council's minute book. To pick just two examples: 15 percent of Protestant leaders and 15 percent of cahier signers were lawyers, and 28 percent of Protestant leaders and 29 percent of cahier signers were cloth workers. The one major difference is that officials and seigneurs seemed to have been more prominent among cahier signers than among early Protestant leaders. These correspondences are remarkable because each provenance is entirely different. It is strong evidence for the reliability of both and for the thesis that there was a close link between politics and religion at this stage of Protestant growth in Nîmes. The Nîmes Protestant community looked the same, whether viewed in a more political incarnation or through a more strictly religious lens. Both sources make it clear why the town council was no longer willing or able to repress the Protestant movement.[3]

Organizing the Protestant Church

Nîmes's Protestants met to found the consistory because the movement had now become so large that it needed a more formal structure. This was particularly important since there were so many new members, who did not necessarily know what their new community expected of them. The consistory was in charge of all aspects of church governance, but it was especially active in disciplining the movement's more wayward supporters. It ordered the town's innkeepers to watch over their customers, for example, to make sure that they did not become "dissolute" and to prevent swearing.[4] The consistory found it difficult to enforce its decisions, however. Sixteenth-century people were, on the whole, undisciplined compared to people today, and this may have been particularly true of French Protestants. After all, if they had been especially law-abiding, they would not have defied the law and joined a heretical church. The Protestant flock may have included a disproportionate share of Nîmes's contrarians. Nonetheless, consistorial discipline cannot be seen simply as the elite men imposing their will on ordinary folk, for three reasons. First, the leadership was not especially elite, and it frequently imposed discipline on its betters. Second, while the consistory was concerned with discipline, it was at least as concerned with self-discipline as with disciplining others. Members of the consistory leadership were determined not to exempt themselves from censure and therefore engaged in periodic self-criticism. Third, the laity wanted the imposition of a new moral order. They just wanted it imposed on society in general, not necessarily on themselves in particular. That is why the cahier's moral reform proposals were so popular and why the bulk of the adult population flocked to hear regular jeremiads from at least two different pastors (Guillaume Mauget and Arnaud Banc and possibly Jean Mutonis, or Mouton, as well).[5] It seems unlikely that people attended the sermons merely for their shock value.

The consistory reserved most of the juiciest discussions for its private meetings. It first discussed how to punish adultery on May 14, 1561, when the minister of Marsillargues raised the issue. One week later, the consistory discussed its first morals cases. Several of these involved religious backsliding: Antoine Triati, a merchant, confessed that "he had been to hear the preaching of the Dominican since his reception in the [Protestant] Church, but had not taken part in the service." He was ordered to make amends. The consistory also ordered Louis de Montcalm, the prior of Millau, to give up his papist benefices. Then there was the case of Raymond Coderc, a cordwainer, who was accused of having been a traitor to the church while he was in prison. While under investigation, he was forbidden to take communion.[6]

The consistory was also concerned with personal morality, although members of the church frequently resisted its intrusions. Doulce Juliane, for example, was the first woman the consistory accused of adultery—which she vehemently denied—on May 21, 1561. This was the beginning of a long dispute in which the consistory was unable to prevail. In October, she refused to come before the consistory, but by December she was asking if she could marry; the consistory insisted that it had to know whether her first husband was alive or not. In the interim, she had to stop seeing Guillaume Felines, a cordwainer, or they would report her to the civil authorities. Apparently, she obtained a document from her supposed husband, saying that they were not married and he was married to someone else, which the consistory proceeded to check. The consistory also interviewed Felines, who admitted that he had promised to marry her, and she added that she had promised likewise. The consistory then ordered them censured and warned that they would be turned over to the civil authorities if they did not stop seeing each other. This was difficult, since apparently Felines boarded with Juliane, but the consistory ordered him not to see her other than at mealtimes. Juliane responded, with admirable vigor, that she would do as she liked, and she would have no other man as her husband. Romantics will be pleased to learn that the marriage contract between the two of them was signed three months later.[7]

Another good example of the difficulties the consistory had in enforcing discipline is the case of Jean Garragues, a student who was accused of making his maid pregnant. When the minister called him to account, he replied by asking: "Did [the minister] have authority in Scripture to ask him that question, and he should prove first whether the minister had the authority to pardon him for his sins, or God. If it was he [the minister], then he would confess to him, and if it was God, he must confess to God and not to men." Eventually, he was brought at least somewhat to heel, since he accepted the consistory's authority, although he continued to deny the accusation, and the consistory seems to have concluded that it did not have sufficient evidence to contradict him.[8]

The consistory, of course, did not give up easily. Guiraud Gaudin, a surgeon, was ordered to stop gaming and to stay out of taverns. Mademoiselle de Carrière was ordered to dress modestly. Jacques Berrason was ordered to stop beating his wife.[9] The consistory was quite prepared to criticize even its most powerful adherents, including Charles Rozel, for example, although even such committed Protestants were loath to be singled out for criticism. The consistory was also anxious to mediate quarrels between fellow Protestants: for example, Barthelémy Garaiche and Guillaume Guiraud promised to come to a compromise in their dispute over the ownership of a house.[10]

At consistory meetings, each officer's behavior was discussed in turn, and summary comments were recorded in the consistory's meeting book. This procedure was derived from Genevan practice, where it was called the *grabaud*. On May 31, 1561, for example, Guillaume Mauget, the pastor, was urged to use more plainspoken language and not to repeat himself, while Jean Bertrand, a wealthy merchant and an overseer, was told to be more courageous, and other members were told to keep their anger in check. Pierre Chabot was ordered "to frequent the assemblies, not to laugh or to think anything frivolous, and not to say anything without being well-informed of the truth." If there was no specific criticism, the members were told to strive for improvement, "to continue to get better and better."[11] The *grabaud* was widely adopted in the Calvinist world, but it was highly unusual, perhaps unique to Nîmes, for the comments to be recorded. This record keeping suggests just how rigorous and committed the Nîmes Consistory was. (After a while, the reporting did stop.)

Not only was it difficult to impose discipline, but the consistory found itself riven by factionalism almost immediately. The cause of the dissension was Jean Mouton, or Mutonis, a pastor who emerged as a rival of Mauget.[12] The consistory first noticed him, on April 7, to censure him for performing a marriage without announcing the banns. They also forbade him to preach in town without Mauget's permission. Nonetheless, he had influential supporters, apparently including several members of the consistory, and the discussion grew heated when early the following month several members attempted to present a petition calling for him to be named co-adjutor with Mauget.[13] The consistory soon decided to assemble a synod of ministers from nearby towns and villages to discuss the question. The meeting was held on May 14; pastor Mauget, who was present, opened the proceedings by noting that they had assembled for "affairs of great importance." After electing one of their number to preside, the ministers attempted to exclude the laity, despite the protests of Pierre Chabot, one of Mutonis's supporters. He insisted, and several others agreed, that since it was an "extraordinary" matter, the meeting should be open to all. This implied that the consistory was analogous to the town council, where only councillors attended ordinary meetings, but extraordinary meetings were open. The majority of the consistory continued to support Mauget. However, when it came to the issue of attendance, they were unwilling to force the public to leave.[14] Mutonis explained that Mauget had given him a *libelle,* attacking him on a number of counts, and he wished to respond to each in turn, which he was permitted to do. He was accused of several main offenses: administering the sacraments to people who had not been properly instructed in the faith, marrying M. de Parinhargues improperly, preaching in Nîmes (by implication, without permission), preaching to anyone who would hear him, from his house, and not being a duly qualified pastor, among other charges.[15] It was also unclear if Mutonis's regular congregation, in Montagnac, had properly released him.[16]

Mauget explained that the lawyers of Nîmes had requested that he accept Mutonis as a preacher. He had attempted to regulate the dispute quietly, while Mutonis had attempted to bring in a notary to swear out a declaration, thus bringing the dispute to a new and more public level. No matter what, only qualified ministers should preach. Mutonis agreed, except to point out that the notary was a fellow Protestant, who presumably would not have made the dispute public. He insisted that Mauget name the person who had accused him of not being a real minister. After considerable debate, the assembled delegates agreed that the matter should be "buried" (*ensepvely*), and the two agreed to reconcile. Fortunately for the consistory, the church of Uzès came to the rescue by requesting Mutonis for itself. But that was not the end of the dispute: in June, it came out that, despite the apparent reconciliation, Mauget had written to Geneva to complain of Mutonis, and several partisans of Mutonis who were members of the consistory attempted to resign. They were persuaded to remain, although ill feelings persisted between the Mauget and Mutonis factions at least until the end of 1561.[17]

At the Nîmes Consistory's first meeting in March, three deacons and ten elders were chosen. Most of them served until the following January, although in late October several of them asked to be relieved of their duties, and one deacon and three elders were indeed replaced. In January 1562, the consistory decided unanimously to nominate ten men to be deacons and twenty to be elders, who would then be asked whether they would accept their positions. Those who did would then be proposed to "the whole body of the Church, and those who had taken part in Holy Communion and had placed themselves under the ecclesiastical discipline, would choose five of the ten [nominees for] deacons, and ten of the twenty elders." (Note that the consistory had decided to increase the number of deacons from four to five.) On February 25, the election was carried out. First, the "women, children and foreigners" left, leaving "all the men received into the Church." They first discussed how to attract more pastors to Nîmes, since the church was too big for Guillaume Mauget alone. They then proceeded to the election, which was done by "marks made on the roll of names and surnames of the deacons and elders which had been shown to all those present in the assembly." Those who were "found to have the plurality of voices" were declared to be elected.[18]

In the elections, upper-middling men triumphed. Figure 6.1 shows the average social status (calculated by using the average dowries of marriages they attended) of the officers of the first consistory when it was established in March

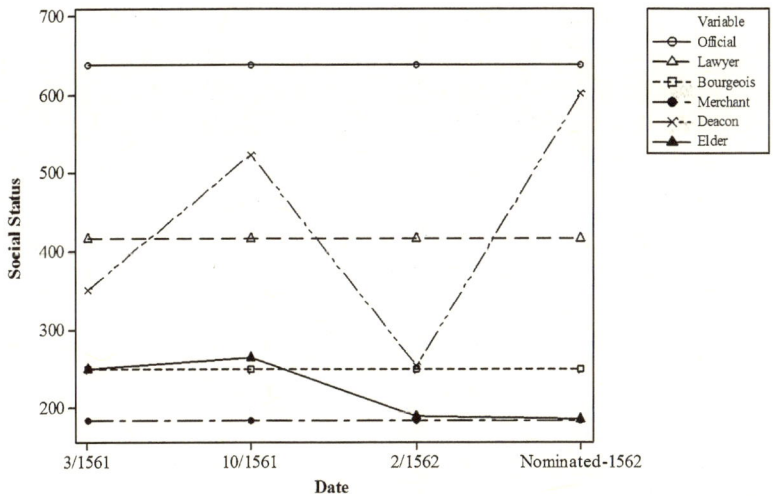

FIGURE 6.1. Consistory elections, 1561–1562. Social status of deacons and elders. Sources: CR, ADG, Series IIE.

1561, the first consistory after it was partially remodeled in October 1561, and the second consistory after the February 1562 elections. The figure also shows the average social status of those who were nominated for the second consistory but not elected. For comparison, the figure also gives the average social status for a few relevant professions. As the figure shows, deacons consistently had a higher social status number than did elders. Elders had an average social status, similar to merchants and bourgeois. Simon Campanhan, a lawyer with a high social status, was chosen in October to become a deacon, replacing Étienne George, a *praticien*. In January, Campanhan left to become a minister. As a result, in the post-October consistory, the average social status of the three deacons increased dramatically; but otherwise, the average social status number of the deacons was below that of lawyers and officials. So, although all of the deacons were lawyers, they were not very rich lawyers, that is, they were below-average lawyers in social status. Furthermore, when elections were held for the second consistory, the nod went consistently to lower-status men, although the consistory had nominated many wealthy lawyers to the prestigious position of deacon.

It is hard to say why the members of the church chose the way they did. For example, the consistory nominated Charles Rozel for both deacon and elder, showing their high opinion of him (he was the only man so honored). Although he and his brother Pierre had been for some time important champions of the Protestant cause in local politics, he was only elected to be an elder, not a deacon. It is possible that the triumph of the upper-middling sorts was made easier because several important people in Nîmes, including Guillaume Calvière the younger, the son of the president of the présidial court, refused to run despite receiving the honor of being nominated. However, some prominent people—including the wealthy lawyer Pierre de Monteils—did accept nomination but lost the election. In the end, the elders included four merchants, a *greffier*, a bookseller, an apothecary, and a farmer (*laboureur*). The consistory remained dominated by men who were at least a notch or two below Nîmes's top elite.[19] The same seems to have been true of the Consistory of Lyon.[20]

Discipline

Nîmes's deacons and elders may not have been among the town's richest lawyers and officials, but they had no fear of their social superiors and meted out stern discipline to many of them. When Guillaume Calvière the younger refused to be nominated as a deacon, the minutes noted that he did so for "highly frivolous reasons," while Jacques Audron, a member of the présidial court, was criticized for not paying his dues to the poor box, for missing church, for refusing to lodge soldiers that the consistory had assigned to him, and for not replacing the Catholic priest in the village of Marguerites with a Protestant minister, although he was the seigneur there. He at first objected, saying (for example) that his servants in Marguerites didn't want to hear a minister, but the consistory was adamant, and he agreed to do his duty.[21] Even Pierre and Charles Rozel were not exempt: Charles was criticized for not putting a Protestant minister in a church to which he had the rights, while Pierre, a member of the présidial, was accused of having his child baptized by a Catholic priest after having been received into the Protestant Church. They too eventually agreed to accept the consistory's correction.[22]

The consistory was equally tough with long-time members. The notary Jacques Ursi probably wrote the first letter from the church of Nîmes to Calvin, in 1547. In 1561, one of the deacons complained that he had heard that Ursi had been carrying on a long-time affair with another man's wife. The consistory called witnesses, who substantiated the story, and Ursi ended up admitting that he had been carrying on the affair for six or seven years. Despite his high status as one of Nîmes's first Protestants, he was excommunicated publicly. Antoine Triati, an elder, was criticized for attending a mass. Roland Vallat, who had stood up at a Nîmes city council meeting in 1560 and at considerable personal risk made a highly Protestant speech, was rebuked for beating his wife and for swearing.[23] In some towns, consistory minutes were censored and their most sensitive cases not written down, but considering how many prominent people were hauled before the Nîmes Consistory, that seems unlikely here.[24]

Nîmes's Protestant judges were not entirely comfortable with the consistory's enforcement of morals. The judges were worried that the consistory was taking power away from them. It is even possible that they were worried about money, since they received fees from their court cases. On October 26, 1562, Guillaume Calvière, the president of the présidial court, presented on behalf of the court an order to the consistory to limit its activities, in order to preserve "the authority of the king and his justice" (*l'autorité du roi et de sa justice*). The consistory, like many others in the Calvinist world, spent a considerable proportion of its time arbitrating disagreements among its members, getting them to withdraw court cases against each other, and making them reconcile their differences. Furthermore, the consistory's cases had some of the flavor of trials, since the consistory called witnesses, put their ages into the minutes just as in legal depositions, and meted out punishments just like judges.[25] Calvière declared that the consistory was prohibited from "making any court, jurisdiction, cognizance, authority or power on the subjects of the king because of differences, controversies, and criminal cases . . . among each other." If the consistory disobeyed the order, it could suffer a £1,000 fine. Protestants were permitted, outside of the consistory, to urge the parties in a Christian fashion not to hate each other on account of any legal proceedings, however. And they were permitted to use excommunication to repress "scandals, atrocious or public faults, whose cognizance and correction could appertain to them according to ecclesiastical doctrine regulated by the Word of God and the Holy Scriptures, without departing from their limits." But the consistory could not make laws and compel members of the church to observe them, nor could it make ecclesiastical ordinances that might lead to "superstition or profanation of things instituted by God." Ministers also had to have permission from the magistrates before taking up their duties, and no synods or consistories could be held without the magistrates' express permission.

Based on the shocked tone of the court order, the judges had probably not imagined this danger when they converted. Despite what Calvière said, the order did not have royal approval: the crown would hardly have recommended that disputes be settled by the word of God. But the language of the order shows that the présidial members did not know that the discipline of the Reformed churches limited the judicial character of consistorial proceedings, since they did not mention it.[26] The whole episode suggests that the magistrates were still unsure of the role of the consistory in a newly Protestant society.

The consistory responded mildly that it "had not thought to contravene the proposed articles and prohibitions . . . and therefore there was no need to present them, but would take them in good part, since it was the court's intention to maintain the obedience of the king's subjects."[27] But the consistory's answer, despite its conciliatory tone, in fact promised nothing. Furthermore, even after this incident, the consistory never asked permission before nominating its ministers or holding its meetings. Nor did it restrict the scope of its activities.

The consistory did not obtain absolute power in Nîmes. First of all, it did take a number of steps to appease the political and judicial authorities. Most notably, in its proceedings it drew a clear division between religious and political matters. The Protestant movement set up the Council of Twenty-Four, which later became the Council of Sixteen, to discuss political affairs, and its members were almost entirely judges and members of the city council, exactly the sort of people who were generally not made members of the consistory.[28] Second, there were occasions when the consistory let its hand be forced, for example, when Protestants began to seize churches in the fall of 1561. The evidence suggests that some prominent people were involved. The consistory was highly uncomfortable with violence and condemned such actions, although it did vote 7–5 to accept the first church to be seized. Finally, there were important episodes where its opinion was simply ignored.[29] However, it must be remembered that, at the same time, on a nationwide scale, religious issues rose to paramount importance, as the country plunged into a civil war between Catholics and Protestants. Nîmes's consistory was rapidly becoming an important institution within the national Protestant movement and received letters and messengers from important national Protestant leaders, although it usually turned to the Council of Twenty-Four to help it decide what to do when it received them.

Despite these significant limitations, the consistory's powers should not be underestimated. First of all, it succeeded in making Calvinist discipline popular: thousands of people turned out to hear sermons preaching moral reform. But people who were enthusiastic about moral discipline in the abstract were not necessarily happy when the consistory focused on their own behavior. Many people brought up for censure were initially truculent, and some refused to submit to the consistory's authority. But most did, despite the consistory's middling social composition. In a highly hierarchical, stratified society, this is quite impressive. The consistory succeeded in creating a climate where community pressure supplemented its own sanctions. Although the most the consistory could do was to bar people from communion, in Nîmes that was sufficient.[30]

The reasons for the consistory's success are not entirely clear, since the laity had no forum in which to testify why they abided by its decisions. Nonetheless, some features of this story are suggestive. First of all, the consistory seems to have been quite impartial, reproving its own members, long-term Protestant supporters, and people from all classes of society. Second, much of what it did was positive and helpful for the parties, since many of its cases involved reconciling people—although mediators are not always welcome. Similarly, the consistory may have received considerable credit for its energetic efforts to help the poor. Poor relief had been a major concern of Nîmes's city council for decades, and municipal leaders were no doubt happy to be relieved of this burden. However, the consistory had to force its members to contribute to the church poor box, which may not have been universally popular. Finally, it may have helped the consistory that its members were not part of Nîmes's upper crust. They could not so easily be accused of using religion to enforce social hierarchy. When they called people to account, they may not have appeared to be agents of the crown or of the elite, but what they claimed to be, namely, humble servants of the Lord.[31]

Taking Over Catholic Churches

Just as there were disputes within the consistory, the consistory found it difficult to get all Protestants to follow the leadership's political policy. Some

Protestants did not always live up to the consistory's high moral standards, and some were also prone to attacking Catholic churches despite the consistory's repeated orders not to do so. The consistory was well aware of the danger of civil war, and it was concerned about the potential for conflicts to escalate. In the heady atmosphere of 1561, when the Protestant movement was making such dramatic gains, hotheads wanted to take matters into their own hands and force the consistory to take a more radical approach. The consistory was delighted by the movement's success, but it did not feel that seizing churches was in the movement's immediate best interests. It firmly attempted to restrain violence, insisting that attacking churches or the established order was wrong and dangerous. In response to a letter from the Protestants of Montpellier on August 9, 1561, the Nîmes Consistory categorically proscribed iconoclasm, saying, "Temples should not be taken without having had a response from the Court." The consistory also decided the same day that "M. Mauget shall admonish the assembly to avoid any sedition on Fridays and other papist holidays, and to admonish them to obey the magistrate in such things which are not contrary to the Word of God and the Confession of Faith." It is necessary to note the qualification here, namely, that Protestants were not bound to obey the magistrate in things that were against the word of God, but the instruction not to interfere with Catholic festivals is much more direct and specific. Furthermore, the consistory repeatedly tried to prevent violence in the months that followed.[32]

Another example of the consistory's wary attitude toward the Catholic Church was the debate about *censives,* liens on private property sometimes held by the Church. Pierre Fournier, a lawyer, asked if he had to pay his *censive* of 25s. to the cathedral chapter, "seeing that the foundation is of the adversary." The consistory decided that he should protest to the civil authorities and ask to pay the money to the poor instead. This might be seen as a tactic, since it preserved the principle that Fournier, and others like him, might have to pay, while giving them an excuse to protest. At the same meeting, however, Étienne George, a *praticien* (legal clerk) and the secretary to the consistory, asked if he could continue to accept business from the Catholic Church, and he was told that he could not.[33] If Protestants gained the right to protest certain payments, thus permitting them to defy authority, that right was both circumscribed and enhanced by context. The new doctrines did not give Protestants the right to do whatever they wanted, but it did give them moral justification so that they could feel that their resistance was principled and not self-interested.

Nonetheless, Protestant mobs attacked Catholic churches at least four times in the fall of 1561, on September 29 (Michaelmas, an important market day in Nîmes) and December 8, 15, and 21. At first, people seem to have resorted to violence for simple, pragmatic reasons: to acquire a place to hold religious services. Over the following months, however, the violence increased and the rioters enlarged their objectives. They wanted Nîmes to become a Protestant town, and they wanted its architecture, its institutions and officeholders, and even its sights and sounds to reflect its conversion.

The first attack, in September, was remarkably restrained. A crowd gathered at the Church of the Cordeliers and demanded admittance, insisting that Protestant services be held there. The crowd did not threaten violence and even offered to let the monks preach there as well, after the Protestant service. The monks refused and prepared to depart, but the crowd insisted that they did not want the possessions of the church, only the space, and, acting on a suggestion from consistory officials who had heard of the disturbance, called for town officials to inventory the church's furnishings, which they refused to do because they did not want to lend any support to the mob's actions. Notaries were called in to put that refusal on the record, which probably pleased both parties: the officials because it was clear that they had refused to take part in illegal activity, and the crowd because it showed that they had tried to act in an orderly fashion. The Protestants in the crowd insisted that they seized the church simply because "n'y avoit lieu" (there hadn't been [a] place).[34] Seizing the church was an expedient solution. People were no longer prepared to meet in private gardens or, more likely, the crowds had grown so large that no private space could hold them. They needed the room. It is unlikely that the Protestant leadership was secretly in favor of the seizure: it is hard to believe that the consistory's explicit statements in its own private records were meant to be disobeyed. Consistory records do show that "several gentlemen" were involved. But there is no evidence that the consistory had a hand in provoking the attack, and once it began, the consistory intervened, trying to restrain the process. Furthermore, although the leadership accepted the church that had been seized on its behalf, with the explanation, "seeing that it has been taken without riot and the necessity we are in," the leaders resolved to punish the offenders. Indeed, only a bare majority of the consistory supported taking the church at all: the vote was 7–5. The minority insisted that the church belonged to the Cordeliers and should be returned to them.[35]

A number of historians have commented that people who resorted to attacks on churches in the sixteenth century frequently implied that they acted to purify the community by ridding it of idolatry. In Nîmes, because Protestantism became the religion of the majority, people did not necessarily need to drive out others to purify the community. Instead, attacks on churches were a way of purging the memory of Catholicism from the community. People wanted to purify themselves as much as rid the community of outside pollution. Attacking churches was a way of marking a liminal moment, that is, a line in time dividing their sinful past from their spiritually reborn present. A good example of this occurred immediately after the seizure of the Cordeliers' church. The priests had departed and the church was in Protestant hands, but some Protestant extremists were not satisfied. On the night of October 5, 1561, they destroyed the stained-glass windows of the church. The consistory, again the agent of restraint, had to put a guard on its new church by night, to protect it from further vandalism. Thus, the violence appears self-directed, an attempt at self-purification. Indeed, it is easy to imagine that a Protestant might consider it scandalous for a *Protestant* church to contain idolatrous symbols. The consistory itself was equally aware that the church needed to be remodeled for Protestant worship and set about hiring carpenters to accomplish the task.[36]

The following week, Pierre Viret arrived in Nîmes for a visit. He was one of the most important Calvinist clergymen and the pastor of Lausanne. His arrival was both a sign of the Nîmes Protestant community's growing importance and a major addition to its strength: he was one of the most powerful preachers of the era. Officially, he was in the south of France for his health, but that did not stop him from lending a hand. He preached in the newly acquired church on October 8.[37]

In Nîmes, people wanted rapid signs of civic conversion, of a collective assertion of the new order wiping away the old. In early November, the consistory resolved, at the behest of Pierre Chabot, one of the more radical members, to ask for the control of more churches. In particular, it decided to ask for "the large temple in the center of town," obviously the new code phrase for the cathedral.[38] Not only did it want to change the religious symbolism of the city's very structure, starting at its heart, but the consistory even refused to admit that a cathedral actually existed. Toward the end of 1561, the situation clearly spiraled out of control, not just for the town but even for the consistory. On December 8, the consistory censured Pierre Gaubert, probably a saddler; his brother Bessede, a cordwainer; and Pierre Bertrand, a baker, after an attack on the Church of the Augustinians, in which people damaged relics and the altars. The Church of the Augustinians was the third most popular church in Nîmes, after the cathedral and the Dominican Church (based on requests in wills for burials there). Taking it over for Protestant worship was particularly symbolic. Nonetheless, the consistory censured the militants who attacked it. From the occupations of the rioters, it seems that they were of relatively low status, although it would be rash to rely too much on such slim evidence. Undoubtedly, the crowd that attacked the church was much larger than the three people the consistory was able to find, or chose to punish. Even so, the consistory's action is further evidence of its cautious attitude. The consistory's relation to the laity in this, however, was marked by the same tensions and negotiations that were evident in morals cases. Five days after censuring the three men, the consistory warned the magistrates to tell the bishop that he must not "provoke the people by the loud clanging of his bells and the multitude of his masses."[39] The consistory appears to have recognized that it could not restrain its more hotheaded members too much without losing its legitimacy. At the same time, it could also use their actions to further the Protestant cause.

The consistory was unable to resist the temptation to accept the property the extremists had seized on its behalf. Some members may even have felt, despite the official line, that the churches really belonged to the body of the Christian church at large, that is, to them. But the behavior of the militants who attacked the churches is also noteworthy. It seems clear that the noise of church bells was annoying Protestant hotheads, since a contemporary diarist makes repeated references to them.[40] The bells were, of course, important for religious purposes, summoning the faithful to mass as well as announcing the hours. Like religious processions, however, they also both fostered and symbolized civic unity, representing the religious glue that held society together. Pierre Goubert, in his celebrated study of Beauvais, for example, uses the town's bell towers to symbolize the authority of its bishop and clergy.[41] But the town of Nîmes had its own clock tower, which regularly summoned councillors to town meetings, for example. Such towers were major, costly feats of engineering and sources of great civic pride for their communities. The concern over the bells thus suggests that townspeople did not like being reminded of the Catholic Church's importance in the life of the town. Its bells commanded attention, perhaps overshadowing the town's own bells, and reminded them of how integral it had once been in their lives. Eliminating the bells would be one more way to symbolically cleanse Nîmes of its Catholic past.

On the night of December 15, a crowd demanded to see the bishop, accusing him of preaching blasphemy. Several notables, including Pierre and Charles Rozel and François de Montcalm, the seigneur de Saint Véran, attempted to meet with the new bishop, Bernard d'Elbène (he had just exchanged positions with Claude Briçonnet, who became bishop of Lodève in d'Elbène's place). The bishop initially refused all compromise, but the following morning, he gave in. After a long meeting held in the présidial courtroom, he agreed to hand over two more churches, St. Eugénie and the Church of the Augustinians, for Protestant use. Protestant crowds had gathered outside the room in order to bring additional pressure to bear.[42]

The bishop's concessions did not stem the tide. On the seventeenth, the consistory again declared that it was unjust to seize Catholic churches. It decided to call in the most prominent members of the assemblies and admonish them to control themselves. Nonetheless, on December 21, after hearing Pierre Viret preach, a group of young people (*enfants*) peeked inside the door of the cathedral and mocked the preacher, calling him "le Beguinier." After several attempts to chase them away, the officials of the cathedral began to use their fists. At this point, a crowd waiting outside descended on the church and, assisted by several notables, destroyed all of the idolatrous images and forced the bishop to flee. The frenzy then extended to the town's remaining Catholic churches. After remaining in hiding for two days, sheltered by the special lieutenant of the présidial, Jacques de Rochemaure, and its president, Guillaume Calvière, the bishop left for Arles. By the twenty-fourth, Viret was preaching in the cathedral "with great tranquility."[43]

Charity

Protestants who seized churches made it easier to evangelize the population, gave the new religion legitimacy, and purged the town of its Catholic past. As the militants took over the churches, the Protestant community was also learning new forms of worship and new behaviors that marked their entry into their new way of life. One of the most noticeable changes was a burst of charitable giving. Ever since Luther, Protestants had criticized monks who lived on charity. The able-bodied should work, and scarce resources should be reserved for the poor who really needed help. In Nîmes, where many people had been suffering from bad economic times for years, it is not surprising that the population was greatly concerned about the poor. Protestantism promised the people of Nîmes that they could master the problem of poverty. This was by no means an exclusively Protestant concern: humanist Catholics and Protestants shared similar ideas on the subject.[44] Nonetheless, it is significant that, at the consistory's first meeting, the leaders of the Protestant movement chose the merchant Arnaud Alizot as treasurer for the poor. Alizot was almost certainly one of the first and most distinguished Protestants in Nîmes, having been charged by the Parlement of Toulouse with heresy as early as 1537. His appointment suggests that the consistory cared a great deal about poor relief. Jacques Nicolas, also a merchant, was chosen to be Alizot's *controlleur*, that is, to watch over his handling of the money. The consistory was determined to establish a reputation for fiscal honesty.

From the beginning, the consistory devoted a great deal of time and attention to poor relief. On April 5, for example, the consistory chose the first people to receive assistance, apparently because they were ill: Panse, a cordwainer; the widow du Pegue; Jean Poulon; and "a poor man in M. Sigalon's district," who was to receive 10s. each week (the range was 5–10s.). Four distinguished women were appointed to search out the poor in their districts and to distribute the alms.[45]

Protestants devised another new means to give to charity: through wills. Help for the poor had also been a part of Catholic wills (see Chapter 1). Typically, poor people would be paid to lead the funeral procession, holding candles and wearing new clothes that they could keep afterward. The deceased also sometimes willed money to distribute bread to the poor on the day of the funeral and on important anniversaries. But most wills did not provide such arrangements. Although early Protestants knew they had to give to charity, the precise mechanisms took some time to be worked out. As early as August 1561, there is evidence that the clients of one notary, Antoine Sabatier, began to feel a new religious imperative to give to charity. Guidon des Georges, for example, made his will on November 13, 1561. It was one of the earliest explicitly Protestant wills in Nîmes, but he used relatively traditional Catholic forms of charitable giving.[46] The consistory established a poor fund, a *bource des pouvres*, at some point in 1561. The first reference to it is indirect, when in early August the consistory decided to fine latecomers to meetings 5s. and give the money to the poor. Starting in the fall of 1561, Protestants began to leave legacies to the poor fund. Giving eventually became nearly universal, at least for clients of some notaries. Just around the time of the iconoclastic episodes, testators who went to Jacques Ursi to make their wills, regardless of social class, began to give alms to the poor. In late February 1562, the consistory decided to remind all the town's notaries to ask testators to remember the poor.[47] After this point, giving increased among the clients of several of Nîmes's notaries, and testators began to mention specifically that their alms should go to the "poor fund" (*bource des pouvres*) or the "poor fund of the Reformed Church of Nîmes" (*bource des pouvres de l'église réformée de Nîmes*). For example, only three of the forty-seven wills drawn up by the notary Jean Mombel in the period 1557–1561 contain any bequests for the poor, but ten of the fourteen drawn up in 1562 and early 1563 do. The amounts vary widely in size: Claude Granié, a weaver, left £1 to the *bource de l'église réformée de Nîmes* before going off on military service, while a traveling provençal seigneur, Antoine de la Roque, left £1,300 to the consistory of Lambesc, his native village. He directed that the consistory use £1,000 either for the poor or to purchase land for a cemetery, at its discretion, and the remaining £300 to provide dowries for poor girls.[48]

Testators were, of course, not required to make bequests, and some began to make them before they were asked to do so. Nor was giving to the poor a new idea: this system probably derived from one popularized by the town of Ypres and endorsed by the Sorbonne as early as 1531.[49] It was not specifically Protestant, although it probably appealed to the new Protestant community at least in part because of its civic character. What is striking is that ordinary Protestants so enthusiastically followed the consistory's suggestion. Ideals, however widely shared, are not always followed in practice. The enthusiasm suggests that people in Nîmes had wanted to do something about poverty for a long time, and now felt that they knew how to solve the problem.

Developing a Protestant Identity

It was in the fall of 1561, when Nîmes was bursting with civic unrest and charitable giving, that the Reformation really took hold in the town. Much more Protestant phraseology began to appear at this time in wills and marriage contracts, showing the Nîmes population's changing religious commitments.[50] Just at the time when preaching moved out from private spaces and into the public sphere, Protestants started acting together in public, and during the period when some aggressive Protestants banded together to take over the town's churches, Nîmes's notarial acts showed, for the first time, people using Protestant language. The timing was not accidental: religious identity seems to have emerged collectively, through the experiences of preaching and iconoclasm. These activities forged a sense of cohesion and turned the movement into a community. Clients of Louis Grimaldi and Guillaume Duchamp stopped being married "before Holy Mother Church" in the second half of 1561, some months after the phrase disappeared from Jean Ménard's registers.[51] As if to emphasize the directness of the link between the Protestant soul and God, many wills recorded simply "having invoked the name of God" (*invoqué le nom de Dieu*) instead of making the sign of the cross.[52] It was also in November 1561 that the first will mentioned the Reformed Church (*Église Réformée*),[53] although the consistory had been founded seven months earlier. Finally, it was at this point that people started to express their hope that they would be among God's chosen (the elect, or *esleus*).[54] When people expressed the hope that they would be among God's chosen people, they were of course stating their adherence to a crucial Calvinist theological concept. But this self-understanding was equally important to developing a Protestant identity, a sense of distinctness from the Catholics around them. Chosenness operated hand in hand with Calvin's theology of the Eucharist to mark the community. Both also reinforced the powerful sixteenth-century tendency to be suspicious of outsiders. Some of the earliest references to the Reformed Church do not refer to it as such. Instead, they refer to it as the local church: for example, Glaude Bernaudon, in his will of November 8, 1561, asked to be buried "where it is the custom to bury those of the Christian Church of the said Nîmes." Similarly, a Protestant from a nearby village who came to a Nîmes notary to make up his will asked to be buried according to "the good custom of Milhau." Many people in Nîmes seem to have been pleased to see that the new church was under greater local control.[55]

Many people in Nîmes slipped into Protestantism and then erected an imaginary line separating themselves from Catholics afterward. For some, the line remained fuzzy for a considerable time. Ysabel Mantesse wrote her will on October 17, 1563, well after iconoclasm had destroyed the religious images that, to Protestants, signified idolatry and papist superstition and after the members of the convents and monasteries had been chased out of town. By this time, Protestants in Nîmes had become accustomed to referring to the Reformed Church and to leaving the term "Catholic" to their opponents. Yet, in her will, Mantesse declared not only that she "wishes to live and die in the Christian and Catholic faith," but also described that faith as "such as has been taught to us by the Word of our Lord Jesus Christ in his holy Gospel." For her, there was not yet a total rupture between the two faiths: she retained faith in the word "Catholic" at the same time as she insisted on the rigor of biblicism. Similarly, another testator "recommended his soul to our Lord Jesus Christ, Creator and Redeemer of the World, let it please Him by the merit of His holy Passion to have pity and mercy on him and place him among his Chosen [or elect], invoking all the Celestial Court of Paradise to pray for him."[56] Here, we see a typical Calvinist view of salvation, where it is simply God's *choice*, not our merits, that determines our fate, combined with a decidedly Catholic view of the value of intermediaries.[57] It would probably be an error, however, to view these people as emotionally torn between Protestantism and Catholicism. Instead, it is likely that they had an emotional identification with Protestantism but were not fully aware of Protestant doctrines, or felt that they were not required to subscribe to all of the new religion's doctrines even if they identified with it.

Well-informed Protestants knew that their movement disdained symbolism of the sort that was common in sixteenth-century France. Ysabel Mantesse, who insisted in her will that she refused to be buried with any "superstition," showed it clearly, and changing attitudes toward charity, discussed above, also demonstrated it.[58] Protestant wills never called for trappings like the colored tapers borne by priests or paupers in front of the caskets in Catholic funerals. Contemporary documents rarely showed Protestants even discussing visual elements or the choreography of their rituals. Their movement disdained Catholic funeral and holiday processions, which were so important for late medieval piety and which helped to bind urban communities. Protestants replaced all this with ceremonies that exalted the pure word of God: they gathered to hear their ministers preach and to sing the psalms of David together, in French so that more people could understand their meaning. The ingrained habits of generations did not change overnight, however, and it was important to some people that civic pageantry come to reflect the new order. On November 1, 1561, the Protestant Consistory debated the question of the hats worn by the officers of the présidial, the highest judicial officials in town and collectively its most prestigious body. They ruled decisively and typically: "concerning the square bonnets, no one can be constrained, as a thing indifferent."[59] Hats were irrelevant. Despite this, according to Jean Deyron, a contemporary diarist, "on Friday the 23rd [of January 1562] Messieurs of the présidial seat, having abandoned the rounded square bonnets, began to wear bonnets with facings, and with them held the session." Apparently, according to another contemporary diarist, the old hats were considered "papal" or "papist."[60] Once converted to the new church, Nîmes Protestants felt obligated to reexamine every part of their pasts, to rip out idolatry root and branch. Excessive zeal was preferable to a moment's laxness. The officers of the présidial had a prominent place in civic processions, for example when the town's officials and citizens marched outside the gates to welcome visiting dignitaries. By changing their dress, they would now symbolize the purification of the social order.

Robert Sauzet has suggested that the people of Nîmes attacked Catholic churches despite the repeatedly expressed wishes of their clerical and lay leaders because "the plebeian followers of the Reformation remained permeated by traditional concepts relative to commerce with sacred objects," which had played a greater role in their religious practices than the more intellectual devotion of the elite.[61] It seems clear that the elite were less likely to commit iconoclasm than the common people. Few of the Protestant hotheads seem to have been rich. It does not follow that the hotheads were more superstitious, however. Iconoclasm is a straightforward consequence of Protestant theology, which (following Deuteronomy) abhorred a local representation of God, whether in a statue or in a wafer. What is surprising is that the consistory should have been so reluctant to seize the churches, compared to the Protestant crowd that did so repeatedly. It is true that the leadership had an interest in preserving respect for authority. They were also more likely to know the doctrines of the new religion, which forbade violent attacks on churches. But the leadership also had a different history than that of many ordinary members of the Protestant movement. Analysis of wills shows that most people in Nîmes had only recently committed themselves firmly to Protestantism. By contrast, consistory members in 1561 were by definition people whose faith burned bright and strong and who had made a conscious commitment, through the offices they held, to the new religion. Unlike the leaders of the consistory, many ordinary Protestants were raw recruits to the movement whose memories of participating in Catholic ceremonies were uncomfortably fresh. If they passed a Catholic church, they were reminded that they had worshiped at the temple of Baal only a short while before. After all, according to Protestant orthodoxy, Catholicism was not just imperfect, but the pope was the Antichrist himself. Thus, converts to Protestantism had to believe that, prior to their conversion, they had sinned most gravely indeed. When they saw a statue in the Augustinian Church, they may have felt considerable guilt. One resolution of this cognitive dissonance was to wipe out the object that brought back the memory of the experience. By contrast, the leaders of the consistory were almost certainly more secure in their religious identities and therefore did not feel a need to erase their pasts. They also had a better sense of the larger political picture and realized that they could suffer considerable harm if they dared to take violent and inflammatory measures. The hotheads destroyed the idols not because they were afraid of the symbols' power, but because they had guilty consciences.

The attack on the cathedral on December 21, immediately after church services, is a good example of this kind of thinking. People in the ambiguous position of new converts or even not-quite converts might naturally feel a certain need to repent as they left church. Furthermore, Calvinist doctrine specifically equated conversion and repentance:

> The whole of conversion to God is understood under the term "repentance." ... The meaning [of conversion] is that, departing from ourselves, we turn to God, and having taken off our former mind, we put on a new. ... it is the true turning of our life to God, a turning that arises from a pure and earnest fear of him; and it consists in the mortification of our flesh and of the old man [the Devil], and in the vivification of the Spirit.[62]

In a relatively brief span of time the people of Nîmes had developed a radically new perspective on their own experience. Before, they had believed they were worshiping holiness. Now, they saw that they had been bowing before corruption and contamination. In moving against the clergy, they were attacking those who had misinformed them. In moving to destroy the symbols of Catholicism, they were wiping clean the slate of their own past, purifying themselves so that they could start anew. It might have been more satisfying to seize Catholic buildings than to build new, Protestant ones, because the act of seizure symbolized the cleansing process. The reverse was not true for Catholics, since for them Protestantism was an intrusion: it would be better to destroy the evidence of Protestant heresy. Protestants believed that their faith superseded Catholicism, while Catholics believed that Protestantism was yet another of the devil's attempts to seduce the hearts of men.

By early 1562, the citizens of Nîmes were clearly trying to create a godly republic. In some ways, this can be seen as a manifestation of age-old localist tendencies and an equally common resistance to paying taxes and tithes. Through mass town council meetings; by listening to their pastors, Mauget and Viret; and, finally, through acts of iconoclastic violence, they had reaffirmed their civic consciousness. They had created a sense of belonging, of community. But how had they changed their beliefs and their behavior?

The first noteworthy point is that the people of Nîmes did not use iconoclasm to scapegoat some outside "other" for their problems. They did not consider marching against the nearby papal stronghold of Avignon, for example. Rather, their concerns were internal: how to make their souls obey a clearly defined moral code. Catholicism also instilled a strong moral code, but the Protestants of Nîmes were clearly morally invigorated by their conversions, proceeding with particular energy to regulate their own social behavior. They supported the consistory's efforts collectively, although individually they might often object when their church criticized their own behavior. The content of Protestant morality was not that different from Catholic morality. Adultery, quarreling, swearing, and other such activities had never been viewed with favor. However, the new emphasis on sincerity required that the townspeople attempt to make reality correspond to their ideas, and they used the institutions they had to do so.

If there is anything specifically Protestant about Nîmes's efforts at moral reform, it is the zeal with which people tried to make their speech and their actions transparent and consistent. Roland Vallat's bluntly honest speech to the town council, discussed in Chapter 4, is an example of this attitude: if people would only speak with excruciating candor, nothing could be hidden. Do not use symbols like elaborate funeral processions to imply that someone was virtuous, for an evil person could easily have himself clothed in the same trappings of sanctity. Through their cahier and their consistory, the people of Nîmes were trying to make their behavior correspond with their principles or, in other words, to live a self-examined life.[63]

The Growth of the Protestant Movement

Throughout 1561 and early 1562, the Protestant movement continued to persuade more and more people in Nîmes to join its ranks. One sign of the growth of the new church was that, starting in August 1561, Mauget and the Church of

Nîmes wrote urgent letters to Geneva to request an additional pastor.[64] In order to understand who was entering the Protestant community during the year following the adoption of the cahier, I compiled a list of every person mentioned in the consistory records, other than the initial leadership discussed above, from its founding on March 23, 1561, through February 28, 1562.[65] Some of these individuals first appeared or spoke at a meeting in this period; others were brought before the consistory because of some moral lapse or because they were poor and were thought worthy of receiving charity. Many of the references are fragmentary, and others could not be identified with sufficient certainty in the database, but in all 113 (7 of them women) could be. The results are given in Appendix A.

Judging from the statistics, the trends noted at the beginning of this chapter only accelerated in 1561–1562, even though the group under examination here was not composed of leaders per se. By 1562, the percentage of lawyers among the Protestants had increased even beyond what it was in 1561, and the percentage of high-status individuals (officials, seigneurs, etc.) was much higher than ever before. The obvious explanation is that officials had far more to lose than other members of the elite and therefore required strong persuasion. By 1562, the social pressure to convert must have been very strong. By contrast, the percentage of agricultural workers dropped even further. The movement had never had much success in that class, and the few farmers it had attracted were drowned by the flood of new, more desirable recruits. The

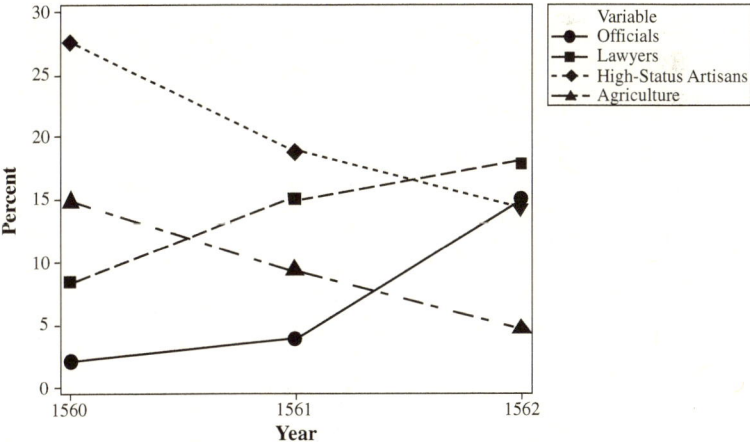

FIGURE 6.2. Changes in the Composition of the Protestant movement: key occupations, 1560–1562. Sources: ADHG, Series B, Geisendorf, Puech, CR.

effect of the rising average status among committed Protestants can be seen if we examine the political careers of the men who joined the church in 1561–1562. Of the 106 new recruits, 22 became consuls, several of them twice, a much larger percentage than in earlier years. Furthermore, while early Protestants were commonly elected third or fourth consul, in this group of new recruits 70 percent became first or second consul, the more prestigious positions.[66] In short, at each stage, Protestantism grew by climbing the social hierarchy, attracting ever more prominent, wealthy, and influential supporters. The trends shown here explain why the city council became pro-Protestant (or, at least, unwilling to engage in the persecution of Protestants) a full year before the présidial.

By 1562, Protestantism had made substantial inroads among Nîmes's most elite families. Of the top 249 families in Nîmes, more than one-third had at least one Protestant member.[67] Among them, the same trends can be seen as among Protestants generally. Protestants were especially numerous in wealthy, prestigious professions, while Protestants were a small minority among those agricultural families wealthy enough to be classified among the elite (see figure 6.3). Protestants at this point were still a minority, but a large one. Given their growth among the most prestigious professions, however, their eventual success was predictable.

In 1564, shortly after Pierre Viret visited Nîmes, he published his summa of Christian theology, *Christian Instruction,* one volume of which he dedicated to the Nîmes Protestant community. In his dedication, he gave a brief description

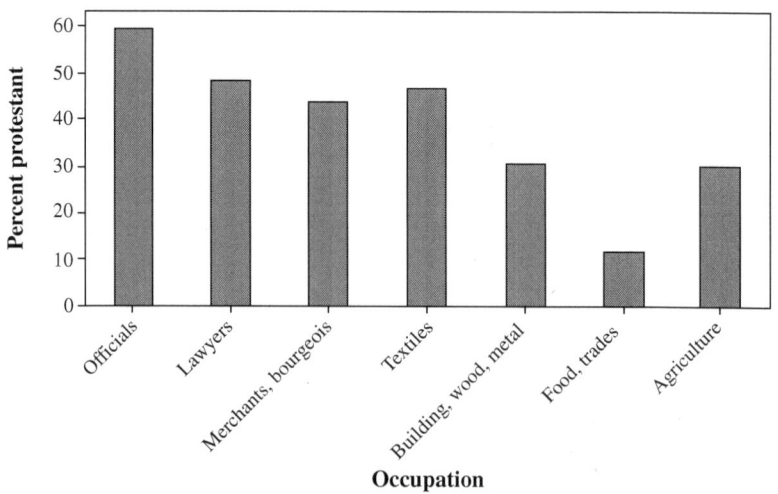

FIGURE 6.3. Protestants among elite families, 1562.

of his impressions of the community. His views conveniently summarized the nature of the Protestant movement at this period.[68] Viret was impressed by what he saw. Indeed, he complimented his hosts by urging them to "persevere always from good to better," which was, as noted earlier, the kindest comment that consistory members gave to each other in the *grabaud*. He also complimented them on their obedience to royal authority. But he closed by making the following comment:

> And insofar as among the other material treated in this volume, it contains a very ample exposition of the Law which God gave to His people, it has seemed to me that I had so much a better reason to dedicate it to you, considering the state of your city. For there are a good and large number of learned men, in your College and in your Présidial Court, who almost entirely make a profession of the law, and the science of law, which is most noble, and most useful and necessary to the Republic, when behavior is well regulated by the laws, and principally by the rule of the Law of God, on which all others must be based.[69]

During 1560 and 1561, the lawyers and officials of Nîmes had to become persuaded of just this point, that their reverence for their profession should include an appreciation for the divine source of legal thinking. In Viret's conception, the crown was not the font of justice, and naturally he would not suggest that it came from the Catholic Church. Rather, as Viret's book proceeded to discuss in detail, God's law came directly from the Bible, and its texts could be analyzed to determine what the law was. Just as Calvin taught in his doctrine of the Eucharist that faith in God, not the intercession of the priest, gave the sacrament its power, the crown did not give the law its power and authority. The power of the law came from God, and it was available to anyone who had the learning to study God's word. It is difficult to know whether Viret's dedication mirrored the thinking of the men he was addressing, but at the very least he presented a powerful argument that was well suited for convincing royal officeholders, including the members of the présidial, that they should follow their consciences rather than the will of the king who had appointed them. Nîmes's elite was more likely to be targeted for prosecution if they converted to Protestantism, and its values emphasized harmony and solidarity—unsurprising, since those on top have every reason to desire stability. The cahier persuaded them because its ideology appealed to them and because it was more divisive to resist its enthusiastic supporters than to join with them.[70]

In addition to the cahier and its ideology, the Protestant movement in Nîmes used personal connections to persuade members of the town's elite to convert. Social network analysis makes this clear. As discussed in Chapter 1,

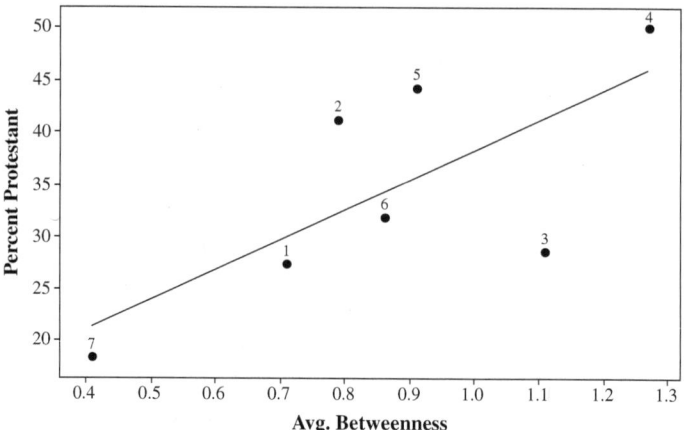

FIGURE 6.4. Betweenness and Protestantism in Nîmes's main factions, 1550–1562. Sources: ADG, Series IIE, ADHG, Series B, Geisendorf, Puech, CR.

Nîmes's elite (defined as its top 249 families) was relatively unified, and its most elite factions had higher betweenness than the others. (As a reminder, "betweenness" shows how well connected people are and is a measure of what sociologists call *brokerage power*.) By 1562, Protestantism had made significant inroads into the elite, since of the 249 elite families, 93 had at least one Protestant member. Despite these impressive gains, one might suppose that Catholicism in Nîmes still had considerable strength, since over 60 percent of the elite families were apparently untouched as yet by heresy. But the Catholic families were distinctly weaker than this raw statistic would suggest, because the 93 Protestant families in Nîmes had higher betweenness than did the 156 Catholic ones and were more prevalent in the factions with higher betweenness. Protestant families had an average betweenness of 1.28, while Catholic ones had an average betweenness of .67. Furthermore, there was a strong correlation between those factions which had the highest betweenness and those which were most Protestant. (The correlation coefficient for the relationship between average betweenness of a faction and the percentage of Protestants in it is .72, with a *p*-value of .07.) There is also some correlation between the wealth of the group and its Protestantism, although this result has a higher *p* value, so it may be due to chance. Faction 7, composed of the 17 small, outlying factions, is the least Protestant and fairly poor. The largest faction, faction 4, was also the richest and included many families closely associated with the présidial court, Nîmes's most prestigious institution. In any case, by early 1562, as figure 6.4

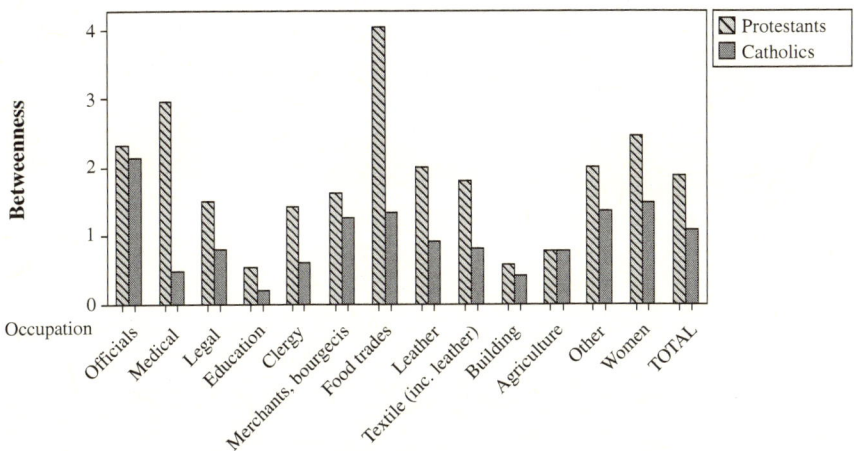

FIGURE 6.5. Comparison of Protestant and Catholic betweenness by occupational category. Sources: ADG, Series IIE, ADHG Series B, Geisendorf, Puech, CR.

suggests, Protestant families had come to dominate the most central positions in the Nîmes elite. Catholics were relegated to more peripheral factions. A modern analogy for this moment in the growth of the Nîmes Protestant movement might be that point in a coup d'état when the coup's organizers have seized the airport, the radio and TV stations, and the presidential palace: even if most of the country remains under the previous government's control, there is no question any more which side will win.

One might suspect that wealthier people would have more social interactions with others and thus higher betweenness. If this were true, it might explain Protestants' high betweenness, since they were better represented in wealthier, more prestigious professions. Interestingly, this is not so. The overall average social status figure for Protestant families is 280 while for Catholics it is 274; the Protestant figure is higher, but only slightly. (Social status was calculated using dowry information. For a more complete description of social status, see Chapter 1 and Appendix B.) Not only did the 93 Protestant families have much higher betweenness scores overall than the 156 other families, this was true regardless of their occupation or wealth. Protestant leather workers were not much wealthier than Catholic ones, but they had much higher betweenness scores. Since betweenness has been shown to be of critical importance in the diffusion of information, high betweenness appears likely to have been a significant asset to the development of the Protestant movement: individuals with high betweenness were likely to be crucial opinion shapers. As has been noted for Normandy, hostile contemporaries frequently accused new Protestants of converting because it was fashionable or faddish, and the betweenness figures suggest that there may have been some truth to this argument.[71]

It is also likely that the leaders of the Protestant movement consciously or unconsciously directed their energies toward converting families with high betweenness, although there is no direct evidence for this theory. Organizing groups need people with wide, diverse networks of friends. For profound, emotional issues like conversion to a new religion, impersonal means such as placards and public preaching are not likely to be successful on their own. Members of the Protestant movement would have sought to make personal contacts with potential converts, because Catholics would be unlikely to join without a sense of connection to the group. Protestants would particularly have wanted to attract, and would naturally have run into, people who could then bring in others—in other words, people with high betweenness. To use another modern analogy to explain this process, consider a group of graduate students trying to form a union. The initial core might come from one academic department (departments here are analogous to occupational groups or factions), and the core members would then meet to come up with contacts in other departments. The core would only know members of other departments who went to lots of interdepartmental gatherings, interdisciplinary seminars, and so forth. Their contact list would therefore naturally concentrate on people with high betweenness, who would also be the best people for their purposes. In short, high betweenness was a natural factor in the organizing process of the Protestant movement in Nîmes, and the existence of high betweenness families made it much easier to convert the bulk of the town. This process may not have been unique to Nîmes, but Nîmes's relatively unified elite (compared to those in other towns) probably helped the movement to succeed.

The Elections for Consul, 1561

The Catholic consuls, imposed by force of arms in late 1560, had found it impossible to impose Catholicism on the people of Nîmes. If the crown had chosen a consistent policy of repression, it is possible that it would have succeeded. However, resentments had built up considerably over the preceding years, and the crown's weakness and indebtedness made it difficult to pursue a military solution to the problem. In any case, under the circumstances prevailing at the end of 1561, it was clear that the monarchy could only keep Catholic consuls in place by force, but the crown was both unwilling and unable to do so. The next consular elections were held on December 6, 1561. Bernard Barrière, the *procureur du roi* at the présidial, took charge of the proceedings. Although he had helped institute the Catholic coup the year before, he explained that it was his duty "to avoid the danger of making the people partial, angry, and seditious."[72] Since the previous year's elections had been irregular, he made a request that this year's elections should be by a special ordinance. Apparently Barrière had switched to the Protestant side and now feared that the new Catholic consuls would simply perpetuate themselves forever. The présidial, apparently with royal permission, therefore ordered that the election proceed by nominating 100 notables to be electors for this one election. Jean Malmazet, the first consul, spoke next, agreeing only under protest, since it was the king's will, to use "a new method" (*une nouvelle façon*) for the elections. "New" was perhaps the ultimate insult in the sixteenth century, and Malmazet's comment bore the same sting that calling Protestantism "the new religion" (*la nouvelle religion*) did. Tellingly, on this occasion, the electors swore to do their duty by the Protestant form of raising their hands, rather than placing them on the Bible.[73]

Although the list of the 100 electors seldom gives occupations, all but 10 of them were identified using the notarial database. However, only 70 electors showed up for the election, and only half of all the Catholics permitted to vote actually did so, while 93 percent of the Protestants did.[74] Still, it can hardly be said that the Protestant movement, whatever hand it had in drawing up the list of electors, was attempting to stack the deck in its favor. Rather, the differing patterns of attendance suggest how much the tide of public opinion had turned in a Protestant direction and how severely the Catholic consuls had discredited themselves in the public eye. Public opinion had shifted sharply in a brief period of time: only eighteen months earlier, Protestant members of the présidial appeared to have avoided meetings because they disapproved of the majority's pro-Catholic policies (see Chapter 4). Now, it was the Catholics who chose the same (non)response. Even Catholics who attended were reluctant to vote for Catholic candidates. The group was highly elite: of the ninety who have been identified, nineteen were lawyers, and twenty-five were merchants or bourgeois. Sixteen were *laboureurs*, which was reasonable, since the fourth consul was usually chosen from among them.

As in every past election, the incumbent consuls spoke first. However, in previous elections, the councillors had generally voted according to the consuls' suggestions, while this time the other voters paid them no heed. The second consul, Pierre de Fabrica, was absent, but the other three, Jean Malmazet, Pons Blanc, and Guillaume Ferrussac, duly nominated their candidates. Malmazet, still unwilling to give an inch, nominated four strong Catholics for first consul: Antoine de Balme, seigneur de Sauzet; Robert des Georges, seigneur de Tharaux; François de Gras; and Honorat Gevaudan—all lawyers as the statute demanded. The other two consuls attempted to compromise somewhat by naming Pierre Rozel instead of Gras.

Then it was the turn of the other electors. Pierre Rozel spoke first, indicating that he was the leader of the group. He nominated his brother Charles and three other lawyers, Pierre Chabot, Louis Bertrand, and Jean Jossaud, all of whom were Protestants. With minor deviations, every elector except one, Bernard Corconne, a *laboureur*, proceeded to follow Pierre Rozel's lead. For the second, third, and fourth consul positions, the same scenario was followed: the Catholic consuls' suggestions were completely disregarded, and Pierre Rozel, as spokesman for the Protestant party, nominated the candidates instead. Again, even Catholic electors appear to have generally followed Rozel. Once the candidates were chosen, one of each group was duly picked by lot: in the end, Louis Bertrand, Vidal d'Albenas, Pierre Cellerier, and Laurens Chantail became the consuls for 1562.[75] The new consuls immediately used their powers to spread Protestant ideas: on December 29, 1561, the consuls decided that the young people in Nîmes should be given instruction in Protestant theology, and they asked Guillaume Tuffan, the rector of the college, to appoint a professor to teach it.[76]

As this narrative should make clear, Bernard Barrière and Pierre Rozel were the two principals behind the engineering of the elections: Barrière ran the proceedings and Rozel proposed the nominees. The episode shows how important family relations are to understanding the underlying dynamics of the Reformation in Nîmes: the two men were brothers-in-law, since Rozel was married to Bernardine Barrière, Bernard's sister. The two families were also frequently witnesses at each other's weddings. When one recalls that Claude Baduel, probably the single most important agent of the early Reformation in Nîmes, was married to Isabelle Rozelle, Charles and Pierre's sister, the Reformation in Nîmes starts to seem like a family affair.[77]

In January 1562, the new consuls faced their first crisis: Catherine de' Medici named Antoine, comte de Crussol, to be the lieutenant general of the kingdom with a mission to pacify Languedoc. In general, Antoine's political and religious views were restrained by two influences, his wife and his mother. His mother, Jeanne de Genouillac, was a firm Calvinist; his wife, Louise de Clermont, was a Catholic, the former governess of Charles IX, and a close friend and ally of Catherine de' Medici. (She was also twenty years older than her husband; they had no children.) In the early 1560s, Antoine pursued a moderately Calvinist course and tried to avoid either outright rebellion or excessively severe measures against Catholics, but he eventually became a Catholic himself, and his policies became more anti-Protestant over time.[78] He ordered Nîmes's consuls to meet him at Villeneuve-lès-Avignon on January 10 to receive his orders. He decreed that Nîmes's Protestants had to return all of the town's churches to the Catholics and that all arms had to be handed in to city hall and put under lock and key. This sounded like a victory for Catholics, but since it did not forbid Protestantism, it amounted to de facto toleration. Since officially the new religion was heresy, punishable by death, this was in fact a major victory for Protestantism. A few days later, Antoine issued more precise orders and extended them to the entire province, ordering both sides not to abuse the other nor call each other "papist" or "huguenot." On the fourteenth, Viret preached a sermon urging Nîmes to obey, and the Protestant party did so, giving the church keys back to the Catholics. They held services at city hall and in a school building instead. President Calvière of the présidial attended, thus officially joining the Protestant church. Calvière was the most eminent man in town, and his conversion strengthened the movement considerably. Calvière was also a cautious man, and his conversion suggests that he knew which way the wind was blowing.

Now that the Protestants had vacated Nîmes's churches, the priests returned, as did the bishop, and despite some difficulties they were able to say mass on January 18. Crussol showed great affection for Viret, which also reassured Protestants. He appears to have passed word to Viret of the Edict of January, which gave Protestants the right to worship outside of towns. This was a remarkable victory for French Protestantism, particularly since other forms of heresy, such as Anabaptism, were still banned. In effect, as long as temples were in the suburbs, Protestants were granted freedom of worship and a preferential status among non-Catholic religions.[79]

Viret had tremendous reason for thankfulness when, on February 1, 1562, he opened a provincial synod in Nîmes. (The same day, he staged a theological disputation with the Dominican monks, but they refused to convert.) The movement, both nationally and locally, had made immense strides in the previous year and a half. The Nîmes Protestant movement, then a small group of true believers, had first written to him fifteen years before. Now, he stood at the head of a united community whose most visible and vocal members were Protestants. Looking out from Nîmes, he saw a province whose Protestant population was everywhere in either the majority or the ascendant, and a nation where Protestantism had grown exponentially and where the practice of Protestantism had for the first time been declared legal. The Synod of Nîmes was a demonstration of the strength of the movement's newly won acceptance. It was time for Viret to move on, to help the movement elsewhere. By instituting the synod, he helped to create an institution that would provide leadership and continuity after his departure.

The principal concerns of the synod were to define duties and avoid disputes. On opening, first the delegates prayed, then the catechism and the ecclesiastical discipline were read. The next order of business was to reconcile every minister and deacon, wherever there had been a dispute. Then, everyone had to submit to the *grabaud*, at which their actions were reviewed by the assembly. To avoid disputes over precedence, the assembly also decided that it would meet at a different city each year.[80]

Between the founding of Nîmes's consistory on March 23, 1561, and Viret's departure nearly a year later, Nîmes's Protestants made enormous strides organizationally. Simply recording their acts took nearly a hundred sheets of large, closely written paper. It is also impressive that Nîmes's testators gave so often, and so generously, to the town's poor. In breaking with Catholicism, Nîmes's Protestants eloquently proclaimed that they were dissatisfied with the established order of things. By reconfiguring their religious life, they hoped to worship more purely and achieve a more just society. By localizing the governance of their religion, they also achieved more control over it. This particularly frightened the crown, already weakened by the deaths of Henri II and François II. The people of Nîmes, in their cahier, had proclaimed themselves to be loyal subjects. The crown was unconvinced. The kings of France were loyal Catholics and bound by their coronation oaths to repress heresy. Furthermore, in Nîmes and elsewhere in France, religious unrest and political defiance were intertwined. Religious unrest was in some ways more dangerous to the crown than was political defiance. Nîmes's Protestants had developed a coherent alternative world view, something much more potent than a mere urban or peasant revolt.[81]

The organizational strength of Nîmes's Protestant movement was linked to its growth. By early 1562, the movement had succeeded in recruiting some of the most socially prominent families in Nîmes, and most particularly many of the officials and men of law who constituted the pinnacle of the town's elite. The key to this growth appears to have been a powerful coalition, centered on political reform, that united the bulk of the community behind the Protestant movement. This nascent majority was then organized around the Protestant temples and the new religion's governing body, the consistory. The movement's strength among the elite can be quantified, and the analysis shows that Catholics were becoming beleaguered, marginalized in low-status occupations like the food and drink trades. Although precise numbers are impossible to come by for the population at large, contemporary testimony about the huge crowds attending Protestant preaching and the changes in the religious formulas in marriage contracts and wills suggest that the new religion was reaching the rest of Nîmes as well. Nîmes's Protestants had every reason to feel satisfied, even triumphant. They also had reason to be pleased with the growth of the religion on the national level: although imperfect, the Edict of January gave Protestants a reasonable facsimile of religious toleration. On March 1, 1562, Nîmes's Protestants moved worship outside the walls to conform to it.[82]

The papacy was not overly displeased with the edict. However, many French Catholics, including some normally classified as moderates, were appalled. The edict did not calm the situation as the queen mother had hoped. Furthermore, the assembly that had passed the Edict of January had not included any representatives of the Guises, who had left the court in disgust some months before. But shortly after the edict was announced, Antoine de Bourbon, who had so far been a somewhat unreliable Protestant supporter, joined the Catholic side. This considerably increased the Catholic party's influence at court, and François, duc de Guise, set out from his estates in Champagne toward Paris. On March 1, at Vassy, he discovered a group of Protestants praying in a barn inside the town, despite the edict's provisions. A dispute ensued. The Protestants locked themselves into the barn, but the duke's guards broke down the doors and began to massacre the worshipers. Between twenty-five and fifty people were killed, including five women and a child, and perhaps one hundred and fifty were wounded. The duke arrived in staunchly Catholic Paris a hero. He had set off a civil war.[83]

7

Rising and Falling

The Protestant Movement in Nîmes, 1562–1570

Despite the initial victory of the Protestant party in Nîmes, the 1560s proved to be difficult, even though Protestantism was now the majority religion in the town. Nîmes did not escape the civil war which broke out in 1562, and for more than half of the decade, Protestants were excluded from government. Thus, the majority of Nîmes's elite, which had converted to Protestantism in the aftermath of the cahier campaign, found its political role not enhanced, but reduced. Nîmes's Protestant elite had to battle for the better part of a decade to restore its position. Seduced by a utopian vision, Nîmes's Protestants eventually killed hundreds of people who stood in their way. Even before Vassy, troops were on the move. A small Protestant troop passed through Nîmes, smashing churches on its way, at the end of February. Nîmes's Protestants received their first warning that civil war was imminent on March 18, when Judge Robert LeBlanc of the présidial came to the consistory with a message from the prince de Condé, Admiral Coligny, and the comte de Crussol. They urged Nîmes's Protestants to live peaceably with their Catholic neighbors, but to watch them carefully. If Catholics began to collect arms, Nîmes's Protestants should do likewise.[1] After this, tensions increased rapidly. At the end of March, the Nîmes Consistory voted money to help the beleaguered Protestants of Paris. In mid-April, the newly returned Catholic canons quit the cathedral and left Nîmes. Within a month, in defiance of the Edict of January, Protestants were holding services in Nîmes proper. On May 19, the Nîmes council ordered that the bells be melted down for cannon, and small Protestant forces attacked various villages in the area. The silver was taken from the cathedral, and the reliquaries were sold in June to raise money for Protestant troops. At the end of September, a Protestant army, after seizing the town of Saint-Gilles, organized a wholesale massacre of Catholics—including children—and dumped their bodies down a well. Preparations were over. War had begun.[2]

The Crussol family provided most of the military leadership in the region: Jacques de Crussol was the local representative of the prince de Condé, who was the most important national political leader of the Protestant party. This relationship would continue: when high political figures in Nîmes planned the massacre of Nîmes's Catholics, they did so because Condé and other principal national leaders had decided on a Protestant uprising, and Jacques transmitted this information to Nîmes. Early in the 1560s, Jacques became the military commander of the Protestant forces of Bas-Languedoc. In early November 1562, meeting in Nîmes, an assembly of the Protestants of Bas-Languedoc chose the head of the family, Jacques's brother Antoine, to become their leader. He then proceeded to name governors for the region's major cities and towns. Jacques de Crussol and his younger brother Gaillot, who was eventually killed in the St. Bartholomew's massacre, appear to have been firmly Calvinist, while Antoine pursued a more moderate course. Antoine, although he had no warrant from the crown for his actions, chose his brother Jacques as governor of Nîmes, which gave Jacques authority over military affairs and a position within the national political leadership of the Protestant movement. The following month, Jacques staged a triumphal entry into town. The consuls gave him the bishop's palace, which had been standing empty, to live in.[3]

The crown saw that letting Nîmes choose its own political leaders was a serious mistake. Indeed, the monarchy was in danger of losing control of the entire province of Languedoc. In 1563, the royal council therefore named a new governor: Henri de Montmorency, seigneur de Damville. After Damville's appointment, he toured the province to survey his new domain. On November 16, he arrived in Nîmes, staging his own entry, accompanied by a small band of troops and a significant entourage of dignitaries, including members of the Parlement of Toulouse and several bishops. He promptly engineered the overthrow of the Protestant party and their replacement with Catholic consuls for the following year, 1564. He also ordered that the Catholic clergy be permitted to return. The new regime was led by Robert des Georges, seigneur de Tharaux. Des Georges and François de Gras were the lawyers for the cathedral chapter.[4] The selection of des Georges showed that Damville was determined to put the Catholic leadership in charge. The new council duly began to rebuild Catholicism in Nîmes: it immediately reestablished the tradition of hiring a preacher for Lent and paid a priest to say mass every day in the cathedral. The council also hired a new, Catholic chaplain for the hospital.[5]

The Catholic consuls could not pursue a completely hard-line policy. First, the council asked that "the garrisons of soldiers be removed, except that the château remain guarded." Even the staunchly Catholic consuls felt that the troops were an expensive menace to local liberties. (Royal troops loose in the town were also likely to do more harm than good. Even if the council members had been prepared to tolerate their presence, they knew well that moderates would be driven into the Protestant party if the troops stayed.) Second, the Observantin friars, whose monastery had been sacked by the Protestants, asked for alms so that they could pay to move back into town. The council replied that, given the expenses for the king's troops, they could not afford to assist them. Third, they never even discussed buying back the Church property which the Protestants had sold off. In short, they were not such zealous Catholics that they were prepared to ignore financial considerations or to renounce local autonomy.[6] The trouble was that reconverting Nîmes would take a substantial financial investment, but the inevitable fiscal burden was likely to provoke so much resentment that the attempt would be counterproductive. Reestablishing Catholic worship, disavowing Protestant emissaries, and removing Protestants from positions of authority were satisfying victories, but they were unlikely to persuade many Protestants to return to the Catholic fold.

In late 1564, the crown was able to repeat its intervention in Nîmes's consular elections, because the king himself, Charles IX, visited Nîmes in December, around election time. He ordered that two nominees be selected by lot for each position, with Governor Damville to make the final choice. Of the two candidates, Damville selected François de Gras to be first consul. De Gras was, along with his predecessor des Georges, the cathedral chapter's lawyer: Damville was still determined to keep the Catholic leadership in power, and he probably manipulated the lottery system to further his goal. (De Gras was eventually murdered in the Michelade.) Furious Protestant protests were of no avail.[7] The new consuls undertook a new initiative: to petition the king for further help. They had three main demands. First, they wanted the mass restored. Second, they insisted that the edicts of pacification be obeyed. Third, they wanted Protestants removed from the présidial court. However, this last demand required a substantial cash outlay, because the judges of the présidial would have to be reimbursed for the purchase prices of their offices. The consuls wanted the crown rather than the town to foot the bill. Unsurprisingly, the crown refused this request.[8]

In March 1565, during a visit to Toulouse, Charles IX issued a decree that redressed Catholic grievances to some degree but that also showed the limitations of royal support for Catholicism. On the one hand, the king ordered that, until Catholic worship was restored, the income from all benefices where the mass was not being celebrated should be seized. On the other hand, he ordered that Protestants not be excluded from office because of their religion, that they be given two lots in Nîmes for building churches, and that royal troops be confined to barracks in the château. The Protestants proceeded to build on the sites allocated to them, and in a demonstration of their members' prestige, the first stones of the foundation were laid by President Guillaume Calvière, the presiding judge of the présidial court; Denis de Brueys, seigneur de Saint-Chaptes, the *juge criminel*; and other members of the court. In Nîmes, however, possession was nine-tenths of the law, and Charles's other commands were not obeyed. Protestants had as little ability to force Catholics to share the council as Catholics did to force Protestants to give up their hold on benefices. If Catholics were going to improve their religious position, they would have to take measures that did not rely on Protestant cooperation.[9]

In late 1565, the crown intervened again and imposed its own group of Catholics on Nîmes's government.[10] But this does not seem to have been enough for Nîmes's increasingly frustrated Catholics: beginning in 1565, their leadership pursued bolder policies. Shortly after Charles IX's decree, the Catholic Church in Nîmes reasserted its authority and reestablished the mass in the cathedral. In May 1566, the chapter published a schedule of masses, indicating which priest was assigned which week. A priest Julien Corbon (later murdered in the Michelade) and a boy were hired to improve the choir; at later meetings, the chapter hired more choirboys and an organist. Although the canons were prepared to vote collectively to restore the mass, they were not necessarily willing to stick their necks out and perform the ceremony; throughout the summer and fall, many of the canons failed to show up when it was their turn to perform the rite. Presumably, standing at the altar, the priests felt like easy targets.

In June 1566, the cathedral chapter also showed its frustration at the failed policy of the preceding years by taking out its anger on the Catholic leadership. It removed Robert des Georges and François de Gras from their positions as the chapter's lawyers, complaining of their "notorious absences." They were replaced by Guy Rochette, another leading Catholic lawyer. He was younger than his predecessors, which may have made him more prepared to pursue extreme policies: des Georges, for example, had first served as first consul in 1546 and thus had long-standing connections with Protestants predating the religious split. Still, the situation for Catholics gradually improved, and in early 1567, the chapter went even further, ordering the revival of a mass in honor of the Virgin and the reinstatement of the town's Corpus Christi procession.[11]

At the end of January 1566, Antoine de Crussol had taken credit for reestablishing the mass in a letter to the king.[12] But the tougher Catholic political line seems to have predated his arrival, and therefore it seems more likely that the new tone was more due to the efforts of local Catholics, whether lay or clerical, who were emboldened by Charles's decree. More plausibly, Crussol, a moderate Calvinist who eventually returned to Catholicism, was happy to make it appear to the king that, despite his own views, he was prepared to grant a certain degree of freedom to Nîmes's Catholics. It is also possible that this letter was part of his gradual shift to the Catholic side. The consistency with which the Church's lawyers became first consul suggests that the clergy was in charge of planning local Catholic strategy: naming them to the position may have been in effect a directive to the Catholic party to make those people its leaders. But that is only an inference, and it seems unlikely that the Church would have risked alienating its embattled supporters with brusque commands. Instead, such decisions were probably the product of a collective process.

Protestants, of course, were unhappy with the new, bolder policies being pursued by their Catholic opponents in the council chamber and the cathedral. Attempting to undo the effects of the royal order, at the end of 1566 Protestants mounted a determined attempt to regain some of the power to which they felt entitled, since they were the majority. They proposed appointing the seneschal, Jean (II) de Senneterre, to preside over the elections. This led to a complex series of negotiations. In the end, the Catholic party agreed to send two representatives to meet with two Protestants. The Protestants proposed splitting the four consul positions evenly between the two religions. The Catholic representatives, once again the lawyers and former first consuls Robert des Georges and François de Gras, refused to make any concessions, and the meeting broke up without any agreement. Instead, the council chose an uncompromisingly Catholic slate for the following year. Guy Rochette, newly chosen to be the lawyer for the cathedral chapter, was picked, by the suspicious workings of the lottery system, to be first consul.[13]

Renewed Civil War

During 1567, increasingly bitter relations between the two religions across France made the resumption of civil war likely. The trouble had begun in 1565, when Spain destroyed a French colony on the Florida coast. This caused a chill in the relationship between Paris and Madrid. In the summer of 1565, the duke of Alva, one of King Philip II of Spain's chief advisers, met with Catherine de' Medici and Charles IX at Bayonne. The talks resulted in no agreement. The following year, a Protestant revolt broke out in the Netherlands, and in the summer of 1567, on his way to repress the revolt, Alva led a Spanish army along France's eastern frontiers. The presence of this large army worried even the French crown, and Alva's purpose was yet more worrisome to the French Protestant party. The crown decided to raise troops, but the Catholic duc de Montmorency and the leading Protestant nobleman, the prince de Condé, fought over who would be in supreme command. Protestants were worried that royal troops would be turned against them if they were not in control. As the dispute continued, they even began to wonder whether Alva and Catherine had agreed on some secret plan of coordinated repression. To forestall any such plot, France's Protestant leadership organized a nationwide uprising for late September, which is called by historians the Second Civil War. A crucial part of the Protestant plan was an attempt (which failed) to kidnap the king.[14]

In Nîmes, tensions were already high. Four successive groups of Catholic consuls had managed to reestablish a significant Catholic ritual presence in the town—and infuriated the town's Protestants—but had not made many converts who might have strengthened their party. Nonetheless, the crown attempted to build up the Catholic party for the coming trial of strength. On April 10, 1567, as renewed civil war loomed, Charles IX issued letters patent directed to the seneschals, granting police powers to Nîmes's consuls and the consuls of a number of other towns in the region. This undercut the authority of Nîmes's Protestant-controlled présidial court. Some Protestants apparently feared that this was the signal for a new round of oppression, and word circulated that the Protestants meant to overthrow the government. In May, the town council informed the royal lieutenant in Languedoc, the vicomte de Joyeuse, about these rumors and asked for his assistance in quelling any potential revolt. He was unable to provide any: the situation was increasingly fragile, and he had few forces to spare. Grain prices also appear to have surged, which could hardly have helped to induce a calmer atmosphere. At the same time, in Nîmes, disputes between the two commanders of the royal forces, Captains Bolhargues and La Garde, endangered the king's peace. In May 1567, the town council became sufficiently alarmed to attempt mediation. Given the increasing levels of hostility between the Protestant and Catholic parties in Nîmes and across France, these disputes were particularly worrisome for the town's Catholic administration. In an effort to placate Bolhargues, the consuls unsuccessfully asked for La Garde's removal, but they failed to obtain it, and in any case their confidence in Bolhargues was misplaced. The dispute between the two captains greatly contributed to the breakdown of Catholic control and to the massacre that followed. The Protestant party was able to exploit the dispute to turn Bolhargues against his Catholic masters, to seize power, and to perpetrate the Michelade.[15]

The Uprising

The uprising in Nîmes was coordinated with the national Protestant plan. On September 27, Jacques de Crussol and his brother Gaillot came to Nîmes to pass the word about the nationwide uprising that was planned for the end of the month.[16] The exact circumstances are hard to determine, but it appears likely that the Crussols met with François de Pavée, seigneur de Servas, who then took a leading hand in organizing the uprising.[17] De Pavée, probably working with Robert LeBlanc, the Protestant *juge ordinaire* of the présidial, managed to turn Captain Bolhargues's anger at his fellow captain into treachery to the Catholic cause. Bolhargues's position was complicated. His name was actually Mathieu Suau, although he was generally known by his title. The language of his 1559 marriage contract was entirely Catholic, and most of the friends whom he chose to be witnesses to it were prominent Catholics, including François de Gras, the future first consul and a victim of the Michelade. Bolhargues had first been appointed captain of the city by Nîmes's Catholic leadership in 1560. However, he had also loyally served the Protestant party after it took power in late 1561 and had served under de Pavée in an expedition to support the Protestants of Beaucaire in 1562. In plotting the uprising de Pavée probably asked LeBlanc to go with him to meet Bolhargues because LeBlanc and Bolhargues had been friends for years: LeBlanc was the only Protestant witness to Bolhargues's marriage contract. It is unclear whether Bolhargues was able to persuade his men to follow him or simply took over the leadership of one of the Protestant companies. In any case, his defection left the Catholic consuls with no armed support apart from the troops in the château, who were soon trapped there.[18]

The uprising began the day after Michaelmas and was called the Michelade. Nearly everyone in Nîmes's Protestant political—but not religious—elite formed themselves into a provisional government called the Messieurs by the populace. Virtually the entire Protestant membership of the présidial was part of it, including President Guillaume Calvière. Several of those who were not members of the présidial were former consuls or otherwise socially prominent. A roster of Protestant perpetrators shows that they were men of high status (see figure 7.1 on page 170). However, this group represented the political rather than the religious leadership of the Protestant movement. Although most of the Messieurs are mentioned in the minutes of the Protestant Consistory, few of them appear there as regular participants or as early deacons, elders, or other officers of the church.[19] By contrast, the consistory promptly sent a representative to de Pavée—which confirms that they saw him as the leader—condemning the uprising.[20] This was consistent with long-standing policy, since the consistory had acted as a moderating force since the movement's earliest days. Furthermore, given the social divide between the members of the consistory and the elite officials of the présidial, who, although Protestants, were only rarely officers of the consistory, certain differences in approach were to be expected.[21]

Given that the leadership of the revolt held so much institutional power in Nîmes, it is not surprising that the violence in Nîmes was fairly well organized. Once it began, the uprising consisted of five main phases. In the first phase, Protestant forces asserted their control by marching in the streets and seizing the keys to the city gates. In the second phase, they arrested many Catholic leaders and clergy. In the third phase, they imprisoned the arrested Catholics, sorted them out based on lists they had compiled, and murdered those whom they had selected to die. In the fourth phase, they remade the sacred geography of Nîmes, polluting the bishop's palace and destroying churches and the homes of leading Catholics. In the fifth phase, they laid siege to the château.

The first phase of the uprising began on September 30, when Protestant forces formed into regular companies and began to march about the city. Little is known of their composition or training, but apart from those who had served under Captain Bolhargues, most probably lacked military experience. The troops were armed, but not identically.[22] As they marched, they shouted crude but effective slogans. Jeanne Auberte reported that she heard loud noises coming from the street, and after shepherding her children inside, she saw armed men heading up the street shouting, "Close the shops!" Other witnesses heard the Protestants yelling, "To arms! To battle!" and "Kill! Kill! Kill the papists!" In one probably exceptional reference to the glory days that would follow a Protestant victory, the troops shouted, "Kill, kill! New world, new world!" All of the surviving reports come from hostile witnesses, but to judge from them the Protestant forces' anger far outweighed any eschatological hopes. Fundamentally, the Protestants marched around town to intimidate the Catholic community.[23]

Seizing the Keys

After asserting their control over the city's streets, the Protestants sought to seize the keys to the town's gates. Protestants and Catholics commonly tried to seize the gates as part of attempts to take over towns; they did so for both practical and symbolic reasons. In Nîmes, Protestant control of the gates meant that royal or other outside Catholic troops could not intervene to prevent the Protestants from taking whatever steps they wished. It also threatened Catholic residents, since they could not escape should the Protestants attempt to arrest or, as in the Michelade, murder them. Furthermore, in Nîmes, Catholics were heavily concentrated in agricultural occupations, which employed about one-third of the adult male population. When Protestants controlled the gates, they also controlled the agricultural workers' access to their farms and gardens, their assets and their livelihoods. At the same time, possession of the keys to the town was an important attribute of sovereignty: normally, Nîmes's consuls held the keys. Possession of the keys conferred legitimacy.[24]

In Nîmes's case, the keys were in the hands of Guy Rochette, the first consul and the lawyer for the cathedral chapter. Our only account of what happened relies on the description provided by Blaise Valon, a servant of Rochette. According to Valon, Rochette took refuge at the house of his stepfather, Jean Gregoire, a merchant who was also a prominent Catholic and a former secretary of the bishop. When Protestant forces, led by Jacques de Possaco, a prominent merchant/draper and early Protestant, showed up at the door demanding the keys, Catherine Valladier, Rochette's mother, lied and insisted that he was not there. Rochette, accompanied by his half brother Robert Gregoire, decided nonetheless to leave the house, hoping to use his authority to order the Protestants to desist. To enhance his authority, Rochette put on the red robes that identified him as a consul and went with Gregoire to summon other town officials to assist him in restoring order, but he did not find any of them. He probably also carried the keys with him. He pleaded with the Protestant companies that he ran across as he walked, including those of Tanequin Finor, a Protestant apothecary, who threatened him for his pains.[25] Similarly, Jean Bonaud, one of the captains of the Protestant forces, and Jean Bertrand, a prominent early Protestant who also took a leading role in the uprising, "turned their backs on him." It seems odd that they did not arrest him; perhaps the leaders of each Protestant company had assigned tasks, and they were afraid of committing the fateful act of arresting the first consul without prior orders. Finally, Rochette went to the bishop's palace, found Bishop Bernard d'Elbène, and cried to him with tears in his eyes that "he did not know what to do." The bishop replied that they should pray, which they did in the front hall. At this point, according to Valon, Captain Bolhargues arrived, along with "two hundred" men, arrested them, brought them back to the Gregoire house, and locked them in the kitchen. Bolhargues soon removed them to the house of Guillaume l'Hermite, an early Protestant who at one time had gone into exile in Geneva. Presumably, Bolhargues also took the keys to Nîmes's gates, which were soon under Protestant control. Valon, some of the other servants, and the bishop managed to escape through a hole in the wall separating the palace from the house of Antoine de Brueys, a *conseiller* of the présidial court. Brueys, a Protestant, hid them for the next several days but was nonetheless eventually condemned to death for his role in the Michelade.[26]

Valon's account seems somewhat improbable, although Rochette's presence at the palace is confirmed by another witness.[27] It seems too perfect. Certainly, it was normal behavior for an official in Rochette's position to clothe himself in the robes that signified his authority and to try to rally the town's officials, but Rochette's attempt to reason with armed Protestant forces seems foolhardy. Similarly, the scene of the arrest, with Rochette and the bishop discovered on their knees in prayer, seems tinged with sanctimony. In short, Valon's account depicts how Catholics wished to imagine their leaders behaving. As such, it is revealing. According to Valon, Rochette was a perfect martyr: he carried no weapon and used no threats. He was a loyal son of the Church, but in this account not its lackey, since he turned to the bishop only when he could do nothing further himself. At the same time, Rochette's actions risked further inflaming the Protestants' anger against the bishop and clergy: since Rochette knew that the Protestants were pursuing him so that they could get the keys, his decision to go to the bishop only ensured that the bishop would be delivered into Protestant hands. Perhaps Rochette meant to warn Bishop d'Elbène that ruin was upon them. Certainly, he did not ask the bishop for assistance, nor did he receive any: if he had wanted something other than prayer, he did not complain when prayer was all he got. The image of the pair at prayer right inside the bishop's front door suggests that they anticipated their arrest. Other Catholic accounts of martyrdom suggest a yearning to die, to replicate and thus to activate in the present Christ's sacrifice on the cross. Something similar seems at work in the report that Father Jean Quatrebars, prior of the Augustinian monastery in Nîmes, when trying to hearten his fellow prisoners on the way to their execution, "exhorted them to patience, telling them that he saw the Heavens open to receive them."[28] It is worth noting that Quatrebars's statement was broadly Christian rather than narrowly sectarian—and therefore he was sending a message as much directed to his Protestant captors as to his Catholic flock.

In some instances, even when Catholics escaped death, they were anxious to show that their deliverance was not due to the merciful behavior of Protestants. That would have given their opponents too much credit. Instead, they attributed their survival to the effects of Protestant vices, including avarice and perfidy. According to Pierre Journet, a clerk who worked for one of the bishop's aides, when Protestant forces came to présidial member Antoine de Brueys's house looking for the bishop and the little troop of Catholics hiding there, de Brueys advised them to bribe the attackers. A bargain was agreed upon. The bishop paid sixty écus for his release, and correspondingly lesser sums were negotiated for the others. The Catholics handed over everything they had, including some of their clothes. The Protestants dumped the bishop and his manservant outside of town. The others were taken away and murdered. Journet explained that he only survived because the Protestants, having wounded him in the side and the thigh, had left him for dead on the stairs in de Brueys's house.[29]

The Arrest of Nîmes's Catholics

In the second phase of the Michelade, after the Protestant forces had taken the keys and thus control of the gates from Rochette, they arrested other prominent Catholics. François de Gras, the ex-consul, was the next target. Guillaume l'Hermite arrived with a body of Protestant forces to search de Gras's house and that of his neighbor François le Roux. After their search was completed, l'Hermite told de Gras that he had to come with them because someone wanted to speak to him. Antoinette de Massilhan, de Gras's wife, then started to cry, but de Gras replied that he had to go see what they wanted, adding, "Our Lord will guard [me] and [I] can only die once." Presumably, this remark was intended to tell his wife to be brave in the face of their enemies; it could hardly have reassured her. L'Hermite wanted to take Jean Canonge, the tutor to de Gras's children, as well, but de Gras prevailed on him to let Canonge stay, saying that there was no other man in the house. De Gras was then taken to l'Hermite's house.[30]

It seems clear that the Protestant leadership intended to conduct a general roundup of Catholic lay and clerical leaders. Protestant forces targeted at least half of the sixteen men who had served as consul between 1564 and 1567, the period in which Catholics had been in power. Although only Rochette and de Gras were killed, all of Rochette's fellow consuls were arrested.[31] Similarly, of the nine Catholic members of the présidial, only two did not appear among the victims, although a number of them managed to escape the city and only one, Jacques Barrière, paid for his religion with his life. He fled to the land he owned near Calvisson, but the Protestants seized him there.[32]

Imprisonment

In the third phase of the Michelade, once the Catholics were under arrest, the Protestant forces imprisoned them while deciding their fate. Some of those arrested were taken to Pierre Cellerier's house, others to the city hall and to Guillaume l'Hermite's house. Cellerier, a jeweler, was, like l'Hermite, an early, prominent Protestant. The conditions of imprisonment were oppressive. Most of the surviving evidence concerns conditions in the city hall, although Nicolas Pradier, the secretary of the town council, who saw Gregoire and Rochette escorted to city hall, refused to watch them leave because "he did not dare leave his room, for fear of being massacred with them." Rochette and Gregoire were kept separately from the many other prisoners, who were confined upstairs and in the basement. The lower chamber, although in the end a safer holding place, had a sinister reputation, since it was used as an abattoir to butcher animals for the sick during Lent. The symbolism was surely not accidental. For much of the first day, while they were waiting to find out what would happen to them, no one came to see or talk to the Catholic prisoners. This must have been disquieting, since it implied that the leaders wanted to kill them, rather than to interrogate them. Apparently, no food was brought to the prisoners: Pradier said that people kept there were "dying of hunger." The Messieurs also taunted the prisoners. Pierre Cellerier, perhaps referring to the abattoir where the prisoners were being held, suggested that they should make a feast (*qu'ilz fissent grand chere*); they replied that they were in no position to do so. Cellerier reassured them with deliberate ambiguity, saying that they would "leave very soon," but he did not say whether they would be released from custody or from life. In short, their imprisonment was designed to terrify even those Catholics who were not destined to be killed.[33]

The leaders of the conspiracy had prepared for the arrests. Guy Rochette's servant Blaise Valon testified that he saw Guillaume Calvière, the president of the présidial, holding a list of Protestants who were to be armed. Similarly, prisoners who were scheduled to die were also placed on a list, although since many of those arrested were not killed, there was probably confusion or conflict among the Protestant leaders about some of the prisoners' ultimate fates. In the middle of the night of September 30, groups of soldiers, including Cellerier, consulting their lists, removed some of the most prominent Catholic officials, including Rochette, and de Gras, as well as the priests whom they had detained in the basement of city hall. The Protestant officers moved the prisoners to the courtyard of the bishop's palace, a large open area with a well in the center. There, they were killed, by sword, dagger, or pistol, and their bodies were dumped down the well. Jean Rovyer, a leather worker, testified that he saw the area the following day, "all covered with blood and the water of the well all red and he saw several dead bodies in it." Jean Vallat, a merchant, claimed that he had gone to see the well afterward, and there were "certain loud noises" coming from it which gave him "a great big fright and made his hair stand on end." Another witness, Pierre Rovyer, claimed that his stepfather, Pierre du Fesc, had told him that he had witnessed the bodies being tossed in and counted 108 of them. Jean Rovyer claimed to have heard from another leather worker that

Jacques d'Estenet, a gardener, and Guillaume l'Hermite were responsible for most of the dirty work. Another witness, Jean Bouze, gave a list of more than a dozen perpetrators. He named some wealthy men, like the important Protestant Jean Bertrand, but most were more humble: leather workers, hosiers, and other artisans. They were more suitable for such disagreeable tasks. There appears to have been an element of inversion in the choice of the bishop's palace for the murders: the aim was to destroy the Catholic party at the site most closely associated with its power.[34]

In one respect, the Protestant party showed both mercy and practicality: they attacked only men, not women. Indeed, the prominent Protestant leader and lawyer Charles Rozel warned some women to lock themselves inside their homes to protect themselves. That does not mean that Catholic women were exempt from suffering: they lost their husbands, sons, and others close to them. When Rochette's and Gregoire's mother and stepfather heard the rumor of their deaths, they broke into loud lamentations, exclaiming that they had "no other children." Furthermore, although women were not targeted for arrest, they were not immune if they did not obey the new regime. Jeanne Corconne attempted to leave town, since her husband had fled for Beaucaire and she wanted to live "according to God's commandments." She was arrested on the road and brought back to Nîmes. On this occasion, Charles Rozel was not so gallant: he told Corconne that her husband was "a wicked papist." She spent several days in jail, along with a number of other women, before being released. The primary goal was to drive Catholics from power, not to kill them all.[35]

The Messieurs claimed that they had no doubt that they would be obeyed. One of them, Jean Bertrand, boasted that "there is no reason to fear the populace, because they will not do anything that we and the other officers and principals of the long and short robes do not make them do." Nonetheless, they performed their most shocking acts at night because, as another Protestant, Jacques Nicot, explained, they did not want to "scandalize the people." Fearing the authorities, they also hesitated to put their signatures to orders that might later incriminate them. When Catherine de Parades demanded a signed order before she would pay a special tax on Catholics, Pierre Rozel, brother of Charles and also a member of the Messieurs, replied, "Would you do it if you were in our place?" Rozel also worried about spies. Most witnesses insisted that the Messieurs were in complete control and therefore completely responsible at all times. One witness, Vidal Caintemesse, a merchant, said that "the ordinary people [menu peuple] were upset on two separate occasions last summer and took up arms against the soldiers of the garrison," but the elite had repressed them then, so it was obvious that, if there were rebellion now, they could have controlled it.[36]

The witnesses were anxious to see as many Protestant leaders as possible punished, but they do not appear to have improved on the evidence. Some Catholics did escape despite the wishes of the Messieurs. Some Protestants, for example, were unwilling to participate in the roundups and even helped Catholics to escape. Pierre Blaise, one of the bishop's servants, escaped by finding refuge with a man named Jean, a Protestant baker. This case is particularly striking, since Blaise's ignorance of the man's last name suggests that they did not know each other well, although it is also possible that Blaise was deliberately keeping the name of this particular Protestant from the authorities. Louis Blachière was on his way to being killed, so he thought, when "someone called Christol, a wool carder, son of Simon Vidalot the butcher," a member of the Protestant companies, came up to him, said "this one should not be killed," took him by the shoulder, and led him back to prison. Blachière was eventually released. Again, the hesitant way in which Blachière named his savior suggests that they were not well acquainted, but it is possible that Christol meant that Blachière should be spared because he was not on the official list. In other cases, friends and neighbors assisted Catholics in making their escape. Jean Roverie, the seigneur de Cabrières, hid in a well while Protestants searched the house; then, he fled to a neighbor's. Father Jean Bompar pretended that he wanted to pay his debts before he died and asked to see Louis Pillet, a tanner, to pay him. Pillet brought his "grand ami le Bastel," who was in Captain Bolhargues's company, and they arranged to bring Bompar to the house of Robert LeBlanc, one of the principal organizers of the conspiracy, where he was hidden. Nor was LeBlanc the only high-ranking Protestant to hide Catholics: Jean-Guy d'Airebaudouze, a Protestant *conseiller* of the présidial, warned his neighbor Jeanne Auberte that she should hide her husband, Jean Vallat, at her brother-in-law's house. D'Airebaudouze was later condemned for his role in the massacre and named as a member of the Messieurs. Unlike LeBlanc, he did not take the risk of bringing a Catholic into his own household. Finally, some Catholics escaped by using their own wits: Father Jean Vincens hid in the suburbs and pretended to be a cook in an inn. In short, despite Protestant efforts at efficiency, events—in particular, who lived and who died—were only partially in their control.[37]

Remaking Nîmes

In the fourth phase of the Michelade, once the town was in Protestant hands and the Catholic leadership either imprisoned, in exile, or killed, the Protestants proceeded to remake the sacred geography of Nîmes to deny the Catholics any focal point for a revival. Over several days following the massacre, the Protestant leaders ordered every church in town destroyed, except one, St. Eugénie, which they used as a space in which to make gunpowder. They destroyed churches even on Sunday. They also destroyed the bishop's palace and houses belonging to priests and some lay Catholics in the city and the suburbs. They burned all of the church furniture and many ecclesiastical records and pillaged the houses of some rich Catholics. Some of the stone from the churches was sold to builders. There were impositions on laypeople as well. While everyone in town was ordered to pay special taxes to support the Protestant forces, Catholics were ordered to pay especially high taxes, to hand over ecclesiastical revenues, and to support soldiers billeted in their houses. Those who complained were given more soldiers to feed. Beyond these semi-legal exactions, there was also out-and-out looting. Jacques Saurin saw one of Captain Bolhargues's servants wearing First Consul Guy Rochette's turquoise ring, and Father Bompar had his purse taken. The leaders of the Michelade had little incentive to repress looting: they wanted to terrify the Catholics into submission. Overall, Protestants directed their destructive energies more at the property of Catholic clergy than at that of the lay leadership.[38] Some of the hatred arose from disgust at the notion of the special holiness that Catholic priests supposedly claimed for themselves but that Protestants believed belonged to all Christians. But at least some Protestant leaders also believed that the Church sustained the Catholic party in crucial ways and hoped that, shorn of this support, it would collapse. As one of the Messieurs, the présidial *conseiller* Jean de Sauzet, commented, "The nests must be destroyed, so that the birds will not return."[39]

The Siege of the Château

Certainly, the killings were in at least one respect counterproductive, because they delayed the fifth phase of the Michelade, an assault on the garrison in the château. The Protestants' delay cost them the advantage of surprise.[40] In any case, seizing the château must have seemed like an extremely difficult undertaking given the inexperienced troops the Protestants had to command. The killings put the garrison on notice that the conspirators meant business. But the defenders refused to be intimidated: the garrison held out for six weeks, despite repeated calls for it to surrender. At the same time, a Catholic force from Tarascon was unable to relieve the defenders. Instead of trying to storm the citadel, the Messieurs ordered trenches dug, at which Catholics were required to work or to pay for substitutes. President Calvière of the présidial court oversaw the digging. On November 10, the garrison, running out of food, gave up, despite the exhortations of Captain La Garde. Terms were eventually agreed upon. The captain and nine soldiers could leave with all of their arms and baggage, while the rest of the garrison was limited to its swords and daggers. The Catholics who had escaped the massacre were promised safety and either permitted to return to Nîmes or to leave, at their choice. The actual surrender occurred on November 15.[41]

Catholics, Protestants, and Motives

It is hard to determine exactly how many people died in the Michelade, but the surviving records indicate that about seventy-five people suffered in one way or another at the hands of the Messieurs, and about half of them were killed (see figures 7.1–3). Witnesses accused 219 people of participating in the massacre in various ways. It is unclear whether the discrepancy between contemporary estimates of one hundred killed and only about one-third that many known victims is due to defects in the statistics, contemporary exaggeration of the death toll, or both. It is also possible that the figure of one hundred killed is too low: one source suggests that eighty to ninety soldiers were killed outside of town, at Sommières and in other nearby villages.[42]

Unnamed victims were probably less prominent than those whose names we do know, but the statistics suggest strongly that the Michelade was a conflict

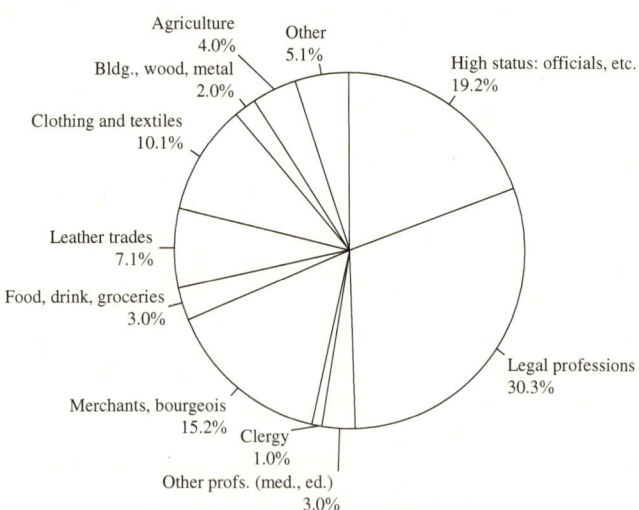

FIGURE 7.1. Perpetrators of the Michelade by occupation. Sources: Ménard, ADG, Series G, 441–442.

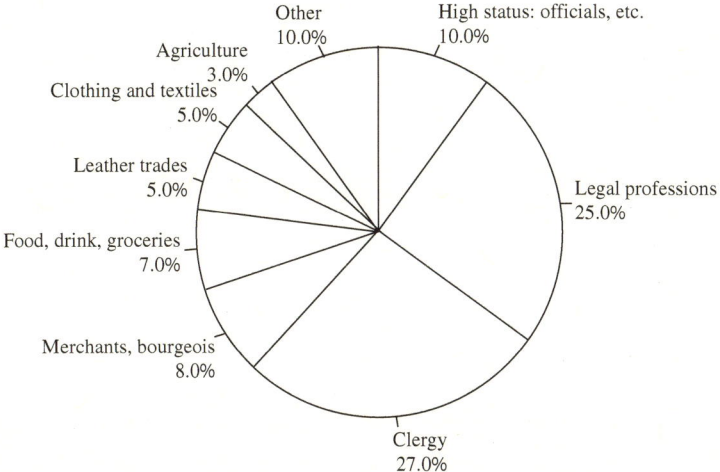

FIGURE 7.2 Victims of the Michelade by occupation. Sources: Ménard, ADG, Series G, 441–442.

among the elite. Three-quarters of both the victims and the alleged perpetrators held high-status occupations, including officials, lawyers, merchants, bourgeois, and—on the Catholic side—clergy. The two groups were also sharply different in other ways. Most important, the relative size of the two groups shows that the Catholic community had become a distinct minority in town, even though most of our information is derived from Catholic survivors, who identified members of their own party more readily than their persecutors. (It is also true that the depositions were collected to assemble a list of those responsible, which may have biased the sample in the opposite direction.) In percentage terms, Catholics were overwhelmingly concentrated in the clergy and legal professions, while the Protestants, although equally well represented in the law, had far more officials on their side than the Catholics did. All in all, Catholic victims in Nîmes appear to have been much more elite than Protestant victims of Catholic massacres elsewhere. Among the alleged perpetrators, the Protestant clergy was notably absent from participation, which makes sense given the consistory's condemnation of the uprising. As noted earlier, about half of all recent Catholic consuls were singled out for arrest, as were more than three-quarters of all Catholic members of the présidial. By contrast, only about one-fifth of Nîmes's priests were imprisoned.[43] Yet their death rate was much higher, since the overwhelming majority of officials were eventually released, while most priests, once caught, were killed. As Josh Millet has noted, many of these were associated with the public performance of the mass,

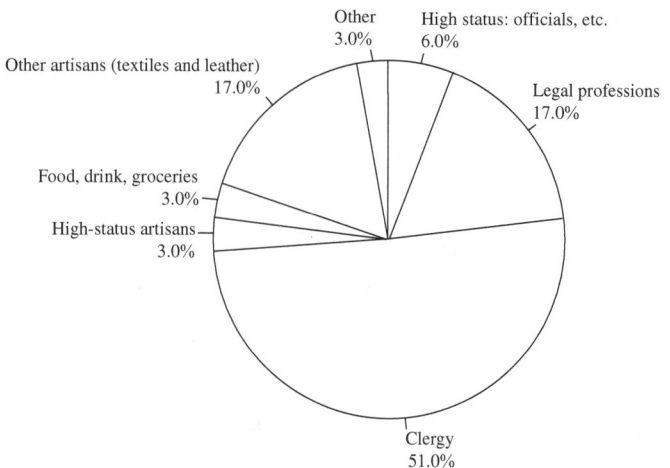

FIGURE 7.3 Deaths in the Michelade by occupation. Sources: Ménard, ADG, Series G, 441–442.

including (as mentioned earlier) Julien Corbon, who was hired for the choir. Millet infers from the unusually high death rate among priests that the primary goal of the killings was to silence the mass in Nîmes forever. He therefore argues that religion was a more important motive than politics in provoking the massacre.[44]

Assessing human motivation is inevitably difficult, particularly in a tumultuous event like the Michelade. Many people were involved in its planning and execution, and there is no reason to believe that any one of them participated for a single reason. Furthermore, religion and politics were thoroughly intertwined in the sixteenth century. There is plenty of evidence for both religious fervor and political passion among the participants. One anonymous contemporary listed six motives for the Michelade: (1) the wrong done to a female gardener, whose harvest was stolen by members of the garrison; (2) the tyranny of the Catholics, who had usurped the consulate; (3) the Protestant prince de Condé's national plan for Protestants to take up arms; (4) quarreling between two leading families, the Catholic d'Albenas family and the Protestant Calvières, headed by Guillaume Calvière, the president of the présidial; (5) the Protestants' getting wind of a plan for a Catholic counterattack, planned for the same time; and (6) the desire to avenge previous massacres of Protestants elsewhere in France.[45] Several of these motives have been discussed already; the first and fifth do not appear to be substantiated by outside evidence, while the fourth is discussed below. Several participants were also quoted in the depositions offering their own explanations. Captain Bolhargues implied that the massacre was a matter of revenge (the sixth reason) because "the papists did the same thing throughout France." Bernard Arnaud, one of the leading Micheladeurs (he was in charge of guarding the Bocarié gate), put it somewhat differently. He saw it as a question of survival: "either [we] will be their heirs or the Catholics will be [ours]." Once Protestants knew that war was coming again, they must have viewed the Catholic elite as the potential nucleus of a fifth column, should Catholic forces threaten the town. Similarly, Jean Vallat reported that he was menaced because he "supported those of [Catholic-controlled] Beaucaire, whom they called enemies." Both of these are rather secular, or political, interpretations of the conflict. Some Catholics failed to see the logic of this position. When Jean Rovyer was threatened by Protestant forces, who said to him that they wanted to cut his throat and throw him down the bishop's well because he was a papist, he replied that he "had not done wrong or displeased anyone in the world." Still, it is striking how many imprisoned Catholic laypeople were released. Some Catholics may have been spared because the Protestants hoped that they were potential candidates for conversion. Vidal Caintemesse was taken to a Protestant service, then taken out to dinner at an inn and urged to sign up. Protestants could also force Catholic laypeople to pay the many onerous expenses of war. Vallat also reported that when people complained to the Messieurs about the impositions, they replied that "they had had too much mercy in saving their lives, and they were papists and they wanted to ruin them entirely."[46]

It seems clear that one cause of the Michelade was that the Protestants of Nîmes felt deprived of what they saw as their right to rule. There was a long history of conflict over the composition of the town council in the years preceding the Michelade, which surely was a major cause of frustration on the part of leading Protestants.[47] Millet argues that the massacre, which he sees as religious, should be distinguished from the uprising, since the Protestants could have taken over the town without bloodshed. But Protestant officials, especially officers of the présidial, also resented the pretensions of the upstart Catholic consuls: the consuls de Gras and Rochette were among those murdered. Furthermore, the Protestant leadership deeply hated those Catholic officials who were not killed: the punishing conditions of imprisonment were clearly aimed at humiliating the victims.

The political and religious rivalry between the two confessions may have turned personal, and leading Protestant families may have wished to purge their Catholic rivals. As noted above, there was a rumor that the Michelade began because a member of one leading Catholic family, the d'Albenas, slapped the face of a member of a leading Protestant family, the Calvières.[48]

Guillaume Calvière was the president of the présidial, while a member of the d'Albenas family also served on the court: there were few more eminent families in town.[49] As discussed in Chapter 6, network analysis suggests that there were six main factions among Nîmes's elites. Thirteen people who were killed, arrested, or molested in the Michelade were members of these 249 elite families; seven of the thirteen (including the d'Albenas) belonged to the most elite faction of all, consisting of 56 of Nîmes's richest and most powerful families. Indeed, the records suggest that the d'Albenas were by far the most prominent Catholic family in town. In the notarial records, the d'Albenas were connected to 22 other families, more than any other family that remained Catholic at the time of the Michelade, and they also comprised the wealthiest Catholic family. Of the 22 families connected with the d'Albenas, 12 converted to Protestantism prior to the Michelade, eight remained Catholic, and two are unknown. For comparison, the des Georges family was connected to six other families, all of whom converted, and the Gregoire family was connected to three other families, of whom two converted. Since the des Georges family and the Gregoires were members of consular rather than judicial families, it is not surprising that they were connected to fewer families than the d'Albenas family, but even the Richiers and the Valletes, also members of the présidial, were only connected to 8 and 14 families, respectively. Of the 13 elite victims in the Michelade, 6 (including Bernard Poldo d'Albenas) were members of families that were tied to the d'Albenas family. Victims in this group included members of the d'Albenas, Richier, Roverie, and Vallete families. It is not surprising that the d'Albenas family was close to the Richier and Vallete families, since all were associated with the présidial; given their prominence in Catholic circles, it is also not surprising that the d'Albenas family was close to Jean Paberan, the bishop's deputy, who was killed.[50] The evidence thus suggests that the d'Albenas family was at the center of a complex of families that included the most elite Catholics in Nîmes; this complex included just under half of the victims of the Michelade who were members of the 249 elite families. Although there is little direct evidence of antagonism between the d'Albenas and Calvière families, it does appear that they headed opposing religious factions on the présidial, and certainly a high percentage of Catholic présidial members were arrested in the Michelade. There is no other evidence for a d'Albenas slapping a Calvière in the face, but it is plausible that members of the two families disliked each other, although in the period before the Reformation there were also ties between them. Perhaps these ties, in addition to the advantages they had owing to their wealth, explain why only one of the Catholic members of the présidial was killed.[51]

As noted earlier, Protestants everywhere had a particular horror of the Catholic clergy. The Protestant leaders behind the Michelade may also have felt that Catholic priests were particularly dangerous because they were the backbone of the opposition. The Catholic clerical and lay leadership worked hand in glove in the period 1564–1567 to maintain Catholic control of Nîmes, and it is certainly a reasonable interpretation of the events of the period to suppose that the initiative came from the clergy. Why else were its legal representatives so often subsequently chosen to be first consul? In short, although Protestant distaste for Catholicism was fixated more on the clergy and the mass than on the Catholic political elite, that does not mean that the extreme frustrations that led to the Michelade were not caused by political as well as religious factors. The Catholic Church in Nîmes could hardly have taken the course it did without political support, and indeed, religion and politics had been jumbled together since the beginning of the Reformation. It is possible that, with more adroit political maneuvering, the Catholic party could have avoided the provocations that led to the Michelade. But Catholic control of the council did make an uprising extremely likely, not least because it would have been well-nigh impossible for the Catholic party to resist taking the decisions it did. Reinstating Catholic ceremonies had been, among other things, a means of asserting their dominance. The Protestant response was violent, ugly, and direct: as several Protestants were reported to have said, Catholics were "papist vermin."[52]

Conclusion

The standard historical interpretation, commonly associated with Natalie Z. Davis, holds that, in the main, Protestants were less violent than Catholics in the French Wars of Religion. In a certain sense, this has to be true, since there were far fewer Protestant massacres of Catholics than the reverse. Davis concludes:

> [T]he iconoclastic Calvinist crowds still come off as the champions in the destruction of religious property. . . . This was not only because the Catholics had more physical accessories to their rite, but also because the Protestants sensed much more danger and defilement in the *wrongful use of material objects*. . . . In bloodshed, the Catholics are the champions. . . . I think this is owing not only to their being in the long run the stronger party numerically in most cities, but also to their having a greater sense of *the persons of heretics* as sources of danger and defilement. Thus, injury and murder were a preferred mode of purifying the body social.[53]

Her argument reproduces sixteenth-century Protestant views, and she cautiously endorses the Calvinist *Histoire ecclésiastique,* whose authors (principally Théodore de Bèze, Calvin's chief lieutenant) wrote: "[T]hose of the Reformed Religion made war only on images and altars, which do not bleed, while those of the Roman religion spilled blood with every kind of cruelty."[54] Davis carefully notes that Protestants were less violent than Catholics for religious reasons in addition to their numerical weakness, but she does not attempt to discover which factor was the more important one.

Denis Crouzet, the author of the most extensive study of religious violence in the period, makes a similar argument:

> There was not, in the beginning and before a perversion that issued naturally from the rituals of war, a Protestant practice of massacre (the celebrated Michelade of Nîmes is a separate case) because the Millennium was dawning for the Protestant party in these crucial years, in the course of which they were engaged with all their being in a war glorifying at every instant the infinite greatness of God.... [Protestant] thought is thus optimist[ic], perhaps utopian, rooted in the power of the Truth finally restored to men, a thought which conceived of a "soft" reconstruction of humanity under the Reign of Christ, without breaking bodies and without torturing flesh.[55]

Crouzet argues that theology alone drove Protestant behavior: Protestants did not massacre Catholics because, at least at first, there was no cultural or intellectual logic leading them to do so. (Crouzet does admit that, over time, as Catholic massacres accumulated, Protestants began to desire revenge and this "perversion" led them to respond in kind.) Crouzet insists that people imbued with utopian or millennial idealism must be reluctant to shed blood. This cannot be true even in the abstract, since we know that revolutionaries in France, Russia, and China were fully prepared to kill people who opposed their utopian visions. In the specific case of the French Reformation, the only way to conclude whether Protestant ideology discouraged believers from bloodshed is to look at the few places, like Nîmes, where Protestants were dominant. If Protestants were reluctant to shed blood when they held power in Nîmes, it would be strong evidence that Protestant ideology, not Protestant weakness, was the reason that there were so few massacres of Catholics in sixteenth-century France. The Michelade suggests that this was not the case.[56] On the contrary, the record makes one shudder to contemplate what Protestant parties might have done elsewhere had they enjoyed the strength they did in Nîmes. Indeed, the events of the Michelade are disturbingly similar to a massacre committed by the Protestant majority in La Rochelle in 1568. Many parallels could also be drawn to Catholic massacres, including that in Troyes in 1572, which also involved using troops to arrest and then murder people, although in Nîmes there was more popular participation. (In Troyes, the men who arrested and murdered the Protestants were few and mostly professionals, members of the town's militia.) Protestant and Catholic massacres were more similar than different, probably because they stemmed from similar anxieties.[57] Protestants elsewhere may have focused their attacks on statues because vandalism can be done at night, with few or no witnesses. A riot against real people requires a superiority of force that sixteenth-century French Protestants rarely possessed. Nîmes was one of the few exceptions. The Michelade suggests that there are two essential preconditions for mass murder: an overwhelming superiority of force and a fear that the weaker party nonetheless poses an existential threat to the stronger one.

While the Michelade shows that Protestants could be just as violent as Catholics in sixteenth-century France, it would be a mistake to reject all of the insights of previous scholars. Protestant anger in Nîmes was especially directed at priests and leading political opponents. The rolls of those murdered in the Michelade thus support one of Crouzet's major conclusions, namely, that priests and the "enemy army-rabble" were the principal targets of Protestant violence. It should be borne in mind, however, that only one-third of the victims can be identified, and if we had a complete list, the percentage of ordinary Catholics would surely be higher. Even without a complete list, given the number of people who died, it seems excessively kind of Crouzet to call Protestant violence "optimistic" and to suggest that Protestants pursued their aims "without breaking bodies and without torturing flesh." If Protestant rage was more narrowly focused than its Catholic equivalent, it was quite capable of being remarkably murderous in comparable circumstances. Furthermore, Crouzet contends that Protestants limited their targets because this view supports his larger thesis that, killing priests aside, Protestant violence was more "rational." It was designed merely to restrain Catholic attacks and to preserve the Protestants' ability to prosclytize, whereas Catholics' burning desire to extirpate the heretics led them to kill Protestants indiscriminately.[58] Crouzet's insistence that Protestant violence was rational is part of a larger argument that Protestantism was a modernizing force. But the Michelade does not support this. When Crouzet emphasizes cool rationality, he downplays the fury of Protestants stuffing bloody bodies down the well at the bishop's palace.[59] When the Protestants conveyed their victims to the room traditionally used as a Lenten abattoir, they demonstrated their hatred and contempt. Catholic crowds elsewhere, who flushed Protestant corpses down the sewers, may have been sending a similar message as much as enacting a rite of purification.

Beyond comparing Protestant and Catholic styles of violence, in "The Rites of Violence" Davis is making an important, broader point: historians need to consider what crowds meant by their actions, rather than dismiss them as irrational. For her argument, one of the prime examples is that sixteenth-century crowds held mock trials of their victims, as Catholics in Montpellier did in 1569, to proclaim the justice of their cause. But, as Davis implies, we need to consider not just the message, but the audience. Explaining this mock-judicial conduct, she comments, "When the magistrate had not used his sword to defend the faith and the true Church and to punish the idolaters, then the crowd would do it for him."[60] In other words, the crowd was sending a message to the authorities, appealing to and rebuking them at the same time. Unlike in Montpellier, in the case of the Michelade the participants do not appear to have intended to deliver their message to the authorities but to their opponents. They were not proclaiming their views to posterity, nor to future historians, but to specific people whom they probably knew well. When we attempt to read the meaning of a sixteenth-century crowd's actions, we should bear in mind that we are eavesdropping. Understanding their meaning thus requires integrating social analysis with the analysis of discourse; unless we know something about the players, we will miss part of the conversation. Once we understand that the people engaged in murderous uprisings like the Michelade and other forms of religious riot were interested in sending messages to specific opponents and potential supporters, it becomes reasonable to conclude that, in many respects, the two groups shared a common language and largely similar symbolism. Religious violence was a form of communication, where the differing parties had different messages but used a common medium to communicate them. In Nîmes, Protestants sent a clear message, by their treatment of the elite and the clergy, that they hated and scorned Catholicism.

Nationwide, the Second Civil War ended in a peace settlement, signed by the king and the prince de Condé at Longjumeau in March 1568. This essentially restored the status quo ante, but was the merest pause, for hostilities resumed in September.[61] Nor did the Michelade inaugurate a long period of Protestant rule in Nîmes. The Treaty of Longjumeau stipulated that the Protestants would surrender all of the towns they held in exchange for a general amnesty. Royal troops entered the city in June. The amnesty did not extend to the time of the massacres, however. The Parlement of Toulouse, in a decree issued on March 18, 1569, condemned more than 100 people to death for their "participation." Many of those condemned had little or nothing to do with the massacre, however: the authorities seem, on principle, to have put every prominent Protestant on the list, including the clergy. Most of those named fled to escape punishment, but four men—only one of whom, Charles Rozel, one of the Messieurs and a long-time Protestant leader, was an important figure in the Michelade—were caught, transported to Toulouse, and executed. Their heads were returned to Nîmes and mounted on the four principal gates of the town. But the Catholic triumph did not last long, either: on November 15, 1569, Protestant forces seized Nîmes again, this time for good. This takeover was accompanied by a second massacre, of equal or greater size. Contemporary accounts suggest that 100–150 more Catholics were murdered. Others were held for ransom.[62] Since the uprising was successful, and the victorious Protestants had no incentive to investigate themselves, this second massacre is poorly documented. After this second bout of violence, Nîmes became a Protestant-dominated town for a century, a situation which was legitimized by the Edict of Nantes in 1598. If most of Nîmes's population had probably converted voluntarily, a significant number of Nîmes's Catholics had emigrated, converted under duress, or been killed. For the majority of Nîmes's Protestants, however, these gruesome tactics were irrelevant, and their commitment to their new religion remained strong. Much of Nîmes's remaining population stubbornly retained a barely concealed allegiance to the Reformed Church even after Louis XIV officially abolished toleration for Protestantism by the Edict of Fontainebleau in 1685. Protestantism in Nîmes had triumphed, politically if not morally.[63]

Conclusion

The Reformation in Nîmes in Comparative Perspective

Nîmes was at the heart of the French Protestant movement, and thus understanding why the movement succeeded there is important in and of itself. This chapter, however, will go beyond the Nîmes case in a brief exercise in comparative history, because the Nîmes experience may also help us to understand the extent and limits of the French Protestant movement's success elsewhere.

In the early phases of the Reformation, the social makeup of the Protestant movement in Nîmes resembled that of other French towns. The central hypothesis of this book has been that Protestant growth in most French towns eventually stalled, while in Nîmes Protestant leaders skillfully exploited the local political situation. They identified arguments that resonated with Nîmes's elite, given the elite's background and circumstances. The background was Nîmes's legal humanist outlook. The circumstances were the crown's indifference to the town's economic difficulties and to established legal procedures.[1] Thus, to test the hypotheses advanced in this book, Nîmes needs to be compared with other towns. This conclusion argues that the factors that have been identified as important in Nîmes were also present in other towns where Protestantism was successful, which is powerful confirmation that the explanation proposed here for the success of the Reformation in Nîmes is correct. Thus, the argument that has been advanced in this book may be extended to create a general model of religious conversion in sixteenth-century France and, in a more limited way, to a model of conversion in other European countries.

The Protestant movement succeeded exceptionally well in Nîmes, but not for idiosyncratic reasons. Instead, urban elites throughout the region held similar views and faced similar problems, and therefore in the Reformation crisis years of 1559–1562 they made similar decisions. I will refer to these as *systemic* reasons for the success of the Reformation in France, reasons that are widespread, regular, and thus to some degree predictable. Indeed, it does seem that the factors or variables that led to the movement's success in Nîmes were present in other cities, although generally to a lesser degree. This conclusion formulates some generalizable determinants in order to create a typology of French towns that will help us to understand not just the specific events in Nîmes, but the general characteristics of pro-Reform and pro-Catholic groups among urban French elites. Seen in comparative context, the Nîmes example gains additional explanatory power.

I wish to emphasize that sixteenth-century people had brains and, in some cases, considerable education. They cannot be reduced to unicellular organisms that acted based on the simplest stimulus-response model. They also cannot be reduced to irrational or wholly alien beings whose thought processes are incomprehensible to modern scholarship. It is my contention that their decisions were carefully thought through and rational within their frame of thought, and therefore they are open to analysis and explanation.[2]

The Reformation as Religious, Political, and Social Event

Historiography after the cultural turn in the 1980s has stressed the religious origins of the Wars of Religion.[3] This trend has been helpful in counterbalancing earlier, crudely materialistic views, but it is also naive in its simplicity. Individuals rarely do anything for one single reason, and large groups by definition act for a variety of reasons. No single explanation will do. Once we admit that different people had different motives, we can move on to the more interesting question: which motives were more important in which cases? By stressing the different phases of conversion, this volume has attempted to answer that question, at least for Nîmes. Mixed motives made life difficult for Nîmes's Protestant movement, but a movement consisting only of the pure would have been dangerously small. The movement was, of course, committed to missionary work on theological grounds. But its adherents were anxious for their own sakes to obtain the allegiance of the elites who controlled Nîmes's political institutions, and therefore they had to devise arguments and strategies to appeal to the town's elites and to the rest of the population.

Denis Crouzet, in his massive and influential study *Les guerriers de Dieu*, has argued that differing sociological analyses have mutually disproved each other, and therefore the social history of the Reformation has come to "une certaine impasse." Others have echoed his opinion. (More recently, Crouzet's opinion of sociological approaches seems to have improved.)[4] The same kinds of difficulties occur in reverse with theological, ideological, or psychological explanations for the Reformation, however. If there are patterns in the picture of religious conversions, such explanations will not work well, since they are inherently applicable to everybody equally. Still, if each local study of the Protestant movement in a French town in the sixteenth century showed that it had a different social profile than the others, Crouzet would have a good argument. But there *are* general patterns, and the Nîmes example, properly understood, clarifies the problem considerably. It is possible that Protestantism succeeded in some localities for random reasons: one village might have had a particularly persuasive preacher. But the overall distribution of Protestants in France was not random.

The Timing of the Reformation in France

The fundamental reasons to suppose that the growth of the Reformation in France was not random are that the movement shows considerable, non-random variation along two axes or variables: time and space. In terms of timing, French Protestantism grew everywhere from the mid-1550s onward, with extraordinary growth after Henri II's death in 1559. French Protestantism did not grow particularly rapidly after the publication of Luther's major works, which date from 1517 to 1520, nor even after the publication of Calvin's *Institutes* in 1536. Clearly, some important change at that time made Calvinism much more attractive throughout France. The growth of French Protestantism after 1559 surely owes something to the ascent of first a fifteen- and then a ten-year-old to the throne, but the growth prior to 1559 suggests that Henri's death only accelerated a process already under way.

These political changes thus cannot fully explain the dramatic growth of French Protestantism in the later 1550s and early 1560s. Instead, this book has argued that the movement grew because it was able to attract additional social groups: first lawyers and then officials joined the movement in the early 1560s. It should therefore be clear that when comparing Nîmes to other towns, it is essential to compare like with like; for example, to compare the social profile of the early Protestant movement in Nîmes with that of the early Protestant movement elsewhere. To illustrate the point, consider figure C.1, which gives the occupational

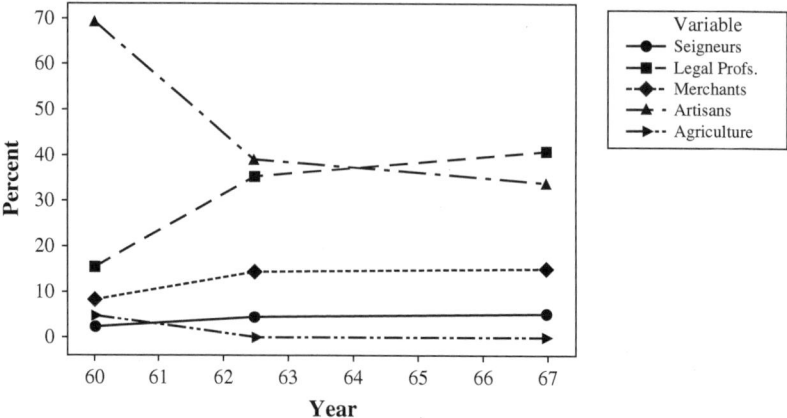

FIGURE C.1 Comparison of occupational distribution of the Protestant movement in Montpellier (1560), Toulouse (1562–1563), and Grenoble (1561–1573). Source: Greengrass.

distribution of Protestants in three different towns: Montpellier, Toulouse, and Grenoble. The information comes from different years, so I have arranged it in chronological order. If all the occupational data had been collected at the same time, it would indicate that the Protestant movement had a different composition in each town. But once the information from the three towns is arranged in order, a different pattern emerges: the Protestant movement was evolving, with the percentage of artisans falling and that of the liberal professions rising, while the others stayed relatively flat (with perhaps a slight rise for merchants and seigneurs and a slight decline for agricultural workers). This picture is similar to the changes that occurred in Nîmes. Other historians, including Henry Heller, Denis Richet, Pierre Imbart de la Tour, Joan Davies (for a slightly later period), and David Nicholls, have noted this general pattern, although it is not as widely recognized as it should be. Indeed, most surveys do not mention it.[5]

For over a century, historians have argued over the social composition of the French Protestant movement. Henri Hauser and, more recently, Emmanuel Le Roy Ladurie argued that the critical component of the movement was the merchant and artisan class. Lucien Febvre argued that doctors of law were crucial. Lucien Romier pointed to the influence of the nobility, who, he argued, tended to take over the direction of the Protestant party from Calvin and the pastors and radicalize it.[6] In Nîmes, true nobles were absent, since most seigneurs were really local lawyers and officials who had bought seigneurial rights and châteaux in nearby villages. This study has suggested that Le Roy Ladurie and Febvre were both correct: both groups were crucial, at different phases of the movement's development. If (stretching a point) we accept Nîmes's seigneurs as true nobility, Romier's argument also has validity. Upper-class men—namely the Messieurs—instigated the Michelade in Nîmes, while the consistory tried to restrain them. The problem with Hauser's, Le Roy Ladurie's, and Febvre's accounts is that they are fundamentally sociological, that is, static, rather than truly dynamic or historical. Once the sequential nature of conversion is understood, the apparent contradictions among their theories are resolvable.

Careful comparison suggests other similarities between the rise of Protestantism in Nîmes and in other French cities. It is noteworthy, for example, that the clergy were generally prominent converts in the early years of the Protestant movement's growth in Nîmes, but not in the later stages. Pierre d'Airebaudouze, the only known cleric to flee from Nîmes to Geneva, did so quite early: in January 1553. Similarly, of the eleven French bishops who converted to Protestantism, at least eight of them probably did so before 1558.[7] A brace of prominent clerical defectors in the crisis years of 1559–1562 would have been highly valuable publicity. But this did not occur, despite the dramatic increase in conversions in those years. This is additional evidence for one of the arguments of this book, namely, the particular importance of theological motives among the earliest converts. A similar logic helps to explain the role of scholars and professors. In Nîmes, there were no known converts among the town's teachers in 1559–1562, despite the prominence of Imbert Pécolet and Claude Baduel in the early years. Many other local studies have pointed out the prominence of scholars among the earliest converts, but none have argued that they were prominent in 1559–1562.

What Philip Benedict said of the early Protestant movement in Rouen could well describe the movement in Nîmes and many other towns: Protestants had a hard time making converts in the food and drink trades and among the poor, as well as from the very top, including lawyers. Protestants tended to come from wealthy artisan families, although from the stratum just below the top in each trade. Members of the town council were, however, well represented in Protestant ranks. More literate trades were generally more Protestant. Protestants, Benedict concludes, were likely to come from "somewhat below the very highest status occupations, but with the degree of literacy, self-confidence, and personal independence needed to reject the tutelage of the clergy and embrace the idea of a priesthood of all believers."[8]

In a well-known article on the Protestant printing workers of Lyon, Natalie Z. Davis has argued that "often there was some novelty" in the trades which were disproportionately Protestant, either because the trade was new, or new to Lyon, or involved new claims to prestige. She argues that these tradesmen had a particular pride in their work: the printers, for example, were regularly called "impudent" by hostile observers, no doubt because they were highly paid and literate, for artisans. Their product was also essential to the learned throughout Christendom. This argument has not been widely accepted, largely because printing workers were not a large part of the population in French towns, and yet other towns had many Protestants in them. Mark Greengrass further points out that the craft pride that Davis's printing workers displayed was actually widespread among Protestant urban artisans, for example, among the weavers of Amiens studied by David L. Rosenberg. Davis's doctoral dissertation provides a remarkable table listing over one thousand Protestants and their occupations. When her figures are considered in detail, her conclusions are actually quite similar to Benedict's. In Lyon, Protestants were underrepresented in the food and building trades, except in a few of the most high-status building trades, such as cabinetmakers. Textile workers, including weavers (but less so carders), goldsmiths, and of course Davis's focus, printing workers, were overrepresented. Merchants were also heavily Protestant.[9] In short, early Protestants in Rouen, Lyon, and Nîmes were a group akin to what would later be called "the aristocracy of labor," plus the *petite* (and perhaps *moyenne*) *bourgeoisie*. Such people were high enough up the social ladder to feel that they were entitled to all the perks of society's elite, but low enough that they did not get them. They were also constantly afraid that they would be pushed lower down the social scale, and therefore extremely jealous of their privileges. One effect of the Reformation, in Lyon and in Nîmes, was that the upper reaches of this social group, most notably the merchants and bourgeois, greatly increased their power in the religious sphere. For example, Davis was able to reconstruct the members of Lyon's Protestant Consistory. She found that it was dominated by merchants, similar to the situation in Nîmes.[10] The difficulty is that, given the rules of the game in southern France, a Protestant movement limited to such people was doomed to remain a minority, and therefore a failure.

One of the goals of the French Protestant movement, like many other movements in Christianity, was to convert the entire world. Had they been entirely successful, there would be no category of person more likely to be Protestant than any other. But it was rare to convert everyone, although in Nîmes they came close. Where Protestants did have a social profile, it was because the movement failed in its mission. One of the conclusions that emerges clearly from the Nîmes experience is that, in order to understand why Protestants in various localities were successful or not, we need to know which categories of people Protestants managed to convert. Protestants needed to convert a sufficient percentage of the population to be successful. In particular, they needed to convert a significant segment of the elites who controlled the machinery of the state. The conversion of the elites was thus part of the strategy used by the initial converts, just as the parlements were particularly anxious to repress heresy among the elites. The consequence of the varying degrees of success of the Protestant movement in different cities is that, even though early Protestants had a similar social distribution in many places, after 1562 the movement's profile varied.

One way to describe the arc of the French Reformation over time is to see it as a form of maturation. The Protestant movement had to come to terms with the world, accepting it while also seeking to change it. This approach is similar to Ernst Troeltsch's. In his terms, the Nîmes Protestant movement began as a sect—a small, tightly bound conventicle of true believers—which evolved to became a church. Such change is essential for religious communities to grow and to continue. It would therefore be silly to say that the later waves of Nîmes's Protestants converted for "political" reasons. Instead, the nature of Nîmes's religious institutions changed as part of a natural, inevitable evolution.[11] The ultimate success or failure of Protestantism in France depended on its ability, given the resources available to it, to negotiate this process.

The Spatial Distribution of Protestantism in France

The second axis or variable along which we can see distinct patterns to the French Reformation is space. Five conclusions can be drawn from the spatial distribution of Protestantism in France: it was most successful (1) in towns; (2) in the south; (3) outside of the largest cities and administrative capitals; (4) in areas that were militarily defensible; and (5) in regions that were long-standing parts of the kingdom, unlike recently acquired areas like Provence or Brittany. In Nîmes, all of these conditions applied, so it should not be surprising that the Protestant movement was particularly successful there. In a few other towns—La Rochelle, Montauban, Montpellier—conditions were similar. Elsewhere, Protestantism was generally less successful, with some exceptions which will be discussed below.

The Role of Towns

Since most historians who have written on the subject would agree that Protestantism was particularly successful in towns, it seems unnecessary to devote an elaborate discussion to the issue. Most commonly, they have argued that towns and cities had sharply higher literacy rates than the countryside, and therefore were more open to a religion which placed a high value on Bible reading. Literacy rates for sixteenth-century Europe are hard to come by. For many regions, including Nîmes, it is impossible to count the number of signatures versus marks on documents—the standard way to calculate literacy rates—because people were not usually required to sign legal and other documents. However, studies for later periods do indicate that people in towns had much higher literacy than those in rural areas, and there is no reason to believe that the sixteenth century was any different, even if it is impossible to give an actual literacy rate.

It should, however, be noted that the rural hinterland near Nîmes, the Cévennes, was one of the few rural areas where the French Protestant movement was highly successful. Although the research for this book was largely limited to Nîmes itself, I did discover some material which suggests why this may have been so.[12] It should be remembered that Nîmes's courts had jurisdiction over a large portion of south central France. Furthermore, much of the local economy, especially the cloth and leather trades, depended on products brought down from the uplands toward Nîmes and the coast, and the whole diocese had a shared tax burden. Immigration from the surrounding countryside was extremely high: at least a quarter of the people who married in Nîmes were born elsewhere (see Chapter 1). Thus, the relationship between Nîmes and its hinterland was largely cooperative, while other cities and towns in France had acrimonious relations with the surrounding villages. The movement of goods and people seems to have created a community of ideas. There were additional reasons for people in the region to be attracted to Protestantism: the bishop of Uzès's conversion may have influenced some people. Protestant preachers circulated in the countryside during the 1550s, when there is no evidence for such activity in Nîmes itself. Nonetheless, Nîmes's effect on its hinterland is striking. If one compares the distribution of immigrants to Nîmes to the distribution of Protestant churches in the map of the region around Nîmes (figure C.2), the similarities are remarkable. The region to the north and east of Uzès sent few immigrants to Nîmes and had few Protestant churches. Villagers in that region tended instead to migrate to Catholic Avignon. Similarly, in the diocese of Mende, almost coterminous with the modern department of the Lozère, the part of the diocese north of Florac was Catholic and unconnected to Nîmes. South of Florac, where immigration to Nîmes began, Protestantism flourished.

The Attraction of Protestantism in the South

Some historians have argued that, since southern France had generally lower literacy rates than the north, it is strange that Protestantism was particularly

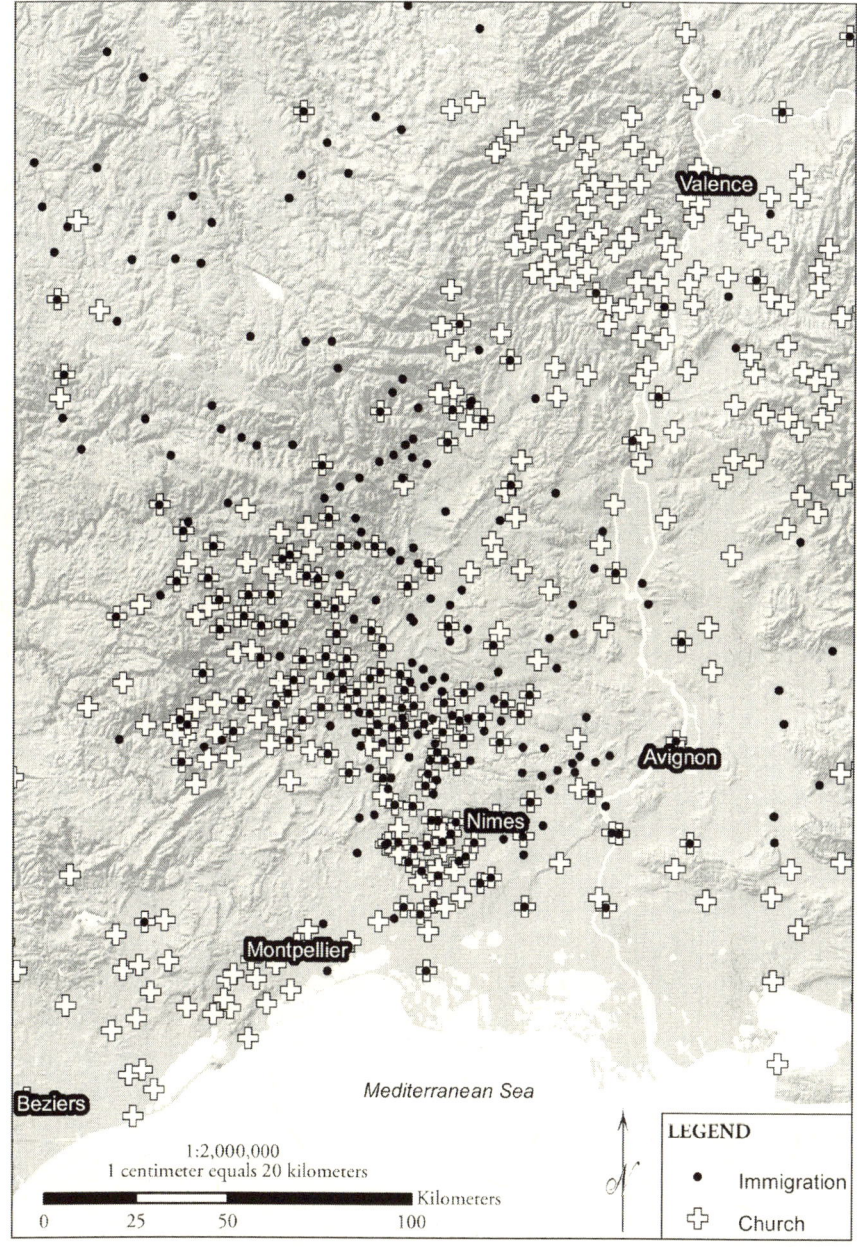

FIGURE C.2. Protestant churches and immigration to Nîmes in the Nîmes region. Sources: Mours and ADG, Series IIE.

successful in the south.[13] After all, almost all Protestant books were published in French or Latin, rather than in any of the various Occitan dialects spoken in southern France. They have concluded that this hindered the spread of Protestantism in the Midi. The lack of books in Occitan may not have mattered much, however. Literacy in this period meant, above all, literacy in Latin or at least French, and therefore most southerners with even a basic education were able to read at least one of those languages. Clergy were prominent among early Protestants because they were interested in theological issues and had the sophisticated literacy required to be susceptible to Protestant theological arguments. Furthermore, among elites, lawyers were especially dominant in southern French cities, although their influence was increasing throughout the country. Both groups needed to know both French and Latin.[14] Thus, southern urban elites were well able to read Protestant books.

In general, the imprint of Roman culture was greater in southern France than in the north. Beyond France, the imperial cities of southern Germany and Switzerland seem to have had the most similar experience of the Reformation to that of Nîmes. The Reformation in the imperial cities has been analyzed in a celebrated series of studies by Bernd Moeller. He argues that the Reformed character of the Reformation there owed something to the region's deep engagement with humanism. In southwestern Germany, the theology was Zwinglian, rather than Calvinist, but the two shared strong affinities. There, too, the Reformation seems to have bubbled up from below. The elites were more cautious. In contrast, the imperial cities had a high degree of autonomy, and therefore resentment of central authority did not play much of a role in their decision to convert to Protestantism.[15]

Southern elites, because they were dominated by lawyers, may actually have been more open to Protestantism than northern ones. In the north, merchants and artisans in guilds tended to have a greater role in civic governance. Merchants certainly had an incentive to know how to read, but only needed literacy to record their business transactions in their *livres de raison*. Lawyers, because of the nature of their profession, had a more sophisticated literacy in general than merchants or artisans did. They needed literacy to do their jobs, and they used reading (and writing) to articulate complicated arguments. Lawyers well versed in the Justinian Code should not have had much trouble following Calvin's theology. Although the south may have had lower literacy rates, its leaders were probably better readers than those in the north, and they were aware of and frequently well disposed toward humanist ideas. Although the Midi had lower literacy rates, its literate classes were probably more susceptible to the Protestant message.

The lawyers of the Midi were also ideologically predisposed to be sympathetic to some aspects of the Reformation. Most studies of the Reformation in France have suggested that southern France was particularly susceptible to the Protestant message because its cities had the physical distance from Paris and the traditions of independence necessary for their residents to convert to a new religion despite royal opposition. Arlette Jouanna in particular has emphasized this, and the role of southern town officials, a point which the case of Nîmes strongly confirms. Furthermore, the ideological trend of legal scholarship, as with other humanist studies at this time, had considerable overlap with Protestant ideas. Both were intent on searching *ad fontes,* to the sources of tradition. Calvin himself also had legal training, and it influenced his theological style. All cities were concerned to protect their liberties, but southern elites, steeped in Roman law, were particularly concerned about legal forms. Indeed, one of the reasons why Protestants succeeded in Nîmes is that they used legitimate political means, rather than violence. Instead, when the crown used troops to overturn the town's established legal procedures, the effect was dramatically counterproductive. Using violence proved that the monarchy had the weaker arguments. Protestants skillfully exploited the situation, built on their popularity with the cahier, and then won the next election. Protestants in Grenoble and Rouen were unable to restrain themselves and paid the consequences. Initially, the movement in the two cities converted something like 20 to 25 percent of the population, but Protestantism in Grenoble stalled after a Protestant army seized the town in the early 1560s, while in Rouen the same process occurred after the local Protestants seized power.[16] Although it was at least partly the Protestant party's initial success which tempted it to resort to violence, it was a temptation the Protestants needed to resist if they wanted potential converts to have a favorable impression of the new religion.

In northern French towns where guilds retained significant political power, governance tended to be significantly more fractured than in southern French towns where one group, usually lawyers, monopolized it. Guild rivalries could be venomous. In guild-dominated towns, Protestants had to adopt a somewhat different recruiting strategy. On the one hand, it was probably easier for them to gain a foothold, perhaps even converting the majority of one occupation. But in a society where everyone was pigeonholed, where hosiers were only friendly with other hosiers, converting the entire town would not be easy. Amiens, as described by David Rosenberg, seems to have been an example of this. There, Protestantism was highly concentrated among weavers and wool carders, who were numerous and included many of the poorer people of the city. The trade, governed by the *sayetterie,* grew large in the late fifteenth and early sixteenth century, but faced increasing economic competition. The city council, which had recently come to be dominated by lawyers, tried to regulate the trade because it wished to increase municipal revenue and because boom-and-bust cycles occurred frequently, leading to high costs in poor relief. However, the *sayetterie* bitterly resented such efforts. In their view, the city was levying especially heavy taxes on a trade whose members were not especially wealthy. The regulations, which the city did not impose on other guilds, were also an infringement of the guild's right to govern itself. By the 1530s, these disputes had led to an immense, costly lawsuit in the Paris courts. The suit necessarily raised fundamental questions of the government's authority versus the guild's autonomy: the city government argued that it needed extra income and special police powers because of Amiens' location close to the frontier with the Spanish Netherlands. The money was necessary to maintain the city's fortifications. The powers were equally necessary because the untrustworthy, turbulent guildsmen could tempt the Hapsburgs to invade. The tradesmen felt singled out and raged against the injustice of it all. If Rosenberg's analysis is correct, it is easy to see how Protestant activists could have exploited these issues analogously to what happened in Nîmes. At the same time, it would have been difficult for them to expand from the *sayetterie* to the lawyers and the other key occupational groups that controlled city government. By contrast, towns without such deep fissures and with one dominant elite were a riskier, but easier proposition. It was nearly all or nothing: convert the elite or be crushed by it.[17]

Legal thinking also influenced the Protestant movement in those places where it assumed power. Many scholars have noted Calvinism's legalistic tone, with its elaborate systems for poor relief and moral regulation. Glenn Sunshine has observed that the hierarchy of French Calvinist governance mirrored the levels of local administration. He also considers, and rejects, the notion that French Protestant synods were modeled on local Estates.[18] It would be more fruitful, however, to compare the various governing councils of the French Protestant church with municipal councils, especially with the consular system used in the south. Protestant delegates had more contact with municipal assemblies than with any other form of governing body.

The Disadvantages of Protestantism in the Largest Urban Centers

Although many of the largest provincial cities in France were administrative capitals and therefore their populations had high concentrations of lawyers, the Protestant movement was not generally successful in them. This might seem to contradict the argument put forward here, namely, that in the troubles of the 1550s, Protestant arguments had a particular appeal to the legal mind. If Nîmes was dominated by lawyers, surely Aix, Grenoble, Toulouse, and Bordeaux, which were the seats of parlements, were even more so. However, although men with law degrees were even more influential in these cities, they were judges and officials rather than advocates, and therefore much more tightly bound to the crown and under much more direct scrutiny. Even in Nîmes, ordinary lawyers converted distinctly sooner than did members of the présidial court. The motives that restrained a judge on the Nîmes présidial acted even more powerfully on the judges of the parlements. In Nîmes, lawyers were the backbone of the consular class and thus much more directly concerned with the town's financial plight. When the town needed to buy grain to prevent starvation and rioting, the consuls had to dig into their own pockets; the judges did not.

Toulouse demonstrates the differing perspectives of lawyers and officials quite dramatically. In Toulouse, the judges of the parlement led the Catholic forces in a mini-civil war against the city council, which was dominated by the town's lawyers. Protestants were (again) especially heavily represented among merchants and the liberal professions, while Catholics were more prominent both higher and lower on the social scale: they dominated the parlement and the lower-status artisan trades. In the end, victory went to the big battalions: the judges were richer, and Toulouse remained largely Catholic.[19] Even if sociological factors alone do not explain why people converted, they are crucial to understanding whether people were allowed to remain in the religion they chose. People and regions with particularly close ties to the crown tended to stay Catholic, which is almost certainly why Paris was always a Catholic-dominated city.

The Role of Geography

In Grenoble, the parlement was one of the main sources of support for the Catholic cause, but military defensibility was even more important. Initially, Protestantism was distinctly successful in Dauphiné, and Grenoble, the capital, was not exempt. Peter France's detailed calculations suggest that approximately 20 percent of Grenoble residents had converted by the early 1560s. Protestants also thoroughly infiltrated the recently refounded university. Furthermore, as figure C.1 shows, a significant percentage of the elite legal families had converted. Grenoble's government was also dominated by lawyers: the first consul was habitually a "noble," which meant in practice a lawyer who represented clients at the parlement. Likewise, the second consul was commonly also a legal official, a *procureur*. Grenoble's lawyers were also sufficiently influential that they were exempt from the *taille*, although in 1539–1541 members of the city council tried to force them to pay extraordinary tax levies.[20] Despite strong opposition from the parlement, the Protestants seized control on April 1, 1562, and were able to hold the city almost continuously for twenty-one months, until December 4, 1563. The Protestants did their best to solidify their rule: churches were cleansed of their idolatrous images, and the representatives of the clergy on municipal councils were replaced by lawyers.[21]

However, although the Protestant party was strong in Grenoble, it was not as strong as in Nîmes. The presence of the parlement was one reason for this. But perhaps more important, Grenoble was much more open than Nîmes was to Catholic military attacks, because it was in a more exposed position at the extreme end of the "Protestant crescent." Social structures do not exist in a vacuum, but within a physical setting—both natural and manmade. This physical setting affected the extent to which certain aspirations could be expressed. While Protestants held Grenoble, the town was besieged twice by Catholic forces and captured once (the Catholics were forced to leave ten days later). It is unclear whether or not Grenoble was sacked on this occasion; accounts differ. After the Catholics fled, the Protestant commander ordered some remaining Catholic troops put to the sword, and the *procureur du roi,* a leading Catholic, was executed. In the second siege, the Catholics used artillery. When a Protestant army arrived and saved Grenoble from further bombardment, the town's Protestant leaders felt obliged to permit them to sack one of the Catholic neighborhoods in town. Another Catholic neighborhood, on the right bank of the Isère, had already been abandoned because it was indefensible, and it was then destroyed by the attackers. Catholics also attempted several other, smaller attacks and *coups de main.* Protestants executed those Catholics whom they found had taken part. On various occasions, both leading Protestants and leading Catholics had to flee the city, and both fled after an outbreak of plague in 1564–1565, which was so bad that consular elections were canceled for the year.[22] Nîmes's Protestants had to endure several years of Catholic rule, but they experienced nothing like this. Although both sides in Grenoble made repeated gestures of reconciliation, it is hardly surprising that over the 1560s attitudes hardened, and the Protestant movement lost momentum.

In Montpellier, Protestants had an advantage over their co-religionists in Grenoble: they were located at the heart of the Protestant crescent, which extended from La Rochelle to Nîmes and then up the Rhone. They were comparatively safe from Catholic armies. Despite this advantage, in Montpellier as in Grenoble, Catholics dominated the highest royal institutions, and those institutions consistently exercised their influence to encourage Catholic worship. Nonetheless, the available evidence suggests that approximately half of Montpellier's population converted to Protestantism. Thus, the new religion there was far more successful than in Grenoble, but less successful than in Nîmes.

Fortified by geography, Protestants were able to maintain their position, and by the later sixteenth century, Montpellier was firmly in the Protestant camp.[23]

The Protestant Advantage in the Older Royal Provinces

Political geography also encouraged or discouraged the Protestant movement. Regions that were long-standing parts of France were markedly more likely to have enthusiastic Protestant movements than were recently acquired regions. In the two generations prior to Luther, the Valois kings added vast areas to the royal demesne: Brittany, Provence, Picardy, Burgundy, the Auvergne. These areas were all strongly Catholic in the Wars of Religion. By contrast, the Protestant crescent can be clearly seen in the strip of older royal territory which stretches from Dauphiné via Languedoc and Guyenne to the Atlantic and then loops around to Poitou. In the north, the three royal provinces of long standing were Normandy, which was heavily Protestant; the Île-de-France, which benefited too much from royal patronage to consider heresy; and Champagne, which was under the firm control of the ultra-Catholic Guises. (Compare, in figure C.3, the territory acquired before 1461 with the distribution of Protestant churches.) Protestantism found adherents everywhere, even in the most ardently Catholic towns, but it made the leap from its initial sociological niche into the crucial governing legal elites much more readily in the older provinces than in the younger ones. It is exceptionally unlikely statistically that this correlation is accidental; systemic reasons are almost certainly responsible. Although there has been little research on the topic, it is plausible that the kinds of frustrations and disappointments that Nîmes's elite felt in the late 1550s and early 1560s were less prevalent in the newly acquired provinces. The crown had every reason to avoid meddling in the affairs of these provinces, to limit its financial demands, and generally not to tamper with local traditions. They were frequently on the border (Provence, Picardy, Burgundy), inaccessible (Auvergne), or spoke a radically different language (Brittany), or the rival Hapsburg family claimed suzerainty (Burgundy). The crown's receipts did increase dramatically in the period, however; if certain regions were exempted for political reasons, the burden must have fallen all the harder on the rest. The most prominent modern American historian of political institutions in sixteenth-century France, J. Russell Major, stresses the comparative mildness of the French state's exactions in the sixteenth century, compared to the absolutism of the seventeenth. Other historians, familiar with his findings, might be somewhat skeptical of the picture of political crisis depicted here. It is worth remembering, however, that the people of sixteenth-century France had yet to experience seventeenth-century absolutism. Even if fiscal demands under Henri II paled by contrast

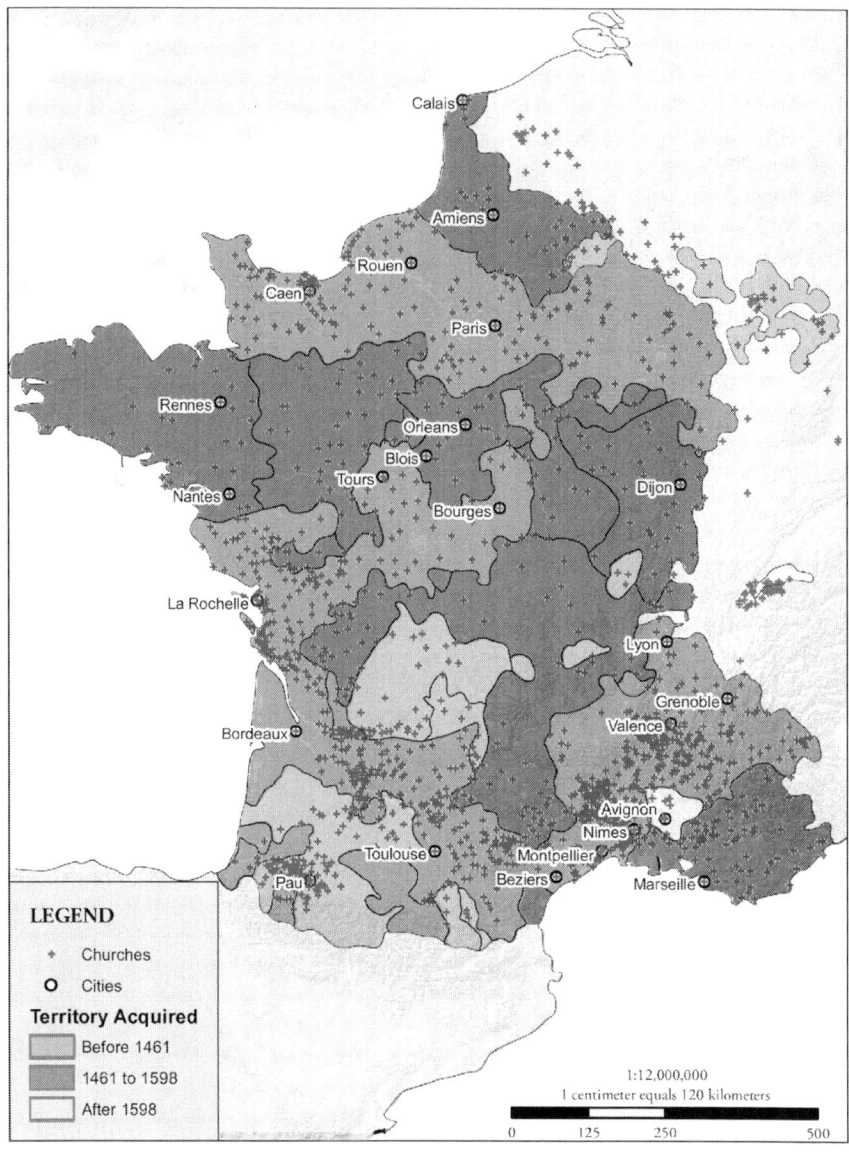

FIGURE C.3 Distribution of Protestant churches in France. Source: Mours.

with those under Louis XIII or Louis XIV, that does not mean that they were not bitterly resented. Seventeenth-century French monarchs also benefited from the response to the disasters of the Wars of Religion, which made France the playing field for the rivalries of the other great powers of Europe and devastated the economy in the latter part of the sixteenth century. As another historian of sixteenth-century France, J. H. M. Salmon, has pointed out, absolutism in the seventeenth century was at least in part a reaction to the chaos of the Wars of Religion.[24]

The Future of Reformation Historiography

In the early 1560s, the townspeople of France had an opportunity to change their religion if they so chose. Like all choices, this one was constrained rather than altogether free, but nonetheless Protestantism was a real alternative. Subsequent generations did not have the same freedom, and social pressures from the Protestant community inhibited conversion back to Catholicism. Even after the revocation of the Edict of Nantes in 1685, Nîmes's Protestants largely refused to succumb to royal pressure to return to the Catholic Church. Instead, their religion went underground. In one respect, this is a quite literal description: they put their church archives in the basement of the hospital, where they remained until shortly before the French Revolution.

Protestant and Catholic identities became part of the social structure of the region. As a result, the Reformation affected every subsequent event, since religious allegiances heavily influenced political ones at crucial periods, such as the French Revolution and the Second World War.[25] In Nîmes, Catholics tended to be more conservative politically and were thus more apt to oppose the revolution in 1789 and more prone to support Vichy in 1940. Protestants, in contrast, saw the revolution as the end of persecution and the beginning of religious liberty. A century and a half later, they were also more suspicious of the Vichy regime and more active in the Resistance. As a result, Protestants, most famously Pastor Étienne Trocmé, were notably active in aiding Jews to escape deportation to the death camps.[26] Even on a personal level, the religious cleavage had important consequences. Dr. Lucien Simon, a pillar of Nîmes's Jewish community until his death in 2003, reminisced once with me about his experiences as a child before the war. He commented that his family had Jewish friends and Protestant friends, but no Catholic ones: the two religious minorities felt joined in solidarity. Similarly, Jean Dumas, my landlord when I lived in Nîmes, was a Protestant. He told me that, through the 1950s, the Nîmes Chamber of Commerce had an informal rule that the presidency of the organization had to alternate between Catholics and Protestants, to prevent bickering between them. Obviously, such distinctions should not be exaggerated; the cleavage, although real, was not absolute. Its persistence over four hundred years is nonetheless impressive.

For these and other reasons, the Reformation is a crucial topic in European and even world history. Between the conversion of the barbarians and the rise of secularism in the modern period, the Reformation is the most important change in the social history of European religion and (largely despite the wishes of the Reformers) a major cause of what most of us still call modernity. It is not just an issue for Protestants or Catholics. However, much of the history of the Reformation has been strongly sectarian: Protestants have written about Protestants and Catholics have written about Catholics, each trying to prove that their side was correct. It took a long time for a more neutral, objective, or secular approach to have adherents, but for a brief while most American historians at least tried to avoid confessionaism, however difficult they found it to achieve in practice. More recently, with the cultural or linguistic turn, Brad Gregory, among others, has criticized even the idea of objectivity for historians of religion. He is afraid above all of reductionism.[27] Gregory's position has some merit: authors can gain a lot when they write on subjects about which they are passionate, even partisan. Although I share little ideologically with J. C. D. Clark, for example, I was impressed by his insight into right-wing Toryism in *English Society, 1688–1832*.[28] The difficulty is that the very passion that gave him such insight into some historical actors prevented him from having insight into many others. If nothing else, historians who choose deliberately to write to exalt their denomination will have a hard time answering Jesus's question: "And why beholdest thou the mote that is in thy brother's eye, but considerest not the beam that is in thine own eye?" (Matthew 7:3).

Surely, the best approach is that historians be self-aware. They should strive at different points in their books to present the world through the eyes of each of the major players, something that this book may not have achieved. My basic assumption has been that people normally remain in their parents' religion (due to cognitive consonance and social pressure, if nothing else) unless they have exceptionally compelling reasons to change. Thus, Nîmes's Catholics needed no positive reasons to remain Catholic. But this strategy has the negative consequence that, since the reasons to remain Catholic seem so obvious, this book has only rarely had the occasion to try to analyze events from a Catholic viewpoint. Despite that, I hope I have avoided some of the excesses of Protestant historiography, which minimizes the Michelade, for example.[29]

Confessional historiography has caused historians of the Reformation to avoid studies of the conversion process in sixteenth-century Europe and to fail to recognize mass conversion experiences even when the evidence for them is plain, as in Nîmes. From a religious perspective, religious conversion must remain a sacred mystery. This approach continues to be influential, even in secular accounts, since the Reformation set the terms of debate on many issues of religious history, even outside of Christianity. This heritage has led historians to underutilize anthropological accounts of religious conversion, despite their obvious relevance. This omission is particularly striking since early modern European history was the first subfield within the discipline of history to open up to anthropological theory. To this day, few local studies have focused on the period covered by this book, which saw the rise of Protestant communities throughout France. Detailed narratives of towns and provinces during the Wars of Religion remain far more common. In them, the origins of the local Protestant movement are frequently ignored, and the crisis years of 1559–1562 are the briefest prologue. Certainly, it is interesting to learn how sixteenth-century communities coped with a new religion in their midst, but it is striking that comparatively few studies have considered why it arose in the first place.

There is a notable tendency, driven by confessionalism, for Christian historians to push conversions backward in time. Pious historians of the early Church attempted to prove that Christianity grew because God favored it. Their proof was that people converted in vast numbers at the very beginning of the movement. The word and Jesus's miracles were enough; the Church did not need Constantine's conversion, which gave it the mundane advantage of state support. Likewise, Abraham Borrel, who wrote the most influential Protestant account of the Reformation in Nîmes, exaggerated the early growth of the Reformation in Nîmes in order to suggest that it was a miracle and thus to show that the rise of the Protestant movement in Nîmes enjoyed divine sanction. In his account, by the crisis years of 1559–1562 most people in Nîmes had already converted. When he discussed the outbreak of mass preaching and the seizure of Catholic churches, he assumed that Nîmes's inhabitants, already Protestants, were merely making their first public profession of their religion, because the weakening of the monarchy after Henri II's death left them free to do so. The underlying logic is that people converted so early—as soon as they heard the new doctrines—because Protestantism is The Truth. No further explanation is needed, and the crisis years of 1559–1562 are not especially interesting. This book asks, following Gibbon: even if we grant the truth of Reformed theology, what were the secondary reasons for its spread?[30]

More secular historians may also have been hampered in studying periods like the crisis years of 1559–1562 in France by the liminal quality of religious conversion. Even people who have directly experienced conversion find it difficult sometimes to speak accurately about their experiences after the event, since the nature of conversion is that it alters their self-perceptions. Historians and anthropologists who wish to understand such experiences have to break down such liminal moments into phases or component parts, as historians of the French Revolution have done. Nîmes's Protestants tried to erase the evidence of their Catholic past when they began to call the cathedral a temple, and then went even further and destroyed first the stained glass in the newly Protestant churches and then eventually the church buildings themselves. It would be unwise for historians to be misled, however: another term for such "liminal moments" is "crucial historical turning points."

Many prominent historians have proposed causes of the Reformation which presuppose that Protestantism is a better religion than Catholicism. Steven Ozment, for example, argues that Protestantism lifted the intense spiritual anxiety induced by late medieval Catholicism, while Euan Cameron argues that Protestantism flattered the laity.[31] These arguments are necessarily incomplete, since avoiding anxiety and enjoying flattery should logically have continued to cause people to convert to Protestantism well after the sixteenth century. Rather, it is surely necessary to look carefully at the people in the historical moment to understand their mixed motives, the choices they had, and what constrained them. In short, a satisfying history of the Reformation requires understanding both sides.

Appendix A

The Evolution of the Protestant Movement in Nîmes, 1560–1562

Occupational Group	Nîmes Population %	Nîmes Population Cases	Protestants to 1560 %	Protestants to 1560 Cases	Cahier Signers %	Cahier Signers Cases	Protestant Leaders in 1561 %	Protestant Leaders in 1561 Cases	Protestants in 1562 %	Protestants in 1562 Cases
1. High-status officials, etc.	3	125	2	1	7	16	4	2	15	16
2. Medical professions	2	86	4	2	2	6	4	2	4	4
3. Legal professions	9	379	9	4	15	37	15	8	18	19
4. Education and books	1	59	0	0	2	4	4	2	2	1
5. Clergy	3	115	6	3	0	0	2	1	3	2
6. Other professions	0.4	20	0	0	0	0	2	1	0	0
7. *All professions* (lines 1–6)	*18*	*784*	*21*	*10*	*26*	*64*	*30*	*16*	*40*	*42*
8. High-status artisans	8	367	28	13	18	45	19	10	14	15
9. *All high status* (lines 7–8)	*30*	*1,276*	*49*	*23*	*44*	*109*	*49*	*26*	*54*	*57*
10. Food, drink, groceries	5	235	0	0	1	3	3	1	3	3
11. Leather trades	8	363	6	3	11	26	15	8	10	11
12. Textiles	12	504	21	10	17	43	13	7	18	19
13. *Clothing: leather and textiles* (lines 11–12)	*20*	*867*	*28*	*13*	*29*	*72*	*28*	*15*	*28*	*30*
14. Building, wood, metal	9	391	2	1	7	17	9	5	9	10
15. *All artisans* (lines 8, 10–12, 14)	*43*	*1,860*	*58*	*27*	*55*	*137*	*59*	*31*	*55*	*58*
16. Agriculture	34	1,466	15	7	13	31	9	5	5	5
17. Other	3	121	6	3	7	16	3	1	1	1
TOTALS	100	4,231	100	47	100	248	100	53	100	100

Sources: ADG, Series IIE; Puech, "Débuts"; ADHG, Series B; Geisendorf, *Livre des habitants*; CR.

Appendix B

Constructing the Notarial Database

Notarial records of wills and marriages are crucial to this study. They open an essential window onto people's lives, and fortunately, they do so at critical, solemn points in the life cycle. At the same time, they give us only certain information, and the window they provide is necessarily somewhat skewed and partial.

In order to make the records useful, they had to be transformed into machine-readable form. Readers who wish to understand the basis for the statistics used in the body of this book are entitled to understand how the database was created; they may also be interested in the details of its creation if they intend to use databases in their own research. This appendix will cover five main issues: (1) bias, (2) coding last names, (3) occupational information, (4) social status, and (5) network analysis issues.

Bias

The database of notarial contracts used in this book is quite large. It consists of every will and marriage contract which survives for Nîmes from 1550 to 1562 Old Style, that is, March 25, 1550, to March 24, 1563. This totals about 1,100 marriage contracts and just under 700 wills. For these contracts, I recorded the principals (husband, wife, testator); the fathers (for marriages); and all witnesses. The result was about 13,000 references to named individuals, the largest database of its kind known to me. The data should therefore be particularly reliable, although no sixteenth-century statistics can be considered absolutely trustworthy. Nonetheless, there are two biases in the sample that are important in some contexts. First, Jean and Jacques Ursi, two notaries who were early converts to Protestantism, account for about half of the surviving acts. The second is that the Ursis' acts are not evenly distributed across the database: instead, wills from other notaries survive in large

	Percentage		
Year	Ursi family	Non-Ursi	Acts
1550	87	13	99
1551	77	23	160
1552	77	23	66
1553	91	9	111
1554	77	23	153
1555	73	27	120
1556	4	96	48
1557	30	70	132
1558	36	64	172
1559	10	90	76
1560	0	100	97
1561	28	72	201
1562	35	65	253
1563	37	63	62
TOTAL	48	52	1750

FIGURE A.1. Surviving acts by notary, 1550–1563. Source: ADG, Series IIE.

quantities for the late 1550s and 1560s, while the Ursis' wills and marriage contracts are the overwhelming majority for the early period (1550–1555). Figure A.1 illustrates how the records of different notaries survive in different quantities.

As noted in Chapter 3, the major consequence of this skewing is that Ursi and non-Ursi acts must be separated when looking at the evolution of religious formulas. In a chart of the use of the phrase "Holy Mother Church," for example, looking at the entire database, use of the phrase would appear to have declined in the early 1550s, as Ursi clients stopped using it, and then seem to have increased again in the mid-1550s, because non-Ursi acts that continued to use it become better represented in the database. There is also another pitfall in compiling data on religious formulas in notarial acts. In draft versions of notarial registers, which sometimes survive, the formulas are frequently omitted. Sometimes, what is apparently an unbroken series of registers is actually a mix of draft and final copies: presumably, at some point, a clerk threw out all the draft registers except for those years when the final copy had disappeared, and he inserted the draft copy at that point. This can wreak havoc, if historians assume that the absence of Catholic formulas is a sign of incipient Protestantism. Fortunately, for Nîmes, there are few surviving drafts (they come from the notaries Rançon Alirand and Jean Lansard); they were included in the database, because it would have made little difference to the statistics had they been excluded.[1]

Coding Last Names

For certain purposes, however, many references did have to be excluded. Unlike a database constructed from a tax roll, it is perfectly possible for people to appear more than once in a database compiled from notarial acts: in fact, some people appear more than twenty times. Multiple references to individuals are both a blessing and a curse. They allow us to get a much better fix on individuals, their professions, friends, and origins. Sixteenth-century documents are much less rigorously exact than those of later centuries, and scribes frequently omitted professions, villages of origin, and so forth from documents. Furthermore, multiple references can help to clarify poor handwriting or a water-damaged page. But it is frequently difficult to be certain that two references are indeed to the same person. All sixteenth-century spelling is highly inconsistent. First names are nonetheless extremely reliable, because the repertoire of first names is relatively small, while there is a much larger repertoire of last names, which makes them very difficult to transcribe. Scribes also clearly had trouble with unusual last names: in a largely illiterate age, they could hardly turn to the person and ask, "Would you spell that, please?" Professions are more reliable, when included, but they frequently are not, especially for witnesses. Furthermore, people could have multiple professions or change professions: a laborer decides to rent an inn, an artisan becomes a town consul for a year, or a rich lawyer buys a property and then becomes entitled to be called seigneur.

Multiple references must be found, however, and aggregated, because even the simplest statistical tests are invalid otherwise. For example, if 2.39 percent of the references in the database are to advocates and doctors of law, that hardly means that 2.39 percent of the individuals in the database, or in the town, were lawyers. In general, more prominent people tend to be referred to more frequently, so not compensating for multiple references would bias the sample. It would also make the analysis of family ties and factions completely impossible.

Unfortunately, establishing that two references are to the same person is not entirely straightforward. Consider the set of references in figure A.2. It is quite clear that these all refer to the same person, although his last name is spelled three different ways. Paleographic difficulties and water damage (and typos in later data entry, of course) only compound an already difficult situation. But, in this case, we have the advantage of an unusual first name (he may have been the only man in Nîmes to bear it) and a precise occupation, seigneur de Sauvinhargues. It is by contrast difficult to determine whether two references to "Jean Dumas, *travailleur*" are to the same person.

In general, it has been assumed that, if two documents mention the same name and occupation, they refer to the same person, unless there is clear evidence to the contrary: this certainly introduces error, but to assume the contrary would be worse and would render the task impossible. Furthermore, multiple references have been exploited whenever possible to fill in missing data in other references: had a reference

Volume	Folio	First name	Last name	Occupation
IIE^{37} 061	139^v	Germengaud	de Faulcon	noble Sr. de Sovinhargues
IIE^1 233	184^v	Hermengard	Falcon	ecuyer, doct. ez dr., Sr. de Savinhargues
IIE^1 234	58	Hermingaud	Falcon	Sr. de Savinhargues
IIE^{36} 320	1009	Hermingrand	Falcone	Seigneur de Sanninhargues

FIGURE A.2. Coding last names. Source: ADG, Series IIE.

to "Hermingard Falcon" been found that did not mention that he was seigneur de Sauvinhargues, it would have unquestionably been marked as the same person. A reference to a name without an occupation was automatically assumed to be the same person unless there were two persons with the same name and different occupations, in which case it was left indeterminate unless there were other clear factors to make a judgment possible.

In order to identify persons and eliminate differences in spelling, an identification system based on the Soundex system was created. Soundex, used widely in the United States, on Illinois driver's licenses, for example, is a system for assigning code numbers to last names, by giving numbers to letters of the alphabet. The initial letter is retained, double letters are eliminated, and consonants are given numbers in clusters: B, V, P, and F are all given the code "1," M and N are "5," and so forth. Only the first three applicable consonants are coded. "Hermingard," for example, would have the code H655, or H-r-m-n. If the name is short, blank spaces are filled in with zeros: "Jack" would be J200. Unfortunately, Soundex could not be applied to the database without some modifications. First of all, consider the case of our Hermingard: is his name "Faucon" or "de Faucon"? Because particles appear and disappear in last names throughout the records with no rhyme or reason, they were eliminated in the coding, except in certain cases: Dumas, for example, and Dupont, although frequently written "du Mas" and "du Pont" in the documents, never appeared as "Mas" or "Pont." Articles ("le" and "la") were more consistent and were generally retained. Women in this period did not bear their husbands' last names, but rather a feminine form of their fathers': Mme. Perrière would be the married daughter of M. Perrier, not his wife, for example. These endings were eliminated, so that they could be properly linked to their male relatives. Finally, because of the difference between French and English pronunciations, final, unsounded consonants were not coded since, not being pronounced, they were frequently omitted. "Jacques," for example, would be coded like "Jack," as mentioned above: J200, since the "s" is not pronounced. (Nasalized "n" was pronounced and therefore always retained for coding.)[2]

Each person received an individual identification number consisting of four parts: a Soundex version of their last and first names; a code for their occupation, grouped into larger categories (numbers between 500 and 599 were used for building, metal, and wood-related trades, for example); and two final digits used to distinguish homonyms, thus normally zero. In this system, Hermingard Falcon's ID code would be F-425-H655-100–00, that is, F for the first letter of his family name, then 425 for the consonants l-c-n, H655 for his given name, and the occupational code "100" for high status. The final zeros indicate that there is no one else in the database with the same name. The next-to-last zero would be changed to a 1 if there were another family of a different last name but with the same Soundex code, while the last digit was used to distinguish people of the same first and last names and occupations, usually fathers and sons. Although Soundex did an excellent job of eliminating spelling differences, occasionally different last names would be given the same code, or the same person was initially given different codes: the whole database had to be inspected (more than once) by hand, or rather, by mouse.

Code	Metier	%	Count
100	High Status: titled, officials	2.45	104
110	Bailiff	0.21	9
130	Greffier (legal official)	0.28	12
200	Professional	0.47	20
201	Medical professions	0.26	11
202	Apothecary	0.85	36
203	Barber	0.17	7
205	Surgeon	0.75	32
220	Legal professions	2.71	115
221	Advocate	0.02	1
230	Notary	0.94	40
235	Clerk	3.21	136
237	Praticien (legal clerk)	1.93	82
238	Hussier	0.12	5
240	Educational professions	0.02	1
242	College professor	0.05	2
245	Student	1.11	47
247	Bookseller	0.19	8
250	Priest	2.48	105
260	Protestant minister	0.24	10
270	Jeweler	0.21	9
280	Merchant, broker	6.46	274
285	Retailer	0.66	28
290	Bourgeois	1.32	56
300	Food, drink, grocery trades	0.14	6
310	Baker	2.38	101
320	Butcher	1.2	51
330	Innkeeper	1.82	77
400	Clothmaking	1.44	61
405	Cutter	0.07	3
410	Dyer	0.09	4
415	Furrier	0.35	15
420	Hatter	0.64	27
425	Hosier	1.08	46
430	Tailor	2.5	106
440	Weaver	3.09	131
445	Woolcarder	3.7	157
450	Leather trades	1.32	56
460	Cordwainer	4.88	207
470	Saddler	0.68	29
490	Tanner	0.59	25
500	Building, wood, and metal trades	0.42	18
510	Mason	2.74	116
533	Woodworking trades	0.02	1
535	Carpenter	1.13	48
540	Furnituremaker	1.32	56
572	Cutler	0.09	4

Code	Metier	%	Count
575	Locksmith	0.78	33
577	Wheelwright	0.83	35
580	Farrier	1.23	52
582	Spurmaker	0.07	3
585	Smith	0.33	14
590	Potter	0.21	9
600	Agriculture (general)	0.66	28
610	Husbandman	24.57	1042
620	Yeoman	6.53	277
630	Gardener	1.89	80
640	Miller	0.85	36
650	Shepherd	0.07	3
700	Servant	0.64	27
800	Military	0.33	14
900	Transport	0.54	23
998	Other	1.34	57
999	Unknown		1547
	TOTAL	100.00	5788

FIGURE A.3. Percentage of men in each occupation. Note: Figures may not add up to 100 due to rounding. Source: ADG, Series IIE.

Occupational Information

Once Soundex numbers were created for the 13,000 entries in the database, identical persons noted, and multiple references consolidated, a statistical profile of mid-sixteenth-century Nîmes could be compiled. The results are in figure A.3. Persons who were described with different but related occupations were usually assigned to a general category: someone described equally often as "yeoman" and "husbandman" was coded for "agriculture," for example. In order to convert these detailed figures into the summary information used in the text, the classification system in figure A.4 was used.

Unfortunately, despite the efforts taken to collate information from every reference, the occupations of fully one-quarter of the adult male population could not be determined (only a handful of women were recorded as having occupations). Since even prominent persons are listed in the records without occupational data, it would be unwise to assume that the unknowns represent exclusively low-status occupations like *travailleur* and *laboureur* (translated as "husbandman" and "yeoman"). For this reason, it has been assumed in the discussion below that the percentages "excluding unknowns" are the best representation of the distribution of occupations.

Some groups are undoubtedly underrepresented. Servants were certainly more numerous than the database would indicate, for example, although servants perhaps should naturally occur less frequently in a chart of men's, and not women's, occupations. The destitute are essentially absent, though some very poor people do appear: some women had dowries in the single digits (£1.5 is the lowest, for the marriage of

Code	Classification	Examples
100–130	High-status	Seigneurs, baillis, judges, officials except consuls
200–260	Professions	Medicine, law, education, clergy
279–290	High-status artisans	Merchants, bourgeois, brokers, retailers, jewelers
300–399	Food, drink, groceries	Butchers, bakers, innkeepers
400–449	Textiles	Dyers, weavers, tailors
450–499	Leather trades	Saddlers, tanners, shoemakers
500–599	Building, wood, metal	Masons, carpenters, armorers, wheelwrights, potters
600–699	Agriculture	Yeomen, husbandmen, gardeners, millers
700–998	Other	Servants, military, carters, other

FIGURE A.4. General categories for coding occupations in the notarial database.

Catherine Fabresse to Jean Michel, *travailleur*), and one bridegroom, Nadal Clemens, did not even know his father's first name.[3]

By contrast, high-status occupations are almost certainly overrepresented: it is plausible that Nîmes, whose présidial was such an important institution, should have a large percentage of lawyers (2.71 percent), but could 6.46 percent of the population really have been merchants? One possibility is that master artisans were recorded as merchants, as some records suggest. Unfortunately, it is difficult to estimate the extent of the practice. Other possible sources of systematic error were investigated but could not be substantiated. For example, was there status inflation, of the sort that promotes a husbandman (*travailleur*) to a yeoman (*laboureur*) on his wedding day? This appears not to have been the case: variation in descriptions seems to have been quite random. As a result, some of the categories have to be read in groups. Weavers and wool carders were occasionally confused, likewise drapers and hosiers (*drapiers* and *chaussetiers*), while carpenters and furniture makers (*charpentiers* and *fûtiers*) were regularly commingled, as were the various branches of the leather trade. As a result, it is perhaps more accurate, as well as easier on the eye, to group occupations into general categories, as is done in the text. The overall percentages given in the text are necessarily imperfect, but they probably represent about as accurate a count as we are likely to get from the sources, recognizing the bias in favor of elites and the undercounting of the poorest (which, after all, still exists, in the United States at least). The one additional difficulty concerns not the results, but their classification: how does one determine what is really a high-status occupation? Determining status is a difficult, interesting question, to which we will now turn.

Social Status

Traditionally, historians have tended to assume, with considerable justice, that status is largely a matter of money. Exceptions are easy to locate: some professions are considered more honorable than their mere earnings may indicate, a point in which contemporary professors of history may well take some comfort. Generally, honor may derive from lineage or education, but money certainly helps, and after all, it has long been customary for the rich but uneducated to remedy their defects in their children. In Nîmes's notarial records, evidence of net wealth is difficult to come by, and estimates of income virtually impossible. Nor is even elementary evidence of education, such as the ability to sign one's name, possible before the very late sixteenth century. Wills only occasionally give legacies of named amounts, usually designating instead a couple of small legacies and then leaving a single heir or a group of persons as residuary legatees.

Dowries, therefore, are one of the few good ways to get a sense of relative wealth and social status. Even this figure, however, is not completely reliable: some marriage contracts do not give an exact figure for the dowry, but instead give the *augment dotal*, which was probably treated as a percentage of the dowry, either one-half or one-third. Such contracts, concentrated at the lower end of the social scale, amount to nearly a third of all cases. Of course, it would be kinder to historians had the percentage been fixed: as it is, it is impossible to use the *augment dotal* to ascertain the dowry figure precisely. For our purposes, where the dowry was unspecified, the *augment* has been used, multiplied by two, to approximate the implied dowry of the wife. This assumes that the husband and wife come from similar social backgrounds. But even if one husband or wife makes a misalliance, the average dowry for wives of bakers, for example, should give a good notion of the rank of bakers within the wealth hierarchy. The plausibility of the results obtained suggests that this system of assessing dowries does provide a good means of ascertaining social status.

It is actually possible to be yet more precise and perhaps to quantify some of the more intangible elements of social status by using dowries. Witnesses to marriages tend to represent important people in the wedding: close relatives of the wealthy, servant women's masters, fellow carders for wool carders, and so forth. A cursory examination shows what should not surprise anyone, namely, that witnesses to marriage contracts vary in prestige according to the social status of the persons getting married. Thus, the field can be usefully widened: the dowry figure can be applied not just to the husband in a marriage contract, but to all the witnesses to that contract. This has the additional benefit of helping to get a good fix on professions where the sample is small and may be unrepresentative. Only six marriage contracts survive in which the grooms are surgeons, for example, but surgeons appear forty times if occasions are included in which they are witnesses.

At this point, it should be remembered, the dowry figure is not being used as an actual sum of money but as a device to clarify social ranking, so that priests' social rank is given by the average dowry of marriages at which they appear, although as celibates they should not have been getting married themselves. This being the Reformation, however, three priests did get married, and it is striking that the average dowry for those three priests was only £50, while it was over £250 when they were witnesses. Here is a good example of the advantages of using witnesses as part of the sample: priests who were getting married were clearly less respectable than priests in general, and that is why the average dowry figure shifted so markedly. Even ex-priests from wealthy backgrounds could not obtain heiresses in marriage.

The data from both methods are worth considering since, as in the case of priests, the differences between them can be quite revealing. However, because the inclusion of witnesses results in a larger sample, a number of small occupations appear in that sample that do not appear when only husbands are considered. For that reason, the results will be presented separately, ranked from highest dowry to lowest, rather than combined in one table. It should also be noted that, for a variety of reasons, the average dowry is slightly higher when all cases are considered, although high-status occupations tend to fall and low-status ones to rise. All money has been converted to *livres tournois* and decimalized (1 sou = .05 livres).

Some results in these figures should not surprise historians of early modern France. For example, lawyers rank above even wealthy merchants and bourgeois, while farmers and agricultural workers rank at the bottom of the scale. In figure A.6, a plausible division would be to mark dowries above £250 as wealthy; £125–250 as an upper-middling group; £50–125 as middling; and below £50 as poor (for figure A.5, it would probably be more reasonable to set figures of £200+, £100–200, £50–100, and below £50, respectively). Thus, professionals, officials, and bourgeois (retired merchants) would rank as rich, while some of the more prestigious occupations like merchants, notaries, other men of the law like clerks and *praticiens,* and apothecaries would be in the upper-middling group.

The middle would consist heavily of those in the cloth trades, with workers in leather goods in the upper half and hatters and wool carders at the lower end. A group of high-status cloth trades, grouped together as "cloth making" (code 400) because there are too few of each of them separately, belong here, too. They include drapers, mercers, embroiderers, and velvet makers. Also prominent in the upper half of the middling group were yeomen, independent farmers who were eligible to be fourth consul. In the lower reaches of the middle group were the food trades: bakers, butchers, innkeepers. The poor consisted of those in the building trades (masons), carters, and above all, poor agricultural laborers.

Certain occupational groups have quite different averages in the two figures. Servants, for example, rank as poor in figure A.5, while relatively high in the broad sample. In this case, figure A.5 almost certainly gives a better picture: servants tend to appear as witnesses only in the marriages of the wealthy families that employed them, thus distorting the average. The lower figures for their own dowries more accurately reflect their real position. By contrast, students, who were mostly from privileged backgrounds, do quite well in figure A.6, as they should, but quite poorly when they themselves are getting married. This is almost certainly because "student" is a life-cycle-bound occupation. Masons can be fifteen years old or fifty, but students are usually fairly young, probably between fifteen and twenty. As witnesses to weddings, they frequently appear with their relatively prominent families, while students who are marrying young appear not to be marrying well. But the sample is also small: only two students married in the period examined. A few other occupations with surprising figures, like college professors, are also probably errors due to small sample size. Similarly, the "military" category consists largely of poor harquebus men and crossbow men, but two groups of army captains are witnesses to weddings of the high aristocracy, with dowries of £3,500 in one case and £500 in the other, thus biasing the results.

APPENDIX B

Code	Metier	Avg.	Cases
100	High Status: seigneurs, officials	1218.41	22
130	Greffier	1150	1
220	Lawyers and legal professions	911.94	18
201	Medical professions	633.33	3
290	Bourgeois	456.72	3
237	Praticien	323.54	13
260	Protestant minister	300	1
230	Notary	300	2
280	Merchant, broker	259.29	40
241	College president	250	1
415	Furrier	206.67	3
590	Potter	150	1
400	Clothmaking	141.5	17
205	Surgeon	130	6
235	Clerk	122.6	5
470	Saddler	113.13	12
202	Apothecary	110	2
425	Hosier	91.25	8
800	Military	90	2
620	Yeoman	86.44	45
450	Leather trades	85	8
535	Carpenter	84.45	11
577	Wheelwright	83.05	6
247	Bookseller	80	1
330	Innkeeper	76.9	16
285	Retailer	72.4	5
460	Cordwainer	67.18	45
420	Hatter	66.67	9
490	Tanner	66.5	4
245	Student	60	2
650	Shepherd	60	2
270	Jeweler	56.67	3
445	Woolcarder	52.25	44
575	Locksmith	50.75	4
250	Priests	50	3
310	Baker	46.81	26
510	Mason	45.74	21
630	Gardener	44.81	27
440	Weaver	42.88	30
998	Other	42.14	7
600	Agriculture	42.03	13
430	Tailor	41.13	30
999	Unknown	40.59	109
580	Farrier	40.52	11
900	Transport	37.5	2
540	Furniture maker	36.52	10
320	Butcher	33.92	13
570	Armorer	33.33	3

Code	Metier	Avg.	Cases
700	Servants	32.14	7
500	Building, wood, and metal	31.5	4
640	Miller	30.14	14
610	Husbandmen	30.09	282
200	Professional (other)	30	6
585	Smith	20	1
300	Food, drink, groceries	13.83	3
405	Cutter	9.73	3

FIGURE A.5. Average dowries by husband's occupation. Source: ADG, Series IIE.

The foot soldiers considered separately have an average dowry of £41, ranking them in the higher ranks of the poor.

Dowry figures have another important use: they can give us an assessment of the relative social status of the clientele of the various notaries whose registers survive. This is particularly important because, as mentioned earlier, the records of the Ursi family of notaries are unusually Protestant in their language early on, and many future prominent leaders of the Protestant party appear there more often than anywhere else. Are the Ursis' clients different in any way? One simple method to evaluate this is to consider the average dowry by notary (see figure A.7).

The figures make it reasonably clear that notaries' clienteles varied dramatically in their social status, with Lansard's, Sabatier's, and Duchamp's clients solidly tending toward the well-to-do, while the Ursis' tended toward the lower middle. The average husband in a contract written by the Ursis married a woman whose dowry was comparable to the wife of an average innkeeper. Interestingly, the dowries in Ursi marriage contracts are not lower because the husbands in them come from different professions than average, but rather because they were poorer members of each profession. Obviously, the percentages are not exactly the same, so, for example, 6.04 percent of the husbands in Jacques Ursi's registers are in the legal professions, compared to 8.93 percent of the whole sample, and 41.41 percent of them are in agriculture, compared to 34.57 percent overall. Nonetheless, the percentage of artisans, for example, is just 0.5 percent lower. In one sense, this is not surprising, since Jacques Ursi's registers, in particular, comprise such an important part of the surviving records: but that only shows how significant the difference in average dowry is. The early Protestant milieu is in some ways sharply different from the general milieu of the Ursis' registers: the percentage of artisans among early Protestants is higher, and the percentage of those in agriculture is much lower. Still, there was a distinct overlap, and the two groups, Protestants and Ursi clients, both contained fewer lawyers and officials than the average.

The result of using the marriages attended for averaging was that 11,000 of 13,000 references could have a social status number assigned to them. This still left 2,000 references, unfortunately, and therefore a significant number of people's status could not be specified. This problem was solved through interpolation: if an individual consistently appeared with high-status people, that individual was assumed also to be of high status. Once I calculated the average dowry of marriages attended for each person in the

APPENDIX B

Code	Metier	Avg.	Cases
100	High status: seigneurs, officials	893.33	254
800	Military	743.78	21
220	Lawyers and legal	509.83	244
201	Medical	447.19	18
130	Greffier	413.6	29
260	Protestant minister	402.79	15
241	College president	360	6
242	College professor	1000	2
290	Bourgeois	287.38	129
250	Priests	266.8	90
410	Dyer	234	10
230	Notary	210.7	49
280	Merchant, broker	198.81	396
237	Praticien	196.26	88
110	Bailiff	190.17	12
415	Furrier	181.43	14
235	Clerk	177.68	103
202	Apothecary	174.56	45
580	Farrier	152.9	51
203	Barber	149.27	5
245	Student	138.86	25
450	Leather trades	131.36	89
270	Jeweler	128.44	19
700	Servants	122.33	23
998	Other	118.3	40
400	Clothmaking	114.7	59
205	Surgeon	112.95	40
247	Bookseller	107.35	17
470	Saddler	106.75	44
490	Tanner	104.29	17
999	Unknown	98.93	1377
430	Tailor	95.86	129
535	Carpenter	89.14	56
590	Potter	85.82	14
620	Yeoman	82.19	373
238	Hussier	81.65	10
575	Locksmith	80.02	41
480	Shoemaker	79.83	30
577	Wheelwright	68.23	50
240	Educational	67	1
460	Cordwainer	64.91	229
330	Innkeeper	64.66	139
420	Hatter	63.32	33
570	Armorer	61.44	9
200	Professional (other)	61.3	27
445	Woolcarder	60.95	193
221	Advocate	60	1
650	Shepherd	60	2

APPENDIX B   215

Code	Metier	Avg.	Cases
310	Baker	58.15	146
285	Retailer	57.96	26
320	Butcher	57.54	94
572	Cutler	57.43	3
630	Gardener	52.37	126
582	Spurmaker	48	5
440	Weaver	47.17	137
510	Mason	45.62	119
640	Miller	45.46	46
540	Furniture maker	43.49	66
585	Smith	39.98	13
600	Agriculture	36.96	57
610	Husbandmen	35.16	1101
500	Building, wood, and metal	34.03	19
300	Food, drink, groceries	32.3	5
900	Transport	22.29	14
405	Cutter	10.07	6

FIGURE A.6. Average dowries of marriages attended. Source: ADG, Series IIE.

database, it became possible to assign each act (will or marriage) an average social status based on the persons participating in it. Acts with high-status people, whether wills or marriages, have high average social status figures; wills of humble tradesmen and agricultural workers, or their widows, rarely do. Because this technique gives a status to every act, not just marriage contracts, it was possible to calculate the average social status, not of marriages attended, but of acts attended, and to assign a social status to all but a handful of references in the database. Interpolating in this way does introduce some errors: one high-status person appearing at a humble marriage can drive the average for that act sharply upward. But if people appear in several acts, that effect tends to dissipate. Interpolation does have one further effect: widening the sample tends to make averages converge toward the center. Agricultural laborers will still be at the bottom of the heap, and lawyers and officeholders at the top, but their average social status numbers will be a bit closer to each other. I call this number "social status by event."

Network Analysis

Properly coding the database and sorting out the names and occupations laid the groundwork to perform network analysis. The crucial steps that had been taken were that each person now had a unique identifier, and so did each event, that is, each will and marriage contract. Two individuals who attended the same event could be considered to be related in some way. Pairs of husbands and wives could be assembled, for example. There were difficulties, however. There is a rigid distinction in network analysis between "actors" and "events." This distinction poses a certain problem in doing a network analysis on the elite of sixteenth-century Nîmes, because many ties could not be

Notary	Avg. Wife's Dowry	Cases
Perret	20.00	1
Malian	57.46	28
Ursi, Jacques	72.82	513
Grimaldi	74.46	127
Ursi, Jean	94.86	79
Alirand	100.34	23
Mombel	109.50	74
Poreau	130.50	7
Menard	177.04	190
Lansard	204.75	15
Sabatier	252.34	28
Duchamp	347.44	27

FIGURE A.7. Average dowries by notary. Source: ADG, Series IIE.

represented by events in the database. Consider the case of a married couple, Anne Durande and Bertrand Favier. Their marriage is the event that ties them together. What is the tie between Anne and her brother Charles Durand, or between Bertrand and Charles? No event—no will or marriage, in the context of the database—joins them. Nor can one consider the sister to be the connecting line between Charles and Bertrand: she is an actor, not an event. The solution was to do the network analysis on the basis of families, not of individuals. Thus, when Anne marries Bertrand, that creates a tie between the Durand and the Favier families, not between the individuals.

While using families solves an important problem, it creates others. The first is a problem of definition: what is a family? It is traditional, for example, to look at a marriage and say that, when Catherine Richière married Pierre Vallete,[4] the marriage created a tie between the Richier and the Vallete families. But to Catherine, Pierre, and their descendants, it may have seemed more a process of establishing a new family, which may not have coincided with the Vallete family name. It is equally traditional to assume that such ties, especially among the elite, represented the desires of the families rather than those of the couple, but that may not be valid in every case. There is the additional complication that the database covers only a narrow band of time, 1550–1562/63, while marriage ties from years or decades before may have created a sense of family connection. Finally, *family* is also a porous term: although a computer might prefer that a person be either a member of a family or not, the experience of family can be, of course, quite different. Distant cousins, for example, may or may not be considered truly "family."

In general, because it would be extremely complicated to do otherwise, I have used traditional, family-name-based definitions of families, which has involved ignoring certain indications of other sorts of family ties. Information gleaned from wills, for example, was used to ensure that persons with the same surnames were indeed from the same family, but similar information about marriage ties in earlier decades was not used to create links between those families, because the references were too scattered and incomplete. Albert Puech, a local historian who was active in the late nineteenth century, compiled extensive genealogical information about over 250 important families, which I also used to assess whether a similar surname really corresponded to a family tie.[5] In general, I assigned people to the same family only if the relationship was reasonably close: parents, children, grandparents and grandchildren, siblings, uncles and aunts, nieces and nephews, and occasionally first cousins when the parties themselves stressed the relationship. I tended to be suspicious of assuming a family tie based on the same surnames when the name was a common one, and I was somewhat more lenient with unusual family names. Because of this use of surnames, it might be more appropriate to refer to "lineages" rather than "families."

Another consideration when using families as the unit of analysis is that some important information relates not to families but to individuals. One might want to know whether weavers, say, tended to be friends with each other, for instance by being witnesses at each others' wills and marriage contracts. But while, for example, Étienne Serre may have been a weaver, one could hardly call the whole Serre family weavers, since other family members did other things, like woolcarding. (And how does one define the female Serres' occupations?) Most important of all, if Antoine Moleri is a heretic, can we make the assumption that everyone in the Moleri family is also heretical? In this last case, the answer has to be yes, because otherwise it would be impossible to compare Protestant to non-Protestant families.

Unfortunately, if family can be a problematic term, so can elite. *Elite* can be defined by reference to power obtained through holding office, through wealth, through education, or through connections to other members of the elite. Defining the cutoff point between elite and non-elite can also be problematic: some families may be more elite than others. When Ann Guggenheim examined Nîmes's elites, she looked at about seventy persons, generally officeholders and men of law.[6] Defining elite status by occupation has certain distinct advantages: occupation is usually easy to determine. But it somewhat arbitrarily excludes some wealthy artisans, for example, who can be shown to have played an active role in town affairs even if most artisans did not. Instead of using occupation to determine status, this book has used the dowry measures discussed above: while wealth is not precisely equivalent to status, it is at least a less crude measure than occupation. In any case, because we will be able to examine a much larger number of families, the overwhelming majority of lawyers and officeholders can be included.

Once I calculated a "social status by event" number for each individual, I selected a smaller group for closer analysis, specifically men with a social status number of 100 or greater and women with a social status number of 80 or greater. The choice of 100 to define the elite was deliberately generous: remember that, using the occupational averages as a guide, I suggested that persons with a social status number above 250 ranked as wealthy, 125–250 corresponding to an upper-middling group, 50–125 indicated the middling, and below 50 was poor. To ensure that a social status number was not just a fluke, however, I required that there be at least four references to each man (since there are many fewer references to women, I did not apply that restriction to them). Very few prominent persons, as judged from town and church records, did not appear at least four times. It would be difficult, in any case, to assign individuals to different factions based on only two or three references to them.

After identifying all probable relatives of the initial sample, I obtained slightly more than 300 families. For technical reasons,[7] an upper limit of 250 was desirable; I there-

Reference	Date of act	Status in act	Social Status	Metier	First Name	Last name
IIE1 244 f. 57	4/25/51	Bride	103.26	Woman	Anne	Borrellon
IIE1 244 f. 48	4/20/51	Witness	101.57	Laboureur	Arnaud	Borrellon
IIE1 245 f. 31v	4/17/53	Witness	101.57	Laboureur	Arnaud	Borrellon
IIE1 244 f. 57	4/25/51	Father of Bride	101.57	Laboureur	Arnaud	Borrellon
IIE1 243 f. 71	5/3/50	Witness	101.57	Laboureur	Arnaud	Borrellon
IIE1 244 f. 49^v	4/20/51	Father of Groom	101.57	Laboureur	Arnaud	Borrellon
IIE1 245 f. 238^v	10/29/53	Witness	101.57	Laboureur	Arnaud	Borrellon
IIE1 245 f. 236^v	8/24/53	Witness	101.84	Travailleur	Jacques	Borrellon
IIE1 247 f. 33^v	4/15/55	Witness	101.84	Travailleur	Jacques	Borrellon
IIE36 326 f. 509	1/21/62	Witness	101.84	Travailleur	Jacques	Borrellon
IIE36 323 f. 321	11/9/59	Witness	101.84	Travailleur	Jacques	Borrellon
IIE1 244 f. 49^v	4/20/51	Groom	220.75	Ropemaker	Jacques	Borrellon

FIGURE A.8. Multiple mentions of family members. Source: ADG, Series IIE.

fore chose to include only families that met at least one of the following criteria: either an average social status of at least 140 or at least nine references. (Again, it is important to remember that this represents an extremely generous conception of what *elite* means.) Therefore, only families who were both relatively poor and had few references in the database were excluded.

It is perhaps worth noting that social status information was originally collected for individuals: in order to convert it to rank families, it must be weighted. Consider the Borrellon family, which includes two brothers, one of whom has two children (see figure A.8). The two brothers, Arnaud and Jacques the *travailleur*, appear much more often in the database than do Jacques the ropemaker and Anne, who are Arnaud's two children. How should the family's social status be calculated? One could add the four social status numbers, 103.26, 101.57, 101.84, and 220.75, divide by four, and use that as the average. But in order to weight the *family* correctly, one must instead take into account how often each member of the family appears in the database.

The use of the two criteria ensured that only poorer families who also appeared relatively infrequently were excluded. Families that contained a notary, a priest, or a Protestant minister were automatically included (clergy because of the nature of this study, notaries in order to ascertain whether faction allegiances could have affected the sample under study). This created a sample of manageable size, with just under 3,000 references to 249 families. Each family was then given a unique identifier, usually the first eight letters of its last name, except for a few cases where there was more than one family with the same name, in which case a number ("Arnaud1" and "Arnaud2," for example) was added. Once all the elite families were identified, families with at least one Protestant member could be compared to non-Protestant families.

Once we have identified a group, if we can determine a way to measure connections between its members, we can measure its cohesiveness, analyze its factions, and so forth. Fortunately, the notarial records in the database were ideal for this, because

Faction	Cases	Avg. Betweenness	Avg. Social status
1	11	0.71	279.99
2	51	0.79	218.73
3	28	1.11	358.65
4	56	1.27	388.79
5	43	0.91	243.08
6	22	0.86	213.64
7–23	38	0.41	227.00
Total	249	0.90	280.43

FIGURE A.9. Basic information about Nîmes' elite factions. Source: ADG, Series IIE.

wills and marriage contracts are, by definition, documents that link individuals in webs of family connections: either one generation to another or one family to another. Furthermore, it is well known that witnesses to these acts were commonly friends of the parties, as indeed the case of the Rozel and Barrière families (see Chapter 6) shows. Because each individual was likely to get married only once or twice, while he might be a witness to friends' marriages and wills fifteen or twenty times, in the end witnessing proved to be a much more powerful tool for measuring family connections.

The mechanics of measuring family connections were reasonably straightforward. Each family had a unique identifier, and so did each event (will or marriage). The unique identifier for each act was the volume and page number where it is located in the archives. Each record therefore could be linked in two directions: to other references to the same family and to other families who were present at the same event. The 3,000 references to members of elite families were divided, therefore, into two groups: (1) principals, that is, husbands, wives, and testators; and (2) witnesses. Each witness family was presumed to have a tie to each principal family if they appeared at the same event. The database program (Microsoft Access) was then programmed to create sets of pairs of families linked by their co-attendance. These pairs were then exported to a spreadsheet program (Microsoft Excel), which created a pivot table, where the sets of pairs were converted into a matrix, where all the families were listed at the top and left-hand edges, and a number was put at their intersection points (1 for one tie, 2 for two, etc.). It should also be noted that the mathematics of network analysis requires symmetrical matrices for many important functions and that the sets of pairs of principals and witnesses are not symmetrical, because the two lists from which the pairs were drawn, principals and witnesses, are by no means identical. To deal with the problem, each pair was entered twice, that is, in both possible orders, before being exported to the matrix. At that point, network analysis became possible, using any standard program; in this case, I used UCINET IV, which created factions. Some basic statistics about the factions are summarized in figure A.9. Social status numbers above 250 (that is, based on average dowries of over 250) indicate that all of the factions were wealthy on average, but of course that means that many of the members were only upper middling in status.

Notes

INTRODUCTION

1. Bossy, *Christianity in the West*, 13.
2. For an alternative view, see Gregory, *Salvation at Stake*.
3. To access this literature, some useful starting points are Spilka, Hood, Hunsberger, and Gorsuch, *The Psychology of Religion*, chap. 11; Buckser and Glazier, *Anthropology of Religious Conversion*; Hefner, *Conversion to Christianity*; Segal, *Paul the Convert*; and Stark, *Rise of Christianity*. All contain good bibliographies. Martin, *Tongues of Fire*, is an excellent local study and is particularly relevant since it deals with conversion from Catholicism to Protestantism.
4. For an example of a sociologist who does propose such rules, see Stark, *Rise of Christianity*, 13–21.
5. Hefner, "Introduction," in *Conversion to Christianity*, 26.
6. Festinger, Riecken, and Schachter, *When Prophecy Fails*. On the use of the term in studies of conversion, see Spilka et al., *Psychology of Religion*, 356. It is risky to state as a certainty that the term has never been used in the context of the Reformation, but a search in the Historical Abstracts database for the terms "cognitive," "dissonance," and "Reformation" produced no hits.
7. Hirschman, *Exit, Voice, and Loyalty*.
8. Spilka et al., *Psychology of Religion*, 348–51. For the notion that structures may be widely applicable but not that constraining, see Sewell, "A Theory of Structure," in his *Logics of History*, 147.
9. Shagan, "Introduction," in *Popular Politics and the English Reformation*.
10. Sewell, "Whatever Happened to the 'Social' in Social History?" 221; Sewell, *Logics of History*, 369–71; and Tucker, *Our Knowledge of the Past*, 33, 131.

11. Bettmann, *A Word from the Wise*, preface.

12. The standard source for monetary values is Spooner, *International Economy and Monetary Movements in France*. His figures indicate that, between 1550 and 1574, the écu had an official exchange rate of 50 sous, but local conditions were often different. As James B. Collins has noted (July 22, 1999, personal communication), "in real life, the écu did not have a fixed but an approximate value." Some examples of variant values: (1) ADG, IIE^1 247, fol. 190^v, 30 June 1555, has a legacy of 100 écus sols, which it notes equals 225 livres (implies 45 sous to écu); (2) IIE^1 250, fol. 235, 12 January 1561/62, has a legacy of £50 over five years, which it notes equals 100 écus sol (implies 50 sous to écu); (3) IIE^{36} 294, fol. 85^v, 22 September 1554, specifies a legacy of 1 ecu of 46s. to each grandchild upon marriage; (4) IIE^{36} 297, fol. 127^v, 15 September 1557, specifies an écu sol of 48s. Baumgartner, *France in the Sixteenth Century*, ix, gives the écu sol a value of 50 sous in this period.

CHAPTER I

1. On dioceses, see Cayla, *Dictionnaire des institutions*, s.v. "diocèse."

2. The classic study is Harding, *Anatomy of a Power Elite*, which lists governors on 219–27. See also Tievant, *Le gouverneur de Languedoc*, 25–26.

3. See Beik, *Absolutism and Society in Seventeenth-Century France*, 34, and the sources cited therein; for European population figures, see de Vries, *European Urbanization*, 31, 36.

4. On the Parlement of Paris, see Roelker, *One King, One Faith*. The *lit de justice* has attracted controversy; see Hanley, *The Lit de Justice of the Kings of France*; and Knecht, "Francis I and the 'Lit de Justice.'"

5. Doucet, *Les institutions de la France*, 1:210–28; Mentzer, *Heresy Proceedings in Languedoc*, 44–52; Davis, *Return of Martin Guerre*, esp. 73–74, 99–100; Monter, *Judging the French Reformation*, 1. There is a useful map of the parlements' jurisdictions in Potter, *A History of France*, 116.

6. Devic and Vaissete, *Histoire générale de Languedoc*, devotes a chapter every year to the meeting of the Estates and gives the meeting places. See also Knecht, *Rise and Fall of Renaissance France*, 230; Major, *Representative Government in Early Modern France*, 59–69. The standard source on taxation is Wolfe, *Fiscal System of Renaissance France*; see also Guéry, "Les finances de la monarchie française," 234, which gives estimates of sixteenth-century gross revenues, net revenues, and expenses.

7. For Nîmes and Montpellier population figures, see Le Roy Ladurie, *Peasants*, 145. Gutherz et al., *Histoire de Nîmes*, 176, following Puech, *Une ville*, 7–8, gives somewhat lower Nîmes figures. Philip Benedict, "French Cities from the Sixteenth Century to the Revolution: An Overview," in Benedict, ed., *Cities and Social Change in Early Modern France*, 24–25, gives French urban population figures; for other European cities, see de Vries, *European Urbanization*, appendix 1. Note that Benedict and de Vries frequently disagree. For modern size-rankings for French cities, see the annual *Dictionnaire national des communes de France*.

8. Puech, *Une ville*, 13. Quotation is from a Latin charter translated in Puech, "Les nîmois à la Renaissance," 425.

9. Sauzet, *Contre-réforme et réforme catholique*, 45–48; and Le Roy Ladurie, *Peasants*, 55–56 (quotation on 55).

10. This was a typical phenomenon, as noted in Braudel, *The Mediterranean and the Mediterranean World*, 1:51, 334. On population density, see Le Roy Ladurie, *Peasants*, 70–71. The figures for immigration statistics come from the notarial database, based on ADG, series IIE. Examples can be found at ADG, IIE^1 245, fol. 81^v, 14 May 1553; IIE^1 245, fol. 284, 1 October 1553; IIE^1 251, fol. 118, 9 August 1562. Many other contracts, although not recording a place of birth for the parties, mentioned that their fathers resided elsewhere, so the actual percentage of immigrants is likely to be distinctly higher. It should also be noted, however, that it is possible that some people who chose to be married in Nîmes subsequently migrated back to their native communities.

11. On olives, see Le Roy Ladurie, *Peasants*, 57–60; for chestnuts, ibid., 66–68. On silk, see ibid., 71–73; Puech, *Une ville*, 320–21; and Teisseyre-Sallmann, *L'industrie de la soie*.

12. On Roman roads, see Gutherz et al., *Histoire de Nîmes*, 86–88, and map after 79. Ménard, *Histoire civile*, I, frontispiece, includes views of Nîmes from the north and the south (the latter reproduced in Gutherz et al., *Histoire de Nîmes*, 154).

13. For elevations, see, for example, the map in Gutherz et al., *Histoire de Nîmes*, 57. A list of Nîmes' churches can be found in Goiffon, *Dictionnaire topographique*, s.v. "Nîmes."

14. Puech, *Une ville*, 31–35 (but compare appendix B, 506–10), indicates buildings from the period that survived into the late nineteenth century. Some have since disappeared.

15. Sauzet, *Le notaire et son roi*, 350–51, has a map showing the major institutions, circa 1700. Except that the college had been taken over by the Jesuits, no major changes had taken place since the sixteenth century.

16. Bodin, *Method for the Easy Comprehension of History*, 220, quoted in Wolfe, *Fiscal System of Renaissance France*, 129. On the expansion of venality, see Wolfe, *Fiscal System*, 101–3, 129–36.

17. Zeller, *Les institutions*, 175–77; Salmon, *Society in Crisis*, 72–73; Ménard, *Histoire civile*, IV:13:33:213–22; and Puech, "Débuts," 35, 85n, 89, for présidial membership.

18. Bonnet, "Visite de Thomas Platter," 189; Puech, *Une ville*, 17.

19. Puech, *Une ville*, 15. The will of Michel Bostaige, ADG, IIE^1 245, fol. 276^v, 26 September 1553, indicates that he was injured by a falling stone from the amphitheater. On dirty streets in the sixteenth century, see Febvre, *Life in Renaissance France*, 5. On the robes, see AMN, LL9, fol. 114^v, 21 January 1557/58.

20. Ménard, *Histoire civile*, VI, *Successions Généalogiques*, has lists of all the consuls. For the locations of their houses, see AMN, QQ12, fol. 89^v; QQ12, fol. 111^v; and QQ14, fol. 20^v.

21. On municipal constitutions, see the general remarks in Zeller, *Les institutions*, 38–44; there is somewhat more detail in Cayla, *Dictionnaire des institutions*, s.v. "consul." For Nîmes, the best account is Angelras, "Le consulat nimois," esp. 130–46.

See also Gutherz et al., *Histoire de Nîmes*, 143; Guggenheim, "Calvinism," 88–116; and Ménard, *Histoire civile*, III:10:56:253–58, and *Preuves*, 328–36. Hauser, "Nîmes, les consulats et la Réforme," 199–202, suggests that the consular regime was an important factor in the growth of Protestantism in France. For a description of the selection of consuls, see, e.g., AMN, LL9, fol. 169^v, 15 November 1559.

22. It was not entirely clear, even to contemporaries, exactly when the meetings were open or closed. It appears that anyone was entitled to attend "general and extraordinary" sessions, or at least during the crisis years of 1559–1562, hundreds of people sometimes showed up for them, and generally no one protested. At one extraordinary session of 21 August 1552 (AMN, LL8, fols. 204^v and 205), the first consul ordered non-council members to leave. Nycolas Galtiny protested, saying, "il estoit habitant de la ville et se pouvoit trouver aux conseils extraordinaires comme les aultres habitans combien qu'il ne soict du nombre des conseillers ordinaires et extraordinaires, et tout le moingz peut estre present à la proposition des matieres desquelles l'on prethend desliberer." The council unanimously agreed that he could stay to hear the first consul present the issues, but he had to leave before they expressed their opinions. He continued to protest that he should be able to hear the entire deliberations, but was escorted out. The council generally seems to have called general and extraordinary meetings when the issue was important, and Galtiny is the only person who appears to have been removed from a session.

23. Chevalier, *Les bonnes villes*, 76.

24. See ADG, IIE^{36} 297, fol. 133, 18 September 1557, will of Louis Gras, *travailleur*, prisoner in the château; IIE^{36} 293, fol. 76, 10 January 1553/54, which includes the jailer among the witnesses; Ménard, *Histoire civile*, IV, *Preuves*, 249 (arms stored there); AMN, LL9, fols. 288^v (mounting a guard over it) and 308^v (poor people who refuse to work should be sent there). On jails, see, e.g., Davis, *Return of Martin Guerre*, 87. For a general discussion, see Chevalier, *Les bonnes villes*, 116–17.

25. Of the 689 wills in the database, 428 request a specific burial place: 27 percent ask for the cathedral, 21 percent for the Dominicans, 11 percent for the Augustinians, and 6–9 percent for the others. ADG, series IIE.

26. Ménard, *Histoire civile*, VI, *Successions Chronologiques*, 1–2, lists the bishops. See also Ménard, *Histoire civile*, IV:11:129:81, and IV:13:49:230–31. On the bishop of Meaux, see Veissière, *L'evêque Guillaume Briçonnet*. The *vicaire* was also called the *prévôt*. Ménard, *Histoire civile*, VI, *Successions Chronologiques*, 2, gives a list of them, but unfortunately it is seriously defective, mentioning neither Suau nor du Caylar (compare with Puech, *Une ville*, 66n). On Suau, see Puech, "Débuts," 45; AMN, LL8, fol. 1; and ADG, IIE^1 244, fol. 59^v, 20 April 1551. Du Caylar was originally the deputy of the *official*, the judge in ecclesiastical cases (the *vicaire* was frequently also the *official*); see Puech, "Débuts," 35. The first mention I can find of du Caylar as the *vicaire* is ADG, IIE^{36} 306, fol. 1, 9 August 1556, but he probably took office several years earlier. On these posts generally, see Venard, *Réforme protestante, Réforme catholique*, 153–56; Puech, "Les anciennes jurisdictions de Nîmes," 161–246; Baumgartner, *Change and Continuity in the French Episcopate*, 105–7; and Doucet, *Les institutions de la France*, 727–28, 741.

27. On the secularization of the chapter, see Ménard, *Histoire civile*, IV:12:72:152–61; on the weakness of the church, see Gutherz et al., *Histoire de Nîmes*,

147–50; occupational information comes from ADG, series IIE. Since the notarial database covers a dozen years, during which some priests may have died and others arrived, the Nîmes figures are not directly comparable to the others; furthermore, priests, especially cloistered monks, are probably the most undercounted profession in the database, since they were unlikely to be used as witnesses to notarial acts. Still, they account for 2.66 percent of the adult males. Troyes figures are from Roberts, *City in Conflict*, 16–17; Rouen and Madrid from Benedict, *Rouen during the Wars of Religion*, 5. Lebrun, in *Du christianisme flamboyant à l'aube des Lumières*, 30, comments that rural clergy felt the lure of the city so strongly that as a result there could be "un prêtre pour cinquante, trente, voire vingt habitants!" in urban areas.

28. On Dijon: Farr, *Hands of Honor*, 254; on Avignon: Venard, *Réforme protestante, Réforme catholique*, 238–42; on Reims and Chalon-sur-Saône: Galpern, *Religions of the People*, 20–43; on Protestantism and poverty: Robbins, *City on the Ocean Sea*, 164–73, and Pugh, "Catholics, Protestants, and Testamentary Charity." On these issues more generally, see Le Goff and Rémond, *Histoire de la France religieuse*, 2:140–42. Nîmes records come from the notarial database, ADG, series IIE.

29. Casteel, "The College and University of Arts in Nîmes," esp. chap. 7. Students were identified using the notarial database, ADG, series IIE; I gave some preliminary results in Tulchin, "Les étudiants au collège des arts de Nîmes."

30. On schools, see Puech, "L'instruction à l'époque de la Renaissance." See also Houston, *Literacy in Early Modern Europe*, 84 (university attendance). On Montpellier, see Le Roy Ladurie, *Peasants*, 161–64.

31. Ménard, *Histoire civile*, IV:11:13:8–11, and IV:12:118:191; Mentzer, "Organizational Endeavour and Charitable Impulse," 5–6; and Puech, *La léproserie de Nîmes*. On consolidation, see Dupâquier, *Histoire de la population française*, 2:260. On bastards in the hospital, see, e.g., Ménard, *Histoire civile*, IV:13:65:240; AMN, LL8, fol. 15, 6 November 1547, and LL9, fol. 83^v, 29 June 1557.

32. Ménard, *Histoire civile*, IV:12:78–79:165; and Jouanna, *La France du XVIe siècle*, 53.

33. On bookselling, printing, and publishing, see Puech, *Une ville*, 356–68, 536–53; Puech, "L'instruction à l'époque de la Renaissance," 126–40; Puech, "La librairie populaire"; and on the facade, Puech, "Les arts à la Renaissance," 333–34. Puech suggests that there were about eleven booksellers in all, but two may have arrived in the 1560s; see "L'instruction," 138–39, and the archival references there. For Bernard's will, see ADG, IIE^{36} 320, fol. 472^v, 21 September 1556.

34. D'Albenas, *Discours historial*. See also Ménard, *Histoire civile*, IV:15:45:384–87; and Puech, *Une ville*, 123–24, on translations.

35. Goltzius, in *C. Julius Caesar*, fols. aa–dd, lists the scholars whom he consulted. For Nîmes, they included "Ioannes, Vicecomes Iocosae, Praefectus Provinciae Narbonensis, Ioannes Poldus Abenas, Bernardus Vallytus, Cyracus Serlonius, [and] Isidorus Assyrus." John Cunnally, *Images of the Illustrious*, 143, probably due to my error, translates "Vallytus" as Vallète; although there was a prominent (legal) family of that name, none appears to have been named Bernard; there was, however, a Bernard Vallat, who was a well-to-do leatherworker (the family comes up several times in this chapter and elsewhere). D'Albenas and Guillaume, vicomte de Joyeuse, are relatively straightforward to identify, while Serlonius and Assyrus are unknown to me. As

Cunnally notes, their foreign names suggest that they may have been travelers, not residents of Nîmes.

36. For general surveys of French urban economic history in the sixteenth century, see Braudel and Labrousse, *Histoire économique et social de la France*, 1:231–479, esp. 249–52 (textiles); and Chevalier, *Les bonnes villes*, 151–71.

37. Le Roy Ladurie, *Peasants*, 159. Day translates *travailleur* as "agricultural laborer."

38. In summary form, the percentage of the population in the legal professions seems remarkably high, although Albert Puech, in his excellent early study of the Nîmes tax roll of 1592, comments that lawyers "pullulated" in sixteenth-century Nîmes. Comparison with his figures suggests that, if nearly 9 percent may be too high a figure, 5 percent is certainly plausible, and a higher percentage is not at all out of the question. Puech, *Une ville*, 17, 119. Although Puech does not give clear statistics, he appears to have found 1.5 percent of heads of households to be doctors of law (more than 40 out of 3,011), plus others among royal officials. He lists 56 *hommes de loi* but comments that the list is sadly incomplete (table on 194; but see the comment on 187), while the association of notaries and clerks called the *basoche* included 80–100 members (p. 183). The 1592 *compoix* is unusually complete, including 3,011 heads of households, of whom 528 were exempt from payment.

39. Puech, *Une ville*, also gives information on the relative status of various professions in Nîmes; more general discussions can be found in Braudel and Labrousse, *Histoire économique et social de la France*, 1:411–23; and for Lyon, see Gascon, *Grand commerce et vie urbaine*, 1:357–406.

40. ADG, IIE^I 245, fol. 453^v, 4 January 1553/54; IIE^I 246, fol. 61, 26 April 1554.

41. Of 1,124 marriages, 479 were signed on a Sunday; the other six days were about equally popular (ADG, series IIE). For Portal: ADG, IIE^I 232, fol. 115, 23 July 1550 (in French, "grand jardin de Gilles Bonaud soubz le grand parqué"). For inns, see, e.g., ADG, IIE^I 249, fol. 293^v, 3 January 1558/59, marriage of Jacques Broudier, *travailleur*; for gardens, IIE^{36} 270, fol. 445. See Hanlon, *Confession and Community*, 111; and Hardwick, *The Practice of Patriarchy*, 61. I thank Edwin Bezzina for the Hanlon reference.

42. Stone, "Social Mobility in England."

43. On betweenness, a nontechnical explanation can be found in Gladwell, "Six Degrees of Lois Weisberg," which is incorporated in his *The Tipping Point*, chap. 2. For a more formal definition, see Wasserman and Faust, *Social Network Analysis*, 188–91. On Florence, see Padgett and Ansell, "Robust Action and the Rise of the Medici," 1304, 1308.

44. On the role of the elite, see Brady, *Ruling Class, Regime and Reformation*; on rural/urban relations, see Le Roy Ladurie, *Peasants*, 164–71; on civic culture, see Moeller, *Imperial Cities and the Reformation*; on localism, see Garrisson-Estèbe, *Protestants du Midi*.

CHAPTER 2

1. Ménard, *Histoire civile*, III:10:62:263, *Preuves*, 341–42. For de Laye's positions, see Ménard, *Histoire civile*, III, *Preuves*, 8, and Ménard, *Histoire civile*, VI, *Successions Généalogiques*, which lists the consuls. This incident is also cited in Otis, *Prostitution in Medieval Society*, 71; and Rossiaud, *Medieval Prostitution*, 44. Note that I cite different

years than Otis does, because she mis-corrects dates when attempting to deal with the problem that sixteenth-century years began on 25 March, rather than 1 January.

2. On Germany, see Roper, "Discipline and Respectability"; Karant-Nunn, "Continuity and Change"; and Schuster, *Das Frauenhaus*. On Toulouse, see Davis, "Reconstructing the Poor," 272; and Otis, *Prostitution in Medieval Society*, 96. For Nîmes, see Otis, *Prostitution in Medieval Society*, 41, 175 (nn. 16 and 18). On closures, see ibid., 40. Brian Pullan has argued, in "Catholics, Protestants, and the Poor in Early Modern Europe," esp. 453–55, that Catholic morality was more accepting of prostitution, but in Nîmes intolerance preceded religious reform.

3. A brief extract of this meeting has been published by Jean Viguié, "Fête de la Réformation," 555, and the incident is discussed in Hauser, "Nîmes, les consulats et la Réforme," 187–202. This article originally appeared in the *Bulletin de la Société de l'Histoire du Protestantisme Français* in 1897.

4. See Strauss, *Nuremberg in the Sixteenth Century*, 107, for similar attitudes.

5. Hauser, "Nîmes, les consulats et la Réforme," 190. The French reads, "Et l'on doyt aller sommer et requerir Monsr. l'evesque de Nismes qu'il ayt à prescher la parolle de Dieu ou faire prescher dans la ville et cité de Nismes par un homme de bien clerc et suffisant, et le requerir qu'il tienne hospitalité aux pauvres, et réside en sond. evesché et maison épiscopalle."

6. For a map of the route, see Knecht, *Renaissance Warrior and Patron*, 126–27.

7. D'Albenas, *Discours historial*.

8. Ménard, *Histoire civile*, IV:12:33–38:123–28; Bardon, "L'entrée de François I à Nîmes," 345 (in French, the quotation reads "une des plus anciennes villes du pays").

9. Crouzet, *La genèse de la Réforme française*, 216–39; Knecht, *Renaissance Warrior and Patron*, 313–23; Jouanna, *La France de la Renaissance*, 312–18.

10. Benedict, *Christ's Churches Purely Reformed*, 132.

11. On Calvin's concern to promote theological unity among Protestants, see Imbart de la Tour, *Les origines de la Réforme*, 4:52, 162.

12. Cameron, *European Reformation*, 117–28, 156–68, is a good source on faith, justification, and the sacraments, as is McGrath, *Reformation Thought*, 87–112, 151–85. See also Elwood, *The Body Broken*, esp. 56–76. Wandel, *The Eucharist in the Reformation*, esp. chap. 4, takes a slightly different view of Calvin's eucharistic theology than I do.

13. Puech, "L'instruction à l'époque de la Renaissance," 243–45; and Casteel, "The College and University of Arts in Nîmes," 15–27. On Pliny, see Nauert "Humanists, Scientists, and Pliny," 80. See also Huppert, *Public Schools in Renaissance France*.

14. On Pécolet, see Gaufrès, "Imbert Pécolet," Maruéjol, "Imbert Pécolet and Casteel, "The College and University of Arts in Nîmes," chap. 2. Hempsall, "The Languedoc," 228, states that Pécolet was arrested for heresy in 1527 in Montpellier. Unfortunately, the reference is not documented in the article nor in his "Reform and Reformation in France." As far as I can tell, Hempsall misread Guiraud, *La Réforme à Montpellier*, 6:41–42, 61, 66, 72 (the last three are the only references to Pécolet).

15. Ménard, *Histoire civile*, IV:12:52–53:137–38. On the role of the college in the diffusion of the Reformation, see Gutherz, *Histoire de Nîmes*, 150: "La voie de pénétration la plus efficace du protestantisme fut l'institution scolaire." See also Casteel, "The College and University of Arts in Nîmes," 1–5. In addition to Casteel, Mathieu-Jules

Gaufrès's articles and his biography of Baduel are also important studies of the college. See Gaufrès, "Les collèges protestants"; and Gaufrès, *Claude Baduel*.

16. Casteel, "The College and University of Arts in Nîmes," 22–38; Ménard, *Histoire civile*, IV:12:54:138–39; AMN, LL6, fol. 116.

17. Casteel, "The College and University of Arts in Nîmes," 39–47. In French, the quotation is "ydoine et souffizant."

18. Ménard, *Histoire civile*, IV, *Preuves*, 136. In French, the deputy replied that he wanted candidates who were "souffisans, ydoines, et non suspectz."

19. To be fair, we know about the complaints against Caihas because Father Antoine reported them; see Casteel, "The College and University of Arts in Nîmes," 54. Ménard, *Histoire civile*, IV, *Preuves*, 145–53, reproduces the letters patent.

20. Puech, "Débuts," 29–36. Puech gives extracts from the *sénéchausée*, which probably refer to the same case as ADHG, series B, 3359, 7 December 1537; and Herminjard, *Correspondance des réformateurs*, 4:316–21, but both of these mention them anonymously, and the letters in Herminjard add that two heretics had been burned at the stake. However, Alizot appears regularly in notarial records, starting as early as 1551, e.g., ADG, IIE^1 244, fol. 86. For his officeholding, see CR, fol. 1. When Arnaud Alizot's daughter got married, Antoine and Jean Moleri, both apothecaries, were among the witnesses; see ADG, IIE^1 250, fol. 359^v, 8 February 1562. Antoine Moleri also fled to Geneva in the early 1550s; see Geisendorf, *Livre des habitants*, 1:23, 34. Similarly, when Jean Ursi, a notary and another early Protestant, made his will, Alizot was among the witnesses; see ADG, IIE^{36} 255, fol. 53^v, 1 February 1553. There is no reference to Bernard Bach in the database of notarial records, although there are two to a farmer named Bertrand Bach, including his marriage contract; ADG, IIE^1 248, fol. 282^v, 7 November 1557. If this is the same person as Bernard Bach, he was back in Nîmes by 1550, when he appears as a witness; ADG, IIE^1 243, fol. 131^v.

21. Hauser, "Nîmes, les consulats et la Réforme," 200–201. See also Bernstein, *Between Crown and Community*, 88 and n. Arlette Jouanna also notes that, for sixteenth-century municipal elites, royal laws only really applied when the local inhabitants could not agree. See her article "La première domination des réformés à Montpellier," 153–54. For the quotation, see AMN, LL9, fol. 186, 25 April 1560. In French, it reads: "aucuns des pais et lieux circomvoysins [qui] se seroient venus randre en la presant ville."

22. Casteel, "The College and University of Arts in Nîmes," 55–62.

23. Ibid., 69–81. Casteel also makes the useful point (79) that the religiously moderate Cardinal Sadoleto had no difficulty writing to Melanchthon as a fellow humanist in 1537.

24. Gaufrès, *Claude Baduel*, 151.

25. For Baduel's marriage contract, see IIE^1 236, fol. 51. Jacques Ursi was the notary. The contract is also reproduced in Gaufrès, *Claude Baduel*, 334–39, where there is also a genealogy. For Sauzet's Protestantism, see Puech, "Débuts," 154. His wife was also accused. On the importance of networks for the spread of religions, see esp. Stark, *Rise of Christianity*, 13–21.

26. See Farge, *Orthodoxy and Reform*, 210–11. Quotation translated from Isambert et al., *Recueil général des anciennes lois françaises*, 12:822.

27. The narrative of the quarrel makes up the heart of Casteel, "The College and University of Arts in Nîmes"; see 138–96. Interestingly, Baduel took the trouble to

apologize to Calvin for taking up the post in Carpentras (Calvin had recently conducted a pamphlet war with the cardinal), explaining that he had "bowed to circumstance." See Casteel, "The College and University of Arts in Nîmes," 147; and Calvin, *Calvini Opera*, 20:col. 374. Casteel, "The College and University of Arts in Nîmes," 194, quotes the letter to Melanchthon. On the meaning of accusations of impiety in the sixteenth century, see Febvre, *The Problem of Unbelief*, 131–51. For Baduel's arrival in Geneva, see Geisendorf, *Livre des habitants*, 1:12. On Tuffan, see Casteel, "The College and University of Arts in Nîmes," 202–4. Casteel, 204, calls Tuffan's religion "impossible to determine" but strangely, he later concludes, 234, that Tuffan was probably a Protestant.

28. Ménard, *Histoire civile*, IV:12:113:188, *Preuves*, 189 (penitential procession). Ménard, *Histoire civile*, IV:12:100:179–80, *Preuves*, 183 (1543 condemnations). See ADHG, series B, 3377, 8 June 1546 (the case of Jehan Vieulx and Anthoine Planhol), series B, 3383, 27 April, 14 June, and 28 July 1548 (which concerns Anthoine Treille), series B, 3387, 28 February 1549/50 (which concerns Jehan Couril and Jehan Gordon), and series B, 3388, 13 March 1550 (which concerns "Pierre Savy dit Ferraudon" and "Jehan Morelet"). Baduel's letter concerning Morlet can be found in two copies, the original at the Bibliothèque Méjanes in Avignon and a fair copy at the Bibliothèque de la Société pour l'Histoire du Protestantisme Français in Paris, ms. 186/1, fols. 8–9. The key passage about Morlet is quoted in French translation in Gaufrès, *Claude Baduel*, 208–9. Baduel is quoting Psalm 41:1.

29. Le Roy Ladurie, *Peasants*, 51–131, esp. 52 (population growth), 56 (plowing poor soil), 63 (falling wine cultivation), 81–82 (draining marsh), 87–97 (subdivision and consolidation of landholdings), 99–100 (falling in-kind wages), 102–6 (dietary changes), 107–10 (falling standards of living).

30. AMN, LL8, fol. 38, 16 February 1547/48. The French reads, "sans jamais varier le pris." AMN, LL8, fol. 231, 18 February 1552/53. See also fol. 57 and verso, 17 March 1548/49.

31. AMN, LL8, fol. 38 and verso, 16 February 1547/48; fols. 41^v to 45^v, 8 April 1548; fol. 57 and verso, 17 March 1548/49. See also fols. 58, 64–66.

32. AMN, LL8, fol. 40, 11 March 1547/48; fol. 410, 11 March 1547/48. The French reads, "pour ouster la malice et obstacle des bouchiers, desquelz tous les ans oun acoustumé geyner la ville par augmentation du pris de la chaire"; fol. 57, 17 March 1548/49. Prices were generally higher in the spring and lower in the fall; see fol. 65.

33. AMN, LL8, fol. 198 to 199 verso, 8 May 1552.

34. AMN, LL8, fol. 235, 30 April 1553; AMN, LL9, fol. 46^v, 9 February 1555/56. Maltraict's occupation comes from the notarial database; no registers by him survive, but his will does (see also AMN, LL9, fol. 128 and verso; Bodet is called a merchant in notarial records). This sort of complaining back and forth would go on and on. For example, shortly after Bodet's complaints, on 2 November 1558, a butcher in turn came to the town council meeting to complain of *his* hardships (AMN, LL9, fol. 129^v).

35. For an excellent description of poor relief in Nîmes during the late sixteenth century, see Mentzer, "Organizational Endeavour and Charitable Impulse."

36. AMN, LL8, fol. 1. The French reads:

> Premierement a esté expausé qu'il y a une grand quantité de pouvres en la pnt. cité de Nismes demandant et serchang l'aulmosne pour l'oneur de dieu

par les maisons des habitans dicelle ensemble par les portes des esglises pour raison de quoy en seroient beaucop de maladies contagieuses tant pour raison des diverses sortes de maldies desd. pouvres que aulcunement, à quoy failloit donner ordre.

37. AMN, LL8, fol. 1ᵛ. The French reads, "il y a plusieurs deliberations de[s] consuls en la pnt. maison consulaire que ne demendre que estre mises à l'exeqution." Robert was the *viguier* of the seneschalsy.

38. In 1563, he was chosen first consul; see Ménard, *Histoire civile*, VI, *Successions Chronologiques*.

39. Vernière was third consul in 1530 and second consul in 1546.

40. AMN, LL8, fol. 2ᵛ.

41. Richier later became a councillor of the présidial court. The de Malmonts were also quite well-to-do and well connected. Robert des Georges was first consul in 1546 and 1554. Pierre de Malmont, a lawyer and *conseiller* at the seneschal court, was first consul in 1531 and 1548. He married the daughter of Jean d'Albenas in 1529, and was therefore quite young when he became first consul. He died in 1575. See Puech, "Débuts," 133n.

42. AMN, LL8, fol. 10 and verso.

43. Despite his degree, Savion is a rather obscure figure. He does not appear ever to have served as a consul, for example. The one reference to him after 1550 is ADG, IIE¹ 244, fol. 121ᵛ, 15 June 1551, where he appears as a witness. For some information about Bonaud, see Puech, *Une ville*, 123–24, and the sources cited therein. He was never a consul, despite his prestigious career. He started out as a poor student, the first member of his family of any distinction, published an edition of an important legal treatise while still a young man, and eventually became wealthy. His two sons also became lawyers, and one, Jean, was first consul twice, in 1573 and 1580.

44. For example, AMN, LL9, fol. 54ᵛ, 20 January 1556/57, where the first consul, Guillaume Martin, noted that there were some poor people who were "habitants natifs de [la] ville," and others who were "estrangiers." He added that only those who were "vrayment pouvres" should be supported.

45. At the meeting of 15 October 1559, AMN, LL9, fol. 160, the suggestion was made that the bishop of Nîmes and the priors of the monasteries should assist with poor relief, and if they did not contribute, they should be sued. The incident is also mentioned in Ménard, *Histoire civile*, IV:13:75:246.

46. AMN, LL8, fol. 45ᵛ, 13 May 1548 (food); fols. 43ᵛ and 44, 6 May 1547 (repairs to the hospital to make rooms for the "pouvres mallades"); fols. 14ᵛ and 15, 6 November 1547; fol. 207, 2 October 1552; and AMN, LL9, fol. 84, 29 June 1557 (clothing). At the 1552 meeting, apparently there was a report that some of the foundlings were "tous neuds."

47. AMN, LL8, fol. 169 (the French reads, "la peste avoit plus longue durée"); fol. 244ᵛ; fols. 43ᵛ and 44, 6 May 1548. The council decided to pursue her in civil rather than in criminal court because it would cost less. It is not clear whether her clerical employer was also suspected.

48. AMN, LL8, fol. 231 and verso, 18 February 1552/53 (the French reads, "faire ce que ung fils est tenu faire a son per"); fol. 64 (the French reads, "aux pouvres des hospitaulx"); LL9, fol. 174ᵛ, 10 December 1559; and fol. 177 (where it mentions du Brana's election).

49. Calvin, *Calvini Opera*, 12:cols. 549–50. On Jacques Ursi's authorship, see Puech, "Débuts," 16n. The original Latin reads, "Sparsus enim rumor de sacramenti ritu innovato deferbuit reseditque." Calvin's previous letter no longer exists.

50. Guiraud, *La Réforme à Montpellier*, 6:284, suggests that d'Airebaudouze was suspect as early as 1545.

51. On the sacrament of the Lord's Supper, see Calvin, *Institutes*, 2:1057, where ministers are defined as those who have the power to administer the sacrament. See also 2:1421, where Calvin's description of the sacrament clearly implies that the minister will perform it, and note also 2:1321, where Calvin denies the right of laypeople (meaning: men) or women to baptize, even in emergencies.

52. Knecht, *Rise and Fall of Renaissance France*, 234.

CHAPTER 3

1. In French: "le peuple n'est à présent si esmue à devotion fervent . . . comme il estoit"; ADG, LL8, fol. 161.

2. Gaufrès, *Claude Baduel*, 229.

3. The records now reside in ADHG, series B. Normally, it would have been a huge task to extract the Nîmes records from the mass of material, but Professor Raymond A. Mentzer, who used them in *Heresy Proceedings in Languedoc*, kindly provided me with the references from his notes. Since the volumes in series B are not paginated, I have adopted Professor Mentzer's practice of citing them by volume and date. On the surviving records, see Mentzer, *Heresy Proceedings in Languedoc*, 3. On total prosecutions, see 163. Two surviving registers cover the period from late 1518 through 1531, and seventy-five more cover the period from late 1535 through 1560. There are a few other small gaps. The parlement prosecuted 257 people in the 1540s, of whom 9 came from Nîmes, and 684 in the 1550s, of whom 68 came from Nîmes. The prosecutions from 1551 come from B 3394, 22 Dececember 1551.

4. Monter, *Judging the French Reformation*, 251–69, lists "heresy executions ordered in France," including five people from Nîmes: two anonymous, Étienne Angelin, Claude Brozier, and Claude Rochier. But there are doubts concerning a number of them. The two anonymous, as discussed earlier, were probably Bernard Bach and Arnaud Alizot, and they were not in fact executed. Brozier was from Alès and his criminal acts were committed in Anduze. There is another, independently verified execution of a monk named Claude Rozier in Anduze (see below). It is possible that the earlier death sentence on Claude Rochier was not carried out, and that all three Claudes are actually one person. Furthermore, as Monter, *Judging the French Reformation*, 141, notes, "it was not specified that [Brozier's] crime was heresy" (see ADHG, B3403, 6 March 1554). Monter includes him because the *arrêt* was ordered to be read in the cathedral. (My thanks to Professor Monter for helping to clarify these points.) Angelin was ordered (series B, 3394, 22 December 1551) to be brought

> audevant l'eglise cathedralle de lad. ville en chemise, teste et pieds nuds, ayant la hard au col et tenant en ses mains une torche de cire ardant, demandera mercy a dieu, au roy, et a justice de son forfaict et ce faict, sera

mys sur une charrete et fera le cours par les roues et carrifours acoustuméz de lad. ville jusques à la place publique ou sera estranglé et boushé, ses biens confisquez sauf le dot de sa femme, desquelz biens seront detraictz les fraiz de justice au profit de ceulx qui les ont expousez.

5. Puech, "Débuts," 59–60, and more generally, 56–58. Since the entry in the présidial minutes is from 8 July, the incident probably occurred on the Nativity of St. John the Baptist, 24 June. Puech confuses Jean Vallat with Roland. For the knifing, see Pierre Vallat's will, ADG IIE^{36} vol. 294, fol. 156 (15 December 1554).

6. Geisendorf, *Livre des habitants*, vol. 1 (vol. 2 concerns the 1570s). Further work in the Genevan archives would surely increase the number of former Nîmes residents known to have been in exile there. See Audisio, "First Provençal Refugees."

7. By analogy with Richard W. Bulliet's terminology, the Protestant movement in Nîmes was still dominated by "innovators" or "early adopters." See his *Conversion to Islam*, 28–32, 51–52.

8. ADG, LL8, fols. 148–54. The first consul's speech reads that the consul

[a] expousé q[ue] la ville a oste et est encores sans raison ne cause eu d'ete diffandu de la secte lutherienne ou se seroit que de quelques de gens p[ar]ticuliers non estans habitans domicillans de ladicte ville et que par iceulx l'on ouyt tousjours mal sona[n]tes parolles d'eulx que pourroient estre cause que le Roy avoit de la pnt. ville malvais content[ment] que seroit chose grandement prejudiciable et dommaigeable a lad. pnt. ville; par quoy a dict estre bon de pourvoir a tout et commectre gens cappables et souffizant pour le aller remonstrer au roy les choses susds. n'estre vrays et affin que la ville ne demeure plus en ceste diffamat[ion] et scavoir s'il est possible quy est celluy l'avoir ainsi diffammée sans rayson ne cause affin de ne tumber ava[nt] en plus grand escandalle et s'en purger par une bonne foys. Aussi ceulx qui s[er]ont depputtes pourront poursuyvre les aultres affaires tant du d'entretienment du siege q[ue] des garrigues et college establi au en la pnt. ville aux artz et aultres chose q[ue] leur s[er]ont bailles p[ar] memoire p[ar] lad. ville.

The final resolution was phrased, "obeissance que lesds. habitans de la pnt. ville ont tousjours heue a sa magesté, ses commandementz et de ses officiers."

9. Ménard, *Histoire civile*, IV:13:14, 21:201, 206, *Preuves*, 1, "journal anonyme." On the d'Airebaudouzes, see Hugues, *Histoire de l'église réformée d'Anduze*, 21–22; and Puech, "Débuts," 76–78, esp. 77n.

10. On the letter to Calvin, see Puech, "Débuts," 16n. An Étienne Ursi was charged with heresy by the Parlement of Toulouse; ADHG, B3394, 23 December 1551. When Jean Ursi wrote his will, ADG, IIE^{36} 255, fol. 53^v, 1 February 1552/53, one of the witnesses was the early Protestant Arnaud Alizot. The notary also crossed out a reference to the Virgin Mary in the will, and although Ursi left £30 for the poor, he specified that, contrary to contemporary Catholic practice, they should *not* accompany his body: "ordonne que soyent abilhes et vestuz douze pouvres neccessiteux a la voulante et disc. desd. execs de son ame soubznommes, sans ce que lesd. pouvres soyent aulcunement tenuz acompagner sond. corps a l'interrement dicelluy."

11. Ménard, *Histoire civile*, IV:13:44:228; and ADG, LL8, fol. 278.

12. Borrel, *Histoire de l'église réformée de Nîmes*, 10–11; and Ménard, *Histoire civile*, IV:13:51:232. But Lavau is not among the people executed for heresy listed in Monter, *Judging the French Reformation*, 251–269. The records of the Parlement are complete for 1554, but four months of 1553 are missing (Mentzer, *Heresy Proceedings in Languedoc*, 5). It is unlikely, but possible, that the trial occurred during the missing period. Deyron reached Geneva in 1556 (Geisendorf, *Livre des habitants*, 1:70); for biographical information, see Puech, "Débuts," 79. This story originally appeared in Crespin's *Livre des martyrs* and in Theodore de Bèze's *Histoire écclesiastique*. Borrel adds that Deyron's friends Pierre d'Airebaudouze and Jean Trigalet "vinrent le joindre," which almost certainly is not true, since they are recorded as having arrived in Geneva well before the supposed date of the execution, on 2 January 1553 and 31 October 1553, respectively (Geisendorf, *Livre des habitants*, 1:26, 28). Borrel adds that Trigalet was caught and executed in 1555 near Chambery, in Savoy. Puech, "Débuts," 80, also notes his suspicions that the story may have been "brodé."

13. Ménard, *Histoire civile*, IV:13:58–60:235–37, *Preuves*, "journal anonyme," 1. See also Devic and Vaissete, *Histoire générale de Languedoc*, 11:321. Information on Rozier comes from Hugues, *Histoire de l'église réformée d'Anduze*, 50.

14. On Lucquet and Bernard, see Puech, "Débuts," 84, 87; and CR, fols. 1^v, 5. On Gouzet, see Geisendorf, *Livre des habitants*, 1:80; and Puech, "Débuts," 85.

15. Puech, "Débuts," 85–89. The French reads: "Il ne treuve poinct y estre faicte mention de la confession ou chose necessere, comme estant l'ung des sacrementz de l'esglise." For biographical information on Lucquet and Bernard, see ibid., 84, 87; and CR, fols. 1^v, 5. For more information on Estiard's *Alphabet; ou, Instruction chretienne*, see Febvre and Martin, *The Coming of the Book*, 311. On Mutonis, see Puech, "Débuts," 74.

16. Benedict, *Rouen during the Wars of Religion*, 93.

17. The statistics on early Protestants were compiled by combining information from ADHG, series B; Geisendorf, *Livre des habitants*; and Puech, "Débuts," 152–55, with ADG, series IIE. Note that, although it is not surprising that agricultural workers in Nîmes were generally resistant to the Reformation, since that was generally the case, there were some exceptions, such as the radical gardeners of Strasbourg, discussed in Brady, *Ruling Class, Regime and Reformation at Strasbourg*, 204.

18. ADG, series IIE. For comparison, see the figures for London in Brigden, *London*, 34.

19. Ménard, *Histoire civile*, IV:13:63:237–38. His account is drawn largely from the anonymous journal he prints in the *Preuves*, 13, from which the quote is drawn. The French reads, "il sembloit que c'estoit un nouveau deluge." The Nostradamus quatrain that "predicted" the flood is also reprinted there. The discussions of the town council meeting of 24 November 1557, AMN, LL9, fols. 89^v–92, largely confirm this account, adding that the road to Montpellier also needed repair.

20. An English case suggests that a natural disaster could indeed play a role in religious change; see Underdown, *Fire from Heaven*.

21. Le Roy Ladurie, *Paysans*, 2:819–20.

22. AMN, LL9, fol. 144^v, fols. 74^v–77. The French reads, "Et premierement qu'en la present ville de Nismes pour raison de la cherté des bleds et aultres fruitz qui

esterellité et rarité diceulx y auroyt grand nombre et quantité de pouvres." (Part of this paragraph is also quoted elsewhere in this chapter.) AMN, LL9, fols. 77ᵛ and 78, 21 March 1556/57; fols. 83ᵛ–84ᵛ, 29 June 1557.

23. AMN, LL9, fol. 116, 2 February 1557/58; and Ménard, *Histoire civile*, IV:13:67:241 (12,000 charges of grain). The conversion from charges to bushels is based on the charge of Béziers, 182 liters according to Le Roy Ladurie, *Paysans*, 2:823. The French reads:

> à occasion de la crainte de la sterillité sur la dernier saison que messieurs les consulz doibvent secretement adviser les quantités des bledz que sont en ville premierement au purvoir de ceulx qui font trafique de bledz pour achepter; et vandre et apres des aultres habitans de la ville doibvent aussi adviser avec les boullangiers et aultres vandans pain de la quantité de bled qu'ilz pourroient à prouficter entre cy et les bledz nouveaux; et s'ilz en sont pourveuz ou non et la quantité que leur deffault jusques lors et encores doibvent adviser la quantité que pourroit estre besoing aux pouvres habitans artisans et aultres.

24. AMN, LL9, fol. 159 and verso, 30 July 1559; and fol. 160, 15 October 1559. In French, the quoted passages read "grand escandalle et emotion de peuple," "grande quantité de pouvres gens qui font desrober les fruitz," and "adviser sy seroit bon de faire saysir le bled des estrangiers qu'este dans la ville de Nysmes."

25. AMN, LL9, fol. 162ᵛ, 15 November 1559; fols. 174ᵛ–175ᵛ, 10 December 1559; fol. 177 and verso, 17 December 1559. The French reads, "que la ville soit porveu et ne tomber en scandalle." AMN, LL9, fol. 179ᵛ, 18 February 1559/60. The French reads, "grand sedition et scandalle."

26. Pin making: AMN, LL9, fol. 46, 9 February 1555/56; and Ménard, *Histoire civile*, IV:13:54:233; cooper subsidized: fol. 91, 24 November 1557; and Ménard, *Histoire civile*, IV:13:65:240; velvet: fol. 89ᵛ, 24 November 1557 (see also fols. 93ᵛ and 125ᵛ); and Ménard, *Histoire civile*, IV:13:65:239–40; silk: fols. 121, 6 May 1558, and 125ᵛ, 29 June 1558; and Ménard, *Histoire civile*, IV:13:59:242. Ménard, *Histoire civile*, IV:13:65:239, comes to a similar conclusion, saying, "On s'attachoit alors à Nîmes à établir en cette ville des manufactures et des fabriques de différents arts et métiers, afin de faire refleurir le commerce, qui languissoit depuis longtemps par la misére generale et les calamités fréquentes du pays."

27. AMN, LL9, fols. 54ᵛ and 55, 20 January 1556/57. In French:

> y aurait grand nombre et quantite de pouvres tant des habitants natifs de ville que l'aultres estrangiers venuz de lieulx [et] villages circumvoysins. Seroit bon de savoir le nombre et apres les loger par les maisons particulieres ou bien leur envoyer certains portion de laquelle se puissent entretenir jusques venu le bons temps.

28. AMN, LL9, fol. 78, 21 March 1556/57.

29. AMN, LL9, fol. 115ᵛ, 2 February 1557/58, and 117ᵛ, 27 March 1558. In French, the quoted passage is "beaucop d'enfans exposués." Also see AMN, LL9, fol. 160 and verso, 15 October 1559; and Ménard, *Histoire civile*, IV:13:75:246. At the same meeting,

the council also considered seizing grain from "extrangieres" in the town. AMN, LL9, fols. 174^v–176, 10 December 1559. The French reads, "y avoit de pouvres en grandissime nombre, de huict cens ou environ et que journellement y en viennent de extrangieres."

30. Baumgartner, *France in the Sixteenth Century*, 124–26.

31. Tax figures come from ADG, C627–29, the records of the civil diocese, which apportioned taxation, confirmed by the accounts in the town council minute books, AMN, LL8–9. National averages are from Jouanna, *La France du XVIe siècle*, 196–97. Regional differences are from Braudel and Labrousse, *Histoire économique et sociale de la France*, 1:148–50. *Taille* exemption is from Chevalier, *Les bonnes villes*, 102.

32. AMN, LL8, fols. 57–64^v, 17 March 1548/49. The quoted passages read in French, "gens forens et estrangiers qui viegnent des montagnes," "dans peu de temps ne se trouvera aulcung boys pour le service dicelle ville," and "les supplians [the cattlemen] sont constrainctz abandonner leur bestail et icell. laisser morir de fem."

33. AMN, LL9, fols. 83^v and 84, 29 June 1557.

34. AMN, LL9, fols. 131^v–136, 17 November 1558; and Ménard, *Histoire civile*, IV:13:72:244. As early as 19 April 1552, the council was discussing possible compromises and attempting to obtain a settlement, so long as the payment would be under 2,000 écus (see LL8, fol. 196). Apparently, the crown finally agreed.

35. Ménard, *Histoire civile*, IV:12:106:184; IV:13:12,18:200–201, 204–5; IV:13:26, 30:208, 211; IV:13:47:230. AMN, LL8, fol. 134^v, 12 April 1551; fol. 205, 21 August 1552; and fol. 285, 14 July 1554.

36. ADG, C629, fol. 90, 7 December 1558. In French, "par ce ques lesd. habitans seroient prives du commerce et trafique qu'ilz ont avec les habitans des montagnes pais du vellay viverois et gevoldan."

37. AMN, fol. 126, 10 August 1558; fol. 131, 6 November 1558; fol. 151^v, 18 December 1558 (the quoted phrase comes from this meeting); fol. 156, 28 May 1559; and fol. 177, 17 December 1559. Also see Ménard, *Histoire civile*, IV:13:71, 73:243, 245–46.

38. AMN, LL9, fol. 177^v, 17 December 1559. The French reads:

> Rembourceme[nt] aussi lad. seroit Impossible de fere en tout ny en partie en duquel aussi lesds. habitans de Nymes n'entendent soubz son bon plaisir se charger po[ur] la povreté et Impuissance en laquelle a cause des grandes charges que par cy-devant ils ont supportees po[ur] subvenir au roy en ses grandz et urgents afferes de guerre. [Et?] pour avoir enduré n'a que environ deux ans par moien de delluge Inurxine? et merveilheux ruyne de la plus part de leur ville, de leurs possessions et biens.

39. Devic and Vaissete, *Histoire générale de Languedoc*, 11:305.

40. AMN, LL9, fols. 148–50 and 201, 13 July 1552. The French reads, "que le Roy estre remis à la guerre par nostre sainct paire le pappe et par l'empereur et que au roy luy estre necessaire faire grand fonds de deniers pour l'entretenement des grands frais de lad. guerre." The loans continued to be a problem. On 31 January 1553/54 (ADG, C628, fol. 65^v), the representatives of the diocese complained bitterly:

Quant aux empromptz a este arreste que sera remonstra a Monrs. le general la pouvrete notoire du diucese de la grand ruyne pour cause des grandz charges qu'il a porté et porte et l'esterillite de l'annee causant les grandz playes et desbordement des rivieres quy non seullement a ceste cause qu'ilz avoit peu semer mays encores ce peu qu'ilz ont semé a esté mys et gasté et aux montaignes toutes chouses dont ilz soulioent tirent argent comme des martinentz? chastaniers ruynez par les eaues et rivieres, les pontz demolez, qu'ilz ne peuvent relever causant leur pouvreté ne scaichant comme ont dict en leurs vigueries personne aysé pour pouvoir prester argent sans vandre son bien ou l'emprompter a l'interest a ce que plaise a mond. Sgnr. le general ayant d'eulx pitié et compassion les vouloir descharger envers le roy et excuser dud. emprompt. Et ou il ne les pourroit relever et excuser de tout luy plaise supplier aud. Sr. le vouloir moderer a moindre somme.

41. AMN, LL9, fols. 119^v–120^v and 124, 12 June 1558. The French reads, "d'aultant qu'il y aura plusieurs qui seroient en impuissance ou difficulté de fournir leurs cottizations."

42. ADG, IIE^1 244, fol. 23, 6 April 1551 (£2,500); IIE^{36} 320, fol. 233, 26 June 1556 (£5,000), and fol. 863^v, 29 January 1556/57 (£3,500); IIE^{36} 296, fol. 239, 2 February 1556/57 (£2,300); and IIE^{36} 277, fol. 294^v, 5 May 1561 (£3,500). The bride in the 29 January 1557 marriage, however, was Marguerite, daughter of François de Montcalm, of a richer branch of the same family as Gaillard de Montcalm, the *juge-mage* who presented the forced loan.

43. Jouanna, *La France de la Renaissance*, 355.

CHAPTER 4

1. Anthropologists have, of course, considered liminal moments extensively, and they are well aware that these moments can occur across society, not just in the life cycles of individuals. For the notion that liminal moments encourage people to think about their society, I am indebted to Turner, "Betwixt and Between," 105.

2. Kingdon, *Geneva and the Coming of the Wars*, 2, 46. On Protestants in Paris, see Diefendorf, *Beneath the Cross*, 49–63.

3. Sutherland, *Huguenot Struggle*, 62–100; and Knecht, *Rise and Fall of Renaissance France*, 328–31. On Catherine de' Medici, see Knecht, *Catherine de' Medici*. On Maillane, see Naef, *La conjuration d'Amboise et Genève*, 222–35, 371–80. Nîmes's pastor Guillaume Mauget called those who were in favor *libertins*. See also Kingdon, *Geneva and the Coming of the Wars*, 73. He cites Naef using different page numbers: presumably, he consulted Naef's original typescript, rather than the printed thesis.

4. Sutherland, *Huguenot Struggle*, 103–14 (quotation on 113); Knecht, *Rise and Fall of Renaissance France*, 331–37; Salmon, *Society in Crisis*, 126. On the parlement, see Roelker, *One King, One Faith*, 241 (Romorantin), 244–48 (the court's religious climate). On L'Hôspital, see Kim, *Michel de l'Hôpital*.

5. Jouanna, *La France du XVIe siècle*, 361–64.

6. Taylor, *Soldiers of Christ*, 28–36.

7. On Mauget's arrival, see Ménard, *Histoire civile*, IV:13:74:246. Puech, "Débuts," 88n, suggests, from a ratification of sale on 5 December 1561, that Mauget was originally from Saint-Valery-en-Caux (Seine-Maritime). But he is described in ADG, IIE³⁷ 083, 201ᵛ, 30 October 1559, as being from Guîtres (Gironde), and that is also his place of origin in Geisendorf, *Theodore de Bèze*, 76. In combination, this makes Guîtres overwhelmingly likely. About Banc and his various names, see Puech, "Débuts," 149n, and on this and his connection to Viret, see Naef, *La conjuration d'Amboise et Genève*, 227 and n. The ministers' movements are somewhat difficult to determine. Puech concludes that Banc came at the same time as Mauget, staying until February 1561 and then returning on 20 June 1562 and staying until at least 26 July 1567; this explicitly contradicts Borrel, *Histoire de l'église réformée de Nîmes*, who suggests that he arrived slightly later than Mauget, left in 1561, returned in 1562, and left again in 1565 (see 15 and table on 477). Borrel appears to be following Ménard, *Histoire civile*, IV, *Preuves*, 1–2. From Naef, *La Conjuration d'Amboise et Genève*, 221 and 371–80, it appears that Banc was in Nîmes in January 1560, and that both he and Mauget visited Geneva, and testified to the authorities there, on 10 and 11 December 1560. CR, fol. 130 suggests that he arrived back in town just prior to 22 June 1562, since he is present at the meeting of that date, asking about his lodging if the consistory chooses to retain him. Banc never appears in the database of notarial contracts (which covers the period up to March 1563) under any of his various names.

8. On the format of Protestant meetings, see Sutherland, *Huguenot Struggle*, 63–64. On preaching in Nîmes, see Ménard, *Histoire civile*, IV, *Preuves*, 1, 14. The French reads, "[Mauget] commençea à prescher en quelques maisons secrettement" and "de nuict, dans la maison de l'advocat Cabot." On Chabot, see Chapter 5. Chabot was fairly well-off, but not politically prominent enough to be named to be a consul. On his office in the consistory, see CR, fol. 1. According to Puech, "Débuts," 211n, his father was a hotelier, and he himself became a minister and died in Pons, in Guyenne, around 1565.

9. For Jacques Maurin's will, see ADG, IIE³⁷ 083, 201ᵛ, 30 October 1559. The French reads, "fait à la maison du jardin du grand parc de Monsr. Me Tristan de Brueys, advocat du roy en la court presidial." For Jean Maurin's role, see CR, fol. 1. Tristan de Brueys, despite his high position, does not appear to have taken part in the consistory deliberations, but he appears to have converted to Protestantism, since in his will, ADG, IIE³⁷ 061, fol. 106, 28 September 1562, he asks that "Almighty God . . . receive him into paradise among the Chosen [or Elect]" (dieu tout puissant . . . le recevoir en son saint paradis parmi les élus). For Protestant preachers passing as merchants, see Kingdon, *Geneva and the Coming of the Wars*, 39.

10. Ménard, *Histoire civile*, IV, *Preuves*, 5 (journal of Jean Deyron). See also CR, fol. 16, 31 May 1561, cited in Ménard, *Histoire civile*, IV:14:26:297.

11. When, at the end of the year, Catholics were banned from the elections for consul, both Bonail and Mombel were excluded, but Granon and de Lubac were included (AMN, LL9, fol. 21, 23 November 1560). Bonail was nominated a deacon on 10 January 1561/62 (CR, fol. 65) and elected 25 February (fol. 72). It is somewhat odd that someone of his high position was not nominated sooner. On Mombel, see CR, fol. 18. The French reads, "Me. Mombel min. [*sic* in transcription; probably "not{aire}."] exhorté de se reconcilier a l'eglise pour l'edification d'icelle, pour autant qu'il a esté à la messe au temps de la

persecution." He refused to comply until 27 December, when he finally, "après longues disputes," submitted (fol. 58). On Cellerier, see CR, fol. 17, 31 May 1561, where he promised to attend the Lord's Supper. Despite Granon's Catholicism, in the 6 December 1561 elections for consul, Granon voted for the Protestant candidates. For his relationship to Dumas, see his will, ADG, IIE[1] 251, fol. 209, 23 December 1562. Other members of the Dumas family were also heretics, and Dumas's house was eventually searched for heretical materials; see Puech, "Débuts," 148 and n., 152 and n. This analysis differs somewhat from Guggenheim, "Calvinism," 193, 223. On the election for fourth consul, see Puech, "Débuts," 89, which points out that Ménard, *Histoire civile*, omits Cellerier from his list of consuls in the *Successions Chronologiques* (vol. 6). However, Granon did become consul later in the year; see, for example, Ménard, *Histoire civile*, IV, *Preuves*, 234. There appears to have been some irregularity about the election, since Cellerier, as a jeweler, should not ordinarily have been eligible for the fourth consul slot, and indeed in 1562 he served, appropriately, as third consul, the position normally held by an artisan or notary. See AMN, LL9, fol. 169^v, which suggests that Cellerier got the fourth consul position because he showed up for the elections, while the others were only represented by proxy; LL9, fol. 297^v, seems to confirm that Cellerier did not serve a full term.

12. Puech, "Débuts," 89–94. The French reads, "tavernes et cabaretz, places publiques et maisons privées, si besoing est." It is possible that nominating both Bertrand and Maure was a compromise. Bertrand converted relatively early to Protestantism: he was named an overseer at the first meeting of the consistory (CR, fol. 1). Maure eventually converted as well and served as a Protestant representative; AMN, LL9, fol. 301^v, 22 March 1562. But he may still have been a Catholic in early 1560, in which case the consuls were nominating one member of each party. On Vallete's Catholicism, see Ménard, *Histoire civile*, V:16:18:14; he was persecuted for Catholicism in the Michelade.

13. Ménard, *Histoire civile*, IV, *Preuves*, 1 (a contemporary diarist). The French reads, "on commencea à prescher de jour," at the house of Guillaume Reimond, "de Maranes." There was a Guillem Reymond in Nîmes, a *laboureur*, but he is only mentioned once in the database, as a witness to a marriage (ADG, IIE[1] 243, fol. 134^v, 8 June 1550), and without the nickname. He does not appear in the records of the consistory; he was never a consul; and Puech does not seem to have found any information on him either.

14. Puech, "Débuts," 94–100. The French reads, "par le grand bruict qui court en la présent ville de quelques désordres et rebellions, afferes contre l'église en aulcuns pays circonvoisins, et que ce ne soient que parolles pour encores."

15. Puech, "Débuts," 100–103. On Alizot, see CR, fol. 1, and the capsule biography in Puech, "Débuts," 34n. On Savy, see Puech, "Débuts," 56 and n. Savy never appears in the database, although a Marguerite Savye, dite Ferrandone, does (ADG, IIE[36] 058, fol. 519^v, 8 May 1559). Guggenheim, "Calvinism," 192–93, argues that Protestant members of the présidial were beginning to avoid attending sessions, starting at this meeting. It is an argument from silence; there is no direct evidence of their religion in this period. Of the ten absentees, two converted by mid-1561, while for the other eight, there is no direct evidence of their conversion before 1562. (By contrast, there is good evidence that at least two consuls were Protestants before the

end of 1560, as discussed above.) Other future Protestants continued to attend. Some Protestant judges in other courts may have absented themselves; see Davis, *Return of Martin Guerre*, 77. If Protestants did choose to absent themselves, it would be more evidence of the strength of the anti-Protestant attitudes among the majority.

16. Puech, "Débuts," 104–8.

17. AMN, LL9, fol. 181^v.

18. Puech, "Débuts," 110–12. The French reads, "le jour d'hier luy auroit esté dict et rapourté les consulz avoir sorty hors la maison consullaire les armes y estans et icelles baillé et presté aux habitans," and "des sédicieulx de Provence et Daulphiné, nos voysins." For Montcalm's letter, see BN, 15641, fol. 40 (fol. 41 contains a copy of the letter cited in Puech). The reply can be found in fols. 44–47.

19. Puech, "Débuts," 113–20 (quotations on 114, 118). The French reads, "Pour ce que M. le juge criminel [Brueys] est absent de cette compaignie, pour ce jourd'hui occupé," and "Me. Pierre Valette . . . protestant que à luy ne tient, ne tiendra pour l'entière exécution de ce dessus."

20. AMN, LL9, fol. 185 and verso. Robert's exact words were:

> Depuis quarante ans en ca il a esté viguier et exercé sa charge durant lequel temps environ douze fois par intervale de temps en temps de guerre auroit esté depputé cappitaine de la ville, suyvant les privilieges donnés par les feuz rois aux habitans de Nymes, mais maintenant de pouvoire exercer la charge de cappitaine est à luy impossible causant sa vielhesse, estant de l'eaige de septante cinq ans ou environ et indisposé en sa personne.

The town's decision was:

> en l'estat et tranquilité que la ville est de present n'y est pas grand besoing de pourvoir de cappitaine à icelle neanmoings pour pourvoir ce que porroit survenir aiant regard aux troubles des lieux et pais circomvoisins, et que certains estrangiers se seroient cy devant gettés en la pnt. ville faisant esmeute et s'estant despuis retirés, pourroient survenir que l'on doibt pourvoir, actendu l'excuse de Monsr. le viguier pour raison de son eaige et indisposition de sa personne, Me. Pierre Robert son lieutenant de continuer lequel qu'il a commencé icele.

See also Ménard, *Histoire civile*, IV:13:79:248, which, unusually, gives the wrong folio number (134 instead of 185) in the footnotes. Something may be wrong with the minutes of this meeting, because this account is not consistent with what had been reported that morning at the présidial meeting, where Pierre Robert the younger had already explained that he was doing guard duty but wished to be excused. On preserving the illusion of unity, see Chapters 2 and 3.

21. Puech, "Débuts," 120–23 (quotations on 122 and 123). The French reads, "quelques assemblées ont été faictes de nuict avec armes prohibées," and "sans favouriser ne exempter personne, de quel estat que ce soit." It is worth noting that the présidial officials said that the assemblies were happening at night, although other sources indicate that they were happening during the day. The officials were probably trying to excuse their lack of success in arresting those responsible.

22. AMN, LL9, fols. 185ᵛ and 186. The French reads, "il leur a dict et faict entendre pour aultant qu'il a esté adverti que en icelle y avoit heu quelque port d'armes et assemblées pour icele fere cesser et obvyer à tumultes ensuivre," and "Et que si aulcunes assemblées ont esté faicte ce n'a esté en public." See also Ménard, *Histoire civile*, IV:13:80:249–50.

23. AMN, LL9, fols. 186ᵛ–187 (18 May 1560); and Ménard, *Histoire civile*, IV:13:85:252–53 (the footnote in Ménard, *Histoire civile*, is to the wrong folio).

24. Devic and Vaissete, *Histoire générale de Languedoc*, 12:cols. 567–69, letter dated 26 April 1560. The French reads:

> en vostre ville de Nismes, le lundy de Pasques, il y fut recogneu grande quantité de estrangers, tant des villages des environs que d'ailheurs, incogneus; et ce soir mesmes, ladite troupe avec plusieurs de la ville, feust recogneu de nuit marchant par la ville en ordonnance, pourtans arquebuses et plusieurs harmes, corcelets et piques.

The letter is also printed in Paris, *Négociations, lettres et pièces diverses*, 361–64.

25. Ibid. The French reads:

> j'en ay trouvé en ladite compagnie [the présidial] qui sont fort affectionnés à vostre service, et gens de bien; mais il en a de sy séditieux que j'ay opinion que leur voix a eu lieu en l'endroit des autres.

> Ils [the council] sont, Sire, si partis en leurs opinions, que je cognois le nombre des zélateurs du service de Dieu et vostre, n'estre souffisant pour regler et conduire le demeurant en ladite polisse.

26. Ibid. The French reads, "donnant la loy, tant aux magistrats de la ville, que consul[s], ce qu'ils auront à faire pour vostre service."

27. Puech, "Débuts," 126–27, 129 (brief cessation of assemblies). Puech, 139n, says that Felix was a doctor of laws, became minister at Le Vigan, and died in 1562. However, in the database, he is mentioned three times, never as a lawyer, but twice as a merchant and once as a bourgeois (ADG, IIE¹ 244, fol. 178ᵛ and 179ᵛ, both 2 August 1551, and IIE³⁶ 299, fol. 26ᵛ, 18 August 1559).

28. Puech, "Débuts," 127–28 (quotations on 128). The French reads:

> il doibt estre commandé aux consuls et principaulx de la ville, sur peyne de leurs vies, ne permetter aucunes assemblées.

> qu'il doibt estre enjoinct à Me. Pierre Robert, lieutenant de viguier, remetters devers la cour par tout le jour ses procès et procédures qu'il avoit faictes, faisant le guet parmy la ville, depuys deux moys en ça; autrement passé ledit jour, à faulte de ce fere doibt estre restrainct au chasateau jusques avoir obéy.

Robert asked to have an extra day to prepare each day's report (136), but the court denied his appeal.

29. Puech, "Débuts," 128–34 (includes the text of the edicts and the minutes of a meeting with the consuls enjoining them to suppress the assemblies on pain of a £10,000 fine; quotation on 128). The French reads, "Me. Richier a esté de l'oppinion de M. le lieutenant en tout, *hoc addito* que Mgr. de Joyeuse, par la letter qui lui sera escripte, sera supplié prouvoir et fere en sorte que la justice aye force pour exécuter les décretz et punitions qui seront décernées." For the religious affiliation of the présidial members, see Guggenheim, "Calvinism," 223.

30. Puech, "Débuts," 137–39. Information on occupations comes from the text, Puech's biographical footnotes, and information in the database of wills and marriage contracts.

31. Puech, "Débuts," 140, 142. Puech notes that a number of Dominican monks turned Protestant, so it is possible that they connived at the use of their enclosure, although a servant may also have opened the gates surreptitiously. These arrests also tend to undercut Guggenheim's argument that the présidial had already divided along partisan lines. If there were so many Protestants among the présidial members (over half, by Guggenheim's count), why was it ready to order an arrest warrant for one member (Pierre Robert, the *lieutenant viguier*) and the close relatives of two others, but not any of the other supposedly Protestant members? It is more likely that most of the officials at the présidial were still Catholics.

32. Puech, "Débuts," 143–48. They also searched the house of Antoine Teyssier, dit Radel, who was not listed earlier.

33. Ibid., 149–50. The list appended to the latter is not identical to the list of houses searched. It adds "La Source," i.e., Arnaud Banc, the minister; Guillaume Saint-Pol, about whom little is known; Pierre Maltret, a lawyer; and Jean Lardet, a furrier.

34. Ménard, *Histoire civile*, IV, *Preuves*, 232–33. The French for the quotation (233) reads, "avoir des espies aux environs de la ville." From this point through late 1562, Ménard, *Histoire civile*, provides a transcription of nearly all of the town council meetings, which will therefore be cited in preference to the original register (AMN, LL9).

35. On the edict's reception in Nîmes, see Puech, "Débuts," 158; and Ménard, *Histoire civile*, IV:13:90:256. On the suspension and then the resumption of preaching, see below.

36. Ménard, *Histoire civile*, IV, *Preuves*, 244. In French:

notoirement en ceste ville, de jour et de nuict, se faisoient assemblées et conventiculles, avec sermons et presches plains de blasphemes contre Dieu et ses sainctz sacrementz, administrant iceulx.

quant à la crainte en quoy vous estes qu'on vous envoyast de la gendarmerye, cela n'avons-nous jamais entendu, d'aultant que telles choses ne se sont qu'aux lieulx où l'on veoyt une apparente connivence du peuple & corps de la ville.

37. Ménard, *Histoire civile*, IV, *Preuves*, 2.

38. Ménard, *Histoire civile*, IV, *Preuves*, 234–35 (quotations on 245). The French reads, "messieurs de la justice," and "chascun se doibt mectre à son debvoir de parler aux ungz et aux aultres des habitans de la ville, et user de toute doulceur pour ne esmouvoir esmocion entre iceulx, et les contenir soubz l'obeissance du roy et de sa justice."

39. Ibid., 236. In French: "le tout se doibt conduire avec prudence."
40. Ibid., 237. In French:

> d'aultant que la ville de Nismes se trouble de ce que ne fault, sellon son advis, & que le remède est fort facille à y remédier, ainsi que le peult entandre sans fere aucung scandalle, d'aultant que sellon son advis le chief de l'assemblée, que l'on appelle le ministre, se presentera à messieurs, quant sera leur bon plaisir l'envoyer querir, là où bon leur semblera, soyt en lieu secret ou public, & sellon le dire les auditeurs, que ne s'en fera poinct abattre pour desduire les choses qu'il presche, & d'icelles veoir s'elles sont véritables ou non.

41. On this point, see Benedict, *Rouen during the Wars of Religion*, 60:

> Much Calvinist agitation therefore took the form of attempting to present the confession of faith to the authorities, the assumption clearly being that, if the king or the parlement were to read these articles for themselves instead of listening to the calumnies of the clergy or the Guises, they would see that ... Reformed doctrine merely embodied the truth of the gospel.

42. CR, fols. 17^v and 18.
43. Ménard, *Histoire civile*, IV, *Preuves*, 237. The French reads:

> despuis quelques jours et en ça se sont faictes, comme se font encores, certaines assemblées en maisons privées, de jour, sans aulcunes armes, avec certain ministre qui presche à grand troppe de gens de toute quallité, tant de la ville que des extrangiers, faisant prieres et chantans les psalmes de David, sans aulcung insult, sedition, et trouble.

44. Ibid., 237–38. The French reads, "ce n'estoit au peuple de inventer et user de novelle religion, sans l'auctorité et permission du roy, et qu'il estoit prohibé par ses édictz de fere assemblées, avec armes ou sans armes," and "le contraire, à son grand regret."
45. Ibid., 239–40. The identification of Pierre de Brueys is tentative, since the records give his name as "le docteur [i.e., of laws] de Brueys," but Pierre is the only member of the family regularly referred to that way in notarial records. Pierre Boys, a bourgeois, and Pierre de Fabrica, a *greffier*, voted in the elections for consul in late 1560, when only Catholics were permitted to vote, as did de Brueys (AMN, LL9, fol. 216). (Rozel was permitted to vote, but did not show up.) Boys also attended a meeting of Catholics in 1562 (Puech, "Débuts," 182). Several other deputies did become Protestants: Jean Bertrand, a merchant (CR, fol. 1); Jacques Ferrand, a doctor of medicine (fol. 107); Pierre Baudan, a bourgeois (accused of swearing, fol. 137); and Laurens Tutelle, a *laboureur* (fol. 70). I have no evidence for the religion of Pierre d'Assas, a merchant and three-time consul. (Occupational information on all of the above comes from the notarial database.)
46. Robert des Georges, seigneur de Tharaux, became a leader of the Catholic party in Nîmes and first consul, before being murdered by the Protestant party in 1569

(see Puech, "Débuts," 181). His brother Guidon, however, was a fierce Protestant, as discussed in chapter 6.

47. Ibid., 240–41. In French, "a dict ne sçavoir aulcungz; mais a dict que a ouy dire." Again, Lansard (CR, fol. 107) and Laurens Tutelle (fol. 70) later appear in consistory records, but Lansard's affiliation is unclear since he also attended meetings of Catholics. His son appears to have been Protestant, since he married into a Protestant family (the daughter of Pierre Robert, the *lieutenant viguier*), and one of his children had a Rozel for a godfather (Puech, *Une ville*, 130). Malmazet was later first consul, and probably remained a Catholic; see Puech, "Débuts," 171; and Malmazet's will, ADG, IIE^{36} 278, fol. 354, 23 February 1561/62. Occupational information on Boys is from IIE^1 250, fol. 267, 2 November 1561, among other references. He was permitted to vote in the Catholics-only election of late 1560; AMN, LL9, fol. 216.

48. In later years, Protestants distinguished themselves from Catholics by raising their hands to swear, rather than laying them on the Bible, but it is unclear if this custom was already established in 1560.

49. Ménard, *Histoire civile*, IV, *Preuves*, 241–42. In French, the quotations read, "recourir à la voye rigoureuse," "aulcune assemblée et force d'armes," "y a plus grand nombre et affluence de gens que ne y eust jamais," "ne se cometant aulcungz larrecins, meurtres, ravissemens, ne aultres insolences, que se souloient fere et comettre plus frequement que ne font à present," and "en ce que touche le service de sa majesté et l'obeyssance que luy debvez, vous usés de limitation."

50. Ibid., 242–46 (quotations on 244): "la ville estoit en malvaise reputation envers le roy et nousseigneurs de son conseil privé," and "que se disoit communement la ville de Nysmes debvoir perir par eaue, qu'il se dobtoit qu'elle ne vint perir par sang et par feu." The "commonplace" was Nostradamus's prediction of the flood; see Ménard, *Histoire civile*, IV:13:63:238. See also BN, 15873, fol. 28, 19 September 1560 (letter from consuls to Montmorency).

51. Devic and Vaissete, *Histoire générale de Languedoc*, 11:336–40. For Villars's letter to Montmorency, see Paris, *Négociations, lettres et pièces diverses*, 656:

> sachent que j'étoez venu sen force ay avecque peu de gens (je lescé mon train derrière pour fère milleure diligence), yl ont reprins queur, de sorte qui sont toujour ensemble, fesent pis que jamés, vivant à leur mode, n'observens heune seulle ordonance du roy, fesent hu maymes les cardes des portes de jour ay de nuit, metent leurs sentinelles à pié ay à cheval ors leur ville. Seux de Monpeliers font encore pis, aytent en plus crent nombre.

52. Tievant, *Le gouverneur de Languedoc*, 27.

53. Ibid., 246. In French:

> Et suivant l'uniforme oppinion d'iceulx, par mesdicts sieur les président et juge criminel conclud, premierement que seront suppliez messieurs de la justice inhiber et deffendre à tous habitans dudict lieu et aultres, fere en icelle aulcunes assemblées et conventicules illicites et prohibées pour presches, ou aultrement se y treuver, bailher pour icelles maisons, lieux, ou aulcune faveur, en façon aulcune, sur peyne de rasement des maisons où se

seront lesdictes assemblées et d'estre chassés, comme infracteurs de paix et du repos public, et punis des peynes des édictz du roy; et ou aulcungz d'iceulx sçauront et descouvriront lesdictes assemblées, soient clandestines ou publicques, soient tenuz les venir reveller, à peyne d'estre reputés pour faulteurs d'icelles, et punis des peynes susdictes.

54. Ibid., 245. Guggenheim, discussing these events in "Calvinism," 114, citing CR, fol. 70 (and see also fol. 106), calls François Barrière the seigneur de Vestric, contradicting Puech, "Débuts," 117n, which states that Bernard Barrière, François's brother, inherited the title from their father, Jean (Ménard, Histoire civile, IV, Preuves, 254, confirms this). I am not sure which is correct. She also calls Jean (I) Boileau the treasurer (chart on 15), rather than Dolon. However, notarial references suggest, despite Puech, "Débuts," 30n, that Boileau only became treasurer in 1562. See ADG, IIE^{37} 084, fol. 198, 13 January 1561/62, where Dolon is called treasurer, and IIE^{36} 327, fol. 20^v, 2 April 1562, where Boileau is the father of the bride, Dolon is a witness, and Boileau is called treasurer.

55. On Abraham, see AMN, LL9, fol. 216; CR, fols. 107 (attended meeting, 29 March 1562) and 141 (25 July 1562, criticized for drawing his sword). On Brun and Arnaud, see Puech, "Débuts," 166–67. On Montcalm, see Puech, "Débuts," 39; and for Barrière, CR, fols. 70, 106 (attended meetings, 14 February 1561/62, 28 March 1562).

56. Ménard, Histoire civile, IV, Preuves, 247. Occupational information is from ADG, IIE^{36} 325, fol. 457^v, 25 January 1560/61 (Baudan); IIE^{36} 295, fol. 46, 16 June 1555 (Bonneterre). Puech, "Débuts," 101, says that Baudan was a Protestant "de bonne heure," and both are later mentioned in the consistory records; CR, fol. 137, 15 July 1562 (Baudan accused of swearing); fol. 153, 26 August 1562 (Bonneterre censured for various offenses).

57. Ménard, Histoire civile, IV:13:10:269–70, Preuves, 248–250. In French, the quotations (249) read:

> il n'entendoit particulariser personne; mais par tous moyens entend faire contenir ung chascun des habitans soubz les commandemens de Dieu, ordonnances de son église, du sainct pere le pape, comme a esté accoustumé par cy-devant, soubz l'obeissance de nostre souverain très-chrestien prince le roy.

> grandes et folles despences pour raison des gens de guerre.

58. Ibid., Preuves, 250–51. In French, the quotations (250) read: "tout ce qui se faisoit en la present ville, comme sont mariages & sepultures en jour et publicquement," and "il luy dict que on y envoyast ung prevost, avec cinquante hommes d'armes, lesquels chasseront le tout, car la justice dormoit, & les consulz connivoient; mais de fere razer la ville, ny prendre à la razer, a dict qu'il estoit faulx."

59. Ménard, Histoire civile, IV:13:109:272–73, Preuves, 265–66; and AMN, LL9, fols. 214–220^v.

60. AMN, LL9, fols. 214–220^v.

CHAPTER 5

1. Puech, "Débuts," 165–67. The seven were Robert Brun, seigneur de Castanet; Bernard Arnaud, seigneur de La Cassagne; Jehan Moleri the younger, an apothecary; Jehan Calvet, a merchant; Tristan Chabaud, a doctor of laws; Gaussent Brozet, a clerk (*praticien*); and Jacques Boys, a *laboureur*.

2. Ménard, *Histoire civile*, IV:14:1:275–76, *Preuves*, 251–52. For Villars's letter (he wrote two copies, which he sent to the duc de Guise and the Cardinal de Lorraine, dated 27 and 29 October 1560), see Paris, *Négociations, lettres et pièces diverses*, 671: "une partie des habitans de Nismes, de trois à quatre mille, s'est retirée dans les montaagnes du Gévaudan, d'où ils menassent de revenir bientost en force dans la plaine." The consuls referred to the Protestants as "ceulx des assemblées."

3. Ménard, *Histoire civile*, IV:14:2–3:276–78, *Preuves*, 252–54. The representatives were Bernard Arnaud and Jean Moleri, who had just stood as guarantors for the community; Pierre Cellerier, the former fourth consul; and Jehan Lucquet, a bookseller. Quotation on 253: they "ont faict semblables assemblées et persisté plus longuement que nulz autres aux assemblées." The only request that the governor did not deny was one where they asked to be able to assemble and nominate syndics so that they could organize payment. (This might have been a way of receiving some official recognition.) The governor agreed to refer this request to Villars. On 6 December, however, despite objections from the incoming consuls, the council agreed that Villars's upcoming visit was a normal event, and the town, not just the Protestants, would be honored to pay the expenses for him and his retinue, as they did for all dignitaries.

4. On the guards, see ibid., *Preuves*, 257–60. The guards consisted heavily of officials, professionals (lawyers, doctors), merchants, and bourgeois. They were probably chosen from these ranks so that they would have as much influence as possible.

5. The standard study is Major, *Estates General of 1560*. For additional information and background, see his *Representative Institutions in Renaissance France* and *Representative Government in Early Modern France*.

6. The chancellor's speech has been reprinted in l'Hospital, *Discours pour la majorité de Charles IX*. See Descimon's preface and Romier, *Catholiques et Huguenots*, 12–17, for analyses of the speech.

7. Lalourcé and Duval, *Recueil des cahiers généraux*, 1:75–77 (noble cahier) 279, 281, 417 (third estate). See also Picot, *Histoire des états généraux*, 2:106–7; and Romier, *Le royaume de Catherine de Médicis*, 2:259 (Romier cites both Lalourcé and Duval and Picot, but his page numbers appear to be in error).

8. Major, *Estates General of 1560*, 83–86 (election of the speaker), 92 (cahiers), 73 (powers of representatives), 102–4 (financial questions and tax proposals), 105 (meeting at Melun). On the letters patent, see Sutherland, *Huguenot Struggle*, 122.

9. The Protestant draft cahier is preserved at BN, 20153, 71–78, and 15881, fols. 376–78. The more complete text is 15881, and it has numbered paragraphs. Noël Valois discovered these documents, and his findings were presented posthumously in "Les états de Pontoise." Some of his conclusions are overstated, and he paints an overly

hierarchical view of the French Protestant movement. Ideologically, the article bears the imprint of the Vichy regime under which it was printed, since it sneers at anything that resembles democracy, but its facts are quite reliable. Romier, *La conjuration d'Amboise*, 262–66, cites a number of other localities where Protestants were able to influence the cahiers, but his sources give no details. For the Protestant synod's proposals, see Aymon, *Tous les synodes nationaux*, 2nd pagination, 1:13–14; and Quick, *Synodicon in Gallia Reformata*, 1:12–13. Quick was scrupulous and thorough, and he occasionally quotes lost, unique documents not in Aymon, so his work, although a translation, is of unusual importance. For the Paris cahier, see Paris, *Négociations, lettres et pièces diverses*, 833–34. Philip Benedict is now researching the wider campaign, and when his research is published we may be able to understand better how the local cahiers were drafted. Brigden, *London*, 173, notes analogously that, in England, Reformers wrote pamphlets with broad political agendas, hoping to encourage conversions.

10. Ménard, *Histoire civile*, IV, *Preuves*, 268. The French reads:

> Maistre Loys Bertrand auroit remonstré que tant en son nom que de ses adherantz, auroit requiz mondict sieur le président et messieurs les consulz d'assembler le present conseil extraordinaire, où il avoyt à remonstrer choses concernantz l'honneur de Dieu, le service du roy, et le reppos et tranquillité du peuple, pour en estre faict rapport aux estatz particuliers du present pays de Languedoc . . . [et] aux estatz-generaulx.

Bertrand's religion is clear since the Protestant Church's governing body, the consistory, named him a *surveillant* of one of the town's ten *quartiers* at its first meeting only eight days later; see CR, fol. 1.

11. Ménard, *Histoire civile*, IV, *Preuves*, 267–68.

12. Ibid. In French, the quotations read, "n'y avoit aulcuns des conseilliers du conseil ordinaire, comme est tout notoire," and to proceed "puisse préjudicier aux transactions, statutz, et ordonnances." On the role of localism in promoting heresy, see Hauser, "Nîmes, les consulats et la Réforme," 201.

13. Ménard, *Histoire civile*, IV, *Preuves*, 278, 280. In French, the quotations read, "en leur deffault seroit procedé," "homme de lettres," and "tant à son de cloche, que particulièrement par les serviteurs; et pour ne retarder les affaires du roy, a commandé ausdictz consulz oppiner." Suggesting that it was unnecessary to send delegates to the national Estates was also a well-calculated hit: the assembly was traditionally loath to spend money, and even Pierre Rozel (although not his brother Charles) agreed that sending deputies to the provincial Estates was sufficient (see ibid., 279).

14. Calvière eventually turned Protestant, but his exact commitment to the movement at this point is difficult to determine. He is first mentioned in the minute book of the Protestant Consistory on 15 November 1561, when the consistory decided to complain to him about the "heresies" preached by the bishop. On 10 January 1562, the consistory tried to elect his son as deacon, but he tried to avoid it for reasons "toutes fois fort frivolles." See CR, fols. 45^v, 65^v, and 67. Ménard, *Histoire civile*, IV:14:75:332, citing *Preuves*, 6, suggests that Calvière first attended services on 21 January 1562.

15. Guggenheim, "Calvinism," 234–61, also analyzes the cahier. She concludes that the cahier "reflected the concerns of persons who favored administrative efficiency and the decentralization of government," and, other than religious grievances, it "contained few notions which had not been supported by moderate Catholics, past and present." The "reform movement" represented by the cahier was a "failure" because its provisions "offered little that had not been said before" (quotations on 247 and 259). For a somewhat analogous situation, see Clifford Geertz, "'Internal Conversion' in Contemporary Bali," in his *Interpretation of Cultures*, esp. 185–86:

> [The elite's] sudden concern with dogma is, therefore, in part a concern to justify themselves morally and metaphysically, not only in the eyes of the mass of the population but in their own, and to maintain at least the essentials of the established Balinese world view and value system in a radically changed social setting. Like so many other religious innovators, they are simultaneously reformists and restorationists.

16. Ménard, *Histoire civile*, IV, *Preuves*, 268.
17. Cited in Major, *Estates General of 1560*, 107. In French, the quotation reads, "le roi doibt prendre à son proffit les annates vacants et depports des bénéfices." The source is a deliberation of the town council, and the actual document, apparently approved by the Estates of Picardy, is not given in full; a speaker quoted the passage I cite, recommending that it be weakened. Several speakers agreed, while others advocated yet stronger measures, but both were defeated.
18. Cited in Major, *Estates General of 1560*, 107. In French, the quotation reads:

> il estoyt fort raisonnable que ceulx qui tiennent la meilleure partye du bien de ce royaulme, comme les gens d'Eglise qui possedent les gros benefices qui ne sont beaucouop chargez, sans y comprendre les pauvres curez et autres pauvres beneficiers qui ont grande peyne à vivre de leurs benefices, aydassent du tiers ou des deux partz du revenu de leurs benefices.

19. Lafaille, *Annales de la ville de Toulouse*, *Preuves*, 2:48–50.
20. Ménard, *Histoire civile*, IV, *Preuves*, 269. In French, the quotation reads:

> afin qu'il ne soyt besoing de charger plus avant son peuple ... seroit bon de prendre deux moyens, l'ung qui n'interesse point et ne touche à personne, l'aultre qui touche le moingz et ne sera resenty: le premier est de prendre le revenu des confrairies, les cloches de deux, ou de troys une, ou plustost toutes, fores une en chascun temple, et le relicles: le second est prendre la tierce partie du revenu des benefices passantz mil livres, et les annates et sequestres des vaccantz, ... et semblable faict, prendre les jurisdictions temporelles des gens d'église, lesquelles ilz ne peuvent tenir, sellon mesmes les decretz, avec saine conscience; et le roy en tirera sommes d'argent, les infeudant, et service au bang et [ar]rière-bang au temps de guerre, ensemble des droictz censuelz fondés sur biens roturiers que le roy pourra extinguer à pris d'argent, que montera aussi beaucoup plus qu'on ne pense.

Cf. BN, 15881, fol. 376ᵛ, par. 12. On poverty, see Ménard, *Histoire civile*, IV, *Preuves*, 277. In French, the quotation reads, "Il n'y a bonnement ordre d'eschauffer le coeur des hommes à cherité & aulmosne, que occasionnera le roy, s'il luy plaict, de retirer, au nom de Dieu, la quatre partie, voyre la tierce, du revenu des benefices, pour la norriture et alimentz des pouvres."

21. On confraternities, see Ménard, *Histoire civile*, IV:12:78–79:165; and Jouanna, *La France du XVIᵉ siècle*, 53.

22. The distinction, still in use today, is equivalent to the British Nonconformist usage of the word "chapel," rather than church, to describe their house of worship.

23. Ménard, *Histoire civile*, IV, *Preuves*, 269–70. In French, "ne soyt faicte cy après reprosche, question, ne moleste, à personne que ce soyt, soubz quelque couleur de conspiration." Compare BN, 15881ᵛ, 376, par. 13.

24. Ménard, *Histoire civile*, IV, *Preuves*, 274. Similarly, Thomas Robisheaux has argued, based on German evidence, that parents were concerned about their children marrying without their consent in the early sixteenth century, since canon law accepted such marriages as valid, although the Council of Trent made clandestine marriages more difficult. Robisheaux, "Peasants and Pastors." See also Diefendorf, "Give Us Back Our Children," 286–88.

25. Diefendorf, "Give Us Back Our Children," 277. In French, the quotation reads "aulcung homme de mestier mecanique, ou n'ayant manifestement de quoy." Gambling was to be permitted to "le gentilhomme faisant honneur à sa noblesse, l'homme d'estude estudiant, et le bourgeois vivent de ses rentes." Dancing should be permitted only at weddings, a provision that the Nîmes Consistory later also endorsed.

26. Hefner, *Conversion to Christianity*, 112, provides an example of this, where the guardian of a spirit shrine in Java, under pressure from orthodox Muslim influences, converted to Christianity while proclaiming it consonant with Javanese custom and the only way to resist orthodox Muslim invasion. Rebecca Sachs Norris, in "Converting to What?" in Buckser and Glazier, *Anthropology of Religious Conversion*, 174, concludes that "conversion is a matter of matching a tradition to an ideal or experience that already exists." Some of the sentiments that Sachs Norris found in her interviews may be a form of post hoc rationalizing to deal with cognitive dissonance, but surely it is easier to shift from Catholicism to Protestantism precisely because the ideals and practices of the two religions are relatively similar. On emergent norms, see esp. Turner and Killian, *Collective Behavior*.

27. Ménard, *Histoire civile*, IV, *Preuves*, 271. In French, the quotations read, "si nous retornons en nostre Dieu, et luy servons purement, sellon sa parolle," "tous ceulx de la langue Françoyse," and "la seulle parolle de Dieu." Parallel clauses appear in the anonymous letter that is the key source for Valois (Valois, "Les états de Pontoise," 241; and BN, 15881, fol. 378, par. 35).

28. Ménard, *Histoire civile*, IV, *Preuves*, 271. In French, the quotations read, "ne sortir hors l'exposition de l'escriture pour ruer les ungs contre les aultres, mais seullement et simplement instruire le peuple en la pure parolle de Dieu," and "ceulx qui croyent ne pouvoir en saine conscience communiquer aux cerimonies de l'église

Romaine soyt donné moyen d'estre instruictz et enseignés en la parolle de Dieu, de peur qu'ilz ne tumbent en atheisme." Cf. BN, 15881, fol. 378ᵛ, pars. 39, 37.

29. Ménard, *Histoire civile*, IV, *Preuves*, 271, 272. In French, the quotation reads:

> Pareilhement pour opposer la lumiere de verité à l'espesseur des tenebres d'ignorance, qui ont remply l'air et la terre jusques aujourd'huy, et donner ouverture à chascun de sçavoir et entendre son salut, sera, si plaict au roy, restitué le catechisme des enfans et des rudes, à tel effect qu'ilz seront clerement et simplement instruictz des articles de nostre foy, de la loy du decalogue, de la maniere de prier Dieu pour esposition de l'oraison dominicale, et enseignée purement la dignité, la fin, et efficace des sainctz sacrementz, à tous qui seront d'aage et discretion competantz.

(There is no parallel paragraph in BN drafts.)

30. The passage from the Orléans cahier reads:

> Que les mêmes curés soient tenus avoir prêches un ou plusieurs avec eux, chacun capable de même capacité, tant pour prêcher que pour instruire la jeunesse de la paroisse, et que à chacun des deux offices qui se diroit par chacun jour de fête, celui qui le dira, après l'évangile parachevé, fasse la prédication, partie de l'évangile ou épître, partie de l'exposition du décalogue ou du symbole ou de l'oraison dominicale.
>
> Plaira à sa majesté enjoindre à tous évêques, curés et autres pasteurs en son royaume, que chacun en son évêché, diocèse ou cure, avant l'administration des saints-sacremens, soient tenus exposer et expliquer au peuple, en langue vulgaire et intelligible, la cause de l'institution, vertu et efficace desdits sacrements, et à cette fin, que par moyen de telle instruction, le pauvre peuple et innocentes personnes les reçoivent plus révéremment et aient en plus grand honneur et respect que par ci devant, sans permettre les insolences et irrévérences qui y ont été faites, mêmement en la célébration des noces et baptêmes, où l'on ne voit que débordemens, risées et moqueries au lieu de penser à la sainte institution d'iceux. (Lalourcé and Duval, *Recueil des cahiers généraux*, 284–85, pars. 14–15)

31. Lafaille, *Annales de la ville de Toulouse*, 2:48. In French, the quotation reads, "longue absence, ignorance et avarice demesurée de plusieurs Prélats."

32. Ménard, *Histoire civile*, IV, *Preuves*, 270 (quotation); and Picot, *Histoire des états généraux*, 1:402. Note that BN, 15881, fol. 378, par. 33, suggests that the Estates should meet every two years, while the parallel paragraph in 20153 has ten years. In French, the quotation reads, "pour veoir mieulx en quel estat seront reduictz sesdictes affaires et le mesnagement qu'on aura faict durant sa minorité."

33. Lafaille, *Annales de la ville de Toulouse*, 2:55.

34. Ménard, *Histoire civile*, IV, *Preuves*, 269–72. In French, the quotation (271) reads, "affin que le roy puisse despartir sa grace et justice jusques au moindre de ses subjectz, sellon son sainct desir et voloir."

35. For Toulouse, see Lafaille, *Annales de la ville de Toulouse*, 2:52. The French reads, "aucun Office de Justice ne sera vendu." On *épices*, see Ménard, *Histoire civile*, IV, *Preuves*, 276.

36. Ménard, *Histoire civile*, IV, *Preuves*, 276. In French, "affin qu'ilz [the judges] puissent honnestement s'entretenir, sellon leur estat et gravité de leur office, leur soyent assignés gaiges bons et competentz qu'ilz ayent occasion de trevailher sans regret."

37. Ménard, *Histoire civile*, IV, *Preuves*, 272, 277. In French, the quotation reads, "longues et inutilles formalités." On disputes with the butchers, see e.g. AMN LL8, fols. 40ᵛ, 57, 60, 64–66, 183ᵛ, 196ᵛ, 198ᵛ-199ᵛ, 235, LL9 58ᵛ, 59, 125–128ᵛ.

38. Ménard, *Histoire civile*, IV, *Preuves* 273, 275, 278. In French, the quotations read:

> heu esgard à la grande corruption & infidelité desdictz notaires, qui sont en grand nombre, sera bon les reduyre à chascune ville & villaige, à tel petit nombre que sera advisé par les habitans de tous estatz.

> Et surtout il ne fault plus souffrir l'impudence des advocatz, qui conseilhent & soubstiennent manifestement une maulvaise cause, ce qu'ilz ne peuvent fere sans honte & grande charge de conscience, ny l'audace & terguiversation de ceulx qui consomment tout le temps en oultrages & faulx faictz qu'ilz alleguent contre les parties.

39. Cf. Strauss, *Nuremberg in the Sixteenth Century*, 169.

40. Ménard, *Histoire civile*, IV, *Preuves*, 277.

41. Moeller, *Imperial Cities and the Reformation*, 64.

42. Compare Ménard, *Histoire civile*, IV, *Preuves*, 267–68, 281–82, with 259–60 (guards); with the présidial list in Guggenheim, "Calvinism," 15; and with AMN, LL9, fol. 216 ("non-suspect" voters). Jean Vigier, who attended a meeting of Catholics in 1562, also signed the cahier; see Puech, "Débuts," 181–82. I do not count Pierre de Fabrica, Pons Blanc, and Guillaume Ferrussac, who attended the cahier meeting and were also voters, because they were consuls and presumably only attended the council meeting because of their position.

43. On preaching, see Ménard, *Histoire civile*, IV, *Preuves*, 2; on the consistory, see its minutes, CR, fol. 1.

44. Chabot quoted in Ménard, *Histoire civile*, IV, *Preuves*, 285. In French, the quotation reads, "en iceulx ne se traitoyt que la subvention des debtes du roy." For summaries of the March 1561 Estates of Languedoc, see Guggenheim, "Calvinism," 240–44; Devic and Vaissete, *Histoire générale de Languedoc*, 11:346–48; and Le Roy Ladurie, *Peasants*, 172–75.

45. *Capitoul* was the term for the town officers of Toulouse, equivalent to *consul* for Nîmes.

46. Gamon, "Mémoires," 34:304 (cited by Le Roy Ladurie, *Paysans*, 1:361). In French, the quotation reads, "l'expedient le plus prompt étoit de prendre tout le temporel de l'Eglise, en reservant aux bénéficiers les maisons et les terres adjacentes de leurs bénéfices." On Chabot's Protestantism, see CR, fol. 1, where Chabot is named

a *surveillant*. Le Roy Ladurie, *Peasants*, 173, calls Terlon "vaguely sympathetic" to the Reformation; Guggenheim, "Calvinism," 241, presents evidence to suggest that he was not a "convinced Protestant"; and Major, "The Third Estate in the Estates General of Pontoise," 470, concludes that he was "at least a nominal Catholic." All three of these are probably true.

47. Devic and Vaissete, *Histoire générale de Languedoc*, 11:347n2; and Gamon, "Mémoires," 304–5. In French, the quotations read:

un perturbateur du repos public

Un air de réforme, dont les prédicateurs de la nouvelle religion faisoient voir la nécessité, séduisoit les uns; la liberté qu'elle favorisoit corrompoit les autres, et dans l'incertitude, ou, pour mieux dire, l'ignorance de la religion catholique et de la religion réformée où on étoit, on ne sçavoit à quelle des deux on devoit s'attacher, et quels pasteurs il falloit suivre.

48. Major, *Estates General of 1560*, 107–14. See also Van Dyke, "Estates of Pontoise."
49. Valois, "Les états de Pontoise," 241, says that the Protestant position "tendait à rien de moins qu'à l'étblissement d'une sorte de gouvernement représentatif," which he concludes the French people did not want. See also ibid., 253–56. Van Dyke, "Estates of Pontoise," 493–95, provides a summary of the political clauses of the Pontoise cahier.
50. Ménard, *Histoire civile*, IV, *Preuves*, 285. In French, the quotation reads, "dans lequel, entre aultres articles, y avoit requisition aux fins de demander des temples, et que ceulx qui desirent vivre sellon la parolle de Dieu se puissent assembler pour estre instruictz en icelle." Chabot also criticized Terlon for not presenting the Nîmes cahier at Pontoise, as Chabot insisted he ought to have done.
51. Ibid., 286. In French, the quotation reads:

acorder à sa majesté toutes impositions qu'il luy aura pleu commander estre faictes sur le pais de Languedoc pour satisfaire à ses debtes, charges, et affaires du royaulme, en usant du debvoir que vrays et fidelles subjectz sont tenus envers sadicte majesté, sans y rien espargner, et pour la quotité concernant ladicte ville; et encores pour aultant que les gens du tiers estat de ce royaulme assemblés aux derniers estats generaulx tenus en la ville de Pontoyse, par leur caher, pour les causes en icelluy contenues, furent d'advis que pour satisfaire à ceulx qui desirent vivre en la pureté de l'évangille, soubz l'obeyssance du roy, leur debvoit estre assigné en chascune ville ung temple.

52. Brady, *Ruling Class, Regime and Reformation*, 233, concludes that Protestantism in Strasbourg also lacked ideological unity until the late sixteenth century. See also Hefner, *Conversion to Christianity*, 118, which describes an analogous process among Christian converts in Java. There, too, the process of negotiating a new religious identity eventually led the converts to jettison some of the beliefs that had led them to convert in the first place.

53. At least it was so in the short term. Philip Benedict, in *The Huguenot Population of France*, has argued that, in the seventeenth century, France's Protestant population was stable or falling, and not because of royal persecution. Lines were clearly drawn, and Protestantism was a known entity. By this period, it was also clear that the Protestant movement needed to offer obsequious obedience to the Crown in order to survive. As a result, it may have cut itself off from being a conduit for discontent, thus hurting its ability to recruit.

CHAPTER 6

1. CR, fols. 1–3. In fact, a rudimentary organization apparently existed earlier. The ministers of the Nîmes church, Arnaud Banc and Guillaume Mauget, mentioned the "consistoire" and the "diacres" when they were interrogated by the authorities in Geneva after the conspiracy of Amboise. See Naef, *La conjuration d'Amboise et Genève*, 372–74.

2. Some men may have been able to use their positions of leadership in the Protestant movement to jump-start their political careers. Of the fifty-three early Protestant leaders, only one, Antoine Triati, had been a consul prior to his election by the consistory (he was third consul in 1553), while four were elected afterward: Jacques Guillon was fourth consul in 1563; Jean Baguard and Jean Jacques were third consuls in 1570 and 1573, respectively; and Pierre Maltraict was first consul twice, in 1577 and 1588. As noted in Chapter 4, only one of the early Protestants ever became a consul. (The information presented here derives from a comparison of CR, fols. 1–5^v, with Ménard, *Histoire civile*, VI, *Successions Chronologiques*.)

3. The close correspondence is particularly important since some of the subsamples in the Protestant leaders group are quite small. Normally, it would be imprudent to generalize about the importance of the legal professions when, after all, 15.1 percent of a sample of fifty-three is only eight people. But the evidence of the cahier signers greatly improves the reliability of these figures.

4. CR, fol. 47, 25 November 1561.

5. Thus, I would disagree with the thesis that such regulations were a form of social control in which elites tried to control the populace, as put forward by Hsia, *Social Discipline in the Reformation*. On the consistory's efforts at morals reform, see Philippe Chareyre, "'The Great Difficulties One Must Bear to Follow Jesus Christ': Morality at Sixteenth-Century Nîmes," in Mentzer, ed., *Sin and the Calvinists*, 63–96; Mentzer, "*Disciplina nervus ecclesiae*"; and more broadly, Mentzer, "Ecclesiastical Discipline and Communal Reorganization."

6. CR, fols. 14^v and 15. In French, the quotation reads, "a confessé avoir esté ouyr le presche du Jacopin depuis sa reception en l'esglise, mais n'avoir assisté à la prière." Occupational information was added from the notarial database.

7. CR, fols. 14^v, 37, 40, 42, 51^v, 53, 58^v, and 59. Contract: ADG, IIE^{36} 326, fol. 536, 11 February 1561/62. Some information is from the notarial database. Juliane appears to have earlier married Pierre Dupont, a surgeon; see contract, 5 October 1551, ADG, IIE^1 233, fol. 237.

8. CR, fols. 48, 51^v–52, 104. In French, the quotation (fol. 48) reads:

a respondu parlant a Monsieur Viret [the minister] s'il avoit autorité en l'Escripture pour luy demander ce qu'il luy vouloit demander, et qu'il le louy prouvast premièrement s'il luy pouvoit pardonner ses pechés, ou Dieu. Si c'estoit luy, il se confesseroit à luy; si c'estoit Dieu, il falloit donc qu'il se confessast à Dieu et non aux hommes.

9. CR, fols. 15, 27. At a later meeting, one of the Rozels, probably Pierre, was criticized and told "d'estre plus court et en oppinant," i.e., he talked too long at meetings (see fol. 105).

10. Ibid., fol. 33, 12 September 1561. For Rozel's difficulties, see below.

11. Ibid., fol. 18. In French, "continuer d'avantage de mieulx en mieulx." The *grabaud* in Nîmes was called the "censures de ceux du consistoire."

12. See also the account in Kingdon, *Geneva and the Coming of the Wars*, 47–48. His sources include Calvin's letters in Calvin, *Calvini Opera*, 18:cols. 446–47, 449–51, 461–62, 496–98; and BPU, 402–3.

13. CR, fols. 4, 5^v, and 6, 5 May 1561.

14. Ibid., fols. 6–10. In French, the quotation (fol. 7) reads, "affaires de grande importance." Chabot's first name is a guess, since it is not given in CR.

15. Ibid., fol. 13. (Mutonis's replies precede the charges in the records.)

16. Kingdon, *Geneva and the Coming of the Wars*, 48.

17. CR, fols. 10–13, 19; and Kingdon, *Geneva and the Coming of the Wars*, 48.

18. CR, fols. 65–67, 71–72.

19. This analysis extends but largely agrees with Mentzer, "*Disciplina nervus ecclesiae*," 91–92. See also Garrisson-Estèbe, *Protestants du Midi*, 94–97. For a good discussion of issues of the consistory and its organization, see Sunshine, *Reforming French Protestantism*, chap. 6.

20. Davis, "Protestantism and the Printing Workers of Lyons," 354.

21. CR, fol. 121.

22. Ibid., fols. 43^v, 63^v.

23. Ibid., fols. 14^v–15, 95, 99, 121. For Vallat's speech, see above.

24. Judith Pollman, "Off the Record: Problems in the Quantification of Calvinist Church Discipline," *Sixteenth Century Journal* 33(2) (2002): 423–38.

25. The Ursi case is a good example of this; for examples of depositions, see those concerning the Michelade massacre, many of which are printed in Ménard, *Histoire civile*, V, *Preuves*.

26. For discussion of this issue, see Sunshine, *Reforming French Protestantism*, 148–57.

27. CR, fols. 169–70. In French, the quotations read:

avons inhibé et deffendu, inhibons et deffendons a peine de mil livres tournois et des autres que de droit pourront estre encores, ausdictz ministres, leurs consistoires, et a tantz autres qu'il appartiendra, de prendre court, jurisdiction, cognoissance, autorité ou puissance aulcune sur les subjectz du Roy pour raison des differentz, controverses et proces criminelz que soyent que lesdictz subiectz ayent ou puissent avoir ensemble, soyt pour

> matieres criminelles ou civiles, exces, injures ou aultrages en consistoire ni aultrement.
>
> aussi n'entendons empecher lesdictz ministres et consistoires esdictes exortations, reprehensions, et en la correction des escandales, des faultes atroces ou publiques, comme la cognoissance et correction leur en peult appartenir par la doctrine ecclesiastique reglee par la parolle de Dieu et par ses Escriptures sainctes, sans sortir hors les bornes dicelle, ny interrompre l'ordre y ordonné, en y uzant pareillement des censures ecclesiastiques, excommunications et aultre autorité appartenant a l'eglize, suyvant la dicte parolle.
>
> l'on n'a onques pensé contrevenir aux articles des inhibitions propozés, comme ny veulent aussi contrevenir cy apres, n'estant besoing pour ce regard lesdictes inhibitions y contenues leur estre faictes, lesquelles neantmoingz prennent a la bonne part, attendu que l'intention de la court n'est aultre que de se vouloir tenir et fere tenir les subiectz du Roy soubz l'obeissance dicelluy, comme se seroient aussi tousiours tenurs et veulent faire.

On the role of consistories in making peace, see Soman and Labrousse, "Le registre consistorial de Coutras," 195.

28. CR, fols. 70, 106.

29. Such as in the Michelade, discussed below.

30. Turner and Killian's concept of an emergent norm, discussed in Chapter 5, also seems relevant here (*Collective Behavior*).

31. See Padgett and Ansell, "Robust Action and the Rise of the Medici," 1260.

32. CR, fols. 28, 27. In French: "on ne prendre temples sans avoir responce de la cour," and "il sera remonstré à l'assemblée par Monsr. Mauget se garder led. jour de vendredi et autres festes pappalles d'aulcune sedition et admonester d'obeir au magistrat ez choses qui ne seront contraires à la parolle de Dieu et confession de foy." Eire, in a generally stimulating book, *War against the Idols*, 74, takes a more cynical view of the Reformers' motives. He argues:

> They would rant and rave against the idols, and work up their congregations to a fever pitch while telling them that they had to wait upon the magistracy to see the idols removed—never saying that the people had obeyed a principle that ought to be followed everywhere, but also never saying that the people had committed an act for which they should repent.

At least for Nîmes, this conclusion does not seem justified.

33. CR, fol. 49^v, 4 December 1561. Fournier's first name and occupation come from the notarial database. I have interpreted George's question somewhat in summarizing the text, because the records are elliptical. The full paragraph reads:

> Monsieur Fournier a demandé advis s'il payeroit une censive qu'il faict au chapitre de vingt cinq solz, veu que la fondation est d'adversaire, et Estienne George a demandé s'il pouvoit escripre à ces matières [i.e., work for the

cathedral's estate managers, since writing such documents was his profession] à saine conscience.

34. Ménard, *Histoire civile*, IV, *Preuves*, 2, 5, 7; and Puech, "Débuts," 169–73. There are other cases where Protestants attempted to give iconoclasm and attacks on churches a legal form. See Christin, *Une révolution symbolique*, 103.

35. CR, fols. 35^v, 36. In French, the quotation reads, "veu qu'il a esté prins sans esmotion et la necessité qu'on en a."

36. On breaking the stained-glass windows, see CR, fol. 36. On notions of pollution, see Davis, "Rites of Violence," in her *Society and Culture in Early Modern France*, 157–60.

37. Ménard, *Histoire civile*, IV:14:37:307–8.

38. CR, fol. 41. In French: "le grand temple au milieu de la ville." This locution was not confined to the members of the consistory; an anonymous diarist referred also to "le temple, appellé esglise Nostre-Dame," and Jehan Deyron calls it "le grand temple de la place de Nîmes"; Ménard, *Histoire civile*, IV, *Preuves*, 3–6.

39. CR, fol. 53^v. In French: "provocque[r] point le peuple par la grand sonerie de ses cloches et la multitude de ses messes."

40. Ménard, *Histoire civile*, IV, *Preuves*, 4.

41. Goubert, *Cent mille provinciaux au XVIIe siècle*, 265.

42. Ménard, *Histoire civile*, IV:14:38–47:308–15.

43. For the consistory meeting, see CR, fol. 53^v. For the attack on the cathedral, see Ménard, *Histoire civile*, IV:14:52:318, *Preuves*, 3. In French, the quotation reads, "avec grand tranquilité."

44. On the similarity of Catholic and Protestant programs for solving the problem, see Davis, "Poor Relief, Humanism, and Heresy," in her *Society and Culture in Early Modern France*, 17–62.

45. CR, fol. 3 and verso. The quotation reads, "ung pouvre de la surveillance de Sigalon." Panse may have been related to Thuffene de Panse, who made her will on 8 October 1561, ADG, IIE^1 250, fol. 238, but she appears to have been well-to-do. Poulon may have been a *travailleur*; see marriage contract, 22 August 1557, ADG, IIE^1 248, fol. 208. The women chosen to distribute alms were "la femme de Me. Guichard, de sire Baudan, la mère de M. Felis et Maltret"; all of their husbands had just been elected to offices in the consistory.

46. See ADG, IIE^{37} 059, fols. 125^v and 152. Note that Guidon des Georges was the brother of Robert des Georges, seigneur de Tharaux, a leader of the Catholic party in Nîmes. The two shared a house. Robert, as discussed in chapter 4, was the first person to state explicitly that there were heretics in the city council. He was later first consul and a leader of the Catholic party, before being killed by the Protestant party in 1569 (for biographical information on him, see Puech, "Débuts," 181). Madeleine Genesie's will simply called for alms to be distributed to the poor on the day of her death, while Privat Vigier's will asked that £10 be spent "en oeuvres pies, mesmes aux pouvres." Although these provisions are not Protestant on their face, they were quite rare in Catholic wills of the period. For Guidon des Georges's will, see, fol. 233^v. He warned his heir and executor that he would disinherit him if he were buried "à la façon des

papistes," perhaps a necessary warning, since the executor was his brother Robert. Nonetheless, although des Georges did give to the poor, he used more traditional means, including giving clothing, that are reminiscent of Catholic wills.

47. For the establishment of the poor fund, see CR, fol. 27. For charitable giving in Ursi wills, see ADG, IIE^I 250. For the consistory's request to the notaries, see CR, fol. 76, which is also cited in Ménard, *Histoire civile*, IV:14:8:337.

48. The first reference is a legacy to the "pouvres de l'assemblée" in the will of André Lombard, a furrier; ADG, IIE^I 250, fol. 232^v. The first direct reference to the "bource des pouvres" is from 28 December 1561, in the same register, fol. 232^v (as usual, it was Jacques Ursi's clients who were the first to use the phrase). Actual references to the "bource des pouvres de l'église réformée de Nîmes" come from 1562, e.g., IIE^I 250, fol. 377, 23 February 1561/62, and IIE^{36} 279, fol. 280, 10 August 1562. For Granié, see ADG, IIE^I 251, fol. 102, 16 July 1562; for de la Roque, see ADG, IIE^{37} 061, fol. 108, 30 September 1562.

49. See Bonney, *The European Dynastic States*, 373; and Davis, "Poor Relief, Humanism, and Heresy," 17, 19.

50. In addition to the examples cited below, see also the statistics on notarial formulas in Chapter 3.

51. ADG, IIE^{36} 277, 325. Grimaldi's clients, however, continued to ask in their wills for the Virgin Mary's intercession on their behalf until early 1562.

52. The first use was by a client of Jacques Ursi's on 4 October 1561 (IIE^I 250, fol. 232^v). It became popular the following summer (see ADG, IIE^I 251) and reached Duchamp the following December (ADG, IIE^{37} 086). Some changes, of course, happened before and afterward: Ménard's clients stopped making the sign of the cross before making their wills in March 1561, and stopped mentioning "père et fils et saint ésprit" a year later. See ADG, IIE^{36} 278, 325, 327.

53. The earliest reference (to the "assemblée de l'église universelle réformée") is in ADG, Antoine Sabatier, IIE^{37} 059, fol. 230^v (11 November 1561). The use of "assemblée" and "universelle" (terms that recur in other early Protestant acts) points again to the collective, civic character of the conversion process.

54. Starting on 13 November 1561, mentioning a desire to be among God's "esleus" became quite common among the testaments in ADG, IIE^{37} 059 (fols. 233^v and following). Other formulas remained ambiguous (usually very Christocentric), suitable for Protestants or Catholics: Guillaume Mombel's clients frequently declared "a recommandé son âme a Dieu le createur que luy plaise avoir mercy de luy par le mérite de la mort et passion de son fils Jesus Christ" (ADG, IIE^{36} 300), while Antoine Malian's clients mentioned Jesus's "intercession" (ADG, IIE^{36} 312). See Vovelle, *Piété baroque et déchristianisation*, 57–59, for a discussion of formulas. He does not conclude that only Protestants asked to be listed among the chosen in their wills, but in Nîmes this was the clear implication. Perhaps circumstances were different elsewhere.

55. ADG, II^{37} 084, fol. 182^v. The French reads, "où l'on a de coustume mectre ceux de l'église chrestienne dudit Nismes." Also see IIE^{36} 312, fol. 141, will of Guilhaumes Cazales, 8 March 1562/63. In French: "la bonne coustume de Milhau." On the role of localism, see, e.g., Strauss, *Nuremberg in the Sixteenth Century*, 161.

56. The French originals of these quotes: "[elle] veult vivre et mourir en la foy chrestienne et catholique," "telle que nous est enseigné par la parolle de notre Seigneur Jesus Christ en son saint Evangille," and "[il] a recommandé son âme à notre Seigneur Jesus Christ, créateur et redempteur du monde, que luy plaise par le mérite de sa saincte passion avoir pitié et miséricorde de luy et le mettre du nombre de ses esleus, invocant toute la court celestialle de paradis prier pour luy." For Mantesse's will, see ADG, IIE^{36} 300, fol. 160^v; the other will is that of Jehan Mombel, a notary, ADG, IIE^{36} 273, fol. 930, 13 November 1558.

57. See very similar phrasing in Brigden, London, 630.

58. ADG, IIE^{36} 300, fol. 160^v.

59. CR, fol. 41^v. In French: "touchant les bonnetz carrés; qu'on ne peult constraindre personne comme chose indifférente."

60. Ménard, Histoire civile, IV, Preuves, 5–6. In French: "le vendredi 23 [Decembre] messieurs du siege présidial ayant laissé les bonnets carrés ronds, commencèrent à porter des bonnets à rebras, & avec iceulx tindrent l'audience."

61. Sauzet, "L'iconoclasme protestant," 13. In French: "les adeptes populaires de la Réforme restent pénétrés des conceptions traditionnelles relatives au commerce avec les objets sacrés."

62. Calvin, Institutes, 1:597 (bk. III, chap. 3, sec. 5). See also Oberman, "Calvin's Critique of Calvinism," in his The Dawn of the Reformation, 264.

63. On the importance of self-examination in Protestant thought, see Elwood, The Body Broken, 164.

64. Calvin, Calvini Opera, 18:cols. 655–58.

65. This day, 28 February 1561/62, was chosen as the terminal date because it marked approximately the first year of the consistory's existence and because the consistory elected its second slate of officers on the twenty-fifth, as discussed below.

66. Ménard, Histoire civile, VI, Successions Chronologiques; cf. CR, fols. 1–80.

67. See Appendix B for information on how "elite" is defined.

68. Viret, Instruction chrétienne. He dedicated volume 1 to the church of Nîmes. The dedicatory epistle can be found on fols. 5^v–8^v. For Viret's activities on his journey, see Roussel, "Pierre Viret en France," 803, and the sources cited therein. Viret also passed through Nîmes briefly while heading from Montpellier to Lyon in May.

69. Viret, Instruction chrétienne, fol. 8 and verso. In French, the quotation reads:

> Et pour autant qu'entre les autres matieres trajttées en ce volume, il contient une bien ample exposition de la Loy que dieu a donnée à son Peuple, il m'a semblé que i'avoye tant plus grande occasion de le vous dedier, considerant l'estat de vostre ville. Car il y a un bon et grand nombre d'hommes savans, tant à cause de vostre college, que du siege presidial dressé en icelle: lesquels font presque tous profession des loix, et de la science de icelles: laquelle est fort noble, et fort utile et necessaire à la Republique, quand l'usage en est bien réglé selon icelles, et principalement selon la regle de la Loy de Dieu, sur laquelle toutes les autres doyvent estre fondées.

70. Moeller, Imperial Cities and the Reformation, 61; and Brady, Ruling Class, Regime and Reformation, 292.

71. Nicholls, "Social Change and Early Protestantism," 294.

72. AMN, LL9, fol. 271^v. In French, the quotation reads, "eviter le dangier de partialiser, esmovoyr, et ceditionner le peuple."

73. Ibid., fols. 273^v and 274.

74. For Protestants, see CR, fols. 1–80; Puech, "Débuts," 152–55; Geisendorf, *Livre des habitants*, vol. 1; and ADHG, series B. For Catholics, see Puech, "Débuts," 181–83; Ménard, *Histoire civile*, IV, *Preuves*, 259–60; AMN, LL9, fol. 216 and (for both Catholics and Protestants) fol. 301^v.

75. It appears likely that Jacques Agulhonet, a merchant, was a Catholic, since he attended a meeting of Catholics on 5 March 1561/62 (see Puech, "Débuts," 182). But apart from Bernard Corconne, who also attended, the other Catholic attendees are so identified because they were electors the previous year, or, in the majority of cases, they had been chosen as guards, which, as discussed in Chapter 4, is not quite as sure a marker. It is therefore possible that some had converted over the course of the year, and indeed a half dozen of them are mentioned in the consistory records of the period. On the voting, see AMN, LL9, fols. 274–81.

76. On the appointment of a professor of theology, see Ménard, *Histoire civile*, IV:14:61:323–25, *Preuves*, 298–300. Tuffan refused to oblige, although he compromised by offering to teach a course in Hebrew. The council appointed Mauget instead; Tuffan resigned shortly thereafter.

77. On the marriage between Bernardine Barrière and Pierre Rozel, see Puech, *Une ville*, 103. For notarial acts linking the Rozels and Barrières, see ADG, IIE^{36} 266, fol. 563, 17 January 1551/52; when Barthélemy Chomieu married Michelle de Barrière, a servant of Jean Barrière and his wife, Pierre Rozel was among the witnesses. The relationship between Michelle de Barrière and Jehan Barrière is unclear from the act, although it is a plausible inference that Michelle was a distant relative employed in the household. She married a second time, on 27 February 1563, to Antoine Boyer, *laboureur* (ADG, IIE^1 251, fol. 287^v). At this point, she was still working for Jehanne de Pavée, Barrière's wife, but no member of the Rozel family appeared as a witness. According to ADG, IIE^{36} 294, fol. 30, 6 May 1554, Pierre Rozel married Françoise de Serres, and Jehan Barrière was among the witnesses. Per ADG, IIE^{36} 296, fol. 239, 2 February 1557/58, Pierre d'Aisse married Tiphene Rozelle, and Bernard Barrière was among the witnesses. According to ADG, IIE^{36} 323, fol. 135^v, 17 July 1559, François de Barrière married Catherine Darlière, and Pierre and François Rozel were among the witnesses. Per ADG, IIE^{37} 61, fol. 139^v, 24 December 1562, Jacques Rozel married Rose de Faucon, and Bernard and Jacques Barrière were among the witnesses. In every case in the surviving records for the period 1550–1562/63, when a member of the Rozel family was a principal (husband, wife, or testator) in a notarial act, a member of the Barrière family was a witness. When a member of the Barrière family was a principal, this was true in two of four instances.

78. The Crussols, a numerous and bellicose family, bore several titles, notably as the seigneurs of Acier and Beaudîner, but the various brothers kept getting killed, so they kept exchanging them. Antoine, who remained the head of the family, had his title elevated from a *comté* to a *duché*, making it difficult to come up with a consistent

formal name even for him. I have therefore used first names throughout. See the *Dictionnaire de biographie française*, s.v. "Crussol."

79. Ménard, *Histoire civile*, IV:14:67–75:327–32; Sutherland, *Huguenot Struggle*, 132–36; Romier, *Catholiques et Huguenots*, 285–300, esp. 291–92 and nn.

80. Arnaud, *Documents protestants*, 40–45. For a discussion that stresses Viret's church order's debt to the Swiss system with which he was familiar, see Sunshine, *Reforming French Protestantism*, 78–81. For Viret's disputation with the Dominicans, see Ménard, *Histoire civile*, IV, Preuves, 6.

81. See Kelley, *The Beginning of Ideology*. In thinking about these issues, I have found Martin, *Tongues of Fire*, to be quite helpful. He has argued that conversion to Protestantism in contemporary Latin America has enabled people to make "innovative shifts shielded behind an apolitical stance" (190) particularly by reinforcing family structures and other avenues to social mobility. Martin notes that the network of small chapels allows people to escape the chaos of their surroundings:

> People are able to devise their own social world for themselves. And as these worlds expand numerically they gain a sense of latent power, which above all becomes manifest as they come together in vast public gatherings. The growing network of chapels represents a walkout from society as presently constituted. The evangelical believer is one who has symbolically repudiated what previously held him in place, vertically and horizontally. He cannot overturn the actual structures and is, in any case, committed to non-violence, but he can emigrate from the ecclesiastical symbol of its all-inclusive claims: Catholicism. (*Tongues of Fire*, 285)

82. Ménard, *Histoire civile*, IV:14:89:338.

83. Guise spoke of the event as an "accident," and standard accounts, such as Jouanna, *Guerres de religion*, 106–10; and Romier, *Catholiques et Huguenots*, 320–21, do not dispute him. Although this may be true, it also served his political purposes perfectly.

CHAPTER 7

1. Ménard, *Histoire civile*, IV:14:88–93:337–40.
2. Ibid., IV:14:95 to IV:15:15:344–64.
3. Devic and Vaissete, *Histoire générale de Lunguedoc*, 11:38:85, 100, 404, 425; and Ménard, *Histoire civile*, IV:15:19–31:368–75.
4. On Damville's appointment, see Tievant, *Le gouverneur de Languedoc*, 94. See Ménard, *Histoire civile*, IV:15:37–48:380–89; and AMN, LL10, fols. 1–3, for Damville's arrival, the elections, and the town council deliberations. For des Georges, see Puech, "Débuts," 181; Millet, "A City Converted," 216n150; and Ménard, *Histoire civile*, IV, Preuves, 240–41. I thank Josh Millet for giving me a copy of his completed dissertation to read
5. On the Lenten preacher, the priest, and the hospital, see AMN, LL10, fols. 7–10.

6. AMN, LL10, fols. 12–13ᵛ; and Ménard, *Histoire civile*, IV:15:48:388–89. In French, the quotation reads, "l'on poursuyvra devers Mond. Sr. Dampville que les garnisons de gens de guerre soient ostées sauf que le chasteau soit gardé." On the sale of church property, see the account in Le Roy Ladurie, *Peasants*, 176–80.

7. On the king's visit, see Ménard, *Histoire civile*, IV:15:58–67:398–404. The original four candidates were François de Gras, Jean Gregoire, Louis Guiraud, and Barthelemy Bastid, dit Odoable. As a result of the Protestant protests, the second and fourth consuls were replaced by Jacques Finor, bourgeois, and Pierre du Fesc, *laboureur*, who were equally Catholic. They all appear on several lists of contemporary Catholics, including that in Puech, "Débuts," 181–83.

8. Ménard, *Histoire civile*, IV:15:68:404–5, *Preuves*, 327–28.

9. Ibid., IV:15:7:406–8, *Preuves*, 11 (laying the foundation stones), 328–30.

10. The new consuls were Jean Saurin, Jean de Combes, Louis Grimaldi, and Bernard Corconne. All of the new consuls except de Combes had attended the meeting in 1561 that marked the formation of the Catholic party in Nîmes. Corconne was also the only elector who defied the Protestant consensus and voted for the Catholic nominees for consul in 1561. On the elections, see Ménard, *Histoire civile*, V:16:1:1–2. For the first meeting of the Catholics, see Puech, "Débuts," 181. For Corconne's voting, see AMN, LL9, fols. 274–81.

11. Millet, "A City Converted," 215–16, and n. 150. For des Georges's previous service as consul, see Ménard, *Histoire civile*, VI, *Successions Généalogiques*.

12. Devic and Vaissete, *Histoire générale de Languedoc*, 11:39:25:473.

13. AMN, LL10, fols. 130–36, cited in Millet, "A City Converted," 188–89. The other consuls included Jean Baudan, François Aubert, and Cristol Ligier. Baudan was also a particularly vehement Catholic, as is evident from his fiercely Catholic will, which disinherited any of his sons should they desert the church (ADG, IIE³⁶ 058, fol. 617, 25 May 1562).

14. See Knecht, *Rise and Fall of Renaissance France*, 397; Salmon, *Society in Crisis*, 68–70; Holt, *French Wars of Religion*, 63–64; and Mariéjol, *La Réforme et la Ligue*, 96.

15. On police powers, see Devic and Vaissete, *Histoire générale de Languedoc*, 9:39:28–29; and Ménard, *Histoire civile*, V:16:11–12:6–7. On dissension between the two captains, see Ménard, *Histoire civile*, V:16:12:7; and AMN, LL10, fol. 191:

> Par M. le premier consul a esté expouzé que en la present ville s'assemblent plusieurs gens qu'on ne peut scavoir à quelles fins ne pourquoi ils y sont et d'ailleurs que entre le capitaine La Garde qui est logé au château et le cappitaine Bollargues ont quelque differant et noise que pourroit causer a la ville une sedition et tumulte bien grand. Et a fin d'y proprement remedier seroit besoing en advertir Monsgr. de Joyeuse lieutenant pour le Roy en pays et gouvernement de Languedoc et depputer gens pour se transporter la part ou il sera. Led. de Gras a esté d'advis qu'il est expedient pour eviter l'inconvenient qui pourroit ensyvre d'envoyer promptement un homme espres par devers mon dit sieur de Joyeuse qui est à Lodun ou en Avignon affin qu'il luy plaise à pourvoir et mesmes de renier [i.e., remove] led.

capitaine La Garde de sa garnison, attendu qu'il y a longuement demeuré et à ces fins a nommé M. le grenetier Combes.

The council followed this suggestion. Also cited in Millet, "A City Converted," 219, 229–30 (also grain prices). For other examples of the role of urban militias in revolts, see Beik, *Urban Protest in Seventeenth-Century France*, 79–94.

16. Ménard, *Histoire civile*, V:16:17:9, *Preuves*, 27–28; Millet, "A City Converted," 195, 200.

17. De Pavée, although a Protestant and an important person in Nîmes's social hierarchy, was not prominent in the consistory (he appears in the records only once, attending a meeting with other notables). Millet, "A City Converted," 200, concludes that Robert LeBlanc, *juge-ordinaire* of the présidial, was the host of the meeting, while Ménard, *Histoire civile*, argues that the rising was discussed at LeBlanc's, but the massacre was planned at a more private meeting at de Pavée's. For de Pavée, see CR, fol. 106^v; and Puech, "Débuts," 211. De Pavée was asked to take on a financial post for the consistory but refused (CR, fol. 154).

18. On Bolhargues's appointment, see Puech, "Débuts," 137. For his wedding, not previously noticed by historians, see ADG, IIE^{36} 323, fol. 390 (contracted on 17 December 1559; the bride was Suffrenete du Valais). The other witnesses to the contract were Tanequin Besserier, Pons Finor, François de Gras, and Jacques Rochemaure. For his actions on behalf of the Protestant leaders of Nîmes, see Ménard, *Histoire civile*, IV:14:104, 15:14, 31, 349, 363, 375. For a summary of Bolhargues's career, see Haag and Haag, *La France protestante*, s.v. "Suau, Mathieu," which concludes, perhaps because the author was unaware that Suau was reappointed captain of the militia, that he converted by 1563.

19. For the list of Messieurs, see, e.g., Ménard, *Histoire civile*, V:16:18; and ADG, G442, fols. 47 and verso; but the most complete list is in Millet, "A City Converted," 260. Millet's list is rather misleading for occupations, however, since he calls all of the doctors of law "lawyers," even those who sat as judges on the présidial; compare it with the list of présidial members in Guggenheim, "Calvinism," 15. The only Protestant member who was not one of the Messieurs was Pierre Bompar, the *avocat du roi* (who is not on Guggenheim's list, since he joined at some point after 1560, according to Puech, *Une ville*, 80). Many of the Messieurs appear just once in the consistory records: at an important meeting called on 28 March 1562, CR, fol. 106^v, which was about military preparations for the beginning of the wars. It seems likely, therefore, that these men had political issues uppermost in their minds. Exceptions include Jean Bertrand (see CR, fols. 1, 106^v), Pierre Maltrait (ibid., fol. 1), and the Rozel family, which was heavily involved; one witness mentioned going to a meeting of the Messieurs which was held at Pierre Rozel's house (Ménard, *Histoire civile*, V, *Preuves*, 43).

20. For the consistory's condemnation, see Ménard, *Histoire civile*, V:16:18:22, citing now-lost consistory deliberations.

21. In this, they were following Calvin; see Foster, "Pierre Viret and France," 40–43. I was able to consult this dissertation at the H. Henry Meeter Center for Calvin Studies, Calvin College.

22. Catherine de Parades saw "a large troop of men at arms, some [with] pistols, arquebuses, halberds, and others" (Ménard, *Histoire civile*, V, *Preuves*, 42). There are a number of lists of the captains of the Protestant companies. See, e.g., Ménard, *Histoire civile*, V, *Preuves*, 30.

23. For the soldiers' cries, see Ménard, *Histoire civile*, V:16:18:11; and ADG, G442, fols. 68^v, 80^v, 91^v.

24. In Poitiers, local tradition held that when a traitor tried to steal the mayor's keys during the Hundred Years' War, the statue of the Virgin Mary in the town's cathedral took them into her hands for safekeeping. See Bernstein, *Between Crown and Community*, 164; for the Protestant takeover, see 153–57. In Dijon, Protestants, who were clustered around the rue des Forgers, raised barricades at each end of the street to protect themselves, according to Farr, *Hands of Honor*, 226.

25. Valon's deposition is in ADG, G442, fols. 42ff. For Jean Gregoire, notarial references refer to him as the bishop's secretary from at least 1555 to 1562. See, e.g., ADG, IIE^{36} 058, fol. 617, 25 May 1562. He was also on a list of Catholic guards chosen to guard the city on 24 December 1560, reprinted in Ménard, *Histoire civile*, IV, *Preuves*, 259. It is also likely that he was the second consul for 1559, although town council minutes give his name as Jean Gregoire, bourgeois (Ménard, *Histoire civile*, VI, *Successions Généalogiques*). Valladier's name comes from Ménard, *Histoire civile*, V, *Preuves*, 71. Jacques de Possaco was named an *advertisseur* at the first meeting of the Protestant Consistory (CR, fol. 2). Valon described Rochette as "portant toutjours son chaperon rouge de consul sur son espaulle." (See also Ménard, *Histoire civile*, V, *Preuves*, 42, 52, which confirm this detail.) Tanequin Finor's last name is not given in the deposition, but he is the only apothecary of that first name known to me. He was a Protestant as of 1562 (CR, fol. 94) and a member of a prominent family that included Jacques (second consul in 1540, 1547, 1558, and 1565) and Pons, a bourgeois. Pierre Finor, a *greffier* in the next generation, was second consul in 1596, and his daughter's godfather was Pierre Suau's son, and therefore had a distant connection to Capitaine Bolhargues (Puech, *Une ville*, 219–20).

26. For Bonaud, see Ménard, *Histoire civile*, V, *Preuves*, 30; for Bertrand, see *Preuves*, 57; CR, fol. 1. L'Hermite is recorded as arriving in Geneva on 16 October 1559 (see Geisendorf, *Livre des habitants*, 1:211); and in consistory records on 28 March 1562 (CR, fol. 107^v). De Brueys was a Protestant. Ménard, *Histoire civile*, V:16:18:13, mistakenly gives de Brueys's first name as André. His assistance is attested to by both Tardeau (*Preuves*, 25) and Journet (46). For his religious affiliation, see CR, fol. 106 (attended consistory meeting). Condemnation: Ménard, *Histoire civile*, V:16:43:44.

27. Ménard, *Histoire civile*, V, *Preuves*, 46–47. The other witness was Pierre Journet; his account lacks Valon's colorful detail. Ménard, *Histoire civile*, V:16:18:12–13, accepts Valon's account absolutely and even heightens it.

28. On Catholic martyrdom, see Gregory, *Salvation at Stake*, 250–314, esp. 274 (killing at prayer) and 279–80 (longing for death). Quatrebars's quote is from Ménard, *Histoire civile*, V, *Preuves*, 52–53. In French, "Cathrebars donnoit coeur auxdicts catholiques, et les exhortoit à patience, leur disant qu'il voyoit les cieux ouverts pour les recepvoir."

29. Ménard, *Histoire civile*, V, *Preuves*, 47.

30. Jehan Canonge's deposition is in ADG, G442, fols. 113^v–118^v. (In French, the quotation reads, "disant que Nre. Sr. le garderoit et qu'il ne pouvoit mourir que une foys.") De Gras's wife's name comes from Ménard, *Histoire civile*, V, *Preuves*, 71. The incident is also in Ménard, *Histoire civile*, V:16:18:14.

31. Ménard, *Histoire civile*, V:16:18, 21. The other consuls who were victims were Étienne André (ibid., V, *Preuves*, 60); Jean Voluntat (ADG, G442, fol. 124^v); Jean Saurin (Ménard, *Histoire civile*, V, *Preuves*, 28); and Bernard Corconne (ADG, G 442, fols. 69^v–71). Interestingly, there is no evidence that Robert des Georges was arrested in 1567, despite his leadership in the Catholic party.

32. The two were Tanequin Besserier and Jean-Poldo d'Albenas. For a list of Catholic members of the présidial as of 1560, see Guggenheim, "Calvinism," 223. Of the eleven she lists, two, Pierre Robert and Robert de Brueys, had died and been replaced by Protestants before 1567 (Puech, "Débuts," 84; and Puech, *Une ville*, 80), unless Ménard, *Histoire civile*, V:16:18:14 is correct and de Brueys had been replaced by George Gevaudan, who was arrested as a Catholic in the Michelade. Guggenheim, "Calvinism," notes, 192n, 193, citing Ménard, *Histoire civile*, V:16:18:10, that Barrière, Ruffi, Montcalm, and Jean d'Albenas fled town during the Michelade. The others were Richier (ADG, G442, fol. 72); Vallete (Ménard, *Histoire civile*, V:16:18:14); and Pierre Saurin (Ménard, *Histoire civile*, V:16:18, 20:10, 26).

33. For evidence of Cellerier's Protestantism, see CR, fol. 17^v. For Pradier's testimony, see Ménard, *Histoire civile*, V, *Preuves*, 55. In French, "tous lesdicts prisonniers furent menés les ungs après les aultres au supplice, mais qui le conduisit, dict ne le sçavoir . . . car n'osoit il qui dépose sortir de sa chambre, de peur d'estre massacré avec eulx." For the use of the basement, see Ménard, *Histoire civile*, V, *Preuves*, 49; for no questions asked, see ibid. For the Cellerier quote, see ADG, G442, fol. 120 and verso. In French, the quotation reads:

> Et ayant ilz [the prisoners, including the witness, Mathieu Raymond] demeuré quelque espasse de temps aud. chambre d'hault [in the *maison consulaire*], il survindrent pleusieurs de lad. nouvelle religion armés d'arquebouses ou pistolles, entre aultres Me. Pierre Celarier, orphevre, quy dit auds. prisonniers qu'ilz fissent grand chere et lhors aulcungs desd. prisonniers leur respondirent qu'il n'estoient en lieu pour se faire, suy quoy led. Cellarier leur dit qu'ilz en sortiroient bien tost.

34. On the list of those to be arrested, see ADG, G442, fol. 120^v; for Jehan Rovyer, see ADG, G442, fol. 89; for Vallat, fols. 52^v–53. In French:

> passant une foys auprès dicelluy ouys quelque grand bruit venant dud. puys comme aussi ceulx de lad. religion novelle disoient publicquement avoir ouy led. grant bruict que occasionna de se arrester ung peu auprès led. puys pour scavoir si cella estoit veritable, et treuva qu'il estoit ainsin, et entendist comme dit est led. bruit tel quy faisoit frayeur bien grande et elisser les poilhz.

For Pierre Rovyer, see fol. 79; for Bouze, see Ménard, *Histoire civile*, V, *Preuves*, 59. For the rest, see Ménard, *Histoire civile*, V:16:18:16–17.

35. For Rochette's and Gregoire's parents' reaction, see ADG, G442, fol. 45^v. For Corconne's story, see Ménard, *Histoire civile*, V, *Preuves*, 40. Ménard, *Histoire civile*, V, 16:18:22, also comments that women were not the principal objects of Protestant aggression. For Rozel's warning to the women, see ADG, G442, fol. 92. Compare Davis, "Rites of Violence," in her *Society and Culture in Early Modern France*, 175.

36. For Bertrand's comment, see ADG, G442, fol. 56^v; Nicot's: fol. 63^v; Rozel's: Ménard, *Histoire civile*, V, *Preuves*, 43, and a similar comment, 38; his concern about spying, 57; Caintemesse's: ADG, G442, fol. 99^v, cited in Millet, "A City Converted," 229.

37. For Blaise, see Ménard, *Histoire civile*, V, *Preuves*, 48; for Blachière, 50. In French, the quotation reads, "ung appellé Christol, qu'est cardeur, fils de Simon Vidalot, le bouchier." Unfortunately, Christol and Simon Vidalot are unknown to me, although there was a Jehan Vidalot who was a butcher. Bompar's testimony is in Ménard, *Histoire civile*, V, *Preuves*, 24–25. For Roverie, see ibid., 36; for Auberte, see ADG, G442, fol. 63^v; for Vincens, see *Preuves*, 41. Roverie escaped this time, only to be murdered in 1569 (Ménard, *Histoire civile*, V:16:51:55).

38. On this point, see also Davis, "Rites of Violence," 159–60, 179. For Rochette's ring, see Ménard, *Histoire civile*, V, *Preuves*, 32; Bompar's purse, 24. For another example, see 55.

39. For the destruction of the churches, see Ménard, *Histoire civile*, V:16:22:27–28, and of houses, see ADG, G442, fol. 88; in suburbs, fol. 104^v; on Sunday, fol. 48; on taxes and billeting, see Ménard, *Histoire civile*, V, *Preuves*, 35, 37–38; and ADG, G442, fols. 58, 60 (a litany of impositions that concludes, "bref, n'ont omis lesd. Messieurs user en endroict desd. catholicques d'aulcune espesse de cruaulté qu'ilz ayent peu exeger").

40. Millet, "A City Converted," 196, makes this point.

41. Ménard, *Histoire civile*, V:16:19–20:24–26.

42. Ibid., IV, *Preuves*, 8 (journal of Jacques Davin).

43. Although only 100 clergy appear in notarial records in the period 1550–1563, judging by population it seems likely that there were at least double that number. Many, no doubt, fled during the troubles, and a good number also converted. Judging from the minutes of the cathedral chapter, whose meetings were fairly well attended, many of Nîmes's priests appear to have returned before 1567. On the occupational breakdown of Protestant victims, see Davis, "Rites of Violence," 177 (here she disagrees with Janine Garrisson-Estèbe); and Benedict, *Rouen during the Wars of Religion*, 76, 128.

44. Millet, "A City Converted," 184–87, 191–92, 207–8, 221–23.

45. Ménard, *Histoire civile*, V, *Notes sur l'histoire de Nîmes*, 1–5, esp. 2.

46. Bolhargues quoted in Ménard, *Histoire civile*, V, *Preuves*, 25. The original reads, "l'on faisoit le samblable par tout le royaume de France, pour aultant que les papistes avoient faict plusieurs massacres contre ceulx de leur religion, volant dire des huguenots, a occasion desquels massacres l'on avoit emeu sedition par tout le

royaume de France." Arnaud quote from ADG, G442, fol. 56: "Il fallot qu'ilz feussent leurs heretiers ou que les catholicques feussent les leurs." Vallat quotations from fols. 52, 60, and verso: "il entretenoit ordinairement ceulx de Beaucaire, qu'ilz appeloient ennemis," and "lors que comme dessus a dit qu'il s'alloit plaindre aud. Messieurs à lad. maison consulaire qu'ilz respondoent à pleuseurs catholicques s'allans plaindre à eulx qu'il leur auvoient faict trop de grace de leur avoir sauvé la vie, et qu'ils estoient papistes et les voloent ryner entierement." Rovyer quote from fol. 90: they said "luy voulloient le couppe la gorge et getter dans le puys, pour ce qu'il estoit ung papiste. Sur quoy, il leur remonstra qu'il n'avoit faict tort ny deplesir à personne du monde."

47. For a different view, see Millet, "A City Converted," 191–92. Such conflict was hardly limited to Nîmes: for the case of Castres, see Christin, *La paix de religion*, 86, and more generally, for the conditions of coexistence in urban areas, chap. 3.

48. Pierre Rovyer reported a similar incident with different participants. He heard Pierre Maltrait say to Guy Rochette that Rochette "payeroit lors le soufflet qu'il luy avoit baillé" (ADG, G442, fol. 70).

49. It is clear that the d'Albenas family remained Catholic, since they appear repeatedly as godparents in AMN, UU1, *Livre des batisés de le glise [sic] catedrale de nostre dame de nismes depuis le moys d'aoust 1568*. It should be noted that one leading member of the d'Albenas family, Jean-Poldo d'Albenas, author of the first description of Nîmes's antiquities, appears to have flirted with Protestantism before returning to the Catholic fold. He probably died in 1566. On him, see Puech, "Débuts," 196.

50. The seven were Honoré Richier, Jacques Barrière, Jean and Bauzille de Roverie, Pierre Saurin, Pierre Vallete, and Bernard Poldo d'Albenas. For some examples of the kind of ties I am referring to, when Pierre Vallete married, Jehan, Jacques, and Galhard d'Albenas were all among the witnesses (ADG, IIE^1 233, fol. 196, 18 September 1551). When Catherine d'Albenas married, Paberan was among the witnesses; ADG, IIE^1 234, fol. 119, 19 July 1552.

51. It should be borne in mind that the notarial database covers 1550–1562 (Old Style). In that era, the elite was fairly unified, and preexisting factional lines do not appear to have had any effect on religious choices. Somewhat surprisingly, the ties between the d'Albenas family and the Calvières persisted right to the end of the period, even when one might think that religious divisions might have started to matter: when Pierre d'Albenas was married, Guillaume Calvière was one of the witnesses (ADG, IIE^1 251, fol 281^v, 21 February 1562/63).

52. ADG, G442, fol. 61.

53. Davis, "Rites of Violence," 173–74 (italics in original). Davis's greater attention to social history is hardly surprising, since (as she acknowledges) she was inspired to work on crowd violence by reading E. P. Thompson and George Rudé.

54. Cited in ibid., 173.

55. Crouzet, *Les guerriers de dieu*, 1:600–601.

56. Millet, "A City Converted," 244, comes to very similar conclusions.

57. Robbins, *City on the Ocean Sea*, 201–4; and Roberts, *City in Conflict*, 145–49. In Troyes, the bodies were then dumped in a ditch.

58. Crouzet, *Les guerriers de Dieu*, 1:607–16 (quotation on 616).

59. Greengrass, "Anatomy of a Religious Riot," 389, is also hesitant to explain violence in ritual terms without considering other factors.

60. Davis, "Rites of Violence," 161 (quotation), 178–79 (purification rites).

61. Holt, *French Wars of Religion*, 65.

62. Ménard, *Histoire civile*, V:16:27:43–44, 51:31–33, 42–45, 50–56, *Preuves*, 70–74. The three others executed were Jacques Andron, a *conseiller* of the présidial court; Lazare Fazendier, a retired legal official (*greffier*); and Claude Garnier, a notary. Ménard, *Histoire civile* (following a journal in IV, *Preuves*, 15), estimates the dead in 1569 at 100–120; Jacques-Auguste de Thou, *Histoire universelle* (London, 1734), 5:652, following La Popelinière, suggests 150.

63. Gerald Strauss, "Success and Failure in the German Reformation," inaugurated a debate on this question, claiming that the only way to evaluate "success" was to use the goals proclaimed by the Reformers in their writings, which were typically millennial. I am on the whole skeptical of this approach, since by this standard most reform movements must be judged to be failures. It is true, however, that Strauss's argument does highlight the slow pace of change, for example, the slow increase of literacy rates in Protestant lands.

CONCLUSION

1. Lawrence Stone's model of preconditions, precipitants, and triggers is useful here. See his *Causes of the English Revolution*.

2. Note that by "systemic," I do not mean "structural." I mean here to rebut suggestions that my arguments in this book deprive sixteenth-century people of "agency," as the usual jargon puts it. On the relationship of structural arguments to agency, see Sewell, "A Theory of Structure," reprinted as chap. 4 in his *Logics of History*.

3. For example, Holt, *French Wars of Religion*; and Crouzet, *Les guerriers de Dieu*.

4. Crouzet, *Les guerriers de Dieu*, 1:74, but see his comments in "Veillée d'armes," which was published in a special ("thematic") issue of a French popular history magazine devoted to "Les Protestants: Leur histoire, leurs valeurs, leur influence." See also Watson, "Preaching, Printing, Psalm-Singing," 10–28, esp. 11.

5. Heller's Marxist rhetoric has unfortunately tended to obscure his real contributions. On the changing demographics of the French Protestant movement, see his *Conquest of Poverty*, 235–36; Richet, "Aspects socio-culturels des conflits religieux," reprinted in his *De la Réforme à la Révolution*; Imbart de la Tour, *Les origines de la Réforme*, 4:467–85; Davies, "Persecution and Protestantism," 37–38; Nicholls, "Social Change and Early Protestantism," 289–92. The picture given in Gascon, *Grand commerce et vie urbaine*, 2:472–77, is also broadly compatible with this progression. One counterexample might be Béziers, where the powerful Protestant movement remained dominated by artisans at a relatively late date (see Le Roy Ladurie, *Paysans*, 1:343).

6. See Hauser, "The French Reformation and the French People"; Le Roy Ladurie, *Peasants*, esp. 149–202; Febvre, "The Origins of the French Reformation: A

Badly-Put Question?" in his *A New Kind of History*, 66; Romier, *Le royaume de Catherine de Médicis*, esp. 2:267.

7. Baumgartner, *Change and Continuity in the French Episcopate*, 131–40. Baumgartner lists twelve converts but eventually concludes that the case against François de Noailles, bishop of Dax, is weak.

8. Benedict, *Rouen during the Wars of Religion*, 72, 88–94 (quotation on 91). For similar descriptions, see Cassan, *Le temps des guerres de religion*, 228–29; Greengrass, *French Reformation*, 54–61; Babelon, *Paris au XVIe siècle*, 406; Guiraud, *La Réforme à Montpellier*, 6:148–52; and Tingle, *Authority and Society in Nantes*, 58–63. Compare, however, Meyer, *Reformation in La Rochelle*, 112–13; Benedict, *Christ's Churches Purely Reformed*, 137; and Boutruche, *Bordeaux de 1453 à 1715*, 243. Meyer's figures present the most serious challenge to the theory proposed here and may indeed represent an interesting exception to the general trend, but they also come from a later period.

9. Davis, "Strikes and Salvation at Lyon," in her *Society and Culture in Early Modern France*, 1–16, esp. 5, 7; and Davis, "Protestantism and the Printing Workers of Lyon," 419–21, and the table on 560–68; Greengrass, *French Reformation*, 60–61; Rosenberg, "Social Experience and Religious Choice."

10. Davis, "Protestantism and the Printing Workers of Lyons," 354–56.

11. This is equally true for the paradigmatic case of Puritan New England; see Pope, "New England versus the New England Mind," esp. 103, 108; Troeltsch, *Social Teaching of the Christian Churches*.

12. For a study of Protestantism's spread to a rural hinterland, see Rambeaud, *De La Rochelle vers l'Aunis*.

13. See Furet and Ozouf, *Reading and Writing*, esp. the maps on 48–49. See also Garrisson-Estèbe, *Protestants du Midi*, 37–39.

14. Jouanna, *La France de la Renaissance*, 134–36. Among major southern French towns, only in Marseille did merchants dominate civic affairs.

15. Moeller, *Imperial Cities and the Reformation*, esp. 99–103.

16. Gal, *Grenoble au temps de la Ligue*, 183–96; Benedict, *Rouen during the Wars of Religion*, 96–103; Jouanna, *Guerres de religion*, 44, 50.

17. Rosenberg, "Social Experience and Religious Choice," esp. 164–172. As in the Nîmes cahier, venal offices were also a major issue in Amiens. Conner, *Huguenot Heartland*, 53, also argues that in Montauban, a unified elite helped the Reformation succeed. Gamm, *Urban Exodus*, argues that white flight proceeded more slowly in the Catholic parts of Dorchester and Roxbury, Massachusetts, than in the Jewish sections because each Catholic parish was its own separate neighborhood. Jews left when their neighborhood was affected, while Catholics only left when their particular parish was. The analogy is that the cellular structure of the guild system made it easier to contain heresy, just as the cellular structure of Catholic parishes enabled them to resist white flight. I owe this notion to a suggestion from Professor John Padgett.

18. Sunshine, *Reforming French Protestantism*, 57–62.

19. Schneider, *Public Life in Toulouse*, 96; Greengrass, "Anatomy of a Religious Riot"; Davies, "Persecution and Protestantism."

20. Protestant statistics from Peter France cited in Gal, *Grenoble au temps de la Ligue*, 186–90; information on consuls from ibid., 79. On the lawyers' exemption, see Prudhomme, *Histoire de Grenoble*, 329–31.

21. Prudhomme, *Histoire de Grenoble*, 349–52.

22. Ibid., 360–66.

23. Guiraud, *La Réforme à Montpellier*, 6:386–87, 430–31. Benedict, *The Huguenot Population of France*, 55, suggests that, in the early seventeenth century, Montpellier was about 60 percent Protestant.

24. Major, *From Renaissance Monarchy to Absolute Monarchy*, xx–xxi; and Salmon, *Society in Crisis*, 326.

25. See Rouvière, *Histoire de la revolution française*; and Zaretsky, *Nîmes at War*.

26. Hallie, *Lest Innocent Blood Be Shed*.

27. Gregory, *Salvation at Stake*; and Novick, *That Noble Dream*.

28. Clark, *English Society*.

29. Garrisson-Estèbe, *Protestants du Midi*, 165–66.

30. Chapter 15 of Edward Gibbon's *Decline and Fall of the Roman Empire* attempts to refute the argument that Christianity grew rapidly because of its obvious truth. For Borrel, see Abraham Borrel, *Histoire de l'église réformée de Nîmes*.

31. Ozment, *Reformation in the Cities*; Ozment, *Age of Reform*; and Cameron, *European Reformation*, 311–13. Crouzet's argument is somewhat similar to Ozment's; Crouzet's term is "désangoissement."

APPENDIX B

1. Thus, Colette Sardinoux, in her M.A. thesis, "Les premières traces de la Réforme à Anduze," was surprised to note that Protestant wills tended to clump in certain registers, not realizing that she was looking at drafts (*brouillards*). Usually, *brouillards* will be noted in the printed inventory (Gouron, *Répertoire numérique des Archives Départementales du Gard*), but not always. I would like to thank Professor Gabriel Audisio for warning me of this probem. For Lansard and Alirand, see Gouron, *Répertoire numérique des Archives Départementales du Gard*, 330, 334.

2. On the issues involved in coding last names, see Harvey and Press, *Databases in Historical Research*, 228–31.

3. ADG, IIE^1 248, fol. 293; IIE^{36} 322, fol. 336.

4. ADG, IIE^1 233, fol. 196, 18 September 1551.

5. Puech, "Débuts" and *Une ville*.

6. Guggenheim, "Calvinism," 2. She states that the elite was composed of "less than thirty-five active policy-makers at any one time and about thirty more persons serving in advisory capacities." In her table of the religious sympathies of officeholders in 1560 (221), she includes thirty-one persons; in an appendix (343–44), she adds thirty-nine more.

7. Family ties had to be codified into a matrix for export to UCINET using a pivot table, which creates a square matrix. For this purpose, I used Microsoft Excel, which permits an infinite number of rows, but only 256 columns, with the practical effect of limiting the matrix to 256 x 256 families.

Bibliography

MANUSCRIPT SOURCES

Archives Départementales du Gard (ADG), Nîmes
Series C, vols. 627–29. Procès-verbaux of the assembly of the diocese
Series IIE^I, vols. 232–34. Registers of Jean Ursi, le vieux, 1550–1553
Series IIE^I, vols. 243–51. Registers of Jacques Ursi, 1550–1563
Series IIE^{36}, vol. 058. Register of Jean Lansard, 1543–1561
Series IIE^{36}, vols. 254–55. Registers of Jean Perret, 1550–1552
Series IIE^{36}, vols. 266–79. Registers of Louis Grimaldi, 1550–1563
Series IIE^{36}, vols. 293–300. Registers of Jean Mombel, 1552–1563
Series IIE^{36}, vols. 306, 308. Registers of Rançon Alirand, 1556–1563
Series IIE^{36}, vols. 311–12. Registers of Antoine Malian, 1560–1563
Series IIE^{36}, vols. 319–27. Registers of Jean Ménard (I), 1555–1563
Series IIE^{37}, vol. 027. Register of Pierre Poreau, 1556–1563
Series IIE^{37}, vols. 055–061. Registers of Antoine Sabatier, 1557–1563
Series IIE^{37}, vols. 083–086. Registers of Guillaume Duchamp, 1558–1563
Series G, vols. 441–443. Chapître de l'église cathédrale de Nîmes, troubles des religionnaires, 1560–1583
Archives Départementales de l'Haute-Garonne (ADHG), Toulouse
   Series B, vols. 3359, 3377, 3383, 3387, 3388, 3394, 3395, 3397, 3400, 3402, 3404–7, 3411, 3415, 3416
Archives de l'Église Réformée de Nîmes, Nîmes. These records have recently been given to the ADG.
   B-90, vol. 1. Transcription of the Nimes consistory register (CR), by Louis Auzière
Archives Municipales de Nîmes (AMN). These records are held as part of the ADG but retain their own classification system.
   Series LL, vols. 5–10. Deliberations du conseil

Series QQ, vols. 9–17. Présage of the compoix de Nîmes, 1544
UU1, *Livre des batisés de le glise* [sic] *catedrale de nostre dame de nismes depuis le moys d'aoust 1568*
Series 42J 26, Transcription of the Nîmes consistory register (CR) by Louis Auzière
Bibliothèque Nationale (BN), Paris
Registres du consistoire de l'église de Nîmes, vol. 1 (1561–1563) (CR; manuscrits français, nos. 8666, 8668, 8669)
Manuscrits français, nos. 15641, 15873, 15881, 20153
Bibliothèque Publique et Universitaire (BPU), Geneva
Manuscrits français, nos. 402–3. Consulted on microfilm at the H. Henry Meeter Center for Calvin Studies, Calvin College, Grand Rapids, Michigan

PRINTED PRIMARY SOURCES

Note: Several secondary sources also include important documentary material. See especially Ménard; Puech, *La Renaissance et la Réforme à Nîmes*; and Devic and Vaissete.

Arnaud, Eugène. *Documents protestants inédits du XVIe siècle: Synode générale de Poitiers, 1557, synodes provinciaux de Lyon, Die, Montélimar, et Nîmes en 1561 et 1562, assemblée des états de Dauphiné de 1563, etc.* Paris: Grassart, 1872.

Aymon, Jean. *Tous les synodes nationaux des églises réformées de France.* 2 vols. The Hague, 1710.

Bèze, Theodore de. *Histoire ecclésiastique des églises reformées de France.* 2 vols. Ed. P. Vesson. Toulouse: Société des livres religieux, 1882. 3 vols. Ed. G. Baum and E. Cunitz. Geneva, 1883–1889.

Bodin, Jean. *Method for the Easy Comprehension of History.* Trans. Beatrice Reynolds. New York: Norton, 1945.

Bonnet, Jules. "Visite de Thomas Platter à Nîmes et au Pont du Gard." *Mémoires de l'Académie de Nîmes*, 7th ser., 2 (1879): 179–192.

Calvin, John. *Joannis Calvini Opera quae supersunt omnia.* Ed. G. Baum, E. Cunitz, and E. Reuss. 59 vols. Brunswick, Germany: C. A. Schwetschke, 1863–1900.

———. *Institutes of the Christian Religion.* 2 vols. Ed. John T. McNeill, trans. Ford Lewis Battles. Philadelphia: Westminster, 1960.

Crespin, Jean. *Le livre des Martyrs . . . depuis Jean Hus jusques à cette année presente . . .* Geneva, 1554–1619; Subsequent eds. bear variant title, *Histoire des martyres . . .* Rpt., 3 vols. Toulouse: Société de livres religeux, 1885.

d'Albenas, Jean-Poldo. *Discours historial de l'antique et illustre cité de Nîmes.* Avignon, 1559; Lyon, 1560. Rpt., Marseille: Laffitte Reprints, 1976.

Gamon, Achille de. "Mémoires." In vol. 34 of M. Petitot, *Collection Complète des Mémoires relatifs à l'Histoire de France depuis le règne de Philippe-Auguste jusqu'au commencement du dix-septième siècle.* 131 vols. Paris: Foucault, 1823.

Geisendorf, Paul-F., ed. *Livre des habitants de Genève.* 2 vols. Geneva: Droz, 1957–1963.

Goltzius, Hubert. *C. Julius Caesar sive historiae imperatorum caesarumque romanorum ex antiquis numismatibus restitutae.* Bruges, 1563.

Goss, John, ed. *The City Maps of Europe*. Chicago: Rand McNally, 1991.
Herminjard, Aimé-Louis, ed. *Correspondance des réformateurs dans les pays de langue française*. 9 vols. Geneva: Georg, 1866–1897.
Isambert, Francois André, et al. *Recueil général des anciennes lois françaises*. 29 vols. Paris: Plon, 1821–1833.
Lafaille, Claude. *Annales de la ville de Toulouse*. 2 vols. Toulouse, 1687–1701.
Lalourcé, Charlemagne, and Duval, eds. *Recueil des cahiers généraux des trois ordres aux états-generaux*. 3 vols. Paris, 1789.
L'Hospital, Michel de. *Discours pour la majorité de Charles IX, et trois autres discours [de] Michel de L'Hospital*. Preface by Robert Descimon. Paris: Imprimerie Nationale, 1993.
Paris, Louis, ed. *Négociations, lettres et pièces diverses relatives au règne de François II, tirées du portefeuille de Sébastien de L'Aubespine, évêque de Limoges*. Paris: Imprimerie Royale, 1841.
Platter, Felix. *Beloved Son Felix: The Journal of Felix Platter, a Medical Student in Montpellier in the Sixteenth Century*. Trans. Sean Jennett. London: Frederick Muller, 1961.
Quick, John. *Synodicon in Gallia Reformata; or, The Acts, Decision, Decrees, and Canons of Those Famous National Councils of the Reformed Churches in France*. 2 vols. London, 1692.
Stil ou Formulaire des Lettres qui se Depeschent ez Cours de Nismes: Amplifié & augmenté en cette derniere impression de plusieurs Requestes & Annotations nouvelles, & des Arrests du Conseil d'Estat, cour de Parlement de Tolose, Jugements & Reglements de ladite Cour, & Siege Presidial. Edition onziéme [sic]. Nismes: Jean Plases, Imprimeur & Libraire ordinaire de ladite ville, 1651.
Thierry, Augustin. *Recueil des mouments inédits de l'histoire du tiers état*. Paris, Imprimerie Impériale,1853–1870.
Viret, Pierre. *Instruction chrétienne en la doctrine de la loy et de l'Evangile*. Geneva: J. Rivery, 1564.
———. *L'interim fait par dialogues*. Ed. Guy R. Mermier. New York: Peter Lang, 1985.

MANUALS AND REFERENCE WORKS

Audisio, Gabriel, and Isabelle Bonnot-Rambaud. *Lire le français d'hier: Manuel de paléographie moderne XVe–XVIIIe siècle*. Paris: Armand Colin, 1991.
Barraclough, Geoffrey, ed. *The Times Historical Atlas*. Maplewood, N.J.: Hammond, 1993.
Borgatti, Steven P., M. G. Everett, and L. C. Freeman. *UCINET IV: Version 1.64*. Natick, Mass.: Analytic Technologies, 1996.
Cannon, John, ed. *The Blackwell Dictionary of Historians*. Oxford: Basil Blackwell, 1988.
Cappelli, A. *Cronologia Cronografia e Calendario Perpetuo*, 3rd ed. Milan: Ulrico Hoepli, 1969.
Dauzat, Albert. *Dictionnaire étymologique des noms de famille et prénoms de France*. Paris: Larousse, 1989.
Dictionnaire de biographie française. Paris: Letouzey et Ané, 1933–. 20 vols. to date.
Dictionnaire national des communes de France. Paris: Albin Michel and Berger-Levrault, 1991.

Du Guerny, Y. *Notariat de Nîmes : Inventaire des actes filiatifs, 1450–1700*. 3 vols. Privately printed, 1995–1996. A copy is available at the ADG.

Germer-Durand, Eugène. *Dictionnaire topographique du département du Gard*. Paris, 1868. Rpt., Nîmes: Lacour, 1988.

Goiffon, Etienne. *Dictionnaire topographique, statistique et historique du diocèse de Nîmes*. Nîmes, 1881. Rpt., Nîmes: Lacour, 1986.

Gouron, Marcel, ed. France. Ministère de l'intérieur. *Répertoire numérique des Archives Départementales du Gard. Série II.E. Minutes notariales*. Nîmes: Imprimerie Chastanier Freres, 1951.

Greimas, Algirdas Julien, and Teresa Mary Keane. *Dictionnaire du moyen français: La Renaissance*. Paris: Larousse, 1992.

Haag, Eugène, and Emile Haag, eds. *La France protestante; ou, Vies des protestants français*. 10 vols. Paris, 1846–1854. Partial 2nd ed., Paris 1877–1888.

Huguet, Edmond. *Dictionnaire de la langue française au seizième siècle*. 8 vols. Paris: E. Champion, 1925–1973.

Lamothe, Bessot de, ed. *Inventaire sommaire des archives communales antérieurese à 1790, Nîmes*. 2 vols. Mende, 1877, and Avignon, 1879.

Morlet, Marie-Thérèse. *Dictionnaire étymologique des noms de famille*. Paris: Perrin, 1991.

SECONDARY SOURCES

Anderson, Benedict. *Imagined Communities: Reflections on the Origin and Spread of Nationalism*. 1983. Rev. ed., London: Verso, 1991.

Angelras, Armand. "Le consulat nimois: Histoire de son organization." Ph.D. diss., University of Montpellier, Nîmes, 1912.

Aubenas, Roger. "Le contrat 'd'affrairamentum' dans le droit provençal du Moyen Âge." *Revue Historique de Droit Français et Étranger*, 4th ser., 12 (1933): 478–524.

———. "Réflexions sur les 'fraternités artificielles' au Moyen-Âge." In *Études historiques à la mémoire de Noël Didier publiées par la Faculté de Droit et des Sciences Économiques de Grenoble* (Paris: Éditions Montchrestien, 1960), 1–10.

Audisio, Gabriel. "The First Provençal Refugees in Geneva." *French History* 19(3) (2005): 385–400.

———. *Les français d'hier*. 2 vols. Paris: Armand Colin, 1993–1996.

———. "Les origines de la Réforme en France: Du nouveau?" *Revue de l'Histoire des Religions* 206(4) (1989): 399–407.

———. Review of *Les guerriers de Dieu*, by Denis Crouzet. *Revue de l'Histoire des Religions* 211(1) (January–March 1994): 108–16.

Babelon, Jean-Pierre. *Nouvelle histoire de Paris: Paris au seizième siècle*. Paris: Hachette, 1986.

Bardon, A. *Ce que couta l'entrée de François I à Nîmes (1533)*. Nîmes: Gervais-Bedot, 1894. Also published as "L'entrée de François I à Nîmes," *Revue du Midi* 7(2) (October–November 1893): 341–60, 440–58.

Barthel, Pierre, Rémy Scheurer, and Richard Stauffer, eds. *Actes du Colloque Guillaume Farel*. Geneva: Revue de Théologie et de Philosophie, 1983.

Baumgartner, Frederic J. *Change and Continuity in the French Episcopate: The Bishops and the Wars of Religion, 1547–1610*. Durham, N.C.: Duke University Press, 1986.

———. *France in the Sixteenth Century*. New York: St. Martin's, 1995.

Beik, William. *Absolutism and Society in Seventeenth-Century France: State Power and Provincial Aristocracy in Languedoc*. Cambridge: Cambridge University Press, 1985.

———. *Urban Protest in Seventeenth-Century France: The Culture of Retribution*. Cambridge: Cambridge University Press, 1997.

Benedict, Philip. *Christ's Churches Purely Reformed: A Social History of Calvinism*. New Haven, Conn.: Yale University Press, 2002.

———, ed. *Cities and Social Change in Early Modern France*. London: Unwin Hyman, 1989; rpt., London: Routledge, 1992.

———. *The Huguenot Population of France, 1600–1685: The Demographic Fate and Customs of a Religious Minority*. In *Transactions of the American Philosophical Society* 81(5) (1991).

———. *Rouen during the Wars of Religion*. Cambridge: Cambridge University Press, 1981.

Bernstein, Hilary. *Between Crown and Community: Politics and Civic Culture in Sixteenth-Century Poitiers*. Ithaca, N.Y.: Cornell University Press, 2004.

Bettmann, Otto L. *A Word from the Wise*. New York: Harmony, 1977.

Bloch, Marc. *The Royal Touch: Monarchy and Miracles in France and England*. Trans. J. E. Anderson. 1924. Rpt., London: Routledge and Kegan Paul, 1973.

Bonnell, Victoria E., and Lynn Hunt, eds. *Beyond the Cultural Turn*. Berkeley: University of California Press, 1999.

Bonney, Richard. *The European Dynastic States, 1494–1660*. Oxford: Oxford University Press, 1991.

———. "France, 1494–1815." In *The Rise of the Fiscal State in Europe, c. 1200–1815*, ed. Richard Bonney, 123–76. Oxford: Oxford University Press, 1999.

Borrel, Abraham. *Histoire de l'église réformée de Nîmes*, 2nd ed. Toulouse, 1856.

Bossy, John. *Christianity in the West, 1400–1700*. Oxford: Oxford University Press, 1987.

———. "The Mass as a Social Institution, 1200–1700." *Past and Present* 100 (1983): 29–61.

Boswell, John. *Same Sex Unions in Pre-Modern Europe*. New York: Villiard, 1994.

Boutruche, Robert, ed. *Bordeaux de 1453 à 1715*, vol. 4 of *Histoire de Bordeaux*, ed. Charles Higounet. 8 vols. Bordeaux: Fédération Historique du Sud-Ouest, 1966.

Bouwsma, William J. *John Calvin: A Sixteenth Century Portrait*. New York: Oxford University Press, 1988.

Brady, Thomas A., Jr. *Ruling Class, Regime and Reformation at Strasbourg, 1520–1555*. Leiden: Brill, 1978.

Brady, Thomas A., Jr., Heiko A. Oberman, and James D. Tracy. *Handbook of European History, 1500–1600: Late Middle Ages, Renaissance and Reformation*. 2 vols. Leiden: Brill, 1995.

Braudel, Fernand. *The Mediterranean and the Mediterranean World in the Age of Philip II*, 2nd ed., trans. Siân Reynolds. 2 vols. New York: Harper and Row, 1972–1973. [Original French ed., 1949]

Braudel, Fernand, and Ernest Labrousse, eds. *Histoire économique et social de la France.* 4 vols. Paris: Presses Universitaires de France, 1971–1982.
Brigden, Susan. *London and the Reformation.* Oxford: Oxford University Press, 1989.
Brown, Elizabeth A. R. "Ritual Brotherhood: Introduction." *Traditio* 52 (1997): 261–83.
Buckser, Andrew, and Stephen D. Glazier, eds. *The Anthropology of Religious Conversion.* Lanham, Md.: Rowman and Littlefield, 2003.
Bulliet, Richard W. *Conversion to Islam in the Medieval Period: An Essay in Quantitative History.* Cambridge, Mass.: Harvard University Press, 1979.
Burgière, André. "The Fate of the History of *Mentalités* in the *Annales.*" *Comparative Studies in History and Society* 24 (1982): 424–37.
Cameron, Euan. *The European Reformation.* Oxford: Clarendon, 1991.
Carpi, Olivia. *Une république imaginaire: Amiens pandant les troubles de religion (1559–1597).* Paris: Belin, 2005.
Cassan, Michel. *Le temps des guerres de religion: Le cas du Limousin (vers 1530–vers 1630).* Paris: Publisud, 1996.
Casteel, Theodore W. "The College and University of Arts in Nîmes: An Experiment in Humanistic Education in the Age of the Reform." Ph.D. diss., Stanford University, 1973.
Cayla, Paul. *Dictionnaire des institutions, des coutumes, et de la langue en usage dans quelques pays de Languedoc, de 1535 à 1648.* Montpellier: Imprimerie Paul Déhan, 1964.
Chareyre, Philippe. "Le consistoire de Nîmes 1561–1685." 4 vols. Thèse d'état, Paul Valéry University, Montpellier III, 1987.
Chaunu, Pierre. *La mort à Paris aux XVIe, XVIIe, et XVIIIe siècles.* Paris: Fayard, 1978.
———. "Niveaux de culture et Réforme." *Bulletin de la Société de l'Histoire du Protestantisme Français* 228 (1972): 305–26.
Chevalier, Bernard. *Les bonnes villes de France, du XIVe au XVIe siècle.* Paris: Aubier Montaigne, 1982.
Chrisman, Miriam Usher. *Lay Culture, Learned Culture: Books and Social Change in Strasbourg, 1480–1599.* New Haven, Conn.: Yale University Press, 1982.
Christin, Olivier. *La paix de religion: L'autonomisation de la raison politique au XVIe siècle.* Paris: Seuil, 1997.
———. *Une révolution symbolique: L'iconoclasme huguenot et la reconstruction catholique.* Paris: Minuit, 1991.
Clark, J. C. D. *English Society, 1688–1832: Ideology, Social Structure, and Political Practice during the Ancien Regime.* Cambridge: Cambridge University Press, 1985.
Conner, Philip. *Huguenot Heartland: Montauban and Southern French Calvinism during the Wars of Religion.* Aldershot: Ashgate, 2002.
Croix, Alain. *Nantes et le pays nantais au XVIe siècle: Étude démographique.* Paris: SEVPEN, 1974.
Crouzet, Denis. *La genèse de la Réforme française.* Paris: SEDES, 1996.
———. *Les guerriers de Dieu: La violence au temps des troubles de religion, vers 1525–vers 1610.* 2 vols. Paris: Champ Vallon, 1990.
———. "Veillée d'armes." *Historia Thématique* (special issue on "Les Protestants: Leur histoire, leurs valeurs, leur influence") 109 (September–October 2007): 30–33.
Cunnally, John. *Images of the Illustrious.* Princeton, N.J.: Princeton University Press, 1999.

Davies, Joan. "Persecution and Protestantism: Toulouse, 1562–1575." *Historical Journal*, 22(1) (1979): 31–51.
Davis, Barbara Beckerman. "Reconstructing the Poor in Early Sixteenth-Century Toulouse." *French History* 7(3) (1993): 249–85.
Davis, Natalie Z. "Protestantism and the Printing Workers of Lyons: A Study in the Problem of Religion and Social Class during the Reformation." Ph.D. diss., University of Michigan, 1959.
———. *The Return of Martin Guerre*. Cambridge, Mass.: Harvard University Press, 1983.
———. *Society and Culture in Early Modern France*. Stanford, Calif.: Stanford University Press, 1975.
Delafosse, Marcel, ed. *Histoire de La Rochelle*. Toulouse: Privat, 1985.
Denis, Philippe. "Viret et Morély: Les raisons d'un silence." *Bibliothèque d'Humanisme et Renaissance* 54(2) (1992): 395–409.
de Bèze, Théodore. *Histoire écclésiastique des églises réformées au royaume de France*. 3 vols. Lille : Leleux, 1841–1842.
de Ruble, Alphonse. *Anthoine de Bourbon et Jeanne d'Albret*. 4 vols. Paris: Librairie de la Bibliothèque Nationale, 1885.
de Thou, Jacques-Auguste. *Histoire universelle depuis 1543 jusqu'en 1607*. 16 vols. London, 1734.
Devic, Claude, and Joseph Vaissete. *Histoire générale de Languedoc*. 15 vols. Toulouse: Privat, 1872–1892.
de Vries, Jan. *European Urbanization, 1500–1800*. Cambridge, Mass.: Harvard University Press, 1984.
Diefendorf, Barbara B. *Beneath the Cross: Catholics and Huguenots in Sixteenth-Century Paris*. New York: Oxford University Press, 1991.
———. "Give Us Back Our Children: Patriarchal Authority and Parental Consent to Religious Vocations in Early Counter-Reformation France." *Journal of Modern History* 68 (1996): 265–307.
———. Review of *Les guerriers de Dieu*, by Denis Crouzet. *American Historical Review* 99(1) (February 1994): 241–42.
Doucet, Roger. *Les institutions de la France au XVIe siècle*. 2 vols. Paris: Picard, 1948.
Duby, Georges, ed. *Histoire de la France urbaine*. 5 vols. Paris: Seuil, 1980–1985.
Dupâquier, Jacques, ed. *Histoire de la population française*. 4 vols. Paris: Presses Universitaires de France, 1988.
Dykema, Peter, and Heiko A. Oberman, eds. *Anticlericalism in Late Medieval and Early Modern Europe*. Leiden: Brill, 1993.
Eire, Carlos M. N. *War against the Idols: The Reformation of Worship from Erasmus to Calvin*. Cambridge: Cambridge University Press, 1986.
Elwood, Christopher. *The Body Broken: The Calvinist Doctrine of the Eucharist and the Symbolization of Power in Sixteenth-Century France*. New York: Oxford University Press, 1999.
Erikson, Eric. *Young Man Luther*. New York: Norton, 1958.

Farel, Guillaume. *Guillaume Farel, 1489–1565: Biographie nouvelle écrite d'après les documents originaux par un groupe d'historiens, professeurs, et pasteurs de Suisse, de France et d'Italie.* Neuchâtel: Delachaux and Niestlé, 1930.

Farge, James K. *Orthodoxy and Reform in Early Reformation France: The Faculty of Theology of Paris, 1500–1543.* Leiden: Brill, 1985.

Farr, James. *Hands of Honor: Artisans and Their World in Dijon, 1550–1650.* Ithaca, N.Y.: Cornell University Press, 1988.

Febvre, Lucien. *Amour sacré, amour profane: Autour de l'Heptameron.* Paris: Gallimard, 1944.

———. *Life in Renaissance France.* Trans. Marian Rothstein. Cambridge, Mass.: Harvard University Press, 1977.

———. *A New Kind of History.* Ed. Peter Burke, trans. K. Folca. London: Routledge and Kegan Paul, 1973.

———. *The Problem of Unbelief in the Sixteenth Century: The Religion of Rabelais.* Trans. Beatrice Gottlieb. 1942. Rpt., Cambridge, Mass.: Harvard University Press, 1982.

Febvre, Lucien, and Henri-Jean Martin. *The Coming of the Book: The Impact of Printing, 1450–1800.* London: Verso, 1990. [Original French ed., 1958]

Festinger, Leon, Henry W. Riecken, and Stanley Schachter. *When Prophecy Fails.* Minneapolis: University of Minnesota Press, 1956

Fogel, Robert W. "New Sources and New Techniques for the Study of Secular Trends in Nutritional Status, Health, Mortality, and the Process of Aging." *Historical Methods* 26(1) (Winter 1993): 5–44.

Fogel, Robert W., et al. "Secular Changes in American and British Stature and Nutrition." *Journal of Interdisciplinary History* 14(2) (Autumn 1983): 445–82.

Foster, Stuart. "Pierre Viret and France, 1559–1565." Ph.D. diss., St. Andrews University, 2000.

Forster, Robert. *The House of Saulx-Tavanes: Versailles and Burgundy, 1700–1830.* Baltimore, Md.: Johns Hopkins University Press, 1971.

Friesen, Abraham. *Reformation and Utopia: The Marxist Interpretation of the Reformation and Its Antecedents.* Wiesbaden: Steiner, 1974.

Furet, François, and Jacques Ozouf. *Reading and Writing: Literacy in France from Calvin to Jules Ferry.* 1977. Rpt., Cambridge: Cambridge University Press, 1982.

Gal, Stéphane. *Grenoble au temps de la Ligue.* Grenoble: Presses Universitaires de Grenoble, 2000.

Galpern, A. N. *The Religions of the People in Sixteenth-Century Champagne.* Cambridge, Mass.: Harvard University Press, 1976.

Gamm, Gerald. *Urban Exodus: Why the Jews Left Boston and the Catholics Stayed.* Cambridge, Mass.: Harvard University Press, 1999.

Garrisson-Estèbe, Janine. *Les Protestants du Midi.* Toulouse: Privat, 1980.

Gascon, Richard. *Grand commerce et vie urbaine au XVIe siècle: Lyon et ses marchands.* 2 vols. Paris: SEVPEN, 1971.

Gaufrès, Mathieu-Jules. *Claude Baduel et la réforme des études au XVIe siècle.* Paris: Hachette, 1880.

———. "Les collèges protestants." *Bulletin de la Société de l'Histoire du Protestantisme Français* 22 (1873): 269–82, 413–23; 23 (1874): 289–304, 337–48, 385–95; 24 (1875): 4–20, 193–208; 27 (1878): 193–208.

———. "Imbert Pécolet." *Bulletin de la Société de l'Histoire du Protestantisme Français* 33 (1884): 49–67.

Geertz, Clifford. *The Interpretation of Cultures*. New York: Basic, 1973.

Geisendorf, Paul-F. *Theodore de Bèze*. Geneva: Droz, 1949.

Gibbon, Edward. *The Decline and Fall of the Roman Empire*. 3 vols. 1776–1788. Rpt., New York: Modern Library, n.d.

Gladwell, Malcolm. "Six Degrees of Lois Weisberg." *New Yorker* 74(41) (January 11, 1999): 52–63.

———. *The Tipping Point*. Boston: Little, Brown, 2000.

Gottlieb, Beatrice. *The Family in the Western World: From the Black Death to the Industrial Age*. New York: Oxford University Press, 1993.

Goubert, Pierre. *Cent mille provinciaux au XVIIe siècle: Beauvais et le Beauvaisis de 1600 à 1730*. 1960. Rpt., Paris: Flammarion, 1968.

Granovetter, Mark S. "The Strength of Weak Ties." *American Journal of Sociology* 78 (1973): 1360–80.

Greengrass, Mark. "The Anatomy of a Religious Riot in Toulouse in May 1562." *Journal of Ecclesiastical History* 34(3) (July 1983): 367–91.

———. *The French Reformation*. Oxford: Basil Blackwell, 1987.

Gregory, Brad S. *Salvation at Stake: Christian Martyrdom in Early Modern Europe*. Cambridge, Mass.: Harvard University Press, 1999.

Grell, Ole Peter, and Robert W. Scribner. *Tolerance and Intolerance in the European Reformation*. Cambridge: Cambridge University Press, 1996.

Guéry, Alain. "Les finances de la monarchie française sous l'ancien régime." *Annales: Économies, Sociétés, Civilizations* 33(2) (1978): 216–39.

Guggenheim, Ann H. "Beza, Viret, and the Church of Nîmes: National Leadership and Local Initiative in the Outbreak of the Religious Wars." *Bibliothèque d'Humanisme et Renaissance* 37(1) (1975): 33–47.

———. "Calvinism and the Political Elite of Sixteenth-Century Nîmes." Ph.D. diss., New York University, 1968.

———. "The Calvinist Notables of Nîmes during the Era of the Religious Wars." *Sixteenth Century Journal* 3(1) (Spring 1972): 80–96.

Guiraud, Louise. *La Réforme à Montpellier*. 2 vols. In *Mémoires de la Société Archéologique de Montpellier*, 2nd ser., 6–7 (1918).

Gutherz, Xavier, et al. *Histoire de Nîmes*. Aix-en-Provence: Edisud, 1982.

Hallie, Philip P. *Lest Innocent Blood Be Shed: The Story of the Village of Le Chambon, and How Goodness Happened There*. New York: Harper and Row, 1979.

Hanley, Sarah. *The Lit de Justice of the Kings of France: Constitutional Ideology in Legend, Ritual, and Discourse*. Princeton, N.J.: Princeton University Press, 1993.

Hanlon, Gregory. *Confession and Community in Seventeenth-Century France: Catholic and Protestant Coexistence in Aquitaine*. Philadelphia: University of Pennsylvania Press, 1993.

Harding, Robert R. *Anatomy of a Power Elite: The Provincial Governors of Early Modern France*. New Haven, Conn.: Yale University Press, 1978.

Hardwick, Julie. *The Practice of Patriarchy: Gender and the Politics of Household Authority in Early Modern France*. University Park: Pennsylvania State University Press, 1998.

Harvey, Charles, and Jon Press. *Databases in Historical Research: Theory, Methods and Applications*. New York: St. Martin's, 1996.

Hauser, Henri. "The French Reformation and the French People." *American Historical Review* 4 (1899): 217–27.

———. "Nîmes, les consulats et la Réforme." In his *Études sur la Réforme française*, 187–202. Paris: Picard, 1909. (This article originally appeared in *Bulletin de la Société de l'Histoire du Protestantisme Français*, 1897.)

Hefner, Robert, ed. *Conversion to Christianity*. Berkeley: University of California Press, 1993.

Heller, Henry. *The Conquest of Poverty: The Calvinist Revolt in Sixteenth Century France*. Leiden: Brill, 1986.

———. *Iron and Blood: Civil Wars in Sixteenth-Century France*. Montreal: McGill-Queen's University Press, 1991.

———. "Putting History Back into the Religious Wars: A Reply to Mack P. Holt." *French Historical Studies* 19(3) (Spring 1996): 853–61.

Hempsall, David S. "The Languedoc 1520–1540: A Study of Pre-Calvinist Heresy in France." *Archiv für Reformationsgeschichte* 62 (1971): 225–43.

———. "Reform and Reformation in France, 1517–36." Ph.D. diss., University of Kent, Canterbury, 1972.

Herlihy, David, and Christiane Klapisch-Zuber. *Tuscans and Their Families*. New Haven, Conn.: Yale University Press, 1985.

Hexter, J. H. *Reappraisals in History*. London: Longman, 1961.

Hilaire, Jean. *Le régime des biens entre époux dans la région de Montpellier du XIIIe siècle à la fin du XVIe siècle: Contribution aux études d'histoire du droit écrit*. Montpellier: Causse, Graille and Castelnau, 1957.

Hirschman, Albert O. *Exit, Voice, and Loyalty: Responses to Decline in Firms, Organizations, and States*. Cambridge, Mass.: Harvard University Press, 1970.

Holt, Mack P. "Attitudes of the French Nobility at the Estates-General of 1576." *Sixteenth Century Journal* 18 (1988): 498–504.

———. *The French Wars of Religion, 1562–1629*. Cambridge: Cambridge University Press, 1995.

———. "Putting Religion Back into the Wars of Religion." *French Historical Studies* 18 (1993): 524–51.

———. "Religion, Historical Method, and Historical Forces: A Rejoinder." *French Historical Studies* 19(3) (Spring 1996): 863–73.

———. "Wine, Community and Reformation in Sixteenth-Century Burgundy." *Past and Present* 138 (February 1993): 58–93.

Horton, Robin. "African Conversion." *Africa* 41 (1971): 85–108.

Houston, R. A. *Literacy in Early Modern Europe: Culture and Education, 1500–1800*. London: Longman, 1988.

Hsia, Ronald Po-Chia. *Social Discipline in the Reformation: Central Europe, 1550–1750.* London: Routledge, 1989.
Hufton, Olwen. *The Prospect before Her: A History of Women in Western Europe*, vol. 1. London: HarperCollins, 1995.
Hughes, Philip E. *Lefèvre d'Étables: Pioneer of Ecclesiastical Renewal in France.* Grand Rapids, Mich.: Eerdmans, 1984.
Hugues, J.-P. *Histoire de l'église réformée d'Anduze.* 1864. Rpt., Nîmes: Lacour, 1993.
Hunt, Lynn, ed. *The New Cultural History.* Berkeley: University of California Press, 1989.
Hunter-Stiebel, Penelope. "Faience: Prelude to Porcelain." *Apollo* 106 (November 1977): 358–63.
Huppert, George. *Public Schools in Renaissance France.* Urbana: University of Illinois Press, 1984.
Imbart de la Tour, Pierre. *Les origines de la Réforme.* 4 vols. Paris: Firmin-Didot, 1905–1935.
Jas, Michel. *Les braises cathares: Filiation secrète à l'heure de la Réforme.* Portet-sur-Garonne: Loubatières, 1992.
Jouanna, Arlette. *La France de la Renaissance: Histoire et dictionnaire.* Paris: Bouquins, Robert Laffont, 1996.
———. *La France du XVIe siècle, 1483–1598.* Paris: Presses Universitaires de France, 1996.
———. *Histoire et dictionnaire des guerres de religion.* Paris: Bouquins, Robert Laffont, 1998.
———. "La première domination des reformés à Montpellier (1561–1563)." In *Les Réformes: Enracinement socio-culturel*, ed. Bernard Chevalier and Robert Sauzet, 151–60. Paris: Maisnie, 1985.
Karant-Nunn, Susan. "Continuity and Change: Some Effects of the Reformation on the Women of Zwickau." *Sixteenth Century Journal* 13(2) (1982): 17–42.
Kelley, Donald R. *The Beginning of Ideology: Consciousness and Society in the French Reformation.* Cambridge: Cambridge University Press, 1981.
Kim, Seong-Hak. *Michel de l'Hôpital: The Vision of a Reformist Chancellor during the French Religious Wars.* Kirksville, Mo.: Sixteenth Century Journal Publishers, 1997.
Kingdon, Robert M. *Adultery and Divorce in Calvin's Geneva.* Cambridge, Mass.: Harvard University Press, 1995.
———. *Geneva and the Coming of the Wars of Religion in France, 1555–1563.* Geneva: Droz, 1956.
———. *Geneva and the Consolidation of the French Protestant Movement 1564–1572.* Madison: University of Wisconsin Press; and Geneva: Droz, 1967.
Knecht, Robert J. *Catherine de'Medici.* London: Longman, 1998.
———. "Francis I and the 'Lit de Justice': A Legend Defended." *French History* 7 (1993): 53–83.
———. *Renaissance Warrior and Patron: The Reign of Francis I.* Cambridge: Cambridge University Press, 1994
———. *The Rise and Fall of Renaissance France.* London: Fontana, 1996.
Lebrun, François, *Du christianisme flamboyant à l'aube des Lumières*, vol. 2 of *Histoire de la France religieuse*, ed. Jacques Le Goff and René Rémond. Paris: Seuil, 1988–1992.

Lemaître, Nicole. *Le Rouergue flamboyant: Le clergé et les fidèles du diocèse de Rodez, 1417–1563*. Paris: Cerf, 1988.
Le Roy Ladurie, Emmanuel. *The Beggar and the Professor: A Sixteenth-Century Family Saga*. Trans. Arthur Goldhammer. Chicago: University of Chicago Press, 1997.
———. *Montaillou: The Promised Land of Error*. 1975. Rpt., New York: Braziller, 1978.
———. *Les Paysans de Languedoc*. 2 vols. Paris: SEVPEN, 1966. Abridged English trans., *The Peasants of Languedoc*. Trans. John Day. Urbana: University of Illinois Press, 1974.
———. *The Territory of the Historian*. Trans. Ben Reynolds and Siân Reynolds. Chicago: University of Chicago Press, 1979.
Linder, Robert D. *The Political Ideas of Pierre Viret*. Geneva: Droz, 1964.
Litzenberger, Caroline. *The English Reformation and the Laity: Gloucestershire, 1540–1580*. Cambridge: Cambridge University Press, 1997.
MacMullen, Ramsay. *Christianizing the Roman Empire*. New Haven: Yale University Press, 1984.
Major, J. Russell. *The Estates General of 1560*. Princeton, N.J.: Princeton University Press, 1951.
———. *From Renaissance Monarchy to Absolute Monarchy: French Kings, Nobels and Estates*. Baltimore, Md.: Johns Hopkins University Press, 1994.
———. *Representative Government in Early Modern France*. New Haven, Conn.: Yale University Press, 1980.
———. *Representative Institutions in Renaissance France, 1421–1559*. Madison: University of Wisconsin Press, 1960.
———. "The Third Estate in the Estates General of Pontoise, 1561." *Speculum* 29 (1954): 460–76.
Mandrou, Robert. *Introduction to Modern France, 1500–1640: An Essay in Historical Psychology*, 2nd ed. Trans. R. E. Hallmark. New York: Holmes and Meier, 1976.
———. *Magistrats et sorciers en France au XVIIe siècle*. Paris: Plon, 1960.
Mariéjol, Jean-Hippolyte. *La Réforme et la Ligue, l'Édit de Nantes, 1559–1598*, vol. 6, pt. 1 of *Histoire de France*, ed. Ernest Lavisse. Paris: Hachette, 1904.
Martin, David. *Tongues of Fire: The Explosion of Protestantism in Latin America*. Oxford: Basil Blackwell, 1990.
McClendon, Muriel. *The Quiet Reformation: Magistrates and the Emergence of Protestantism in Tudor Norwich*. Stanford, Calif.: Stanford University Press, 1999.
McDonald, Terrence J. *The Historic Turn in the Human Sciences*. Ann Arbor: University of Michigan Press, 1996.
McGrath, Alister E. *Reformation Thought: An Introduction*, 2nd ed. Oxford: Blackwell, 1993.
McNeill, John T. *The History and Character of of Calvinism*. Rev. ed. New York: Oxford University Press, 1967.
Maruéjol, Gaston. "Imbert Pécolet et l'ancienne école de Nîmes," *Nemausa* 1 (January 1883): 8–28.
Meeks, Wayne A. *The Origins of Christian Morality: The First Two Centuries*. New Haven, Conn.: Yale University Press, 1993.

Ménard, Léon. *Histoire civile, ecclésiastique et littéraire de la ville de Nîmes.* 7 vols. Paris: 1750–1756. Rpt., Marseille: Lafitte Reprints, 1976. There is another edition available (Nîmes, 1874) which was also reprinted (Nîmes: Lacour, 1988–1990), but it lacks the *Preuves,* a selection of original documents. To help anyone wishing to check a reference using the 1874 edition, which has different pagination, in the notes I give the volume, book, and chapter number as well: Ménard IV:13:59:242 is vol. 4, bk. 13, chap. 59, in either edition, and p. 242 in the original edition.

Mentzer, Raymond A., Jr. "*Disciplina nervus ecclesiae:* The Calvinist Reform of Morals at Nîmes." *Sixteenth Century Journal* 18(1) (Spring 1987): 89–115.

———. "Ecclesiastical Discipline and Communal Reorganization among the Protestants of Southern France." *European History Quarterly* 21 (1991): 163–85.

———. *Heresy Proceedings in Languedoc, 1500–1560.* In *Transactions of the American Philosophical Society* 74(5) (1984).

———. "Organizational Endeavour and Charitable Impulse in Sixteenth-Century France: The Case of Protestant Nîmes." *French History* 5(1) (1991): 1–29.

———, ed. *Sin and the Calvinists: Morals Control and the Consistory in the Reformed Tradition.* Kirksville, Mo.: Sixteenth Century Journal Publishers, 1994.

Merrick, Jeffrey W. *The Desacralization of the French Monarchy in the Eighteenth Century.* Baton Rouge: Louisiana State University Press, 1990.

Meyer, Judith Pugh. *Reformation in La Rochelle: Tradition and Change in Early Modern Europe, 1500–1568.* Geneva: Droz, 1996.

Millet, Joshua E. "A City Converted: The Protestant Reformation in Nîmes, 1532–1567." Ph.D. diss., Harvard University, 2000.

Moeller, Bernd. *Imperial Cities and the Reformation: Three Essays.* Ed. and trans. H. C. Midelfort and Mark U. Edwards Jr. Philadelphia: Fortress, 1972.

Molinier, Alain. "Aux origines de la Réformation cévenole." *Annales: Économies, Sociétés, Civilizations* 39(2) (1984): 240–64.

———. "De la religion des œuvres à la Réformation dans les Cévennes." *Revue de l'Histoire de l'Église de France* 77 (1986): 245–63.

Monter, William. *Calvin's Geneva.* New York: Wiley, 1967.

———. *Judging the French Reformation: Heresy Trials by Sixteenth-Century Parlements.* Cambridge, Mass.: Harvard University Press, 1999.

Mours, Samuel. *Les églises réformées en France.* Paris: Librairie Protestante, 1958.

Mours, Samuel, and Daniel Robert. *Le protestantisme en France.* 3 vols. Paris: Librairie Protestante, 1959–1972.

Mousnier, Roland E. *The Institutions of France under the Absolute Monarchy, 1598–1789.* 2 vols. 1974–1980. Rpt., Chicago: University of Chicago Press, 1977–1984.

Naef, Henri. *La conjuration d'Amboise et Genève.* Geneva: Jullien and Georg; and Paris: Édouard Champion, 1922.

Nauert, Charles G., Jr. "Humanists, Scientists, and Pliny: Changing Approaches to a Classical Author." *American Historical Review* 84(1) (1979): 72–85.

Newcomb, T. M. *Personality and Social Change.* New York: Dryden, 1943.

Nicholls, David. "Social Change and Early Protestantism in France: Normandy, 1520–62." *European Studies Review* 10(2) (1980): 279–308.

———. "The Social History of the French Reformation: Ideology, Confesion and Culture." *Social History* 9(1) (1984): 25–44.
Novick, Peter. *That Noble Dream: The "Objectivity Question" and the American Historical Profession.* Cambridge: Cambridge University Press, 1988.
Nugent, Donald. *Ecumenism in the Age of the Reformation: The Colloquy of Poissy.* Cambridge, Mass.: Harvard University Press, 1974.
Oakley, Francis. *The Western Church in the Later Middle Ages.* Ithaca, N.Y.: Cornell University Press, 1979.
Oberman, Heiko A. "Calvin and Farel: The Dynamics of Legitimation in Early Calvinism." *Journal of Early Modern History* 2(1) (1998): 32–60.
———. *The Dawn of the Reformation: Essays in Late Medieval and Early Reformation Thought.* Grand Rapids, Mich.: Eerdmans, 1986.
———. *Luther: Man between God and the Devil.* Trans. Eileen Walliser-Schwarzbart. 1982. Rpt., New Haven, Conn.: Yale University Press, 1989.
Otis, Leah L. *Prostitution in Medieval Society: The History of an Urban Institution in Languedoc.* Chicago: University of Chicago Press, 1985.
Ozment, Steven. *The Age of Reform, 1250–1550: An Intellectual and Religious History of Late Medieval and Reformation Europe.* New Haven, Conn.: Yale University Press, 1980.
———. *Protestants: The Birth of a Revolution.* Garden City, N.Y.: Doubleday, 1992.
———. *The Reformation in the Cities.* New Haven, Conn.: Yale University Press, 1975.
Padgett, John F., and Christopher K. Ansell. "Robust Action and the Rise of the Medici, 1400–1434." *American Journal of Sociology* 98 (1993): 1259–1319.
Pettegree, Andrew, Alaistair Duke, and Gillian Lewis, eds. *Calvinism in Europe, 1540–1620.* Cambridge: Cambridge University Press, 1994.
Picot, Georges. *Histoire des états généraux.* 4 vols. Paris: Hachette, 1872.
Pope, Robert G. "New England versus the New England Mind: The Myth of Declension." *Journal of Social History* 3(2) (Winter 1969–1970): 95–108.
Poton, Didier. "Aux origines du protestantisme en Basses Cévennes." *Bulletin de la Société de l'Histoire du Protestantisme Français* 128 (1982): 469–88.
Potter, David. *A History of France, 1540–1560: The Emergence of a Nation State.* New York: St. Martin's, 1995.
Prestwich, Menna, ed. *International Calvinism, 1541–1715.* Oxford: Clarendon, 1985.
Prudhomme, Auguste. *Histoire de Grenoble.* Grenoble: Alexandre Gratier, 1888.
Puech, Albert. "Les anciennes jurisdictions de Nîmes." *Mémoires de l'Académie de Nîmes* 12 (1889): 155–91; and 13 (1890): 161–246.
———. "Les arts à la Renaissance." *Revue du Midi* 4(2) (November 1890): 329–59. In his *La Renaissance et la Réforme à Nîmes.*
———. "Les débuts de la Réforme à Nîmes, d'après des documents inédits." In his *La Renaissance et la Réforme à Nîmes.*
———. "L'instruction à l'époque de la Renaissance." *Revue du Midi* 5(1) (February–March 1891): 119–45, 234–55. In his *La Renaissance et la Réforme à Nîmes.*
———. *La léproserie de Nîmes.* Nîmes: Gervais-Bedot, 1888. Originally published in *Bulletin du comité de l'art chrétien.*

———. "La librairie populaire avant la Révolution d'après des documents inédits." *Revue du Midi* 1(1) (January 1887): 22–38.

———. "La musique et les musiciens à Nîmes aux XVIe et XVIIe siècles." *Revue du Midi* 2(2): (July 1888): 44–65. In his *La Renaissance et la Réforme à Nîmes*.

———. "Le potier nîmois Sijalon ou Sigalon: Son atelier de céramique au seizième siècle." *Réunion des Sociétés des Beaux-Arts*, 15th sess. (1891): 84–89.

———. *La Renaissance et la Réforme à Nîmes*. Nîmes: Gervais-Bedot, 1893.

———. *Une ville au temps jadis; ou, Nîmes à la fin du XVIe siècle*. Nîmes: Grimaud, 1884.

Pugh, Wilma J. "Catholics, Protestants, and Testamentary Charity in Seventeenth-Century Lyon and Nîmes." *French Historical Studies* 11 (1980): 479–504.

Pullan, Brian. "Catholics, Protestants, and the Poor in Early Modern Europe." *Journal of Interdisciplinary History* 35(3) (Winter 2005): 441–56.

Rabb, Theodore K. *The Struggle for Stability in Early Modern Europe*. New York: Oxford University Press, 1975.

Rambeaud, Pascal. *De La Rochelle vers l'Aunis: L'histoire des réformés et de leurs églises dans une province française au XVIe siècle*. Paris: Champion, 2003.

Raveau, Paul. "La crise dex prix au XVIe siècle en Poitou." *Revue Historique* 162 (1929): 1–44, 268–93.

Rice, Eugene F. *The Foundations of Early Modern Europe, 1540–1559*. New York: Norton, 1970.

———. "The Meanings of 'Evangelical.'" In *The Pursuit of Holiness in Late Medieval and Renaissance Religion*, ed. Charles Trinkaus and Heiko Oberman, 472–75. Leiden: Brill, 1974.

Richet, Denis. "Aspects socio-culturels des conflits religieux à Paris dans la deuxième moitié du XVIe siècle." *Annales* 32 (1977): 764–83. Reprinted in his *De la Réforme à la Révolution: Études sur la France moderne*, 15–51. Paris: Aubier, 1991.

Rivals, Georges. "Les conditions économiques et sociales de la Réforme dans le Bas-Languedoc." *Cahiers d'Histoire et d'Archéologie* 13 (1938): 41–66.

Rivet, Bernard. *Une ville au XVIe siècle: Le Puy en Velay*. Le-Puy-en-Velay: Cahiers de la Haute-Loire, 1988.

Robbins, Kevin C. *City on the Ocean Sea: La Rochelle, 1530–1650: Urban Society, Religion, and Politics on the French Atlantic Frontier*. Leiden: Brill, 1997.

Roberts, Penny. *A City in Conflict: Troyes during the French Wars of Religion*. Manchester: Manchester University Press, 1996.

Robisheaux, Thomas. "Peasants and Pastors: Rural Youth Control and the Reformation in Hohenlohe, 1540–1680." *Social History* 6 (1981): 281–300.

Roelker, Nancy L. *One King, One Faith: The Parlement of Paris and the Religious Reformations of the Sixteenth Century*. Berkeley: University of California Press, 1996.

———. *Queen of Navarre: Jeanne d'Albret, 1528–1572*. Cambridge, Mass.: Harvard University Press, 1968.

Romier, Lucien. *Catholiques et Huguenots à la cour de Charles IX.*, 2nd ed. Paris: Librairie Académique, 1924.

———. *La conjuration d'Amboise*, 2nd ed. Paris: Librairie Académique, 1923.
———. *Les origines politiques des guerres de religion*. 2 vols. Paris: Perrin, 1913.
———. *Le royaume de Catherine de Médicis: La France à la veille des guerres de religion*. 2 vols. Paris: Perrin, 1922.
Roper, Lyndal. "Discipline and Respectability: Prostitution and the Reformation in Augsburg." *History Workshop Journal* 19 (1985): 3–28.
Rosa, Susan, and Dale Van Kley. "Religion and the Historical Discipline: A Reply to Mack Holt and Henry Heller." *French Historical Studies* 21 (1998): 610–29.
Rosenberg, David L. "Social Experience and Religious Choice: A Case Study: The Protestant Weavers and Woolcombers of Amiens in the Sixteenth Century." Ph.D. diss., Yale University, 1978.
Rossiaud, Jacques. *Medieval Prostitution*. Trans. Lydia Cochrane. Oxford: Basil Blackwell, 1988.
Roussel, Bernard. "Pierre Viret en France (septembre 1561–août 1565)." *Bulletin de la Société de l'Histoire du Protestantisme Français* 44 (Fall 1998): 803–38.
Rouvière, François. *Histoire de la revolution française dans le département du Gard*. 4 vols. Nîmes: A. Catélan, 1887–1889.
Russell, Conrad. *Parliaments and English Politics, 1621–1629*. Oxford: Oxford University Press, 1979.
Salmon, J. H. M., ed. *The French Wars of Religion: How Important Were Religious Factors?* Boston: Heath, 1967.
———. *Society in Crisis: France in the Sixteenth Century*. New York: St. Martin's, 1975.
Sardinoux, Colette. "Les premières traces de la Réforme à Anduze." M.A. thesis, University of Montpellier, 1971.
Sauzet, Robert. *Contre-réforme et réforme catholique en Bas-Languedoc: Le diocèse de Nîmes au XVIIe siècle*. Louvain: Nauvelaerts, 1979.
———. "L'iconoclasme protestant dans le diocèse de Nîmes aux XVIe et XVIIe siècles." *Revue d'histoire de l'Église de France* 176 (1980): 7–15.
———. *Le notaire et son roi: Étienne Borrelly (1733–1718), un nîmois sous Louis XIV*. Paris: Plon, 1998.
Schneider, Robert A. *Public Life in Toulouse, 1463–1789: From Municipal Republic to Cosmopolitan City*. Ithaca, N.Y.: Cornell University Press, 1989.
Schuster, Peter. *Das Frauenhaus: Städtische Bordelle in Deutschland, 1350–1600*. Paderborn: Schöningh, 1992.
Scribner, Robert W. "Is There a Social History of the Reformation?" *Social History* 2 (1977): 483–505.
Scribner, Robert W., and Gerhard Benecke, eds. *The German Peasants' War, 1525: New Viewpoints*. London: Allen and Unwin, 1979.
Segal, Alan F. *Paul the Convert*. New Haven, Conn.: Yale University Press, 1990.
Sewell, William H., Jr. *Logics of History: Social Theory and Social Transformation*. Chicago: University of Chicago Press, 2005.
———. "A Theory of Structure: Duality, Agency, and Transformation." *American Journal of Sociology* 98(1) (July 1992): 1–29. Reprinted as chap. 4 in his *Logics of History*.

---. "Whatever Happened to the 'Social' in Social History?" In *Schools of Thought: Twenty-five Years of Interpretive Social Science*, ed. Joan W. Scott and Debra Keates, 207–26. Princeton, N.J.: Princeton University Press, 2001.

Shagan, Ethan H. *Popular Politics and the English Reformation*. Cambridge: Cambridge University Press, 2002.

Soman, Alfred, and Elizabeth Labrousse. "Le registre consistorial de Coutras, 1582–1584," *Bulletin de la Société de l'Histoire du Protestantisme Français* 126 (1980): 193–228.

Spilka, Bernard, Ralph W. Hood Jr., Bruce Hunsberger, and Richard Gorsuch. *The Psychology of Religion: An Empirical Approach*. New York: Guilford, 2003.

Spooner, Frank C. *The International Economy and Monetary Movements in France, 1493–1725*. Cambridge, Mass.: Harvard University Press, 1972.

---. "The Reformation in France, 1515–1559." In *The New Cambridge Modern History*, 2nd ed., ed. G. R. Elton, 223–61. Cambridge: Cambridge University Press, 1990.

Stark, Rodney. *The Rise of Christianity: A Sociologist Reconsiders History*. Princeton, N.J.: Princeton University Press, 1996.

Stone, Lawrence. *The Causes of the English Revolution, 1529–1642*. London: Routledge and Kegan Paul, 1972.

---. *The Family, Sex and Marriage in England 1500–1800*. London: Weidenfeld and Nicolson, 1977.

---. "Social Mobility in England, 1500–1700." *Past and Present* 33 (April 1966): 16–55.

Stouff, Louis. *La table provençale: Boire et manger en Provence à la fin du Moyen Age*. Avignon: Barthélemy, 1996.

Strauss, Gerald. *Nuremberg in the Sixteenth Century: City Politics and Life between Middle Ages and Modern Times*. Rev. ed. Bloomington: Indiana University Press, 1976.

---. "Success and Failure in the German Reformation." *Past and Present* 67 (May 1975): 30–63.

Sunshine, Glenn S. *Reforming French Protestantism: The Development of Huguenot Ecclesiastical Institutions 1557–1572*. Kirksville, Mo.: Truman State University Press, 2003.

Sutherland, Nicola M. *The Huguenot Struggle for Recognition*. New Haven, Conn.: Yale University Press, 1980.

Taylor, Larissa. *Soldiers of Christ: Preaching in Late Medieval and Reformation France*. New York: Oxford University Press, 1992.

Teisseyre-Sallmann, Line. *L'industrie de la soie on Bas-Languedoc, XVIIe–XVIIIe siècles*. Paris: École des Chartes, 1995.

Tievant, Claude. *Le gouverneur de Languedoc pendant les premières guerres de religion (1559–1574): Henri de Montmorency-Damville* Paris: Publisud, 1993.

Tingle, Elizabeth C. *Authority and Society in Nantes during the French Wars of Religion, 1559–1598*. Manchester: Manchester University Press, 2006.

Tracy, James D. *Erasmus: The Growth of a Mind*. Geneva: Droz, 1972.

Trocmé, Étienne, and Marcel Delafosse. *Le commerce rochelais de la fin su XVe siècle au début du XVIIe*. Paris: Armand Colin, 1952.

Troeltsch, Ernst. *Protestantism and Progress*. Philadelphia: Fortress, 1986. [Original German ed., 1912]
———. *The Social Teaching of the Christian Churches*. 2 vols. New York: Macmillan, 1931. [Original German ed., 1911]
Tucker, Aviezer. *Our Knowledge of the Past: A Philosophy of Historiography*. Cambridge: Cambridge University Press, 2004.
Tulchin, Allan A. "Les étudiants au collège des arts de Nîmes au XVIe siècle." *Bulletin de la société de l'histoire moderne et contemporaine de Nîmes*, n.s., 10 (October 1994): 33–35.
———. "The Reformation in Nîmes." Ph.D. diss., University of Chicago, 2000.
Turner, Ralph, and Lewis M. Killian. *Collective Behavior*, 3rd. ed. Englewood Cliffs, N.J.: Prentice-Hall, 1987.
Turner, Victor. "Betwixt and Between: The Liminal Period in Rites de Passage." In his *The Forest of Symbols: Aspects of Ndembu Ritual*, 93–111. Ithaca, N.Y.: Cornell University Press, 1967.
Ullman, Chana. *The Transformed Self: The Psychology of Religious Conversion*. New York: Plenum, 1989.
Underdown, David. *Fire from Heaven: Life in an English Town in the Seventeenth Century*. New Haven, Conn.: Yale University Press, 1992.
———. *Pride's Purge: Politics in the Puritan Revolution*. Oxford: Oxford University Press, 1971.
Valois, Noël. "Les états de Pontoise." *Revue d'Histoire de l'Église de France* 39 (1943): 237–56.
Van de Put, Albert. "The Nîmes Faience: I, II, and III." *Burlington Magazine* 62 (March 1933): 108–14; (April 1933): 157–60; (July 1933): 16–21.
Van Dyke, Paul. "The Estates of Pontoise." *English Historical Review* 28 (1913): 472–95.
Veissière, Michel. *L'évêque Guillaume Briçonnet, 1470–1534*. Provins: Société d'Histoire et d'Archéologie, 1986.
Venard, Marc. *Réforme protestante, Réforme catholique dans la province d'Avignon (XVIe siècle)*. Paris: Cerf, 1993.
Viguié, Jean. "Fête de la Réformation." *Bulletin de la Société de l'Histoire du Protestantisme Français*, 2nd ser., 18 (1868): 552–60.
Vovelle, Michel. *Piété baroque et déchristianisation en Provence au XVIIIe siècle*. Paris: Plon, 1973.
Wandel, Lee Palmer. *The Eucharist in the Reformation: Incarnation and Liturgy*. Cambridge: Cambridge University Press, 2006.
Walzer, Michael. *The Revolution of the Saints*. Cambridge, Mass.: Harvard University Press, 1965.
Wasserman, Stanley, and Katherine Faust. *Social Network Analysis: Methods and Applications*. Cambridge: Cambridge University Press, 1994.
Watson, Timothy. "Preaching, Printing, Psalm-Singing: The Making and Unmaking of the Reformed Church in Lyon, 1550–1572." In *Society and Culture in the Huguenot World, 1559–1685*, ed. Raymond A. Mentzer and Andrew Spicer, 10–28. Cambridge: Cambridge University Press, 2002.

Weber, Max. *The Protestant Ethic and the Spirit of Capitalism*. Trans. Talcott Parsons. 1920–1921. Rpt., New York: Scribner's, 1958.
Wolfe, Martin. *The Fiscal System of Renaissance France*. New Haven, Conn.: Yale University Press, 1972.
Wrightson, Keith. *English Society 1580–1680*. New Brunswick, N.J.: Rutgers University Press, 1982.
Zaretsky, Robert. *Nîmes at War: Religion, Politics, and Public Opinion in the Gard, 1938–1944*. University Park: Pennsylvania State University Press, 1995.
Zeller, Gaston. *Les institutions de la France au XVIe siècle*, 2nd ed. Paris: Presses Universitaires de France, 1987.

Index

Note on the alphabetization of names: royalty and crowned heads are referenced under their first names, major nobles by their titles, and everyone else under their last names. Members of one family are listed together. Particles "de" and "d'" are not alphabetized, but "des" and "du" are. Thus: des Georges, Robert, but Airebaudouze, Jean-Guy d'.

Airebaudouze, Jean-Guy d', 168
    Pierre d', 47, 52, 185
Aix-en-Provence, 16
Albenas family, 173–174
    Jacques d', 29
    Jean d', 11, 50, 80–82, 84–86, 173–174
    Jean-Poldo d', 11, 17, 80, 94, 98
    Vidal d', 85, 150
Alès, 7, 28, 40
Alesti, Jean, 56
Alexi, Étienne, 78
Alizot, Arnaud, 36, 80, 83, 85, 122, 136, 228n.20
Alva, duke of, 159–160
Amboise, conspiracy of, 73–74, 107
Amboise, edict of, 74, 79
Amiens, 105–106, 186, 191–192
anciens. *See* Nîmes consistory, overseers
Anduze, 7, 40, 53, 56, 98
Angelin, Étienne, 51
Annales school, xvii–xviii
Antoine de Navarre, 73, 75, 100, 153
arena. *See* Nîmes, amphitheater
Arnaud, Bernard, 93, 173

Aspères, Pierre d', 52
assemblies. *See* Nîmes Protestant movement, preaching
Assembly of the Clergy, 75, 100
atheism, 108
Avignon, 15, 44, 64, 142, 188

Bach, Bernard, 36
Baduel, Claude, 36–39, 47, 50, 36–39, 47, 50, 52, 60, 150, 185
Banc, Arnaud, 77, 124
Barrière, Bernard, 95, 149–150
    François, 93
    Jacques, 165
    Jean, 24, 38
Baudan, Jean, 80
begging. *See* Nîmes, poverty in
bells. *See* Nîmes, church bells
Benedict, Philip, 58, 185–186
Bernard, François, 17, 56–57
Bernaudon, Glaude, 138
Bertrand, Jean, 79, 125, 163, 167
    Louis, 103–104, 150
Besserier, Tanequin, 80
Bettmann, Otto L., xviii

betweenness, 59, 146–148
    defined, 25
Bèze, Théodore de, 176
Bible, 33, 35, 50, 57, 108, 118, 149, 198. *See also* psalm-singing
Bigot, Guillaume, 37–39, 50
Bloch, Marc, xvii
Bodet, Nicolas, 43
Bodin, Jean, 10
Bolhargues, captain. *See* Suau, Pierre
Bonail, François, 78
Bonaud, Gilles, 24
    Jacques, 45
    Jean, 163
Bonfar, Antoine, 64
books, heretical, 56, 86, 93
books, publishing, 17, 56–57
Borrel, Abraham, 199
bread. *See* Nîmes, economic conditions
Briçonnet, Claude, bishop, 13
    Guillaume, bishop, 13
    Michel, bishop, 13
Brueys, Antoine de, 163–165
    Denis de, 43, 53, 56, 80, 82–83, 86, 158
    Pierre de, 91–92, 95, 98
    Robert de, 84
    Tristan de, 77
Bucer, Martin, 37, 50

cahier de doléances. *See* Nîmes cahier de doléances, Paris cahier de doléances, etc.
Caihas, Gaspar, 35
Caintemesse, Vidal, 167, 173
Calvière family, 172–174
    Guilaume, 11–12, 43, 91, 104, 129–130, 136, 151, 158, 161, 166, 169, 172–174
    Guilaume, views of, 43, 91, 104, 129–130, 151
    Guilaume, the younger, 128
Calvin, Calvinism, 25–26, 32–34, 37, 50, 72–74, 112, 119, 138–139, 141, 183. *See also* ecclesiology, sacraments

Calvin and Viret, letter to, 47, 54
Camargue, 4, 7, 40
Cameron, Euan, 200
Cateau-Cambrésis, treaty of, 65
catechizing, catechism, 108, 151
Catherine de' Medici, 30, 73–75, 101–102, 105, 114, 150, 153, 159–160
Catholic reform, 31, 110, 115. *See also* humanism
Cellerier, Pierre, 78, 113, 150, 165–166
censives, 132
Cévennes, 7–8, 26, 40, 42, 67–68, 98, 188
Chabot family, 60
    Pierre, 77, 114–115, 117, 125–126, 134, 150
charity. *See* Nîmes, poverty in; Nîmes consistory, poor fund
Charles IX, 75, 101, 150, 157–160, 178
Cheylane, Louis l'Estrange, vicomte de, 93–94, 97–99
children, attitudes toward, 46
chosenness, 138
church organization. *See* ecclesiology, Nîmes consistory
city council. *See* Nîmes town council
Civil War, First, 153–156
Civil War, Second, 159–160, 178
Clark, J. C. D., 198
cognitive dissonance, xvi–xvii, 107, 112, 145
Coligny, Gaspard de, Admiral, 74, 155
Collège de France, 30
Colloquy of Possy. *See* Poissy, Colloquy of
community, sense of. *See* Eucharist
conciliarism, 111, 116–117
Condé, Louis, prince de, 75, 155–156, 160, 178
Confession of Faith, 72
consubstantiation, 32–33
consuls. *See* Nîmes consuls, Nîmes town council
contractualism, 116
conversion
    explanations of, xvi–xvii, 141, 179
    of French bishops, 185

Copier, Antoine, 85
Corconne, Bernard, 150
   Jeanne, 167
Corpus Christi, 33, 158
Cosme, Benoît, 34
court factions, 73, 153
cross. *See* sign of the cross
Crouzet, Denis, 176–177, 183
crown, fiscal problems of, 71, 75, 101, 104–106, 109–110, 114–115, 117, 148
   policy towards Nîmes, 95
   religious policies of, 31–32, 38, 70, 72–74, 79, 86–87, 90, 95, 102, 151–152
Crussol, Antoine, comte de, and vicomte d'Uzès, 6, 115, 150, 155–156, 159
   Jacques de, 156, 161, 258–259n.78

Damville, Henri de Montmorency, seigneur de, 4, 156–157
database. *See* notarial database
Davis, Natalie Z., 175–176, 178, 185–186
deacons. *See* Nîmes consistory
debt, royal. *See* crown, fiscal problems of
des Georges, Guidon, 137
   Robert, 44, 91, 94, 156–159, 174
Deyron, Dominique, 56
   Jean, 140
Dijon, 15
discipline. *See* Nîmes consistory, morals regulation
dowry, dowries, 21–24, 58, 69, 107, 137, 208–215
du Brana, Guichard, 12, 45–46
du Caylar, Jean, 13, 79, 87–88, 95
Dumas, Étienne, 78, 85

ecclesiology, 109, 116, 119, 121
Écouen, edict of, 70
edicts, royal. *See* Fountainebleau, edict of; Nantes, edict of, etc.

Elbène, Bernard d', bishop, 13, 135, 151, 163–164
elders. *See* Nîmes consistory
election. *See* chosenness
Elizabeth de Valois, 70, 73
emergent norms, 107–108
Emmanuel Philibert of Savoy, 70
endogamy (in marriage), 22–23
Erasmus, Erasmian, 27, 31, 105
Estates General, 5, 73, 75, 88, 99–105, 107, 110, 115–118, 122
   powers of representatives, 101
Estates General of Languedoc. *See* Languedoc, Estates General of
Estiard, Pierre, 56
Eucharist, 32–34, 38, 47, 60, 84, 138, 145

factions
   within consistory. *See* Mutonis, Jean
   See also Nîmes, factions in
family structure, 107, 216–217
Febvre, Lucien, xvii, 184–185
Felix, François, 84–85
Ferrandon. *See* Savy, Jacques
Festinger, Leon, xvi
Florac, 7, 188
Florence, 25
Fons, Jean de, 80, 85
Fontainebleau, edict of, 179
France, Peter, 193
François I, 10, 29–32, 48
François II, 58, 70, 72, 75, 100
French Protestant movement, 76–77, 102, 183–197. *See also* synods

Gamon, Achille, 115
Garragues, Jean, 125
garrigues, 7, 40, 42, 66–67
Geneva, 6, 39, 47, 53–54, 57, 72–74, 84, 108, 125–126, 143
   immigration to, 32, 36, 47, 52–53, 56–58, 113, 163, 185
   Company of Pastors, 53–54, 72, 77

292   INDEX

Ginzburg, Carlo, xv
Goltzius, Hubert, 17
grabaud (self-criticism sessions). *See* Nîmes consistory
grain prices. *See* Nîmes, economic conditions
Granon, Claude, 78, 91
Gras, François de, 150, 156, 157–159, 161, 165–166, 173
Greengrass, Mark, 186
Gregory, Brad, 198
Grenoble, 7, 184, 191–194
guilds, 191–192
Guilhon, Pierre, 44
Guinefort, St., xv
Guise, François, duc de, 73, 87–88, 98, 153
Guises, 73–75

Hapsburgs, 63, 65, 67–70, 192, 195
harvest. *See* Nîmes, economic conditions
Hefner, Robert, xvi
Heller, Henry, 184
Henri II, 10, 30, 48, 65, 70–72, 101, 152, 183, 195, 199
Henri II d'Albret of Navarre, 35
Henri IV, 73
Henry VIII of England, 30
heresy, 4, 14, 97, 104, 109, 121–122, 151–152, 187, 195
  cases of, 15, 28–29, 35–36, 38–39, 49–52, 58, 113, 136
  royal policy on (*see* crown, religious policies of)
  See also Nîmes town council; Nîmes présidial
historiography, xvii–xix, 195–197
  of the Reformation, 176–178, 182–186, 198–200
humanism, 26, 29–31, 34, 112, 190. *See also* Catholic reform
husbandmen. *See* Nîmes, agricultural workers

iconoclasm, 39, 134, 140
identity formation. *See* Nîmes Protestant movement
Imbart de la Tour, Pierre, 184
immigration. *See* Geneva, immigration to; Nîmes, immigration to

January, edict of, 151–153, 155
Jeanne d'Albret, 73
Joussaud, Jean, 44
Joyeuse, vicomte de, 79, 81–86, 88–90, 92, 160
Juliane, Doulce, 124–125

L'Hospital, Michel de, 74, 100, 102
La Garde, capt., 160, 170
La Rochelle, 176
laboureurs. *See* Nîmes, agricultural workers in
Languedoc, 3–4, 66
Languedoc, Estates General of, 5, 7, 92–93, 114–118
Lansard, Jean, 42, 44, 91–92
Lausanne, 36, 77
Lavau, Pierre de, 56
Le Puy, 68–69
Le Roy Ladurie, Emmanuel, 184–185
Le Vellais, Jacques, 63
LeBlanc, Robert, 67, 155, 161, 168
L'Estrange. *See* Cheylane, comte de
liminality, 72, 115, 133–134, 199–200
linguistic turn, xvii
literacy, 15–16, 60
localism, 26, 138–139, 152. *See also* xenophobia
Longjumeau, treaty of, 178
Lord's Supper. *See* Eucharist
Lorraine, Charles, cardinal de, 73
Louis XIV, 179
Louvain, Univ. of, 37
Lubac, Jean de, 78, 81, 91
Lucquet, Jean, 17, 56

Luther, Lutheranism, 31–33, 53, 94, 136, 183, 195
Lyon, xv, 30, 57, 75, 90, 92, 94, 128, 186

Madrid, 14
Maillane, Arnaud de, 74
Major, J. Russell, 195
Maligny, Edmée de, 75
Malmazet, Jean, 91, 95, 149
Malmont, Pierre de, 29, 45, 60
Maltraict, Antoine, 43
Mantesse, Ysabel, 139
Marguerite de Navarre, 31, 35–36, 73
Marguerite de Valois, 70
marks of the Church, 33
marriage contracts, 18, 21–22, 24, 38, 54, 58, 69, 125, 138, 152, 161, 203–204, 210, 213, 215, 217, 219
Marsillargues, 124
Martin, Guillaume, 6
Mary, 39, 54–55, 57, 158
mass, masses, 14–15, 24, 32–33, 35, 61, 78, 129, 135, 151, 157–159, 175
Mauget, Guillaume, 77, 79, 122, 124–127, 132, 142
Maure, Jean, 79
Maurin, Jacques, 77
Maurin, Jean, 77
Medici family, 25
Melanchthon, Philip, 31, 34, 37–38, 50
Menocchio, xv
Michelade, 161–178
  1st phase (seizing keys), 162–165
  2nd phase (arrests), 165
  3rd phase (selection), 165–168
  4th phase (sacred geography), 168–169
  5th phase (siege), 169–170
  motives for, 172–175
  victims, 170–172
Midi, 4, 18, 26, 30, 190–191
migration. *See* Nîmes, immigration to; Geneva, immigration to
militia. *See* Nîmes, guards in

Moeller, Bernd, 190
Moleri, Antoine, 36, 50, 52
Mombel, Jean, 78, 113
monarchy. *See* crown
Montcalm, François de, 83, 93, 135
  Françoise de, 50
  Gaillard de, 69
  Isabeau de, 50
  Jean de, 80, 82–83
Montgomery, Gabriel de, 70
Montmorency, Anne de, 86, 93, 160
Montmorency, Henri de. *See* Damville
Montpellier, 4–5, 19, 27–28, 34, 38, 44, 93, 4–6, 15–16, 115, 178, 184, 187, 194–195
Morlet, Jean, 39
mountains. *See* Cévennes
municipal council. *See* Nîmes town council
Mutonis, Jean, 57, 125–126

Nantes, edict of, 179
Netherlands, 150
Nîmes
  agricultural workers in, 19, 41, 58–59, 143
  agriculture in, 18, 40
  amphitheater, 11, 45
  anticlericalism in, 29, 45–46, 101, 105–106
  arms in (bearing, stockpiles of), 81, 84–85, 90–91, 151, 164
  artisans in, 58–60
  Augustinians in, 13, 28, 134–135, 141, 164
  avocat des pauvres (lawyer for poor), 16
  bakers in, 42
  bourgeois in, 20, 58, 128
  butchers in, 42–43
  Catholic Church in, 13–15, 29, 175
  Catholic clergy in, 14, 60, 81, 151, 156, 171–172, 175, 224n.27

Nîmes (*Continued*)
  château in, 8, 13, 85, 157–158, 161, 162, 169
  church bells, 135, 156
  churches, 8–9, 151, 158
  churches seized, 130–136
  clothing trades in, 19–20
  coat of arms, 31
  confraternities, 17, 106
  Cordeliers in, 56, 133
  Dominicans in, 9, 13, 49, 56–57, 64, 85, 124, 151
  economic conditions, 40–41, 43, 60–64, 92
  economic regulation in, 41–43, 64
  economic strains, 1557–1560, 61–65
  economy of, 18–22, 39–46
  education in, 15–16, 34–38, 60, 108
  elites of, 15, 24–25, 28–29, 31, 38, 42, 58, 64–65, 144–149
  factions in, 25, 59, 146
  fiscal pressure in, 65–69
  fishmongers in, 42
  flood in, 61
  food trades in, 42–43
  forced loans demanded of, 69
  geography of, 5–9
  guards of, 44, 78, 80, 82, 85, 93, 98
  guilds in, 16
  hospitals in, 16, 46
  immigration to, 7–8, 40
  inns, innkeepers in, 24, 91, 93
  institutions of, 9–17. *See also* Nîmes présidial, Nîmes town council, etc.
  jail, 13, 85
  lawyers, legal professions, 20–21, 113, 122–123, 128, 143, 226n.38
  legal mentality, 28–29, 111–112, 190
  Lenten preacher in, 28, 44, 56, 156–157
  monasteries in, 8–9
  notaries in, 12, 18, 20–22, 35, 58, 111, 122, 126, 133, 204, 216
  popular piety in, 14–15, 49, 61
  poverty and charity in, 16, 39, 41, 43–46, 63–64, 104, 112
  prostitution in, 27–28
  Roman monuments in, 8
  royal entry of 1533, 30–31
  royal troops in, 7–8, 13, 38, 69, 90–94, 97, 156–158
  silk production in, 8, 64
  social hierarchy and stratification in, 22–25, 122, 131, 147, 209–219
  taxation in, 65–66, 75, 94, 98, 102
  University and College of Arts of, 15, 36–39, 61, 103
Nîmes cahier de doléances, importance of, 103, 113
  debated, 103–104, 117
  financial provisions, 106
  introduced, 103
  legal provisions, 111–112
  political provisions, 110–111
  religious provisions, 106–110
  social and educational provisions, 106, 112
  summary of provisions, 105
Nîmes consistory, 77, 78, 89, 114, 122–137, 155, 161–162
  deacons, 122, 127–128, 161
  elders (overseers), 36, 122, 127–128, 161
  elections, 122, 127–128
  grabaud (self-criticism sessions), 89, 125, 145, 152
  ministers of, 76, 84, 86, 89, 93
  morals regulation, 123–125
  poor fund, 122, 136–138
Nîmes consuls, 11–13, 16, 26, 28–29, 35, 46, 60, 64–65, 78–84, 88, 91, 94, 98–99, 103–104, 117, 144, 150, 156–157, 159, 165
Nîmes présidial, 10–11, 57–58, 71, 88, 129–130, 140, 155, 157, 161, 165
  debates on heresy, 78–86
  absences from, 80, 82, 86, 149

Nîmes Protestant movement, expansion,
after 1559, 75–78
extremists, 74, 114, 117, 132–135,
140–141, 184
first converts, 36
formation of community, 46–48
growth, in 1550s, 55–58
identity formation, 46–47, 54–55,
118–119, 121, 134, 138–142
organizing strategies, 102, 116–118,
122, 148, 181
political leadership, 130–131, 161
preaching, Protestant assemblies, 52,
56, 72, 77–79, 81–84, 86–87, 89–90
religious leadership, 47, 122–123, 125–128
social profile (prior to 1560), 58–61
social profile (1561), 122–123
social profile (1562), 142–148
See also iconoclasm; Nîmes, churches
seized; Nîmes cahier de doléances
Nîmes town council, 11–13, 121, 224n.22
complaints of, 68, 98
conflict, dislike of, 83
debates on heresy, 29, 35–36, 53, 71,
52–53, 81–83, 86–94, 98–99
debates on poverty, 43–46, 62–64
elections, 72, 78, 95, 148–150, 157–159
legitimacy of, 95
pays bribes, 67–68
See also cahier de doléances
nobility, 73, 100
Normandy, 66
Nostradamus, 61
notarial database, xvii, 24–25, 58–61,
122–123, 143, 149, 201
bias in, 203–204
coding last names in, 204–206
network analysis in, 215–219
occupational information in, 207–209
social status in, 209–215

Olivier, François, 74
Orléans Estates. *See* Estates General

overseers. *See* Nîmes consistory, elders
Ozment, Steven, 200

Parat, Hugon, 64
Paris, xxi, 7, 26, 30, 31–32, 38, 72, 153
cahier de doléances, 105
Parlement of, 4, 10, 74
University of, 15, 31, 36–39, 56, 137
parlement of Paris. *See* Paris,
parlement of
parlement of Toulouse. *See* Toulouse,
parlement of
parlements, 192–193
Pascal, Geoffre, 45
paternalism, 29, 46, 65, 112
Pavée, François de, 94, 161
Pierre de, 38
Pécolet, Imbert, 34–36, 52
Philip II of Spain, 70, 73
pious bequests. *See* wills
placards, affair of the, 31–32
Platter, Thomas, 11, 17
Pliny the Elder, 34
Poissy, Colloquy of, 108
Poitiers, Diane de, 70
Poitou, 40
Pontoise Estates. *See* Estates General
poor relief. *See* Nîmes consistory, poor
fund; Nîmes, poverty in
population growth, 39–41
poverty. *See* Nîmes consistory, poor fund;
Nîmes, poverty in
preaching. *See* Protestant movement
predestination, 32
présidial. *See* Nîmes présidial
priests. *See* Nîmes, Catholic clergy in;
Nîmes, Lenten preacher in
Protestant church. *See* Nîmes consistory
Protestant movement. *See* French
Protestant movement; Nîmes
Protestant movement
Protestantism, doctrines, 32–34
growth of, in France, 183–187

Protestantism (*Continued*)
  spatial distribution of, in France, 187–197
psalm-singing, 83–84, 90, 108, 140

quantitative history, xvii–xix
Quatrebars, Jean, 164

Reformation debates, 89, 113
Reims, 15
relics, reliquaries, 106, 134, 156
Renaissance, 30
Richier, Honoré, 44–45, 80, 85, 88, 174
Robert, Jean, 35, 44
  Pierre, 29, 44, 78, 82
  Pierre, the younger, 82–85
Roch, St., xv
Rochemaure, Jacques de, 88, 136
Rochette, Guy, 158–159
Romier, Lucien, 184–185
Romorantin, edict of, 74, 86–87, 90, 92
Rosenberg, David L., 186, 192
Rouen, 14, 191
Roverie, Bauzille, 94
Rovyer, Jean, 166, 173
royal council 73, 75, 99. *See also* court factions
royal policies. *See* crown
Rozel family, 37–38, 88, 150
  Charles, 91, 125, 128–129, 135, 167, 178
  Pierre, 43, 88, 91, 114, 129, 135, 150, 167
  Isabelle, 50, 52
Rozier, Claude, 56

sacraments, 32–34, 88, 109
Sadoleto, Cardinal, 38
Saint-André, marshal de, 93–94
Saint-Gilles, 17, 156
saints, cult of the, 16–17, 38, 54–55, 57, 139
Salmon, J. H. M., 196–197
Saurin, Pierre, 80
Sauzet, Jean de, 38, 53, 85, 86, 169
Sauzet, Robert, 140
Savion, Louis, 45
Savy, Jacques, 80, 83–85
schools. *See* Nîmes, education in
servants, 24
Snow, C. P., xviii
social network analysis, 17, 24, 59, 145–148, 174, 215–219. *See also* Nîmes, factions in; betweenness
social status. *See* Nîmes, social hierarchy in
soldiers. *See* troops, royal
Sorbonne. *See* Paris, Univ. of
speech, Protestant style of, 89, 107, 142
St. John's Day, harvesting on, 51
standard of living, 39–41
Stone, Lawrence, 24
Sturm, Jean, 37
Suau, Pierre, capt. Bolhargues, 83, 85, 160–163, 168–169, 173
surveillants. *See* Nîmes consistory, elders
synods, Protestant, 72, 102, 151–152, 192

Terlon, Claude, 114–115
textiles, 186. *See also* Nîmes, clothing trades
Third Estate, 101
Toulouse, 4–5, 28, 30, 57, 68, 114, 184, 192–193
  cahier de doléances, 105–107, 109–110
  parlement of, 5, 7, 28, 36, 39, 49, 56, 58, 60, 81, 84, 86, 156, 178, 192
Tour Magne, 31, 52
travailleurs. *See* Nîmes, agricultural workers
Triati, Antoine, 124, 129
Troeltsch, Ernst, 187
Troyes, 14, 177
Tuffan, Guilaume, 39

University and College of Arts. *See* Nîmes
Ursi (family of notaries), 15, 36, 47, 50, 54, 58, 61, 129, 203–204

Uzès, 6–8, 17, 47, 126, 188
Uzès, Antoine d'. *See* Crussol, comte de

Vallat, Jean, 51, 166, 168, 173
　Roland, 88–90, 129
Vallete, Pierre de, 78–80, 174
Valon, Blaise, 163–164, 166
Vassy, 153, 155
venality, 10, 67
Vernière, Vidal, 44
vicaire, 13
Villars, Honorat de Savoie, comte de, 92, 94–95, 98
Villers-Cotterêts, edict of, 16–17, 106
Viret, Pierre, 36, 47, 77, 134, 136, 144–145, 151–152
Vives, Juan Luis, 37
Vovelle, Michel, xvii

wage rates, 40
Waldensians, 38
Wars of Religion. *See* Civil War
weapons. *See* Nîmes, arms in
wedding receptions, 24
wills, 14–15, 54–55, 57–58, 61, 77, 137
　pious bequests in, 14–15, 61
　sign of the cross in, 55
Wittenberg, Univ. of, 34
women, status of, 44, 125, 127, 137

xenophobia, 45, 138

yeomen. *See* Nîmes, agricultural workers
Ypres, 137

Zwingli, Zwingianism, 32